SIMULCAST

SIMULCAST

Four Experiments in Criticism

Benjamin Friedlander

THE UNIVERSITY OF ALABAMA PRESS
Tuscaloosa and London

The University of Alabama Press
Tuscaloosa, Alabama 35487-0380

Manufactured in the United States of America

Typeface: New Baskerville

∞

The paper on which this book is printed meets the minimum requirements of American National Standard for Information Science–Permanence of Paper for Printed Library Materials, ANSI Z39.48—1984.

Library of Congress Cataloging-in-Publication Data

Friedlander, Benjamin, 1959–
Simulcast : four experiments in criticism / Benjamin Friedlander.
p. cm. — (Modern and contemporary poetics)
Includes index.
ISBN 0-8173-1166-1 (cloth: alk. paper) — ISBN 0-8173-5028-4 (pbk.: alk. paper)
1. American poetry—20th century—History and criticism. 2. Experimental poetry, American—History and criticism. 3. Avant-garde (Aesthetics)—United States. I. Title. II. Series.
PS325 .F75 2004
811′.5409—dc21
2004010652

British Library Cataloguing-in-Publication Data available

Contents

Acknowledgments

Many thanks are due to the editors of the following publications where much of the work in *Simulcast* originally appeared: *DIU (Descriptions of an Imaginary Universe)* (Chris Funkhouser) for "Mr. Daly's Polemic," "The Anti-Hegemony Project" (Poe's introduction), and "The Literati of San Francisco" (entries on Benjamin Friedlander, Lyn Hejinian, Nathaniel Mackey, Tom Mandel, Michael Palmer, Ted Pearson, Larry Price, Kit Robinson, Andrew Schelling, and Barrett Watten); *Lagniappe* (Graham Foust) for "Mr. Rasula's History"; and *Qui Parle* (Barrett Watten) for "A Short History of Language Poetry" (in excerpt). Earlier versions of "Letter to B——" and "The Poetic Principle" were privately circulated in pamphlet form under the imprint "MS. in a Bottle." Ken Sherwood published an uncollected Poe review in his pioneer electronic journal *R/IFT* and commissioned the review of Jed Rasula's *American Poetry Wax Museum* for *Chloroform* (it unfortunately did not appear there). Thanks are also due to Charles Bernstein for permitting use of the Poetics List in staging "The Anti-Hegemony Project."

As Poe's example teaches, there is nothing more dangerous to a friendship than affection without respect, and nothing more dangerous to a community than respect without affection. Let me take this occasion, then, to affirm my respect *and* affection for the numerous friends, fellow poets, teachers, and colleagues who offered their assistance. Charles Bernstein was the first to appreciate the metacritical possibilities in my method. His later suggestion that I collect this work into a single volume was galvanizing. Hank Lazer guided me adroitly through several stages of drafts. Nick Lawrence, Bob Perelman, and

Barrett Watten offered their invaluable readings. Alan Gilbert fought deep misgivings to offer this manuscript his reasoned response. I value his judgment—and friendship—immensely. Thanks are also due to Michael Alpert, Michael Basinski, Robert Bertholf, Don Byrd, Susan Clark, Joseph Conte, Henry Friedlander, Nada Gordon, Tom Hull, Cristanne Miller, Tom Orange, Lisa Robertson, Jill Robbins, Stephen Rodefer, Neil Schmitz, and Martin Spinelli. I am also indebted to the staff of The University of Alabama Press, Kevin Fitzgerald, and Mary Lawrence for their superb work in shepherding my manuscript through publication. Finally, Chris Funkhouser and Belle Gironda gave this project their unconditional support from the very beginning, while Carla Billitteri provided guidance—and a stabilizing influence—throughout; this book would not exist without them.

SIMULCAST

Introduction

Criticism as Applied Poetry

I began the four experiments gathered in this volume for my own amusement in 1995 and published them intermittently under assumed names, primarily on the Internet. Their principal subject is avant-garde American poetry of the last twenty-five years, especially language writing, but the styles of approach and conclusions vary markedly from piece to piece. The first, "The Anti-Hegemony Project," borrows its language from journalism and fan-group chitchat in order to satirize SUNY Buffalo's "Poetics List," the earliest collision of literary print culture with the World Wide Web. The second is a series of essays in ornate (some would say purple) prose, on subjects ranging from Gertrude Stein to Charles Bernstein. Unambiguously polemical, these essays move freely from broad statements of principle to close readings of specific poems to summary judgments of entire careers. The third experiment, "The Literati of San Francisco," is written in the same voice, only now the focus shifts from individual poems and poets to a detailed portrait of a particular poetic community. This altered emphasis continues in the last piece, "A Short History of Language Poetry." Here, however, the polemic is abandoned entirely in favor of sober, even deferential, analysis.

I describe these works as experiments because all four are based on source texts and thus inaugurate a species of criticism in which the findings emerge only after struggle with predetermined forms. Sometimes this struggle took shape as an exercise in translation, not unlike the re-creation of a sonnet's rhyme scheme and meter. Often, translation was impossible, and the struggle resolved itself instead in an act of controlled imagination—not unlike the sonnet's original creation. In each case, the production of my text had less in common with the ordinary practice of writing an essay than it did with the composition of metrical verse. For this reason, I coined the phrase "applied poetry" to characterize *Simulcast*'s somewhat scandalous methodology: the creation of criticism through the strict re-creation of an earlier critic's text (or, more precisely, through as strict a re-creation as the discrepancy between my source text and chosen topic would allow). Thus, my "Short History of Language Poetry" follows the arguments (and even wording) of Jean Wahl's *A Short History of Existentialism,* while "The Literati of San Francisco" takes Edgar Allan Poe's *Literati of New York City* as its template. Not all of my sources were so distinguished. The twenty-four documents that make up "The Anti-Hegemony Project" were inspired by syndicated news reports and email postings to alt.fan.madonna. In this way, a bug museum became a home for "creepy" poets and tainted containers of baby formula a noxious form of language writing.

But satire is one thing, serious criticism another. What risked scandal in my method—what marked my project as a kind of poetry and not merely an antic form of poetics—was its privileging of style over substance, artifice over rigor, mere plausibility over truth, an inversion of the hierarchy of values that ordinarily (and sensibly) obtains in criticism, an inversion that in effect ceded control of my writing to the writing itself. Although I was predisposed in each of these pieces to certain arguments and conclusions, I willingly abandoned these when they became incompatible with the critical approach demanded by my source. The results were emphatically *not* what I would have written if left to my own devices, one reason I opted for pseudonymous attribution. Sincerity in Pound's sense ("a man standing by his word") was simply not at issue. The issue, instead, was a compositional practice in which criticism derives less from a given set of facts, opinions, and interpretive strategies than from a collision between *two* such sets: one fixed in the form of a source text, the other still inchoate in my chosen topic.

If the experiments in *Simulcast* were all produced through collision, the end results were neither accidental nor confused, in part because I matched source to topic with care, in part because the process of composition itself registers as a legible stratum of meaning. Although a function of violent synthesis, each experiment in *Simulcast* bears the scar of its construction in a neat seam that runs through every sentence, along the boundary dividing form from content. Thus, in "A Short History of Language Poetry," the shape of my narrative, its idiosyncratic style, and its anachronistic tone were appropriated from Wahl's account of existentialism. The narrative's substance and theoretical vocabulary were determined instead by the specific character of language writing and its various poetic antecedents. Where Wahl, for example, declares of Hegel: "He tells us that our thoughts and feelings have meaning solely because each thought, each feeling, is bound to our personality, which itself has meaning because it takes place in a history and a state, at a specific epoch in the evolution of the universal Idea."[1] My own text (attributed to "Hecuba Whimsy") offers a comparable claim regarding Robert Creeley:

> He tells us that form is only an "extension" of content; that our thoughts and feelings have form solely because each thought, each feeling, is bound to experience, which itself has form only because it takes shape in history and as a habit of speech, at a specific moment in the evolution of language.

And where Wahl writes of Heidegger:

> The notion of the experience of anguish, and marked Kierkegaardian influences, lead to a definition of human existence as anxious, bent over itself, making plans. On the other hand, the Heideggerian individual is in-the-world, an idea which is foreign to Kierkegaard and may have come in part from Husserl.[2]

"Whimsy" provides a similar accounting of the itinerary of Lyn Hejinian:

> The importance in her work of self-reflexivity—the image of herself "as a spectator of the spectating," a marked influence of Gertrude Stein—leads to a definition of poetry as spectacle, and recognition that "Western curiosity is addicted to the theatricality of seeing and being seen." On the other hand, Hejinian's "spectating" always occurs in a particular locale, an idea that is foreign to Stein and may have come in part from Williams, a rarely remarked influence, and from her fascination with the nineteenth-century novel.

Such revisions (especially the second) indicate just how much amplification was sometimes required in order to maintain a coherent argument within the constraints of my method.

It would have been possible, I suppose, to simply take my source texts as a starting point. I could have abandoned their structures of argument whenever necessary in order to preserve the internal coherence of my own arguments and in order to maintain a stricter fidelity to the facts pertaining to my subject. Certainly, from the standpoint of serious criticism, any other decision would have to be considered frivolous—"coherence" and "fidelity to the facts" being the very principles on which criticism's claims to truth (and hence, its claims on a reader's attention) are founded. But consistency of argument was only one half of the task I set myself. Consistency of method was the other half, and my unwillingness to depart too freely from this method was in large part the consequence of a different sort of rigor than the one that holds sway in what writing instructors term "argumentative and persuasive prose." This rigor, as already noted, is much more familiar to the art of translating poetry than the practice of literary criticism as ordinarily conceived. In translation, the coordination of sound and sense is a matter of constant negotiation, with one or the other value continually compromised in a process of discovery whose findings are better evaluated according to their overall use than the bare accuracy of this or that word. A similar negotiation occurs in *Simulcast,* only here the give and take between "sound" and "sense," between form and content, is absorbed into the work as a content in its own right, albeit a hidden one. This hidden content—for example, my struggle to reconcile Wahl's *Short History* as "form" with the actual history of language writing as "content"—likewise has a usefulness independent of its bare accuracy. Let me note, however, that "accuracy" has a very specific meaning in this context: it refers to the exactness with which I followed the twists and turns of my original text's argument. Moreover, since an *in*accuracy was sometimes required in order to produce a coherent argument in the new text, it was neither feasible nor desirable to view "accuracy" (or, for that matter, "coherence") as an absolute value. The transformation of "Wahl" into "Whimsy" was precisely a matter of *negotiation*. In this sense, the composition of this book made literal Foucault's well-known definition in "What Is an Author?": "Writing unfolds like a game that inevitably moves beyond its own rules and finally leaves them behind."

Indeed, because of the way this particular game unfolded, my experiments further corroborate another of Foucault's dicta: that the author is a "function" of discourse, "a projection . . . of the operations we force texts to undergo."[3]

In translation, of course, the end result is a text whose explicit aim is to minimize the differences between original and copy. In *Simulcast,* the differences are lovingly preserved, however invisibly to the casual reader. The experiments collected here are only *like* translation. What mattered most to me in the metamorphosis of my source texts was the process of metamorphosis itself—the application of a poetic methodology in contexts where poetry is only allowed to speak under the most codified of social and cultural controls. If the end results were irresponsible, disruptive, or unpleasant, this is largely because poetry itself is irresponsible, disruptive, and unpleasant, at least when judged by ethical rather than aesthetic criteria. But before taking up these questions of ethics, a more detailed account of this project's origins is perhaps in order.

THE CULTURAL WORK OF PLAGIARISM

I do not want to give the mistaken impression that the experiments in *Simulcast* were composed to illustrate a method arrived at theoretically beforehand. Far from it. The pieces gathered here were written entirely for pleasure, utilizing a method deduced intuitively from a variety of influences, many going back a decade or more. First and foremost was the resonant phrase "appropriation art"—the phrase itself more than any example. "Appropriation art" sounded definitively postmodern, a step beyond Walter Benjamin's dream of a book comprised entirely of quotations, though Benjamin certainly played a role in my increasingly perplexed notions of originality.[4] Borges too; his "Pierre Menard, Author of the *Quixote*" was a metaphysical joke that left serious echoes in my head, not so much on account of the story's conceit (a word-for-word re-creation of a portion of Cervantes's novel), as from the meaning Borges derived from that conceit.[5] For Borges, Menard's painstaking recreation of *Don Quixote*—an act of "deliberate anachronism" and "erroneous attribution"—is most noteworthy in its impact on "the halting and rudimentary art of reading."[6] The literary text, he suggests, however marvelous in its own right, is only a raw material. What shapes this material into something meaningful vis-à-vis world literature and world history is the act of attention performed by a reader. Unfortunately, this act is usually constrained by such factual considerations as chronology and context. We read only what we imagine it *possible* to read, adhering to a fixed order of reality even when reading the most fantastic of texts. But texts, for Borges, are not parasitical to reality; rather, reality is parasitical to texts. Like Wallace Stevens, he not only believed that "the imagination adheres to reality, but, also, that reality adheres to the imagination and that the interdependence is essential."[7] Borges, however, went further than Stevens. He recognized that readers, if freed from factual constraints, would be able to shape reality anew, in accordance with their own imaginations. Approaching the *Odyssey* "as if it were posterior to the *Aeneid*" or the *Imitatio Christi* as a composition by Céline or Joyce would alter one's understanding not only of the work, but of the history within which the work magically appears. Stripped of its metaphysical trappings, then, Menard's "technique" is little more than an act of reframing. Of course, reframing alone is insufficient to convince most readers to abandon their belief in chronology and context, hence the metaphysical trappings. But even those who discount Borges's conceit as a mere joke can appreciate the seriousness of its underlying argument: that the difference between "a plausible description of the universe" and mere "caducity" is discernible within texts as well as between them, and that the discernment of this difference is precisely how we produce what we call reality in our heads.

Another influence, albeit an indirect one, was Kathy Acker. I say indirect because my reading of Acker came many years after I first developed an impression of her work. In the early 1980s, I overheard a conversation at a poetry reading about Acker's pervasive use of textual "thievery." More precisely, I heard that her 1982 novel *Great Expectations* was built up from the work of other authors, most notably Charles Dickens. Stumbling in this way upon Acker's method was especially appropriate given her own improvisational approach to writing. As she would tell an interviewer several years later, "*Great Expectations* was the first one where I tried to use other texts purely, and I really didn't know yet what I wanted to do and what I was doing—I just knew I was interested in plagiarism. . . . I didn't have any theory."[8] Like feedback solos in rock and roll, the idea was strikingly original and strikingly obvious at one and the same time—a combination that no doubt obviated the need for conscious articulation.

Almost immediately after learning of Acker's method, I began acquiring copies of her books. Steadfastly, however, I failed to read more than a few pages of any. Strangely, this did not deter her influence. Although I only glimpsed a hint of what Acker had actually accomplished, this hint took root deep in my imagination, where I set about tending it with care, sensing intuitively that the gestation period would be quite lengthy. Why? Why did I feel the need to protect myself from undue influence? I couldn't have said so at the time. In retrospect, however, I would guess that I needed to distinguish between Acker's "thievery" as an instance of punk transgression (surely her work's most easily copied quality) and as a means of befuddling the difference between reading and writing, criticism and art. Put in postmodern terms, Acker's pervasive use of plagiarism offered a practical solution to two problems posed by my reading of Borges: how to produce a text like Pierre Menard's, and how to produce a text like "Pierre Menard."

Acker's solution to the first of these problems was surprisingly straightforward: "deliberate anachronism" and "erroneous attribution." A disparate set of uncredited texts of varying length is absorbed into a new narrative with little regard for stylistic or even logical coherence. Thus, in *Great Expectations,* Acker absorbs the work of Dickens, Proust, and Pauline Reáge, among others, and impedes our recognition of what she has done through insistent disjunction and strategic revision—by changing the names of characters or their genders, for instance, or by recasting or modernizing the settings. Martina Sciolino's description of this method is perhaps the most evocative. Drawing an analogy from nature, she speaks of Acker as a "kleptoparasite," that is, as "a spider [who] appropriates another's web and eats the prey entrapped" there. Sciolino goes on to argue that the important question raised by Acker's method is not what texts Acker has stolen, but "what victims are coiled in these already woven fictions."[9] Implicit in this question's formulation, however, is the notion that Acker's texts are primarily concerned with issues originating in her source texts; or, to put this in kleptoparasitic terms, that her borrowings exploit an historical content available to any reading daring enough to inhabit Acker's dangerously sticky forms. Acker herself seems to conceive of her project in just these terms when she speaks of her work as "a simplistic example of deconstruction." She says, "You just take other texts and you put them in different contexts to see how they work. You take texts apart and look at the language that's being used, the genre, the kind of sentence structure, there's a lot of contents here that most readers don't see."[10] But if Borges teaches us anything, it is that old webs attract *new* content as well, and this too is an aspect of Acker's work. In her 1986 novel *Don Quixote,* for example (for Acker, like Pierre Menard, has usurped the place of the spider Cervantes), the title character's quest begins with an abortion:

> From her neck to her knees she wore pale or puke green paper. This was her armor. She had chosen it specially, for she knew that this world's conditions are so rough for any single person, even a rich person, that person has to make do with what she can find: this's no world for idealism. Example: the green paper would tear as soon as the abortion began.[11]

Taken as an allegory of her method, the passage tells us quite a bit about Acker's relationship to her source texts. The clearest point of contiguity here between Acker's *Don Quixote* and Cervantes's is the armor, but if we conceive of the "armor" as the stolen text—torn as soon as Acker's operation begins—then the ultimate focus of attention is surely something Acker herself introduces into Cervantes's narrative: the abortion. "Deconstruction" is irrelevant. The abortion is hardly something Acker discovers *in* Cervantes (it was not, in Sciolino's terms, stolen prey); rather, the abortion is something that Acker has captured by using Cervantes's text as a trap.

Acker's solution to the second problem—how to produce a text like "Pierre Menard"—proved more complex. But then, the problem itself was more complex: how to produce reality instead of a text, since, according to Borges, the text itself is only raw material shaped into something more meaningful by the reader. Borges's own solution in "Pierre Menard" was to write his story in the form of an essay. What, after all, is a critic, if not a reader who takes pen in hand in order to substantiate the reality produced in his or her head? Adopting the stance of a pseudo-critic, or of a real critic of a false work, Borges was able to shape his own raw material into . . . into what? A pseudo-reality? The argument is absurd on its face. Even so, read as an essay, "Pierre Menard" does manage to cast its shadows beyond the text, altering our perceptions—if not quite the substance—of its underlying context.[12] Acker's solution is less elegant, but less cumbersome as well, and it holds the additional advantage of organizing her work according to two distinct logics: a surface logic of representation, as found in her novels' narratives, and a hidden logic of performance, as seen in her appropriation and rewriting of other texts, which creates secret dialogues between her narratives and their various sources. The advantage of this two-tiered system is the clarity it brings to our reading. Beginning at the surface, on the level of representation, we have literature as "raw material" (and in Acker's case, the material is very raw indeed). Persevering in our reading, we discover Acker's deeper intentions, made manifest in her writing as performance. She seeks to shape her raw material into something even rawer: not a picture of the real, but an intervention within it. More pervasive than allusion, surreptitious than quotation, cunning than collage, Acker's parasitic method enacts what Rebecca Moore Howard calls "The Cultural Work of Plagiarism." Her method becomes a "patchwriting" that emphasizes thought as performance rather than object, and that reconceives authorship as "collaboration" rather than "autonomy, originality, proprietorship."[13]

My own first attempt at such "cultural work" occurred in 1987 when I reviewed Bob Perelman's *The First World*. Perelman published this collection of poems when he was still negotiating the turn from austere lyricism (in *Primer*, 1981) to a raucous political poetry (announced in *To the Reader*, 1984). Only a few years earlier, Fredric Jameson had made Perelman's poem "China" (from *Primer*) his textbook example of postmodern poetry.[14] Perelman's "China" and his early work, however, seemed to me unabashedly modern, if only because of his unexamined repudiation of popular and mass art forms. Later, Perelman would come to question this repudiation and the high versus low art distinction on which it was founded. He did this first in his political reading of Pound's *Cantos*, and then in his acceptance of commodity culture as the necessary ground for political poetry *after* Pound. But although this acceptance was already underway in *The First World*, Perelman was not yet ready to distinguish between the positive and negative elements in his relationship to mass culture's products. Later works (most notably, "The Manchurian Candidate," 1998) would find models and not just objects for critique in these products, but *The First World*'s erosion of the divide between high and low art led only to a repudiation of the high along with the low.[15]

At the time, I found the question of high versus low art especially pointed and relevant, as I was trying to draw on the Raymond Williams-influenced writings of rock critic Robert Christgau in order to formulate a critical approach to poetry that did not begin and end in the formalism I saw in the critical and poetic work of the language poets.[16] I use the word "formalism" loosely here. In those days, formalism was not so much a method as a cause. It united under a single banner a wide range of critical stances that included, for example, belief in "the materiality of the sign"; suspicion of "reference," "representation," "stable meaning," and "transparency"; interest in "the I" as a "construct of language" only; a tendency to speak of "language as such" rather than this or that particular language; a tendency also to treat history as pure abstraction, as a conceptual foundation rather than a context. It is not difficult to imagine just how prim and anti-poetic this critical discourse could sound. (A friend of mine, only partly in jest, used to refer to the language poets as "the A students").[17] There were reasons for this investment in formalism, as well as for the earnestness and studiousness it seemed to demand. For Perelman and his contemporaries, formalism's technical vocabulary and scientific posture offered an escape from what must have seemed, in the mid-1970s, the bottoming out of the New American Poetry (NAP), in particular, the NAP's increasingly anti-intellectual reliance on personality as the origin and horizon of all poetic utterance. By the mid-1980s, however, especially in the Bay Area, the field had undergone substantial revision. Language writing's own prominence had undercut the oppressiveness of the NAP in its decadent phase, making reappraisal possible, and making possible (if not necessary) an initial appraisal of language writing itself. Not surprisingly, this "initial appraisal" soon took on a variety of forms, some of them quite nasty. In retaliation, Ron Silliman coined the phrase "language bashing," which subsequently became a slur hurled, at least in conversation, at even the friendliest of critiques.[18] (I cite this fact only to indicate how quickly the discourse became charged.) I myself was a staunch advocate of language writing. But having come to the work along a route different than the one traveled by the language poets themselves, I found in this moment of shifting definition an unexpected but welcome occasion for recasting its formalist poetics in terms more credible vis-à-vis my own experience.

Rock criticism came to my aid here. For a short while, I devoured everything I could find, from the nearly anonymous fan-driven writing in various underground zines to the Bay Area's local rock journalists, from genre specialists and star biographers to cultural critics and historians, from *The Boy Looked at Johnny* to *Blissed Out*.[19] As with the language poets' turn to formalism, there were many reasons for my enthusiasm, not least the strength and intelligence of the writing itself, but two reasons in particular help to explain why rock criticism proved so useful to me in appraising my relationship to an older generation of poets. First of all, my undergraduate years at Berkeley coincided almost exactly with the early phase of the punk scene in San Francisco. Although I was not a participant in that scene in any meaningful sense (I turned down a chance to see the last Sex Pistols show at Winterland, much to my subsequent chagrin), I had close friends who were, which meant that I often found myself at the edges of activity. Willy-nilly, punk became for me a model of artistic ferment, and it was natural that I turn to punk's critics and chroniclers when trying to understand such ferment in the context of poetry. I also looked to rock criticism because I needed a critical method capable of accounting with equal clarity for both the work and the scene that produced it. Language writing was not simply a moment of artistic ferment, but also an experiment in community. Here my interest in rock criticism expanded to include writings on jazz, a genre of music in which the relevance of social history has long been affirmed by practitioners and critics alike. It helped, of course, that the correlation of jazz and poetry has a rich (if recent) tradition, and was thus intellectually respectable in ways that the correlation of pop music and poetry was not. So far as I could tell, there was no poet who had done for rock and roll what Amiri Baraka had done for jazz, and Baraka's attempt to extend his analysis into the realm of mass-produced, mass-distributed soul music thus became something of a model.[20]

Even more significant than Baraka, however, was Robert Christgau. This was partly because Christgau's primary means of expression was the short record review, a superficially modest form that seemed to require precisely the skills I had developed as a poet, and partly because Christgau struck so exemplary a balance between social analysis and aesthetics. Compact as any utterance of Adorno's, Christgau's reviews—published every month or so under the heading "Consumer Guide"—subjected a seemingly endless stream of "product" to theoretical scrutiny and rigorous grading. Didn't poetry need just such a monitor? Even those aspects of Christgau's work that did not seem relevant—most notably, his steadfast attention to sales—suggested useful directions for my own analysis. Language writing in the Bay Area might not have been "product" in the same sense that the Bay City Rollers were product, but it was still a function of its engagement with an audience, not simply a phenomenon in the history of ideas. Socially speaking, the work's most immediately verifiable dimensions were those of its readership, which was for the most part a white, middle-class intelligentsia (one that most certainly included myself). This readership fathomed the work's meaning in ways that the poets themselves could neither foresee nor control, and that a formalist reading could scarcely illuminate.

I stumbled in this manner on an ad hoc version of cultural studies; that is, I came to see language writing as a "subculture" in Dick Hebdige's sense: a "style" with "subversive implications," "alternately dismissed, denounced and canonized."[21] From Baraka I had learned that forms have social content, and that their transformation is never simply a matter of aesthetic development. From Christgau I added the insight that the relationship between writer and reader is also a matter of form, and thus also participates in the construction of meaning. Logically, the next step would have been an immersion in the sociology of art. But at just the moment when that step should have been taken, I became disenchanted with the scene and withdrew into my own work, taking my developing interest in poetry's structures of address in a different direction altogether.[22]

But that was not until 1990; in 1987, I was still committed to a critical practice in which popular music provided a model for understanding poetry as both aesthetic artifact and social phenomenon.[23] Engaged in this critical practice during a time when language writing had begun to insist upon its own authority, I was also hypersensitive to hints of snobbery. "Seriousness" was the ultimate badge of honor at that time, and several poets made a point of telling me I was lacking in that quality—a judgment I attributed entirely to my extraliterary engagements. (I brooded for weeks over an innocent joke from Michael Palmer about my skateboard.)[24] This sensitivity, perhaps, more than any intellectual principle, explains my brashness in writing to Bob Perelman, shortly after *The First World* appeared, to share my mixed feelings about what was, in effect, his own attempt to think free of the strictures of formalism. "Though *The First World*'s chief target seems to be repression," I noted, "these aren't really a libertine's poems." The problem with this, I suggested, was that his intellectual rather than visceral approach led him to reject the visceral out of hand, unfairly. And what could be more visceral, I wondered, than pop culture? Having taken issue, however, with what I perceived to be his poetry's elitism, I concluded with sincere praise. "But all qualms aside, *The First World* is an eye-opener—more than a collection—and the liveliness of its oratory, the inventiveness with which it gives expression to outrage, is pretty inspiring."[25]

The key phrase here is "more than a collection." What distinguished the language writers from other poets in my eyes was not the efficacy of their program, but the fact that they *had* one. Descendents of Pound and Olson, they treated the poem as a means rather than end, that is, as a site for enacting an intellectual project that was not itself poetic, or was not necessarily so. This was what made their formalism so maddening: it seemed to countermand the very development of thought their work proposed. Like Parmigianino's self-portrait in John Ashbery's famous homage, the marvel of their forms became a lens for viewing an exaggerated gesture of entrapment. In Parmigianino's case, the gesture is literal: an outsized, outstretched hand bent back by the invisible limits of representation. In the case of the language poets, the gesture was instead a matter of attitude: an outsized, outstretched ambition bent back by the opacity of "language as such." Of course, if any of the poets shared my sense of constriction, it was Perelman. Rereading my note to him today, I cannot help but feel that I was really criticizing him for being "too straight." Perelman himself must have picked up on this, for his generous if understandably protective reply concludes: "I still want to defend myself against charges of elitism: Ann Landers, Pinocchio, Dynasty—I'm just using them as material—pretty neutrally I think. I'm certainly not rejecting your sharper sense of 'cutting edge' pop culture. I don't even know much about it yet really."[26]

The complexity of my mixed feelings seemed to require fuller explanation; and so, sparked by Perelman's response, I began a proper review. In this review, I retracted my earlier charge of elitism, for Perelman had been right to claim neutrality vis-à-vis pop culture. Instead, I noted the beleaguered status of human agency. Comparing

The First World to his previous volume, *To the Reader,* I noted a systematic leveling of distinctions that turned Perelman's "enraged irony" on his own practice as a poet. As I put this in my review:

> *To the Reader* questioned the legitimacy of the irrationally rule-bound society that defines and maintains our culture, but implicitly privileged culture's "top end," if only by leaving art out of the attack. Happily, Perelman's newest collection, *The First World,* makes this contradiction its central theme. To wit, a head-on confrontation with "The Art Machine"—Duchamp, Bach, literary theory, Sophocles, even Pinocchio—everything that smoothes over the brutal acts of what Allen Ginsberg once called (misogynistically, but with psychosexual implications similar to those emphasized in Perelman's work) "the one-eyed shrew of the heterosexual dollar." Unlike *To the Reader, The First World* claims complicity, singing in its chains like the sea.[27]

What bothered me was the book's hyperbole. In leveling distinctions, Perelman was also, to some degree, leaving them intact. After all, if every stratum of our culture, high and low, is rotten to the core, there nonetheless remains the fact of consciousness regarding this corruption. By claiming complicity, *The First World* already distinguished itself from Perelman's other objects of critique, which was fine, except that I could make the same claim for other cultural artifacts as well. Why didn't Perelman? Why could he not see the consciousness of corruption in pop culture?

In reading *The First World,* I wanted, for polemical reasons, to argue that the difference between engaged and disengaged thought cut across all precincts of artistic activity—that rock musicians were just as capable as language poets of self-consciousness regarding their cultural predicament. Perelman, for his own polemical reasons, wanted to ignore the difference between engaged and disengaged art altogether. At the time, it did not occur to me that Perelman was *suffering* from disengagement and that the leveling of distinctions was precisely how he fought off the ensuing sense of powerlessness. I could only see a celebration of powerlessness that surreptitiously let poetry off the hook, as if the self-consciousness of powerlessness exempted poetry from the full force of Perelman's critique, that is, as if including poetry excluded it. What I did not say, although I thought it, was that Perelman's stance reminded me more than anything of the attitude of certain rock stars. Jameson, in his essay on postmodernism, had drawn an oblique correlation between Perelman's work and the Clash, Talking Heads, and Gang of Four. A more pointed analogue, it seemed to me, was Steely Dan, a group of cynical, self-reflexive hipsters who were brilliant at crafting a pop music for which they often expressed an undisguised disdain. It was with this parallel in mind, in fact, that I ended the paragraph cited above with the literary phrase "singing in its chains like the sea"—a silent allusion to the first line of Robert Christgau's review of Steely Dan's *Aja:* "Carola suggests that by now they realize they'll never get out of El Lay, so they've elected to sing in their chains like the sea." Even more pertinent, however, was the next sentence, a rhetorical question that characterized the result in terms that severely undercut Perelman's ostensible antagonism to his own *personal* "El Lay" (i.e., the first world): "After all, to a certain kind of reclusive aesthete, well-crafted West Coast studio jazz is as beautiful as anything else, right?"[28]

"Reclusive aesthete" was manifestly unfair but I was pretty pleased with "well-crafted West Coast studio jazz," and for two reasons. First of all, it named with just the right mixture of respect and dismissal the combination of formal constraint and conceptual limitation that *The First World* both struggled against and entertained. Second, and more importantly, the phrase didn't even appear in my review; for notwithstanding my brashness in writing Perelman in the first place, I was wary of controversy. Cowardice was not the issue. I had no qualms about expressing myself in public or answering critics should they take exception to my remarks. What gave me pause was the intense polarization of the scene in those days. Christgau's cavalier tone—the combination of respect and dismissal in his appraisal of Steely Dan—would only have registered as "language bashing." In the charged environment of the Bay Area writing community circa 1987, primness had become essential as a kind of armor against criticism. My own, like Acker's, was puke green and easily torn, but I needed it all the same.

Although I had yet to absorb Acker's work with any seriousness, her mention in this context was hardly an accident. Contemplating with satisfaction my silent allusion to Christgau, it occurred to me that I could underscore my point (i.e., that the critical imagination appropriate to popular music was no less appropriate for poetry) by utilizing what I did know of her method. Going beyond hidden reference, I decided to end my review by rewriting an entire paragraph from the liner notes to a jazz record—an appropriation that paid further homage to music criticism while signaling more emphatically (if only to myself) my rejection of poetry's privileged status vis-à-vis popular art forms.[29] After all, if the same words could be applied with equal exactness to both a jazz record and book of language poetry, the difference between one "LP" and the other could not simply be attributed to disparities of intellectual currency. This, in any event, is the point I wanted to make—however evasively—in summarizing my response to Perelman with words "plagiarized" from Blue Note.

Alas, the grafting was not successful; the paragraph does not appear in the published version of my review. For the first time, however, I had a visceral understanding of the value of Acker's method. Her thievery, I now saw, was not simply a trick for generating text (as I originally imagined); it was also a form of engagement, a means of bringing into conversation culturally disjunct and seemingly incommensurate discourses. Given my own sense of disjunction at the time—my feeling that important elements of my intellectual life had no place in the poetry scene—this method proved immensely attractive, not least in its surreptitiousness. To be sure, the sheer transgressiveness of Acker's method was also attractive (especially her extension of transgression beyond subject matter into form), but even more attractive than her punk sensibility was the possibility of a secret project—of a project kept secret, like Poe's purloined letter, in plain sight. Several years would pass before I again took up "the cultural work of plagiarism," but when I did, Poe himself would play a prominent role.

DESCRIPTIONS OF AN IMAGINARY UNIVERSE

The experiments in *Simulcast* evolved out of these influences, but even as I set this genealogy down, earlier instances of artistic activity come to mind, childhood experiences in which this book's method was glimpsed, though from afar. When I was thirteen, for example, a friend and I made drawings of naked men and women by tracing the underwear ads in the *New York Times*. (Homemade pornography, it was later intercepted by our homeroom teacher, who hid her amusement in a sharply worded letter to our parents.) A few years before, I had an unfortunate encounter with a summer-school art instructor—a fastidious gentleman who took back his admiration of my butterfly sketch once he learned that it was copied from a book. Drawing from life, apparently, was his preferred method; drawing from the imagination, his one acceptable alternative. Readymades, detourned images, and loving simulations all fell under the heading of fraud.

My source text for the butterfly sketch was *The Golden Book Encyclopedia,* and having recently reacquired a set from the Salvation Army, I am tempted to argue that the 1959 publication of that series marks a small but decisive step in the development of a postmodern sensibility. More precisely, I am tempted to argue that the *Golden Book*'s "Sixteen Accurate, Fact-filled Volumes" ("ENTERTAININGLY WRITTEN AND ILLUSTRATED TO MAKE LEARNING AN ADVENTURE") exemplify what Jean Baudrillard would later term *hyperreality:* "the generation by models of a real without origin or reality."[30] Such a heightened state of artificiality might seem a strange result for a compendium of factual information, even a compendium intended for children. But let us recall that one of the principal signs of hyperreality, according to Baudrillard, is the active role information plays in the dissolution or neutralization of meaning—something that is especially evident when we compare the *Encyclopedia* with its companion set, *The Golden Book Picture Atlas of the World*. Both the *Picture Atlas* and *Encyclopedia* were cold-war documents perfectly attuned to the needs of the time. However, where the *Atlas* remained fixed in its rationality and focused on such tropes of modernity as industrialization, exploitation of natural resources, and the classification of exotic cultures, the *Encyclopedia* gave free reign to the imagination. This is clearest in the types of illustration the two series favored: photographs in the *Atlas,* paintings in the *Encyclopedia*. Thus, where the latter's entry on "erosion" ("Wind carrying grains of sand can wear away even solid rock") featured a psychedelic monument valley further embellished with cowboys and Indians, the *Picture Atlas* showed a cotton field near Tucson, Arizona, with the sober caption: "Irrigation turned desert into fertile farmland."[31]

As this disparity of aim begins to suggest, the end of the fifties and beginning of the sixties were a period of momentous change. Two modes of apprehending and representing experience were vying for supremacy, with pedagogy only one of the many battlefields. Even at the time, however, it was possible to see which mode was going to win.

Thus Daniel Boorstin, in his 1961 classic *The Image,* prophesized a world in which reality itself would become a manmade commodity: mass-produced and sold at a profit, then greedily consumed (with increasing disregard for the shoddiness of its manufacture) by a mesmerized populace unable to reckon the cost. Sounding remarkably like Baudrillard, he identified what we would now call postmodernism, but in terms that recall the paranoia of fifties science fiction films:

> The American citizen . . . lives in a world where fantasy is more real than reality, where the image has more dignity than its original. We hardly dare face our bewilderment, because our ambiguous experience is so pleasantly iridescent, and the solace of belief in contrived reality is so thoroughly real. We have become eager accessories to the great hoaxes of the age. These are the hoaxes we play on ourselves.
>
> Pseudo-events from their very nature tend to be more interesting and more attractive than spontaneous events. Therefore in American public life today pseudo-events tend to drive all other kinds of events out of our consciousness, or at least to overshadow them. Earnest, well-informed citizens seldom notice that their experience of spontaneous events is buried by pseudo-events. Yet nowadays the more industriously they work at "informing" themselves the more this tends to be true.[32]

Is it any wonder that the Kennedy years were called Camelot? When facts and fantasies become interchangeable, the world necessarily begins to recede in favor of an idea of the world. This, indeed, is precisely what occurs in *The Ugly American.* A crude caricature of American blundering in Southeast Asia, this book passed itself off as informed documentary.[33] Published in 1958, it became an immediate best seller, and perhaps the most influential political novel in American history, not excluding *Uncle Tom's Cabin.* Eisenhower reportedly ordered an investigation of foreign-aid programs after reading it, while John F. Kennedy, still a Senator, helped to purchase copies for all ninety-nine of his colleagues, which in effect endorsed fantasy as a reasonable basis for foreign policy.[34]

What marks the *Encyclopedia* as an instance of hyperreality is not simply its confusion of fact and fantasy. Advertised as "THE ONLY ENCYCLOPEDIA FOR YOUNG GRADE-SCHOOL CHILDREN," the series offered itself, quite consciously, as a means of initiating the young into post-war consumer culture—a culture where information was no longer a means of *understanding* the world, but was, instead, the world one needed to understand. This emphasis on initiation is put most bluntly in the introductory letter, "To Our Readers." There the *Golden Book*'s authors informed their target audience:

> Every day, there are times when you want to know more about something. It may be about how plants grow, or how electric motors work. You may want a certain fact about Abraham Lincoln, earth satellites, Bolivia, the invention of the piano, or what causes colds—to take just a few examples. Sometimes you need more information than a teacher, your parents, or a schoolbook can give. That's the time to turn to your GOLDEN BOOK ENCYCLOPEDIA. . . .
>
> Into this encyclopedia have been put the most important facts of modern knowledge. The thousands of articles and color pictures, charts, diagrams, and maps make all this knowledge clear and exciting. Here is an endless parade of fascinating facts—facts you can depend upon for up-to-dateness and accuracy, because world-famous experts have checked them. Get into the habit of looking things up in your GOLDEN BOOK ENCYCLOPEDIA. . . .
>
> Watch newspapers and television for important news about science and government, foreign countries, famous people, sports, plants and animals, literature and art, weather and exploration. Look up these subjects in the index, which is in the last volume of your GOLDEN BOOK ENCYCLOPEDIA. Then read about them.
>
> In the evening, or on a rainy day, pick up any volume of your GOLDEN BOOK ENCYCLOPEDIA. Open it anywhere and start reading. Notice how interesting just about any subject can be when it is clearly explained and well pictured. You will find yourself getting interested in more and more kinds of information.

That the *Golden Book*'s "endless parade of fascinating facts" was a fantasy in Boorstin's sense—a "contrived reality"—is suggested by the appearance of Walt Disney's name on the roster of "world-famous experts" in child development and education listed at the beginning of each volume (this roster includes Glenn T. Seaborg, "Co-winner of Nobel Prize for Chemistry, 1951," along with Willy Lee, author of numerous books on rocketry, and the inspirational minister Norman Vincent Peale). Not surprisingly, Disney's identifying note ("Motion Picture and Television Producer") was the simplest and most direct of the bunch. Of the book's prominent contributors, he alone worked in the entertainment industry, without need of degrees or proliferating institutional affiliations. How great a role he played in the *Encyclopedia*'s construction remains uncertain, but the overall effect of the series does, at the very least, give a *hint* of the Magic Kingdom.[35] Indeed, if the *Picture Atlas* depicts the world as imagined by Wall Street or the State Department, then the *Encyclopedia* is a guide constructed under the sign of Disney.

Pointedly, Disneyland is one of the few examples of "pseudo-event" and "hyperreality" that Boorstin and Baudrillard both cite. In *The Image,* Boorstin writes:

> Disneyland in California—the American "attraction" which tourist Krushchev most wanted to see—is the example to end all examples. Here indeed Nature imitates Art. The visitor to Disneyland encounters not the two-dimensional comic strip or movie original, but only their three-dimensional facsimiles.[36]

Baudrillard's analysis goes further. In "The Precession of Simulacra" he argues:

> Disneyland is a perfect model of all the entangled orders of simulacra. It is first of all a play of illusions and phantasms: the Pirates, the Frontier, the Future World, etc. . . . But what attracts the crowds the most is without doubt the social microcosm, the *religious,* miniaturized pleasure of real America. . . . Disneyland exists in order to hide that it is the "real" country. . . . Disneyland is presented as imaginary in order to make us believe that the rest is real.[37]

Never mind that "Disneyland as example" is itself an example of an historical artifact preserved in facsimile like one of the artifacts preserved in Disneyland. Although surpassed in 1971 by Disney World, and in 1994 by Celebration (Disney's model city, inhabited year round by "real" Americans), the original site—if I may put it so—remains a convenient marker of cultural shift. It is no surprise that the primary theoreticians of postmodernism were at the cusp of adulthood when Disneyland opened its gates. Their achievement was to live in two distinct cultural epochs and come to terms with the difference.

My own location in history is substantially different. Indeed, for poets of my age and background—say, Americans born between Disneyland's opening and the opening of Disney World, that is, between 1955 and 1971—the shift in consciousness we have had to assimilate has not been from modernism to postmodernism, but *within* postmodernity from an intuitive action to self-reflexive practice. This, in any event, is how I have come to understand my own trajectory. Whether copying butterflies from the *Golden Book Encyclopedia* or tracing underwear ads from the *New York Times,* rewriting news stories as a form of satire or philosophy books as a form of literary criticism, I have invariably come to a point of crisis (often, but not exclusively, brought on by the work's reception) where the aesthetic or intellectual value of my "means" and the social value of the "ends" become the primary focus of attention rather than the work itself. This deflection of attention from "the work itself" to its methods, ethics, and utility—from poetry to poetics—was often maddening, but it has led, through introspection, to a heightened self-consciousness, and through self-consciousness to a heightened understanding of what I might use the practice to accomplish. The experiments in *Simulcast* exemplify this development by moving slowly but surely from more or less spontaneous play (the satires of "The Anti-Hegemony Project"), to a playful criticism in which the method triumphs over its findings ("Poe's Poetics and Selected Reviews" and "The Literati of San Francisco"), to a form of criticism in which the findings achieve a measure of triumph over the method ("A Short History of Language Poetry").[38]

But before taking up this trajectory in detail, I must say a few words about Chris Funkhouser's Albany-based electronic journal *DIU (Descriptions of an Imaginary Universe),* surely the most immediate instigation for these experiments. Begun in the summer of 1994 when Chris and I were in graduate school, *DIU* came to a natural end some twenty-eight months later, after forty-five issues. Together, these issues now comprise nearly four hundred pages of printed text.[39] Far less labor-intensive than an ordinary journal, *DIU* still absorbed an enormous amount of energy. Using a standard UNIX text editor, Chris would prepare "galleys" in the middle of the night, multiple versions of which would flood my email account before dawn as minor glitches were caught and corrected. The publication schedule was brutal, especially in the beginning. The first issue was dated July 4th, 1994, and eighteen more appeared before the end of November, when we paused to catch our breath. Yet there was method in our madness, for what seemed, in the short run, a mere distraction from schoolwork, turned out, in the long run, to be a kind of R&D lab for ideas in poetry and poetics. There was even a kind of method in our pause for breath, for shortly after the slowdown (in February of 1995), "The Anti-Hegemony Project" was born, and shortly after that the essays and reviews of "Edgar Allen Poe" began to appear. By the time the journal folded on "election day 1996," Chris had worked out in detail what came to be his dissertation (on digital media and poetics), and I had composed the majority of the work you now hold in your hands.

Such usefulness was hardly predictable at the magazine's inception. To all outward appearance, *DIU* was an anarchic compendium of improvised poetry, in-jokes, and dada manifestos. Much of the writing was silly or sloppy, and much was of little interest to outsiders (for instance, issue 21 contained a long list of poets matched to country-western singers, inspired by Jonathan Williams's similar matching of poets to movie stars in the 1960s). But an undeniable vitality ran through all of it. Like Jill Stauffer's roughly contemporary *H_2So_4*, *DIU*'s style owed something to the zine culture that sprang up around punk. But where *H_2So_4* celebrated a particular present (the post-punk counterculture), *DIU* fixed its sights on the imaginary. Poems, letters, syllabi, notes, reviews, and essays were intermixed in no particular order, with no distinction drawn between fact and fantasy. Topics ranged from the pedagogical value of fast food on college campuses (no. 13) to prophesy (nos. 20 and 27.2) to poetry conferences (nos. 34 and 36). Cecil Taylor's transcribed conversation (nos. 10 and 13) appeared alongside stoned-serious discussions of made-up words (nos. 12 and 13), and a list of things missing from American poetry (no. 21) provoked compensating works on higher mathematics and machine language (nos. 22a, 25, and 32). The journal featured, as well, playlists from several radio shows (most notably, Nathaniel Mackey's "Tanganyika Strut," broadcast in Santa Cruz on KUSP-FM). There were regular musings on philosophy and politics signed "Thus, Albert or Hubert" (Don Byrd), a serialization of Will Alexander's "To the Bloodless Refugees of Emptiness," installments of Beth Russell's "Theses for a *Neo-Luddite Militia" and Stephen Cope's "From *The Annals of Multikulti,*" and an ongoing series called "The Last Days of the White Race," modeled on Mackey's radio playlists and the "Editor's Quotron" in John Clarke's *Intent: Letter of Talk, Thinking & Document.* And beginning with issue 22c, there was Poe.

Maddening in its erasure of context, the work in *DIU* often came across as ephemera floated back in time from an unrealized future, as an alternative culture's debris rather than its finest achievements. This was, in fact, precisely the point, but the point was frequently disguised by the magazine's reliance on anonymity. This anonymity proved a big obstacle for readers who were used to ordinary poetry journals, where the matching of style or stance to author (and the subsequent placing of author on literary map) often takes the place of reading. In *DIU,* all contributions were unsigned, signed with initials, or attributed to fanciful characters, and if this weren't enough to thwart the mapping instinct, many of the journal's contributors went by several names. (I myself was "Black Hole Sun," "Patriarchal Poetry," "Guantanamo Bey," "Kimberly Filbee," "Hecuba Whimsy," and "Edgar Allen Poe," among others.)[40] There were reasons for this cavalier disregard for the niceties of attribution. We were trying to confuse the difference between documentary and science fiction, and this required both a defamiliarizing of the given and a naming of the possible. Thus, what appeared, at first glance, to be improvised poetry was often an elaborate fantasy of how poets in the future *might* improvise. Likewise, what appeared to be an in-joke was sometimes an attempt to create a community out of thin air *with* a joke. And when one looked closely, the dada manifestos often turned out to be Heideggerian, or feminist, or multicultural, or cybernetic. "Can't take the culture offline while you tinker," wrote Greg Keith in issue 10, and this sense of tinkering amid the deafening roar of the culture's machinery gave *DIU*'s mix of fact and fantasy its particular tonality of exhaustion and desire. As in the *Golden Book Encyclopedia,* the world disappeared in favor of an idea, but here the "idea" in question was precisely the world's disappearance. To chart this disappearance—filling the resulting void with something other than nostalgia—was our ultimate aim, and the ultimate justification, of our labor.

This aim was made abundantly clear in the opening issue, which began with an epigraph from Eileen Myles ("I have the same / birthday as John / Milton. Did / you know that? / So I don't have to / write long poems about heaven & hell—everything's / been lost in my lifetime") and continued with a manifesto by "Thus, Albert or Hubert":

> Everything is lost. We have the advantage of worldlessness & more. Even nothing is lost. DIU celebrates the emptiness. We don't have an idea. We don't have time or space. I or I cannot say it, but we don't have a noun. And I or I say it any way.
>
> We cannot make a *thing*. Everything could be lost because there never was any thing (you can lose only illusions). The man said, "No ideas but in things," and we laughed our heads off. There are no ideas, there are no things. . . .
>
> You don't get to be somewhere just by showing up. The place must be constructed, and its compositions and concepts and correlations and technologies must be made up, not out of need (we do not need anything we do not already have) but out of love of life.
>
> Our ignorance is of epic proportion, and it can be overcome only with an epic. The epic of the single body, however, will not suffice—the epic of Joyce, Pound, Olson, the epic of Whitehead, Lacan, Althusser, epics of single bodies. Homer was many (we can now know this for certain). No matter how I or I manage these events of knowing you are always another actor of my act.
>
> Exercise for today: rewrite the above paragraphs, substituting verbs for nouns.

The pseudo-Rastafarian "I or I" in this passage suggested that the quizzical attribution ("Albert or Hubert") was more than just a passing joke, that even though identity and authorship were part of the all-encompassing emptiness, they were nonetheless worth speaking into existence, especially if their existence could be taken with a grain of salt. Hyperbolic and contradictory, the manifesto sought, as manifestos often do, to resolve its contradictions—and justify its hyperbole—through sheer force of will. A will in the legal sense too, bequeathing its force to the reader in the form of a command: "rewrite."

The injunction to participate through revision in the creation of an epic, or better yet, *encyclopedic* "description" of an "imaginary," or better yet, a *virtual* "universe" was especially appropriate given the immediate context of the journal. One of the first poetry journals on the Internet, *DIU* was also a collectively improvised prospectus for what was often called, in a wildly inappropriate metaphor, "life on the information superhighway."[41] This metaphor, no doubt, was meant to be reassuring, to serve as an evocation of industrial America for those of us who, like myself, were anxious about their adaptability to a post-industrial future. But nothing could have been further from the interstate highway system (with its well-lit rest stops and service areas) than the Internet in its early inception. In those days you could not simply point with your mouse, click, and have your function performed. Even with written instructions, I often found myself staring blankly at my screen—stymied at a crucial moment by the intractability of the program or by my own inability to conjure the right command. Things would soon change, of course, but in 1994, when *DIU* appeared, the Internet was poised at a moment of tension and transition: *after* the initial period of experimentation, when nearly everyone online was an enthusiast (if not expert) in the use of computers; yet *before* the arrival of the World Wide Web, which would drastically reduce the problems of access while dramatically increasing the possibilities of display.[42]

It is no accident that the majority of *DIU*'s contributors were students of Don Byrd at SUNY Albany and Charles Bernstein at SUNY Buffalo. Byrd first went online in 1986, and had been using computers in his teaching since 1984. Bernstein went online in 1992, but by 1993, he had founded the "Poetics List."[43] Byrd and Bernstein thus fit the profile of first-generation experimenters in "virtual community," and so did many of their students. But not all. Many of us (I studied with Bernstein at the time) had only gone online in order to participate in seminar discussions and we barely had enough expertise to manage an email account. Contributing to an ongoing experiment in community seemed a far-fetched possibility, as the experiment seemed to require a knack for technology. We brought instead our bewilderment and suspicion, which placed us at odds with the generally utopian spirit of the venture. Considering this predicament, *DIU*'s most *useful* contribution to Internet culture may have been its ability to introduce an uncertain, even hostile readership of poets into the pleasures and possibilities of the "virtual." The journal accomplished this by exaggerating the medium's most frequently noted aspects (anonymity; self-invention; erasure of geographic distance; occlusion of gender, ethnic, and age differences) within a quasi-fictional frame that both highlighted and rendered safe the Internet's still alienating strangeness.

I cannot overestimate the intensity of this strangeness. In those days, online publishing was in its infancy, and though I had heard of "popnetting" and "bbs's" many years before, I was an easily befuddled "newby."[44] I owned a computer and modem, and I had network access from home, but I still preferred using a manual typewriter for poetry. I had not yet made the leap from DOS to Windows, and I had not yet become acquainted with what was happily called (to my nineteenth-century trained ears) "a graphical browser." Yet much of *DIU*'s character came from its anarchic relationship to the befuddling medium of the Internet, and from the friction between the journal's high- and low-tech features. Restricted in design possibilities by the "text only" format, *DIU* was a newsletter whose primitive layout paid deliberate homage to the corner-stapled mimeo and xerox magazines of the sixties and seventies, and like those magazines, *DIU* was available by subscription only.[45] Electronic journals would subsequently take shape as "sites" rather than "email," but in those days of incompatible VAX and UNIX accounts, of "gopher" and "telnet" and VT100 terminals, I was pleased as punch just to be able to navigate my own mailbox. More demanding forms of engagement—for instance, requesting and downloading "zipped" files—often brought me to an impasse I could only overcome by rebooting my computer.

Oddly enough, the often alienating aspects of the journal's underlying technology only fed my fascination with minor aspects of presentation peculiar to the medium: unexpectedly "wrapped" text, the replacement of individual pages with a seemingly unending "scroll," "chevrons" for quoted material, signature files, "emoticons," subject headings, routing codes, minimal maneuverability between "screens," blocks of radiant letters bouncing angrily against invisible "buffers," and a typographic monotony (via "ASCII") more familiar to the typewriter than computer. Longtime users, especially those engaged in theorizing the Internet, were, by contrast, eager for the next leap in technology. Murry Christensen in a letter to the editor of *Ejournal* asked:

```
Is ANYBODY else out there as frustrated (to the
point of beating my head against the monitor)
by the absolute paucity of communication tools
*actually* available to the _cyberspace_ communi-
cator? :-(
```

Adding:

```
Look at this last sentence . . . what a pathetic
arsenal of communication tools. And that pretty
much exhausts what's available! This in a world
that gives any user of any reasonably-competent
word processor scaleable typefaces, embedded
graphics, at least simple text linking. Yet the
instant you want to make that "document" avail-
able to others on-line all the meaning inhering
in anything other than raw ASCII text gets
stripped away. Put it on the wire and instantly
we all become visually disadvantaged (and I
wouldn't be afraid to propose perhaps in some
way intellectually-mangled also).
```
[46]

For me, as well, the experience of a "visually disadvantaged," "intellectually-mangled" discourse community was a source of frustration, but I also found the textual characteristics of this discourse a valuable means of understanding and articulating what the experience was teaching me. This may sound like a tautology, but it's really not, for the particular community with which I was trying to communicate was made up almost entirely of poets, and I found that the arrival of this community on the Internet was far more revelatory of *the community* than of the Internet. As I came to terms, then, with this "discourse network" (first on the Poetics List, as a practitioner; later, as a practitioner and theorist in *DIU*), my ultimate object of attention was not the network, but the discourse community that had taken this network as its site of activity.[47]

"The Anti-Hegemony Project" (or AHP, as it quickly became known) developed these reflections improvisationally in a series of satires that extended certain aspects of the *DIU* project beyond the journal's own borders by appearing in unannounced installments over a one-month period on the Poetics List.[48] The rate of appearance was slow for the majority of this time (thirty messages in twenty-five days), but sped up considerably at the end (twenty-four in two days). These two varying rates of activity corresponded to two phases of satire. Both phases of the satire were based on rewritten texts found on the Internet, a provenance that the individual installments emphasized by mimicking meticulously the typographic peculiarities of the source material.

The first sequence was based on wire-service stories from the "clari.* news net," a series of Usenet groups whose characteristic look (based on a computer screen sixty-five characters wide and twenty-six lines high) included an elaborate frame of "headers" and "footers." The frame, of course, bore no relation to any known page size; it did not even match the oddly shaped accordions of newsprint that my university's computing center favored. This meant that the headers and footers appeared mid-page in any printout. Adding to the peculiarity were the "chevrons" running down the left-hand side of the page, which were a consequence of the method I used to retrieve the stories. Rather than print them directly from the news group, I would forward them to my email account. The end result, when sent to the Poetics List, looked something like this:

```
> Subject: AHP Correction on Lean Times Story
> Copyright: 1999 by The Anti-Hegemony Project
> Date: 31 Feb 99 26:30:13 PST
>
> Lines: 10
>
>   LOS ANGELES (AHP) -- In a story yesterday
> about a study examining how shortages of
> inspired language and increasing population
> will affect U.S. poetics production and
> Americans' diet of subsidized corn porn lyrics,
> The Anti-Hegemony project erroneously reported
> the corporate affiliation of a researcher.
>   Marjorie Perloff is employed by Lang-Po
> Labs, not Arithmetrick Frozen Yogurt Co. Down
> Under.[49]
```

The second sequence of posts, which appeared over the last two days of the project, was also based on Usenet material: messages posted on the electronic bulletin board "alt.fan.madonna." But where the clari.* texts were relatively staid in appearance and language, the alt.fan.madonna material was exuberant, disputatious, freewheeling in typography, overblown in rhetoric, lax in what English teachers call "mechanics," and wildly adolescent in attitude. This was, in fact, part of the material's appeal. I wanted to create a distorted image of the Poetics List, using Usenet language to exaggerate the exuberance, disputation, and so forth of Listserv discussion.[50] (Since 1995, and the emergence of the World Wide Web, the difference between the two networks is much less pronounced.) The result was an imaginary news group devoted to language writer Ron Silliman:

```
> Rating: PG13
> <poetic guidance for readers over 13 suggested>
> From: nathanthewiseguy@ARIBADERCI.ARIZ.AHP
> Newsgroups: alt.fan.silliman
> Subject: Desperately seeking Silliman . . .
> Date: 14 Feb 1999 06:06:06
> Organization: The Anti-Hegemony Project
> Lines: 23
>
>      Ok . . . back in '84 or '85 (when langpo
> was only ten years old or so, whatever you
> consider to be the movement's origin), an Ohio
> fan club released among other things, a book
> called "The Silliman Issue" with a picture on
> the cover of Silliman smoking a cigar.
>
>      I DESPERATELY want to get hold of this
> item. Is there anyone that can give me some
> clue/hint, etc. as to how I can purchase or
> swap for this item????
> I would be eternally gratefull!!!!!  THANKS.
>
>
```

```
>         "Each duck was called Cause & Effect, and
>  their progeny swim in the same pond today."
>                                  David Bromige
>
>
>                               Happiness? to all,
>
>
>                                       Nate[51]
```

The rates of deployment between the two sequences differed for reasons of content. The news satires were dispatches, portraits of the poetry world unified by their general reference to members of the Poetics List. On the other hand, the alt.fan.silliman material was a portrait of the Poetics List itself. The outpouring of messages was meant to approximate the list's ordinary flow of communication.

As mentioned earlier, several characteristics of the AHP posts extended the *DIU* project. First of all, the force of will evident in both the volume of the messages and the aggressiveness of their content; second, the masking of their authorship (the messages were sent to the list from a variety of email accounts, none of them mine); third, the fantasy and science fiction elements of the individual satires (debris from an unruly future, they were all dated "1999"); and fourth, the attempt to both describe and create a literary culture specific to the Internet (most notably in the "alt.fan.silliman" pieces). The first two were major sources of criticism, and I will take them up in a moment. Of more immediate concern to me in the AHP's production were the other two. *DIU*'s fantasy and science fiction elements had always been more prominent in my contributions to the journal than in those of the other writers. This was perhaps a consequence of my reading interests; more likely, it was due to my relationship to the enabling technology. Unskilled and even inept, I was necessarily more inclined to concoct elaborate scenarios for the future than manipulate present possibilities. Simply put, the Internet was less real to me as a locus for community than as a screen for projecting an *idea* of community. My fascination with the textual characteristics of the Internet's various modes of communication derived from the same source; because my negotiations were so severely restricted, it seemed to me more useful to explore the logic of representation that controlled my access than the Internet itself. Thus, where other contributors to *DIU* elided the emphasis on "description" in the journal's name, treating *DIU* as a kind of "squat" within the Internet—a "temporary autonomous zone," or "TAZ," in Hakim Bey's terminology—the generative possibilities of description were precisely what held my fascination.[52] Of course, it is ironic that, where *DIU*'s "Temporary Autonomous Zone" became reified into mere description by virtue of its containment within the frame of a literary journal, the descriptions put forward by the AHP, slipping free of that frame, did, in fact, create a kind of "TAZ," at least within the narrow context of the Poetics List.

Within this "narrow context," the AHP was bound to be controversial. What surprised me was the focus of this controversy, for although the satires were provocative (and did, on occasion, draw blood), the primary cause of complaint was their mode of dissemination. At the project's end, especially, when the AHP's pace of production picked up, the criticism became quite heated: the list had been taken over by interlopers, serious discussion drowned out; the satires were malicious, their anonymity cowardly. Only some of this criticism was posted on the list. The vast majority filtered back to me by word of mouth. And this indicates something else worth noting about Poetics: unlike other "virtual communities" in which I then participated (the Derrida and Sixties Lists, most notably), the members of Poetics were connected by a skein of relationships that had nothing to do with the Internet per se. Especially in its first two years of operation, the list was driven by, and in turn exaggerated, social dynamics that originated elsewhere (for instance, in classrooms, reading groups, and poetry scenes).[53]

Public or private, the criticism leveled at the AHP was valid, and having witnessed a number of similar (but never quite the same) intrusions on other lists, I appreciate the bewilderment and irritation that greeted the AHP all the more. Yet the content of this criticism is worth exploring in detail, and certain distinctions worth emphasizing. First of all, if the AHP was unwanted, then so was every other contribution to the list, for they were also unsolicited. In Listserv parlance, Poetics had an "owner," Charles Bernstein, but apart from his administration of subscriptions and resolution of technical problems, his involvement was decidedly hands off. What, then, constituted an unwanted message? If "list owner" approval was the issue, then the

AHP was fine. Bernstein was amused by the satires and gave them his tacit approval by discussing them with me without any particular reference to their appropriateness.[54] Of course, the problem of distinguishing between wanted and unwanted messages was not simply a matter of top-down control; the members of the list were also part of its administration. This was the point, or perhaps the justification, of Bernstein's hands-off approach. But how, in *practical* terms, was this alternative method of administration to operate? How were the list's members to decide on a day-to-day basis whether this or that particular message—or set of messages—was "wanted"? Before the AHP, the list's members had "voted with their feet." Any message that provoked conversation was wanted; messages met with stony silence were not. But conversation and silence were hardly foolproof criteria, since desirable participation need not require a response while undesirable communications might well demand it. Indeed, for many people, the most unwanted messages of all were those that provoked the most insistent discussion: taunts and insults, exhibitionist displays of wit, irrelevant tangents. How, then, distinguish between an interruption of discussion and a discussion when both took the same form and public complaint merely added to the blurring of the difference? Unless the matter was put to a vote, the membership-as-administration was better placed to *discuss* a matter than *decide* it.

As it happens, discussion of the AHP remained rudimentary, partly because the satires ceased and the list moved on to other topics, partly because those responsible for the postings weren't interested in demanding such discussion. Unlike other provocations that would later shake Poetics, the AHP was not intended as a permanent alteration to the list's dynamics, only as a comment upon them.[55] Nor was this "comment" intended as a challenge to the legitimacy of the list's overall mission. This mission, according to Bernstein's "Welcome Message," "while provisional, and while open to continual redefinition by list participants," was nonetheless quite specific in aim: "to support, inform, and extend those directions in poetry that are committed to innovations, renovations, and investigations of form and/or/as content, to the questioning of received forms and styles, and to the creation of the otherwise unimagined, untried, unexpected, improbable, and impossible."[56] To my mind, the AHP *fulfilled* this mission. In form and content alike, the satires sought to extend the possibilities of innovative poetry both by questioning received forms and values and by creating new ones. To be sure, the AHP was more interested in social formations than books of poetry or ideas in poetics, but the formal symmetry between the individual satires and the work satirized was never exactly hidden. One story blamed the first wave of the AHP on an ordinary computer inspired to a new stage of evolution by *The Norton Anthology of Postmodern American Poetry.*[57] Another (no. 8) blamed the second wave on a toxic spill of "Simulac," a substance earlier identified as a "formula" developed by "Lang-Po Labs" in California (no. 3). In the context of prior Poetics List discussion, the AHP's interest in poetry as social formation was not unusual. The policing of poetry's discursive borders (no. 1), the taming role of the academy (nos. 5, 6) and the nature of Internet discourse itself (nos. 10–24) were all familiar topics to the list's membership. In what sense, then, was the AHP an interruption or drowning out of serious discussion? If anything was drowned out, it was the serious discussion that the AHP could have inspired: about group dynamics, about the intersection of "real" communities in "virtual" space, about the relationship between critical and creative writing, about the nature of authorship on the Internet, about the Poetics List itself.

The major reason given for repudiating the AHP was its "anonymity": though the satires did arrive from identifiable senders, these "senders" were universally discredited as little more than camouflage. Most of the list's members required as a prerequisite for serious engagement the signed name of a person who could be held responsible for the post. But "responsible" in what sense? And "required" toward what end? I was prepared, at least in theory, to step forward as the AHP's primary author, but none of the arguments that encouraged such a step convinced me that "serious engagement" would be the result. The most common of these arguments, by far, was that the anonymity was "cowardly," a claim I dismissed, far too quickly, as mere machismo. The assumption guiding this line of thought *seemed* to be that a satire's accuracy was of less importance than the satirist's willingness to risk opprobrium. "If you were a *real* man," these critics seemed to be saying, "you'd come out and take your lumps—or whip us all in a fair fight."

Complicating my response to this criticism was a growing irritation at the imputation of "camouflage" in the AHP's dissemination. By prior arrangement with Chris Funkhouser—who administered the postings to Poetics, one of the many ways that the satires functioned as an extension of *DIU*—the installments were sent from a number of different email accounts in order to suggest a collective enterprise. The enterprise was, in fact, collective in the sense that the postings to Poetics were made possible by a network of friends, the majority of whom enjoyed the satires and approved of their method of dissemination.[58] By and large, however, I alone authored the pieces, and this state of affairs—guessed almost immediately by a number of the AHP's readers—was taken as evidence that the collectivity of the project was a sham.[59]

Up to a point, the inference was justified, as my own email address was notably absent from the list of senders. An early member of the Poetics List, I had quit in 1994 after a "flame war," vowing never to return, and stubbornness held me to this vow during the reign of the AHP. Nor was my departure from Poetics an irrelevant fact. After all, the AHP was *directed* at Poetics, both literally (as a potential readership) and figuratively (as an object of the satires themselves). Members of the list who guessed my authorship understandably interpreted this direction of energies as an act of vengeance. And perhaps they were right. The AHP's *fictive* erasure of the difference between Listserv and Usenet cultures was certainly derisory from the point of view of those satirized. Never mind that this erasure was prophetic; that the merging of Listserv and Usenet styles of discourse (what Charles Bernstein would later term "tabloidization") would lead to a momentary shutdown of Poetics in the *real* 1999. The AHP's imaginary future was a far from flattering extrapolation from lived experience.[60] Like Bob Perelman's similar erasure of the divide between high and low art in *The First World,* my leveling of distinctions was born of disengagement—a disengagement I did not revel in, but suffered. Imaginary collectivities were a necessary placebo.

Hostile reception notwithstanding, the AHP was an exhilarating, even joyful experience. Intellectually challenging and poetically pleasing, it gave me an occasion for camaraderie (not to mention a break from schoolwork). I felt as though I had taken a crash course in "textual appropriation" (fifty odd texts in thirty odd days), but far from exhausting my interest in the practice, the crash course only whetted my appetite for more. Here and there, I had been able to make complex statements about the poetry I was satirizing, but by and large the source material had limited me to burlesque. The burlesque was meaningful in the sense that it drew an analogy between the poetry world and the world at large in such a way that the latter illuminated the former. Nonetheless, other, more meaningful forms of illumination were certainly possible. My ambition now was to find those forms, to go beyond satire toward criticism proper, but without abandoning the practice of textual appropriation. Having sharpened my technique on the clari.* news net and alt.fan.madonna material, I was eager to test my skill on something more intricate and more rewarding stylistically—on something like the essays of Edgar Allan Poe. In terms of sheer craft, I had come a long way since 1987, when a single paragraph of rewritten text proved too unwieldy for inclusion in my Bob Perelman review; but when measured in terms other than craft, the AHP was something of a backward step. I had mastered the transgressiveness of Acker's method, but not its ability to engage in surreptitious dialogue. This would now be my goal.

FROM SATIRE TO CRITICISM

My fastening on Poe was not arbitrary. I had played with the notion of rewriting his essays for some time; the AHP developed as a consequence of this play. The game of rewriting (or should I say "thought experiment"?) began with a problem, a difficulty I was having in reading Poe's essays end to end. The problem, for me, was not Poe's own writing, but the writing of the authors he discussed. Minor figures for the most part, their works invariably awful, his principal targets of rebuke (for rebuke was Poe's most characteristic gesture) were a murky pool of stagnant water into which Poe cast away his most polished thought like a stone. Not always, of course. When he gave grudging praise to William Cullen Bryant, forced himself to speak ill of Mrs. Browning, or waged his ongoing border war with Longfellow, the inherent interest of the subject buoyed up for me the weight of his attentions. These subjects, however, were exceptions to the rule. Generally speaking, his essays take up the likes of J. F. Dalton, Cornelius Mathews, and S. Anna Lewis—and takes them up with an unrelenting detail that makes casual reading difficult, at least if one is unprepared to think long and hard about *Peter Snook, Wakondah,* or *Child of the Sea*.

One day, reading aloud to my wife, I fell upon an accidental solution. If the difficulty of Poe's criticism was the tedium of its subject matter, why not change the subject? I cannot remember which essay I was reading at the time—it does not really matter—but halfway through a sentence—a juicy one-liner—I caught the hint of a resemblance between the subject of Poe's remarks and a living poet my wife and I both happened to detest. Without missing a beat, I made a quick substitution of names and earned an instant laugh. This in itself was noteworthy, since I had already read aloud several similar sentences, receiving little more for my trouble than a bored "that's great" (meaning: "leave me alone, I'm busy"). More noteworthy still was the impact this substitution had on *me*. Now, instead of continuing on as before—lazily skipping ahead to the next *bon mot*—I found myself paying close attention, following out in my head the improvised analogies between living and dead authors. To be sure, these analogies did not remain parallel all the way through, but even the divergences proved enlightening.

A question immediately arose. Would this game remain interesting with another essay? I tried right away and discovered that it would. Informative too? More so than I hoped. The formulation and pursuance of analogies not only illuminated the individual essay; the overall shape of Poe's relationships to his contemporaries came into focus as well. And this, of course, induced me to see my own relationships in Poe-esque terms, even when the analogies broke down. If the playful substitution of one name for another was already a kind of game (subsequently perfected in the AHP), this could not compare with the role-playing game that quickly developed once I began rewriting Poe in earnest. In the AHP, the correlations I had sought between my source texts and the poetry world were entirely thematic. Underage drinking had suggested powerful ideas abused by underage poets; safe sex and retroviruses had suggested "safe discourse" and retro thinking.[61] My earliest experiments with Poe worked the same way: imitators of Wordsworth and Coleridge suggested second-generation language poets; talentless hacks suggested talentless hacks. Slowly, however, my approach began to change, accelerated by the AHP and by my increasing boredom with pure satire. The translation of Poe's insults into a contemporary context through the substitution of names was no longer enough. In seeking a fit between past and present, I no longer based my judgment solely on the quality or character of the work under review. I now gave equal weight to the quality or character of Poe's relationship to that work.

The evolution of my reading of Poe coincided with the appearance of Lew Daly's *Swallowing the Scroll,* the first (and last) supplement to *apex of the M,* a Buffalo-based poetry magazine best known for the anti-language poetry editorial in its inaugural issue.[62] *Swallowing the Scroll* amplified on this editorial's primary thesis: that "the rhetoric of innovation as proclaimed by the avant-garde" had become as untenable as "the suburban vacuity of mainstream poetics and verse," and that the only viable alternatives were either "the mystical and prophetic traditions," or romanticism. Dense, impassioned, even moralistic in its denunciation of experimental writing, *Swallowing the Scroll* was nonetheless framed as an appreciation of two writers who were themselves experimentalists, Susan Howe and John Taggart—a fact that marked both the magazine and pamphlet as defiantly in-house acts of aggression, letter bombs sent by one member of a household to another. This I knew because I myself was a member of that household, having published an essay in the first issue of *apex* and having talked to Daly at length about his pamphlet before it went to press. Was I sympathetic to his argument? Not especially. But I took a rooting interest in his tussle with received values, and in *our* household (the Buffalo Poetics Program), no value was more complacently received than the inherent goodness of experimentation. With this in mind, I did my best to help Daly edit his pamphlet into a readable form. Alas, to no avail. Fearful that I was trying to water him down, he declined to change more than a phrase or two.

Daly's pamphlet had the feel of an antique document. This was partly a function of its emphasis on prophecy—*Swallowing the Scroll* was deliberately modeled on religious tracts of the seventeenth century, the subject of Daly's dissertation—and partly due to the pre-modern flavor of Daly's prose, a lugubrious argot that bespoke of old-spelling Bibles, old political movements, and old translations of continental philosophy.[63] Indeed, there was even something old-fashioned about the deliberateness of Daly's provocations, something in his dogged antagonism to language writing that reminded me of Poe—of the Poe who dogged Longfellow with trumped-up accusations of plagiarism. And then, in a flash, it occurred to me: If Lew Daly wanted to wage war in pamphlets, why not answer him in kind?

Heretofore, in reading Poe's essays, I had asked myself which living author best fit the parameters established by Poe's critique. I now found myself asking the same question in reverse: Which of Poe's essays best fit the parameters established by Daly's pamphlet? The answer was not immediately obvious. I thought at first of an 1840 review of Thomas Moore's *Alciphron, a Poem* ("Amid the vague mythology of Egypt . . . Anacreon Moore has found all of that striking *materiel* which he so much delights in working up"), but this was not one of Poe's more amusing outings, and humor was decidedly required.[64] I next thought of his 1836 review of *Paul Ulric* by Morris Mattson ("In itself, the book before us is too purely imbecile to merit an extended critique"), but too much of this essay was given over to plot summary and I saw no easy way to pursue an analogy between novel's plot and pamphlet's argument. In the end, I settled on Poe's dismantling of the clergyman-poet William Wilberforce Lord, in part because Lord's miscues reminded me of Daly's, in part because Poe's opening paragraph allowed an extended allusion to the Poetics Program. Thus, where the original begins:

> Of Mr. Lord we know nothing—although we believe he is a student of Princeton College—or perhaps a graduate, or perhaps a Professor of that Institution.[65]

I have:

> Of Mr. Daly we know nothing—although we believe that he is a student in SUNY Buffalo's Poetics Program—or perhaps a graduate, or perhaps a Professor of that Institution.

The reference to Buffalo tied in especially nicely to my source text, for one of the poems taken up at length by Poe was Lord's "A Hymn to Niagara" (an exercise in solipsism, Poe declared, in which "the little figure of Mr. Lord, in the shape of a great capital **I,** gets so thoroughly in between the reader and the waterfall that not a particle of the latter is to be discovered").[66] No less serendipitous, however, was the cheap joke Poe used to bring his essay to a close, for here he introduced a religious note much more appropriate to *my* subject than *his:*

> But enough of this folly. We are heartily tired of the book, and thoroughly disgusted with the impudence of the parties who have been aiding and abetting in thrusting it before the public.

> To the Poet himself we have only to say—from any farther specimens of your stupidity, good Lord deliver us![67]

Translated, this last sentence yielded the analogous pun:

> To the poet himself we have only to say—from any farther specimens of your stupidity, God give us daily deliverance!

Here Poe's facetious "good Lord" (another jab at Lord's solipsism) became a literal appeal to the Lord almighty, an alteration forced by the difference in names, but fortuitous withal since Lew Daly's ostensible flaw was not self-regard, but zealotry.

Appropriating Poe's invective in these opening and closing paragraphs was immensely satisfying, and almost effortless. The real work of transformation occurred in between, in the fitting of Poe's particular remarks—his criticism proper—to the particular case of *Swallowing the Scroll*. Here I was forced to attend closely to the logic and structure of Poe's attack. At the same time, in order to fit this attack to the case at hand, I was forced to attend closely to the formal properties of Daly's prose. As noted above, I had already read the pamphlet carefully in manuscript. After publication, I read it again, but more aloofly. Now I found myself reading a third time, in a strange manner that felt, at once, both careful *and* aloof. Scouring the text for passages matching those in Lord, I studied the workings of Daly's argument as never before; and yet, never before had his argument worked *on me* with so little effect. I found this freedom from entanglement a welcome relief, but recognized (with no little sense of irony) that this freedom was aided by my rigid adherence to a source text; for precisely when a phrase or thought might have goaded me into response had I only been writing with a free hand, the template of Poe's commentary held me fixed on matters alien to my own interests as a critic.

The most important of these alien matters was what Poe elsewhere terms "the minor morals of the muse," by which he meant a writer's technique.[68] I myself have trouble conceiving of craft in moral terms, perhaps because the difference between ethics and aesthetics seems unbridgeable, perhaps because so many writers suspected of a lapse in technique have called into question the very terms of our critique. For Poe, however, for whom the "ideality" of art was a virtue in its own right, passing judgment on a writer's technique acquired the character of a moral crusade. This was not a sad duty. Rather, the merciless exposure of a writer's deficiencies (however "minor") provided Poe with one of his favorite pastimes. The nature of the deficiencies varied widely—from bad rhyme and broken meter to poorly worked-out metaphors and mistakes in grammar—but the fascination with technical incompetence remained constant. Indeed, the monotony of this fascination would often stymie me when trying to read Poe end to end. When translating or rewriting Poe's work, however, I was stymied for a different reason, for finding equivalent deficiencies proved difficult at times, and not simply because the quality of writing has improved over the years. The nature of error itself has changed. After all, when it comes to free verse, the basic requirements of craft are scarcely matters of unambiguous law. When the writing is disconnected by design, poorly developed metaphors or inconsistent plots can no longer be taken as matters of deficiency. Surrealism's violations of logic are virtues. Pound's slippage into prose, a point of interest. Are there grammar mistakes in Gertrude Stein? Usage errors in language writing? To say of Lyn Hejinian, as Poe once wrote of Margaret Fuller, "Perhaps only the scholastic . . . would be able to detect in her strange and continual inaccuracies, a capacity for the accurate," is to encompass in one huge breath the caesura dividing nineteenth- and twentieth-century lines of thought.[69] And this, indeed, is what my Poe translations try to do: speak across the disjunction between Poe's universe and our own, allowing the ostensibly silent caesura to become audible as a subject matter in its own right—to become an alteration in the meaning of Poe's prose quite apart from any alteration done *to* his prose. Dealing with the alteration became a practical problem of the first order. Should I change the terms of Poe's response and make a serious critique? Or keep to his terms and risk farce? Should I highlight the modernity of the work under discussion or expose its anachronism? Play up Poe's pertinence or his bluster?

Happily, these particular difficulties did not obtain in my rewriting of Poe's Lord review. Indeed, one of the reasons I matched Daly's pamphlet with Lord's poetry was the exaggerated attention Poe pays to the technical aspect of the writing (exaggerated even for Poe). "Of that species of composition," he tells us, "that comes most appropriately under the head, *Drivel,* we should have no trouble in selecting as many specimens as our readers could desire."[70] The same was assuredly true of *Swallowing the Scroll:* the gumminess of the prose—mannered to the point of self-parody—was by all accounts the pamphlet's most noteworthy feature. Even so, the pamphlet's *notoriety* was due almost entirely to Daly's dogged attack on experimental poetry (readers of such poetry being uncommonly forgiving when it comes to gummy prose). It therefore appealed to me—to my sense of humor, if not my sense of justice—to attack Daly's pamphlet with equal doggedness in an essay that was itself a species of experimental poetry, and to base this attack almost entirely on his pamphlet's quality of expression. In *apex of the M,* Daly had set himself in opposition to "the self-conscious opacity practiced by most poetries today."[71] What better response, then, could I possibly make to his magazine's program than to cast a sharp light on the opacity of his own prose?

One example will suffice to indicate the difficulties involved in bringing Poe's critique to bear on a subject other than his own. Here, first, is a brief passage from the beginning of Poe's review, a pretense at granting Lord's "particular merits—such as they are":

> At page 6 . . . we meet . . . a passage of high merit, although sadly disfigured:
>
> Thee the bright host of Heaven,
> The stars adore:—a thousand altars, fed
> By pure unwearied hands, like cressets blaze
> In the blue depths of night; nor all unseen
> In the pale sky of day, with tempered light
> Burn *radiant of thy praise.*
>
> The disfiguration to which we allude, lies in the making a blazing altar burn merely like a blazing cresset—a simile about as forcible as would be the likening an apple to a pear, or the seafoam to the froth on a pitcher of Burton's ale.[72]

Poe makes no effort to explain what he means by "high merit." The gesture toward praise is a feint; his real point comes after, in exposing the silliness of Lord's comparison. Playing with his victim, he deals out disdain in little jabs, saving the full force of his contempt for later (and in this respect, even his exposure of Lord's silliness is a feint, a preparation for the far sharper critique at essay's end). Here now is my translation:

> At page 10 . . . we meet . . . a passage of high merit, though sadly disfigured:
>
> > I will provisionally describe by the word "prophecy" here a poetry that might be said to permit—on a stage of public hierarchy, and under the full weight of our disgrace as citizens on such a stage—enunciation in an encounter with the supra-hierarchical, the power of God.
>
> The disfiguration to which we allude lies in making poetry's "stage" less solid than the emotions of those who would ascend to speak. Concrete froth on a pitcher of beer could not effect a more ridiculous image. Moreover, by giving less weight to history's "stage" than the actor's "disgrace," our author betrays an overweening aestheticism. In Mr. Daly's scenario, the Poet does not so much bear witness to the Age as the Age to the Poet. "Enunciation" occurs less as an encounter with God than as the aftertaste of God's "power." (This "power," alas, has little to do with revelation, but is merely the bombast of any competent preacher.) The poetry in question is not *really* prophecy, but only allows itself to be *described* as such.

The rewrite is longer and more heavy-handed than the original, but the general idea (ridiculous imagery) and even some of the language (froth on beer) remains the same. My divergence from Poe has its source in the difference between the two authors. Lord's flaws are straightforward, his poetry simple, and his ideas largely beside the point. The silliness of his imagery is evident from the imagery itself. Not so with Daly, whose flaws are anything *but* straightforward. His writing and thought are far more complex than Lord's; his work's nobility or silliness is inextricable from its larger ambitions—all of which takes time to expose. A single, graceful thrust was thus insufficient.

The "disfigured" passages quoted above—Lord's and Daly's—are hardly the most egregious. For *egregious* error, one must turn to the essays' parallel conclusions, crescendos of unflattering quotation that prod the two critics—Poe and his twentieth-century echo, me—to announce in unison, "The only excuse we can make to our readers for annoying them with specifications in this respect is that, without the specifications, we should never have been believed."[73] Transcribing this "we" for the first time, in the midst of recreating Poe's essay for a new audience, I felt a shiver of fear and excitement, as if a ghost had suddenly taken possession of my hand. Never before had I written anything with so much rhetorical power. I was hardly sure I had written *this*. The voice was Poe's through and through; only its distorted reproduction was mine. Nor were these distortions intentional. In giving myself over to Poe's rhetoric, I was eager to experience that "extinction of personality" Eliot describes in "Tradition and the Individual Talent." I was aiming, at best, to become an echo, albeit an echo that took liberties with its originating command. Signing my own name seemed presumptuous. When it came time, then, to publish the review, I decided after a brief period of reflection to credit the essay's authorship to "Edgar Allen Poe"—inadvertently misspelling Poe's middle name along the way.[74] The error stuck and became a kind of signature: a means of distinguishing (however silently) the historical Poe's essays from my own.[75] Apparently, the extinction of personality is not so easily accomplished.

Given the sharpness of Poe's critique, it did not shock me that this essay should generate strong response, nor that this response should follow the pattern already established by the AHP. There were three principal attributes of this pattern: First was the near-universal certainty that I was the author. Second, a near-total silence regarding the *content* of the work (the manner in which the work was rendered was something else again). Third, a complete absence of any direct engagement with me, the presumed author (or with "Poe," the identified author) regarding *either* the content *or* the manner. To be sure, I was queried many times as to whether or not I was Poe, but I did not count this as a serious engagement. "Was Poe right or wrong in his judgment?" This, to my mind, was the essential question, not "*Who* is Poe?" or "*Why* does he have to be so nasty?" Here, however, I was missing the point of my own project, for the problem posed by anonymity—by the institution of authorship at its most unstable and thus most socially disruptive—was intimately connected to the problem of writing a "true" criticism, though not in the manner I then imagined. At the time, I viewed the emphasis on "who" and "why" rather than "what" as a form of corruption, a sign that the poetry world was primarily concerned with reputation and power. Criticism, I reasoned, has two functions: intellectual exchange and social mapping. In the first, ideas and arguments are what matter—their truth or falsity, rigor or slackness, fluency or clumsiness. In the second, what matters is the correlation of ideas and arguments with their exponents. Truth, rigor, and fluency may still be valued, but motive and affiliation take precedence. It was a sign of my naiveté, I suppose, that I viewed the inevitable entanglement of these two functions as a trap rather than condition of engagement for thought. Of course, it was more than naïve, it was *foolish* to think that this "trap" could be evaded through anonymity, not only because my authorship was assumed in any case but also because this evasion itself became the focus of public attention.

If I heard it once, I heard it fifty times: *anonymity is cowardly*. I understood the argument in theory. Attacking someone in print without signing your name takes less courage than a signed critique because one need not fear retaliation and need not worry that one will gain a reputation as a scandalmonger. The problem with this argument, in my particular case, at least from my own vantage point, was that I *had* developed a "bad reputation." What then was I evading? Foolish as I was, I was not *so* foolish as to think that anonymity alone could give me the freedom to speak truth. Indeed, my method of composition precluded such a thought, since the ideas expressed in my essay were not mine to speak, and were not free in any event, in the sense that they did not arise from free inquiry, but were instead traced from the template of someone else's inquiry. Moreover, even if this tracing *was* "true," it was true only by accident, since a different template would have yielded a different tracing, hence a different reading. What then was my game?

Apparently, I was demonstrating to my readers what my readers already knew, that criticism is powerful, while demonstrating to myself that this power should not be trusted. No doubt, I should have been doing the opposite: teaching my readers to read skeptically, while teaching myself to handle this power with greater care. Unfortunately, the ruse of anonymity kept this from happening, enticing my readers into imagining that I imagined myself to be speaking daring truths, while enticing me into imagining that I could speak and disavow my speech in the same breath. My mistake—my delusion if you will—was to think that I could enter ideas into the world with the same freedom and control with which I might enter them into a novel. Yes, I was the author, but the "I" of my essay was not necessarily me, it was a narrator speaking. Was he trustworthy or untrustworthy? This, in fact, is what I wanted my readers to decide by asking if Poe was right or wrong in his judgment.

I said above that I misunderstood my own project. A more accurate way to put this would be to say that my review was born of mixed motives, a confusion of aims I would only work out—I won't say resolve—in subsequent rewritings of Poe. What were these mixed motives? There were two primarily, but their relationship was as fluid and as symbiotic as the relationship between form and content in a poem, and this makes it difficult to refer to them with any specificity in isolation. Rather than speak, therefore, of two different motives, I will speak of two different *mixtures* of motive. In one, the impulse toward satire was predominant—defining satire, in Horatian terms, as "the art of 'telling the truth in a jest.'"[76] In the other, the method of composition took precedence. The difference between the two was crucial. In satire, the "I" who speaks, no matter how fictional, aims to speak honestly. The rewriting of source texts, by contrast, reduces honesty to a fiction by treating the "I" (no matter how truthful its "speech" might end up being) as nothing more than a textual effect. Only in the latter instance does criticism *truly* become what I earlier termed "applied poetry." This does not mean, however, that an impulse toward satire does not persist, even there, if only for a fleeting moment (in a sentence bent to my will against the logic of my source), or only by happy accident (the source saying exactly what *I* would have said, if only I had thought of it first). Moreover, even those essays that were not satirical in aim often turned out to be satirical in effect, a function of the comical inappropriateness of Poe's ornate language when brought to bear on contemporary subjects. For this reason, the opposition I am drawing here between "satire" and "applied poetry" might just as well be described, in Steven Weisenburger's terms, as a shift from "generative" satire to a postmodern "degenerative" variety, that is, from "a closely targeted, normative and corrective aggression" that takes "for granted satire's power to punish vice and uphold liberalist norms" to a "delegitimizing" satire that aims instead "to reflect suspiciously on all ways of making meaning, including its own" and which "displays language as an enclosed, self-reifying system constantly in need of demolition through laughter from positions further and further outside."[77]

These "mixtures of motive" and their textual effects are especially evident in "The Literati of San Francisco," a series of sketches of the Bay Area poetry scene as constituted in the early 1990s. My source in this instance was Poe's *Literati of New York City,* a similar series of sketches first published in *Godey's Lady's Book* between May and October 1846. Poe's sketches were similar, but not quite the same, for where *his* literati included novelists, playwrights, essayists, editors, scholars, reformers, and theologians, mine were all poets. This dissymmetry introduced a note of anarchy in my correlation of figures, since a poet translated more smoothly into a poet than did a scholar, reformer, or theologian. Turning "Fitz-Greene Halleck," for example, into "Robert Duncan" was a much simpler proposition than making "Michael Palmer" out of "Charles Anthon." Halleck—the most famous New York poet before Whitman, secretary to John Jacob Astor—was an obvious doppelganger for Duncan, an equally Byronic figure who at one time also made his living as a secretary. Anthon—a professor of Greek and Latin—necessitated a more devious rhetoric.

Another dissymmetry was due to gender. Only twelve of Poe's thirty-eight portraits were of women writers, a proportion that severely limited my options when it came time to match contemporary writers with nineteenth-century prototypes. Not that there was any reason to translate women as women or men as men. But what to do about Poe's habitual gallantry? How should I approach the fact that the two longest and most judicious entries—notwithstanding a certain amount of uncontrollable dislike—belonged to "Frances Osgood" ("Norma Cole") and "Margaret Fuller" ("Lyn Hejinian")? Even more pressing: what to do about Poe's habitual abusiveness toward men? The problem was not simply a choice between positive and negative judgments. The issue—going beyond gender—was sympathy. Poe is often remembered as America's first original literary theorist, as a professional reviewer who struggled to impose rigorous standards in a marketplace overrun with subliterary artifacts. Careful survey uncovers a much more ambiguous record. His animus toward Longfellow—sometimes ascribed to sectional or class conflict, sometimes to creeping insanity—is the stuff of legend, but there are certainly other examples of unbalanced judgment.[78] René Wellek cites several in *A History of Modern Criticism:*

> He disparages Greek tragedy for its "shallowness and uncouthness" and speaks of the "dramatic inability of the ancients." He finds the older English poets overrated and tells us that "for one Fouqué there are fifty Moliéres." . . . He detests Carlyle and Hugo as "asses," Emerson as a "mystic for mysticism's sake." He has no love for Cooper . . . and turns sharply against Lowell for a gibe against him, asking that "no Southerner should ever touch a volume by this author," since Lowell is an abolitionist.[79]

My point here is not to discredit Poe, who certainly knew the difference between "literary criticism" and "the flippant *opinion* which so long has been made its substitute."[80] Rather, I want to emphasize Poe's continual temptation as a working journalist to promote the latter as the former. This is nowhere more apparent than in his *Literati of New York City,* subtitled "Some Honest Opinions at Random . . . with Occasional Words of Personality." As Poe wrote in a letter to George Eveleth, a young admirer, "Do not trust, in making up your library, to the 'opinions' in the Godey series. I *meant* 'honest'—but my meaning is not as fully laid out as I could wish. I thought too little of the series myself to guard sufficiently against haste, inaccuracy or prejudice."[81] Readers will no doubt find my Poe equally guilty of irrational grievances and double standards, of inconsistencies in standards of judgment or fairness.[82] Whether these inconsistencies were random, motivated, or—as in the original Poe—some capricious combination of the two is best left to others to decide. I'll only note that the treatment of friends in these sketches ranged from harsh (Stephen Rodefer) to brusque (Andrew Schelling) to affectionate (Eileen Corder), repeating a pattern of attention equally discernible in my treatment of those for whom I felt no affection at all. In this way, the distribution of sympathy, whatever its moment-to-moment motivation, became, in effect, a matter of aesthetics. It became a compositional problem; a problem of critical standards consistently applied, not a problem of ethics.[83]

The range of approaches encompassed in the "Literati" is partly owing to the series' piecemeal structure, a trait that invited a trial and error approach. With no apparent logic to the arrangement or interrelation of sketches, the portraits were inherently separate and separable. If a translation did not work, I could junk it and try again ("Reverend George Bush" was "Norman Fischer" before he became "Bob

Perelman") or simply absorb the lesson and move on. At the same time, a finite number of portraits made it inevitable that some of the fits would be better than others, leading some sketches toward serious criticism, others toward burlesque. Yet even arbitrary conjunctions yielded interesting results. "Prosper M. Wetmore" became "Barrett Watten" primarily because both names begin with W's. Wetmore was a General, though, which I thought a fitting and suitable mark of distinction given Watten's abject treatment by the press during the "Bay Area Poetry Wars."

As the project moved forward, the matchups became more strained, which tested my powers of translation. The strain worked in both directions: from the source text forward, toward its new subject matter; and backward from the present poetry world toward its prototype in the nineteenth century. Sometimes, I would read and reread one of Poe's portraits, ransacking my memory for a plausible stand-in; other times I would start with my stand-in, thumbing pages of Poe in search for a plausible source. The goal was a thick description of the Bay Area poetry scene. Yet the number of potential subjects was far too great for the available material, even when supplemented with passages from Poe's other writings. Who then to exclude?

I originally hoped to make forty portraits: all thirty-eight of Poe's plus two more excavated from the *Marginalia*. But some of the material proved intractable, and some required so much cut and paste that only tatters of text were left when I was done. Completeness became an idle dream (and not only for me: Poe himself abandoned the project, defeated in part by negative reactions). Moreover, even if adequate source texts could have been found, the subject was too large for its frame. Poe's scale of attention was deliberately small. His original installments—three to six sketches—took up at most seven pages in *Godey's Lady's Book* (about twenty pages in ordinary print), and though he contemplated a sequel involving the literati of all America, he never followed through, sensing, perhaps, that an entire volume of breezy portraits would have been less effective than a small selection. Poe's perpetual problem as a professional writer—how to escape "the Magazine Prison-House"—is thus inscribed in the very structure of his series, in the give and take between scale and size, between the intimate glimpse and sustained critical scrutiny.[84] And as a structural element, this problem was passed down to me: a scale and style that I could stretch to cover my topic, but only at risk of tearing the original fabric. This meant, in practical terms, an arbitrary restriction of focus. As a consequence, several significant writers, even whole circles of writers (though some of these survive, albeit in ghostly fashion, in the figure of a single author) are missing from my final survey.[85] Sadly, the poets who are missing most invisibly are those of my own immediate circle (Michael Anderson, Halliday Dresser, Steve Farmer, Jeff Gburek, Nada Gordon, Jessica Grim, Andrea Hollowell, David Sheidlower), terrific writers and integral members of the community who were too often overshadowed by their elders. Early on, however, I could see that Poe's signature combination of gossip and misinformation would not be especially useful in advertising their talents. Too few readers possessed enough information to measure Poe's inevitable distortions, and too many would take his cavalier appraisals at face value. By and large, then, the focus of my "Literati" is on language poetry (broadly conceived to include both fellow travelers and notable opponents). The exceptions—if there are exceptions—should be seen as gestures toward an impossible completeness.

That said, in composing my translations the only limitations I set myself were geographic and chronological. All of the writers had to share some sort of connection with the Bay Area scene as it stood at the end of the 1980s.[86](The one possible exception to this rule was Nathaniel Mackey, who was from nearby Santa Cruz). This meant, of course, that when I began the series in the mid-1990s, my view was already retrospective. This, in itself, was not a problem. Although Poe's New York sketches were decidedly present-tense reflections, the San Francisco scene had entered a temporary lull. Taking stock of the scene made sense. The problem arose with later installments, which labored to maintain the posture of a recent retrospective even as the S.F. scene recomposed itself and old members moved on to new phases of development. The artificiality of that posture is indicative, moreover, of a general tendency that extends all through the "Literati": a complicity with the imaginary that transformed even truthful elements into something fictional—a "generative" fiction in some instances, "degenerative" in others. In some portraits, in other words, I aimed for maximum accuracy—notwithstanding distortions forced on me by my adherence to a source text—while in others I made use of distortion for critical ends to which accuracy was only tangentially related.

A good example of the latter would be my sketch of "Benjamin

Friedlander." Based on Poe's portrait of "Thomas Dunn English"—a second-rate poet and novelist with whom Poe briefly enjoyed friendly relations—my self-analysis was dismissive and insulting by design. I wanted, for starters, to show my readers (those who guessed that I was "Poe") that I was not using the "Literati" to settle old scores, that the harshness of the rhetoric was a literary construction, and that this "construction" was the real focus of my interest. After the AHP, and even more so after the appearance of the essay on Lew Daly, friends and acquaintances would suggest I wrote out of bitterness. I would counter that by saying that if I really wrote for revenge, I would surely not attack my friends or myself with equal harshness, but that, too, struck my friends as strange and curious, if not terrible and cruel. Nonetheless, rigor—not to say fairness—required that I be as merciless with myself as with others. In the AHP, this had meant depicting myself as a tapeworm. In the "Literati," it meant turning loose Poe's most disdainful language on my own labors. Accuracy as such was not the point. The point was to put "Benjamin Friedlander" in an uncomfortable relationship to "Poe."

My choice of Thomas Dunn English was not arbitrary. Poe's English portrait was the most controversial of the series and had the most far-reaching results. In January 1846, some six months before publishing his sketch, Poe found himself embroiled in a public dispute that involved compromising letters that may or may not have been sent by Elizabeth Ellet, a poet who was spreading rumors about Poe's relationship with Frances Osgood. Under threat from Ellet's brother, Poe went to see English to borrow a pistol for self-defense. English refused, and even took Ellet's side in the quarrel, leading to a fistfight that both parties later claimed to have won. Not surprisingly, these events would play a decisive role in Poe's framing of the English portrait, and not only by goading him into an undisguised expression of contempt. Unwilling, apparently, to cite English's insults publicly, Poe was further goaded—a disastrous miscalculation—into hiding the *personal basis* for this contempt, thereby opening himself up to charges of dishonesty. His argument, in essence, was that English plagiarized other poets, and that his knowledge of "English" grammar was deficient ("although an editor should certainly be able to write *his own name*").[87] English very quickly replied in print, and his answer—elaborating on the theme of dishonesty—far outdistanced Poe's original statement in both the scurrilousness of its charges and the intensity of its contempt. The end result was a libel suit against English's publishers, which Poe subsequently won—a Pyrrhic victory, as English and his allies continued to smear Poe in print.[88]

In translating Poe's most controversial sketch and turning loose its dishonesty and contempt on myself, I aimed, among other things, at making a point about criticism: that precisely when a text appears to be reaching most definitively outward, it may well be tracing a gesture inscribed in its origin.[89] This is not to argue in a tired hyperbole that the world is unreal or only a text, or that texts cannot refer to anything outside themselves. The reception of my Poe translations—not to mention Poe's own reception in the nineteenth century—proves otherwise. My argument is rather that engaging reality independent of texts—independent of prior models—is so difficult a task, and so rare an achievement, that one must read with the greatest vigilance and skepticism at precisely those moments when immediacy is most tempting. In such moments, it is not enough to read between the lines: one must read beneath them as well. More precisely, one must read both "between the lines" of the given text, and "between the given text and the hidden one beneath it." This "hidden" text, an abstraction in most criticism, is a concrete entity in *Simulcast*. Although *Simulcast* has abstract origins as well (many of them enumerated earlier in this introduction), the purpose of this book—the "cultural work" performed by its "plagiarism"—is to encourage a skeptical reading of texts in relation to their origins. To do that I have necessarily created a text whose origins have exaggerated legibility.

SIMULCAST

In TV and radio parlance, a "simulcast" is a concert or other live event simultaneously broadcast in video and audio. Given the resemblance, however, between the words "simultaneous" and "simulation," "simulcast" might also be defined as a *false* broadcast. The four experiments collected in this book are "simulcasts" in both senses. Credited to fictional authors, all four perpetrate elaborate frauds, thus putting forth what I earlier termed "descriptions of an imaginary universe."[90] They do so by appropriating and rewriting a series of source texts (a practice of "applied poetry") whose own itineraries are interrogated, complicated, and even overturned. I conceive of this latter task as the enactment of a dialogue simultaneously broadcast from two distinct intellectual contexts—one belonging to my source text, the other to a subject matter particular to my own interests as a poet. Thus, in "Mr. Rasula's History," I transform Poe's invested survey of Francis L. Hawks's *Contributions to the Ecclesiastical History of the United States—Virginia* into a comparable study of Jed Rasula's *American Poetry Wax Museum*. In the process, I set in motion a surreptitious dialogue between poetic and religious cultures, and between my own investment in history and Poe's. In "The Anti-Hegemony Project," I transform the adolescent chitchat on alt.fan.madonna into a fantasy discussion of Ron Silliman. Delineating in this way the social and discursive complexity of the so-called "low end" of Internet culture, I parody the shallowness that often characterizes the "high end" as well. Here too, the fact that my text derives from two distinct contexts establishes the grounds for a critical dialogue.[91]

These various modes of "simulcast" are enacted and coordinated most consciously and most purposefully in the last experiment, "A Short History of Language Poetry." Here I divest my method of all but a few traces of satire, in favor of a criticism that takes on the task of describing the poetics of language writing in all its philosophical complexity. Wahl's study of existentialism made a good source text for such a study. A philosopher of no small note (his writings influenced Emmanuel Levinas), Wahl was also a poet whose totality of interests caught the attention of Wallace Stevens. In *A Short History*, Wahl's poetic side shows itself, most notably, in the *texture* of his argument, which sustains a relationship to its subject matter that is much more attractive (and much more durable) than the argument itself. It was this relationship above all that I sought to capture in my rewriting. Wahl's characterizations could be as summary as any judgment of Poe's, but his emphasis in *A Short History* is resolutely analytic. Here, the matching of subject to source text proved especially felicitous. Other poets would have sounded ridiculous if presented in the manner of Wahl's discussions of Jaspers, Heidegger, and Sartre, but the language poets were themselves creators of a specialized discourse. More to the point, their emphasis on poetic language as a mode of thought (and not simply form of expression) marked them as inheritors of existentialism's own poetics. Different as the two movements might have been, their shared fascination with the poetry-philosophy threshold made the translation workable and end results illuminating.[92]

Such points of convergence proved essential to the task of translation. In a purely mundane sense, they supplied me with a relatively simple means of narrowing my subject. This narrowing was the first of many problems that beset me, for while Wahl's *Short History* takes up only three existentialists (Jaspers, Heidegger and Sartre), plus two forebears (Hegel and Kierkegaard), there are thirty-nine poets in Ron Silliman's language-writing anthology *In the American Tree*. Even if I divided Wahl's extensive discussion of Heidegger in half, I was left with a template that allowed room for only six poets to be treated in any detail. But which six? The choices were far from inevitable. Although guided in some measure by my own sense of what matters, the fortuitous characteristics of Wahl's account were of equal importance. His decision, for instance, to speak of existentialism as a German and French phenomenon led to an emphasis on language writing's bicoastal character, and this in turn made other decisions simpler. The calculations were practically algebraic. If "Heidegger" (or half of Heidegger) was to be my "Hejinian," then "Germany" would have to be "California," and "Sartre" a New Yorker. Moreover, if "Sartre" was to be my "Charles Bernstein"—and the match worked for many different reasons—then there would be no space for Bruce Andrews, Alan Davies, Hannah Weiner, or any other East Coast language writer, save by incidental mention.

The parallels between Wahl's subject and my own were not always so superficial; his descriptions of existentialism were often uncannily accurate in their evocations of certain aspects of language writing. Sometimes, these evocations were purely formal, as when Wahl's account of the "in-itself" and "for-itself" in Sartre provided a blueprint for discussing "absorption" and "impermeability" in Bernstein (the key terms in Bernstein's 1987 essay "Artifice of Absorption"). More frequently, however, the point of convergence was a turn of phrase that required no revision at all in order to make sense or be accurate in the new context. An example of this occurs in Wahl's brief discussion of Karl Jaspers. Elaborating on what he means by Jaspers's "secularization and generalization" of the philosophy of Kierkegaard, Wahl writes:

> In the philosophy of Jaspers, we are no longer referred to Jesus, but rather, to a background of our existence of which we may glimpse only scattered regions. Humanity has multiple activities, and each of us has multiple possibilities. But we develop one, we

> sacrifice another, and we never attain to that Absolute which Hegel prided himself on being able to reach through the unwinding of the Idea to its necessary conclusion. The absolute, in Jaspers's philosophy, is "something hidden," revealing itself in fugitive fragments, in scattered flashes like intermittent strokes of lightning. We have the sensation of a night into which our thought or non-thought plunges. Consequently, we are doomed to "shipwreck," *naufrage;* our thought fails utterly, yet fulfills itself in this very disaster by sensing the background of Being from which everything springs.[93]

Inspired by the references in this passage to "fugitive fragments" and "scattered flashes," I quickly settled on Ron Silliman as my Jaspers. The principal characteristic of Silliman's poetry is the epic accumulation of minutely observed details—"fragments" and "flashes"—in a non-narrative structure whose coordinating principle remains no less "hidden" than the "absolute" in Jaspers. Samuel Delany, in an essay on Silliman, describes this accumulation of detail as "sentential cascade," a phrase that likewise resonates with Wahl's "sensation of a night into which our thought or non-thought plunges."[94] Building on these fleeting points of convergence (and on my previous decision to make Clark Coolidge my Kierkegaard), I transposed the terms of Wahl's argument from "Jesus" to "music," from "existence" to "language," from "humanity" to "speech and writing," from "*naufrage*" to "ideological entanglement," from "Being" to "form." This is the result:

> We may consider the poetics of Silliman as a sort of politicizing and generalizing of the poetics of Coolidge. In the poetics of Silliman, we are no longer referred to music, but rather, to deep structures of our language of which we may glimpse only scattered regions. Speech and writing have multiple functions, and each utterance has multiple meanings. But we respond to one, we ignore another, and we never attain to that absolute physical location in words Creeley hoped to reach through the unwinding of the mind to its necessary conclusion. The absolute, in Silliman's poetics, is instead the social totality, which reveals itself only partly—in bits of torn paper, in scattered flashes, like intermittent strokes of a pen. We have the sensation of a tunnel into

> which our thought plunges like a subway. Consequently, we are doomed to "ideological entanglement"; individual identity is refracted utterly by language, yet fulfills itself in this very fragmentation by sensing the background of form from which everything we know or feel emerges.

I hope that statements like this one illuminate the work in question, but their ultimate usefulness depends upon the reader's recognition of the argument's synthetic construction. Highlighting the relationship between poetry and philosophy, language writing and existentialism, Silliman and Jaspers, this hidden content, borne by my text in its very structure, maintains a probative value accessible to any reader who takes the trouble to set Wahl's original text side by side with Whimsy's simulacrum.

When poets articulate their poetics discursively—whether in book reviews, essays, or theoretical statements—their formal decisions and stylistic idiosyncrasies necessarily influence what is said. The stylistic and formal aspects of the work, however, are generally muted and rarely discussed. This is partly a consequence of a prejudice against form and style, which many critics treat as more contingent and more ornamental than content, and partly because contingency and ornamentation are not seen as having a content worthy of discussion in their own right. There are exceptions, to be sure, most notably Charles Bernstein, who refers in *A Poetics* to an "applied poetic," by which he means a criticism in which contingency and ornamentation are prized rather than scorned, in which the visibility of form and style is heightened, and their role as *determinants* of sense emphasized.[95] My own project, indebted to Bernstein's, is more conceptual. In describing *Simulcast* as a form of "applied poetry," my interest is not in the content produced by form, but in the form produced by content.

The hybridity implicit in the phrase "literary criticism" has always been an awkward fact for critics who take seriously their claims to truth, and essays that flaunt their own literary qualities are often greeted with suspicion. *Simulcast* suggests that the most suspicious writing of all *masks* its literary qualities—and that all writing is literary insofar as it traces a form susceptible to literary appropriation. Lyn Hejinian, in one of her earliest essays, writes: "Any thought can be kin to another. The agility of the imagination and its whimsy make this possible."[96] The work in *Simulcast* puts this "agility of the imagination" to the test. My method recalls, more specifically, Charles Bernstein's declaration: "I am a ventriloquist, happy as a raven to preach with blinding fervor . . . in a voice of pained honesty that is as much a conceit as the most formal legal brief." Adds Bernstein: "But my art is just empty words on a page if it does not, indeed, persuade."[97] More literally than Bernstein, my "Short History" is an act of ventriloquism, but it too aims at "persuasion." At the same time, *Simulcast* aims to throw *suspicion* on "persuasion." Persuasive or unpersuasive, critical texts should elicit more from their readers than mere assent or dissent. Calling into question criticism's ostensible transparency, the essays in *Simulcast* promote a particular kind of engagement, not a particular set of judgments or particular body of work. Without such engagement—so this book would argue—poetry and poetics are scarcely worth thinking about at all.

In reworking these essays, I have often thought ruefully of Godard's great dictum, "Letting others tell you what to think is a crime." In coming to terms with the evidence of *my* crime (if that is indeed what it was), *Simulcast*'s readers would do well to remain on alert. In art—indeed, in all that art seeks to comprehend—the least suspicious meanings are the ones that pose the greatest risk. To borrow a phrase from another avant-garde filmmaker: "Trust, but verify."

NOTES

1. Jean Wahl, *A Short History of Existentialism,* trans. Forrest Williams and Stanley Maron (New York: Philosophical Library, 1949), 3.

2. Wahl, *Short History,* 24.

3. Michel Foucault, *Aesthetics, Method and Epistemology,* ed. James D. Faubion, trans. Robert Hurley and others (New York: New Press, 1998), 206, 211, 213. To be precise about it, "A Short History of Language Poetry" involves itself in *three* games: existentialism, language writing, and the correlation of the two in a single text. Since obedience to one of the games often required abandonment of one or both of the others, the inevitability of a break in play was itself part of the play.

4. More Benjaminian than "appropriation art" was the increasingly common use of borrowed snippets of sound in popular music (generally known today under the umbrella term "sampling"). Recordings that pointed beyond such a practice, toward something closer in spirit to "appropriation," were Ciccone Youth's "Into the Groovy" (1986), Laibach's *Let It Be* (1988), and

the Pooh Sticks' *Great White Wonder* (1991). These three works served as deeper influences on *Simulcast* than comparable work by Mike Bidlo, Jeff Koons, and Sherry Levine, perhaps because the musicians were less inclined than the visual artists to treat appropriation as an end in itself.

5. Fredric Jameson, in a cutting comment, says of Borges: "In the high theory of the postmodern [he has] all the vulgarity and lack of distinction of Escher prints on the walls of middlebrow college students" (*Postmodernism, or, The Cultural Logic of Late Capitalism* [Durham: Duke University Press, 1991], 430 n. 60). This remark certainly gave me pause when I set about writing this introduction. The remark hit home, in part, because I first read Borges in Terry Carr's *New Worlds of Fantasy No. 2* (New York: Ace Books, 1970), a very Escher-friendly context. Let me reiterate, however, that my present purpose is to trace this book's *actual* evolution (no matter how lacking in "distinction"), not to fabricate a surprising, sophisticated lineage, though fabrication would certainly be in keeping with the book's underlying method.

6. Jorge Luis Borges, *Labyrinths: Selected Stories & Other Writings*, ed. Donald A. Yates and James E. Irby (New York: New Directions, 1964), 44. *Labyrinths* is the work of a number of translators; James E. Irby prepared the English version of "Pierre Menard." My subsequent quotations from this story are taken from pages 43 or 44.

7. Wallace Stevens, *Collected Poetry and Prose* (New York: Library of America, 1997), 663.

8. "Kathy Acker Interviewed by Rebecca Deaton," *Textual Practice* 6:2 (Summer 1992), 281. "Plagiarism" is in fact the title of the first of the novel's three sections.

9. Martina Sciolino, "Confessions of a Kleptoparasite," *Review of Contemporary Fiction* 9 (1989): 63.

10. Kathy Acker, *Hannibal Lecter, My Father* (New York: Semiotext(e), 1991), 13–14.

11. Kathy Acker, *Don Quixote: Which Was a Dream* (New York: Grove Press, 1986), 9.

12. For a study of these shadows, see Daniel Balderston's remarkable *Out of Context: Historical Reference and the Representation of Reality in Borges* (Durham: Duke University Press, 1993).

13. Rebecca Moore Howard, "Sexuality, Textuality: The Cultural Work of Plagiarism," *College English* 62:4 (March 2000): 475, 485, 486. Howard's subtitle has two contrary meanings. On the one hand, it refers to the cultural work done by the *word* plagiarism, which, as Howard's title suggests, draws a correlation between textual and sexual transgression. Howard states, "Embedded in the discourse construction of plagiarism are metaphors of gender, weakness, collaboration, disease, adultery, rape, and property that communicate a fear of violating sexual as well as textual boundaries" (474). On the

other hand, the *activity* of plagiarism ("authorship run amok" [486]) can undermine the "regulatory fictions that consolidate and naturalize power regimes of gender and sexuality" (485). Howard's essay is written in the context of composition studies. Her call to distinguish fraud and insufficient attribution from patchwriting represents an attempt to extricate herself from "the argument-by-metaphor that helps define modern authorship" as what Adrienne Rich has termed "compulsory heterosexuality" (485). In Acker, then, "the cultural work of plagiarism" is at once an appropriation of the word "plagiarism" analogous to queer theory's embrace of the word "queer," and an assault on authorship as institution.

14. See, e.g., chapter one of Jameson's *Postmodernism;* the Perelman poem is cited in full at 28–29.

15. Yunte Huang has proposed an allegorical reading of "The Manchurian Candidate" in which Perelman's selection by Jameson as the representative poet of postmodernism becomes the basis for Perelman's identification with the brainwashed agent of John Frankenheimer's 1962 movie. The reading plays on the title of the Perelman poem ("China") that forms the basis for Jameson's discussion. For samples of the Perelman work cited above, see *Ten to One: Selected Poems* (Hanover, Wesleyan University Press, 1999) and "Good & Bad/Good & Evil: Pound, Celine, and Fascism," *Poetics Journal,* no. 6 (1986): 6–25.

16. See, e.g., "Living in a Material World: Raymond Williams's Long Revolution," originally published in the *Village Voice,* April 1985, now available at the invaluable Robert Christgau web site (http://www.robertchristgau.com/xg/bkrev/williams-85.php).

17. The comment was perhaps inspired by the language poets' favorite locution when one of their peers gave an especially well-conceived lecture: "So-and-so really did a lot of homework."

18. Ron Silliman, "Flashback," *Poetry Flash,* no. 136 (July 1984): 7.

19. The books cited are Julie Burchill and Tony Parsons, *"The Boy Looked at Johnny": The Obituary of Rock and Roll* (London: Pluto Press, 1978), and Simon Reynolds, *Blissed Out: The Raptures of Rock* (London: Serpent's Tail, 1990). Writers I admired at the time included Vince Aletti, Gina Arnold, Tom Carson, Chuck Eddy, Greil Marcus, Dirk Richardson, R. J. Smith, and Greg Tate.

20. Apart from "The Changing Same: R&B and New Black Music" (in *Black Music* [New York: Morrow, 1967]), I found the excerpt from Baraka's still-unpublished Coltrane book in his *Selected Plays and Prose* (New York: Morrow, 1979) especially influential. My immersion in jazz and rock criticism occurred just before the appearance of Nathaniel Mackey's *Bedouin Hornbook* (Lexington, KY: Callaloo Fiction Series, 1986), an epistolary novel that

upped the ante considerably on what a correlation of writing and music might require, and long before the appearance of Joshua Clover (whose two-fold career—innovative poet and freelance rock journalist—bodes well for future evolutions of poetic thought).

21. Dick Hebdige, *Subculture: The Meaning of Style* (London: Methuen, 1979), 2, 117. Around this same time, Andrew Ross, an early champion of language poetry, made a more emphatic and more enduring transition into cultural studies, but his earlier and later interests were never assimilated. Which is too bad; if any critic could have taken up Jameson's halting discussion of postmodern poetry as one of many commensurate cultural activities, it was Ross.

22. The disenchantment was primarily a consequence of the so-called "poetry wars," which wrenched apart the Bay Area writing scene in the mid-1980s and left a lingering suspicion that eventually strangled all collaboration between writers of different affiliation or generation, at least for a while. But my withdrawal was not simply due to disenchantment. I also drew inward for a variety of personal reasons. Friendship with Benjamin Hollander accelerated these changes. His edited volume of essays on Paul Celan (*Translating Tradition: Paul Celan in France* [*Acts* 8/9 (1988)]) led to an exchange of letters, and eventually to a projected book on Celan and the Holocaust, which was only set aside when I began graduate school. By then, I was already far removed from earlier concerns, having recognized a more emphatically pop orientation in the work of two younger poets, Jeff Gburek and Halliday Dresser (their serialized *Prolegomena to the Study of Rock-n-Roll Spectacle* was published in the first three issues of *'Aql*), and having discerned in the difference between their work and mine a directive to explore more deeply the relationship between poetry and experience (in particular, the experience of history). In the long run, this exploration proved more useful to me and better suited to my interests than the study of poetry's disposition within popular culture.

23. This commitment manifested itself in a variety of critical and poetic texts read or circulated in a variety of contexts: in brief essays on rock and roll published in *Jimmy & Lucy's House of "K"* (a poetics journal I edited with Andrew Schelling between 1984 and 1989); in a long collaboration with Jean Day, one portion of which appeared in the second issue of *Ottotole;* in a talk on poetry and music at the home of Jessica Grim and Michael Amnasan (part of a series organized by David Sheidlower); and in a paper delivered as part of a panel on "The Poetics of Everyday Life" organized by Carla Harryman at Small Press Distribution (a revised version of which subsequently appeared in *Poetics Journal,* no. 9, under the title "Lyrical Interference").

24. Who would have guessed that Barrett Watten would be publishing ar-

ticles on electronic dance music a decade later? Certainly not I. See "The Constructivist Moment: From El Lissitzky to Detroit Techno," *Qui Parle* 11:1 (Fall-Winter 1997): 57–100.

25. Private correspondence, 5 June 1986.

26. Private correspondence, 9 June 1986.

27. Benjamin Friedlander, "Guide to Kulchur," *Revista Canaria de Estudios Ingleses* 18 (April 1989): 97.

28. *Christgau's Record Guide: Rock Albums of the '70s* (New Haven: Ticknor & Fields, 1981), 371.

29. The distinction between hidden reference and appropriation is examined by Kevin H. J. Dettmar in an essay on Acker, "The Illusion of Modernist Allusion and the Politics of Postmodern Plagiarism," in *Perspectives on Plagiarism and Intellectual Property in a Postmodern World,* ed. Lise Buranen and Alice M. Roy (Albany: State University of New York Press, 1999): 99–109.

30. Bertha Morris Parker, *The Golden Book Encyclopedia* (New York: Golden Press, 1959) title page; and Jean Baudrillard, *Simulacrum and Simulation,* trans. Sheila Faria Glaser (Ann Arbor: University of Michigan Press, 1994) 1. Although Baudrillard shuns use of the word "postmodern," it is clear from his writing as a whole that the phenomenon he describes under the rubric "hyperreality" is precisely the collapse of the social brought on by modernity, and hence post-modern literally.

31. *The Golden Book Encyclopedia,* 6:483; Phillip Bacon, *The Golden Book Picture Atlas of the World* (New York: Golden Press, 1960), 1:65.

32. Daniel Boorstin, *The Image: A Guide to Pseudo-Events in America* (New York: Vintage Books, 1992), 37.

33. Echoing *Dragnet,* the authors begin: "This book is written as fiction; but it is based on fact. The things we write about have, in essence, happened." Their book ends with "A Factual Epilogue." See William J. Lederer and Eugene Burdick, *The Ugly American* (New York: Norton, 1958).

34. These details come from John Hellmann's superb account of the novel in *American Myth and the Legacy of Vietnam* (New York: Columbia University Press, 1986).

35. Consider Disney's own description of the Magic Kingdom, offered at the opening ceremonies in 1955: "The idea of Disneyland is a simple one. It will be a place for people to find happiness and knowledge. . . . Disneyland will be something of a fair, an exhibition, a playground, a community center, a museum of living facts, and a showplace of beauty and magic." Quoted by Henry A. Giroux in *The Mouse That Roared: Disney and the End of Innocence* (Lanham, Md.: Rowman & Littlefield, 1999), 35–36.

36. Boorstin, *The Image,* 103. Sadly for Krushchev, the U.S. government blocked the visit.

37. Baudrillard, *Simulacra and Simulation,* 12.

38. This development has not come to a final resolution. A recent experiment, devised with Graham Foust, is based on the writings of Clement Greenberg, taking on, surreptitiously, the repressed question of taste. See, e.g., the following reviews by "Wyman Jennings" in *Lagniappe* (http://www.umit.maine.edu/~ben.Friedlander/lagniappe.html): "John Ashbery, *Wakefulness*" (issue 1:2), "Spicer Writ Large" (1:3), "Dale Smith, *Texas Crude*" (2:1), and "Jeff Conant, *The Evacuated Forest Papers*" (2:2).

39. The entire run is now archived at SUNY Buffalo's Electronic Poetry Center (EPC), at http://wings.buffalo.edu/epc/ezines/diu.

40. Several of these alter egos make an appearance in *Simulcast:* Poe and Whimsy directly (as authors of entire sections), Bey and Filbee as participants in the roundtable discussion at the end of Whimsy's "Short History." Filbee would subsequently slip free from my control, writing the introduction to a collection of poems by Bill Howe (*Floor Them All* [Austin: Center for the Study of Accelerated Aesthetics, 1994]) and the epilogue to a pamphlet by forgotten beatnik "Bernie Fox" (*Pensive as a Faint Scrawl on a Faint Pencil* [Buffalo: The Echinacea Society, 1995]). She would also edit two of my own books, *Partial Objects* (Buffalo: porci con le ali, 1999) and *A Knot Is Not a Tangle* (San Francisco: Krupskaya Press, 2000). In this respect, she drew inspiration from Samuel R. Delany's "K. Leslie Steiner" (author of several essays on Delany now gathered in Delany's *The Straits of Messina* [Seattle: Serconia Press, 1989]). Two other inspirations were "Rrose Sélavy," about whom Donald Judd once quipped, "Rrose Sélavy is all right, but I don't know about Duchamp" (*Complete Writings 1959–1975* [Halifax: Press of the Nova Scotia College of Art and Design, 1975], 166); and Philip Roth's "Philip Roth," who performs an unspecified Mossad mission at the end of *Operation Shylock* (New York: Vintage, 1993). The suggestion of spycraft in Kimberly Filbee's name was in fact an undercover salute to Roth.

41. Online poetry journals preceding *DIU* include *Inter\Face* (Katie Yates, Nancy Dunlop, and Ben Henry, eds.), *Grist-On-Line* (John Fowler, ed.), *Experioddi(cyber)cist* (Jake Berry, ed.), and *R/IFT* (Ken Sherwood and Loss Pequeño Glazier, eds.), all founded in 1993. Also noteworthy is *TREE (Taproot Reviews Electronic Edition)* (Luigi-Bob Drake, ed.), which made its appearance in 1992. No doubt, other early journals appeared on commercial networks such as Delphi, AOL, or the WELL, but they have not yet come to my attention. Unfortunately, the early history of Internet *content* remains unwritten.

42. The Web was available for use in 1992, but it was not until the development of browsers for PCs (beginning with Mosaic in 1993) that traffic began to pick up. According to James Gillies and Robert Cailliau in *How the Web Was Born* (Oxford: Oxford University Press, 2000), "Web traffic was at number eleven in the Internet charts [in January 1994]. By the time the first version of [Navigator] was released [in October], it had moved up to number

five, and in April 1995 the Web reached number one with over a fifth of all of Internet traffic, overhauling the long-time leader, FTP" (258). The ban on commercial use eased up at precisely the same time, with "[a]ll pretenses of limitations . . . disappear[ing] in May 1995 when the National Science Foundation ended its sponsorship . . . and all traffic [was made to rely] on commercial networks" (*The Internet,* ed. Gray Young [New York: H. W. Wilson, 1998], 6).

43. "Poetics" was and is a Listserv-based discussion group. Although definition is probably not needed at this late date, Listserv "is a service whereby anyone can set up a discussion forum on any subject they want and like-minded people can subscribe. Subscribers send e-mails to the listserver, which then forwards them on to all subscribers." An alternative service developed on Usenet, where "instead of sending e-mails to every subscriber, subscribers read and posted messages on a kind of electronic bulletin board" available "to any computer subscribing to a particular service" (Gillies and Cailliau, *How the Web Was Born,* 77–78). The difference in style between Listserv and Usenet communication—the former academic, the latter commercial—is precisely what "The Anti-Hegemony Project" explores. For a selection of messages from the first two years of the Poetics List, see *Poetics@,* ed. Joel Kuszai (New York: Roof Books, 1999). The entire archive is available through the EPC, at http://epc.buffalo.edu/poetics.

44. David Sheidlower, a high school friend and fellow writer in the Bay Area poetry scene, used "popmail" (one of the earliest email systems with a user-friendly interface) to participate on electronic bulletin boards in the mid-1980s. He wrote about this technology and its relevance for poetry in "Popnetting," *Jimmy & Lucy's House of "K,"* no. 7 (December 1986): 48–51.

45. The mimeo-Internet parallel was made more explicitly by *Grist-on-Line,* an electronic revival of *Grist,* an underground poetry magazine of the 1960s.

46. *Ejournal* 2:3 (August 1992) (http://www.ucalgary.ca/ejournal/archive/ej-2-3.txt).

47. I take the phrase "discourse network" from Friedrich Kittler, who uses it to mean both "the network of technologies and institutions that allow a given culture to select, store, and process relevant data," and literature understood as a function of such technologies and institutions (one era's "technologies and institutions" inevitably surviving as another's "data"). *Discourse Networks 1800/1900,* trans. Michael Metteer, with Chris Cullens (Stanford: Stanford University Press, 1990), 367.

48. Nick Lawrence and I coined the phrase "Anti-Hegemony Project" for one of our many abandoned collaborations.

49. Circulated on the Poetics List, 28 February 1995. The piece alludes

to a memorable early essay by Perloff, "The Corn-Porn Lyric: Poetry 1972–73," *Contemporary Literature* 16 (Winter 1975): 85–125.

50. Although it was a portrait of the Poetics List, the "alt.fan.silliman" discussion satirized people who were not necessarily on the list (or even the Internet) at the time. I saw no reason to draw a sharp distinction between online and offline members of the poetry world. For the purposes of satire, what interested me was not the Poetics List per se, but the entry of a well-defined poetic subculture into uncharted electronic space.

51. Circulated on the Poetics List, 1 March 1995.

52. Hakim Bey himself equivocates between a conception of the TAZ as "an *essay* ('attempt'), a suggestion, almost a poetic fancy," and as "a guerilla operation which liberates an area (of land, of time, of imagination) and then dissolves itself to re-form elsewhere / elsewhen, *before* the State can crush it." The two conceptions blur (without quite erasing) the distinction I am making here between "description" and "squat." I myself associate the TAZ exclusively with the latter. *T.A.Z.: The Temporary Autonomous Zone, Ontological Anarchy, Poetic Terrorism* (New York: Autonomedia, 1991), 99, 101.

53. As Joel Kuszai would subsequently remark, "For me, this list has always been an extension of the poetry and poetix communities, graduate school programs, etc. It isn't about VIRTUAL anything—that is a bunch of cosmic cyber hype." Message to the Poetics List, 3 December 1998.

54. In one of the satires, I absolved Bernstein of any collusion—and all but admitted authorship—by describing myself as a "26-foot long tapeworm" extracted "from a gaping terminal in Charles Bernstein's office." According to this story, "Bernstein, away on a reading tour, had left the terminal unattended and during this time the tapeworm—nicknamed 'Benji' by engineers—apparently nestled into an intractable position." See document no. 7 of "An AHP Dossier." Further citations identified by document number.

55. Spiraling crisis would cause a brief shutdown of the list for some three weeks beginning December 20th, 1998, followed by the imposition of a new policy in January. As Bernstein notes in his preface to *Poetics@*, "Starting at the beginning of 1999, Christopher Alexander became the list moderator and editor; under a new format, subscribers were no longer able to post messages directly to the list. Unfortunately, as the list became bigger and more prominent, it became impossible to continue with unrestricted posting. Simply put, we were too easily open to abuse" (7). For comments on the change, see Kent Johnson, "Buffalo '99," *Skanky Possum*, no. 3 (Autumn 1999), available electronically at http://www.flashpoint.com/skanky.htm; and William Gillespie, "Is Charles Bernstein a Political Poet?" *Electronic Book Review*, no. 11 (2001) (http://www.altx.com/ebr/reviews/rev11/Gillespie/index.htm).

56. Quoted in *Poetics@*, 6–7.

57. Circulated on the Poetics List, 16 February 1995.

58. One or two simply sent the posts as a favor, without paying any attention whatsoever to the content. The majority of those involved were regular contributors to *DIU*.

59. Don Byrd, Nick Lawrence, and Martin Spinelli wrote three messages not collected here.

60. "By tabloidization I mean persistent posts that are big on attitude but little else; that are more focused on generating attention than provoking thought." Charles Bernstein, message to the Poetics List, 28 November 1998.

61. See, e.g., satires circulated on the Poetics List, 12 February and 15 February 1995.

62. "State of the Art," *apex of the M*, no. 1 (1994): 6, 7. The controversy over this editorial is alluded to in the AHP.

63. See Lewis C. Daly, *"Saith the Spirit to This Shattered Earth": Mid-Seventeenth Century Puritan Radicalism and the History of Religious Forms of Class-Struggle* (Ph.D. Thesis, SUNY Buffalo, 1996).

64. Edgar Allan Poe, *Essays and Reviews*, ed. G. R. Thompson (New York: Library of America, 1984), 333. The line from Poe's Mattson review (quoted below) appears at 838.

65. Poe, *Essays and Reviews*, 797.

66. Poe, *Essays and Reviews*, 803.

67. Poe, *Essays and Reviews*, 808.

68. Poe, *Essays and Reviews*, 453. The phrase appears in a review of William Cullen Bryant's *Complete Poetical Works*, appropriated in the present volume for an essay on Charles Bernstein.

69. Poe, *Essays and Reviews*, 1175–76.

70. Poe, *Essays and Reviews*, 800–1.

71. "State of the Art," 5.

72. Poe, *Essays and Reviews*, 799.

73. Poe, *Essays and Reviews*, 808.

74. The essay appeared in *DIU*—appropriately so, given the appearance of the original in a magazine similarly disposed to Poe.

75. The spelling created Poe with a difference or should I say "différance"? For Derrida, the interchange of an "a" and "e" marks "a lapse in the discipline and law which regulates writing and keeps it seemly." *Margins of Philosophy*, trans. Alan Bass (Chicago: University of Chicago Press, 1982), 3.

76. Gilbert Highet, *The Anatomy of Satire* (Princeton: Princeton University Press, 1962), 47.

77. Steven Weisenburger, *Fables of Subversion: Satire and the American Novel, 1930–1980* (Athens: University of Georgia Press, 1995), 3, 14, 27, 136.

78. When Poe died, Longfellow savored the last word: "My works seemed to give him much trouble . . . but Mr. Poe is dead and gone, and I am alive

and still writing—and that is the end of the matter." Quoted by Stanley Moss in *Poe's Literary Battles: The Critic in the Context of His Literary Milieu* (Durham: Duke University Press, 1963), 189.

79. René Wellek, *A History of Modern Criticism: 1750–1950* (New Haven: Yale University Press, 1965), 153.

80. Poe, *Essays and Reviews*, 1027.

81. *The Letters of Edgar Allan Poe*, ed. John Ward Ostrom (Cambridge: Harvard University Press, 1948), 2:332.

82. In critical focus and tone, the Poe of *Simulcast* varies as widely as the historical Poe, ranging freely from the purely factual ("Mr. Rasula's History") to the vitriolic ("Mr. Daly's Polemic"), from the high-minded and judicious ("The Poetic Principle") to the journalistic and inflammatory ("The Literati of San Francisco"). In some pieces, he seems to have made up his mind long in advance of writing ("Gertrude Stein: A Retrospective Criticism"). In others, we seem to see Poe engaging his subject with an open mind ("Blockage, Breakdown, Baffle"). He remains decidedly unfixed in his *particular* opinions. Dismissive of Pound in one piece ("Letter to B——"), he is supportive in another ("Mr. Rasula's History"). Opposed to opacity in theory ("The Poetic Principle"), he surreptitiously readmits it into his vocabulary when writing on particular poets (Charles Bernstein, Norma Cole). These inconsistencies exacerbate or literalize tendencies implicit in the original Poe. The comment on Pound in "Letter to B——" is based on a swipe at Samuel Johnson, and although the original Poe never devoted an entire essay of approval to Johnson as mine does to Pound, he did, on occasion, make reference to Johnson as an authority. Likewise, the opposition to opacity in "The Poetic Principle" is based on an analogous opposition to didacticism, a quality that continually reappears in Poe, and that Poe occasionally readmits in others.

83. This development was not surprising given my source text, for the same approach to sympathy was ever present, if latent, in Poe. See, for example, "A Reviewer Reviewed," in which Poe (writing under the pseudonym "Walter G. Bowen") retracts sympathy from himself, but precisely in order to decry such retraction as incompatible with honest critical practice: "Real, honest praise is a thing not to be looked for in a criticism by Mr. Poe. Even when it is his evident intention to be partial, to compliment in an extravagant manner some of his *lady* friends (for he never compliments a gentleman) there always seems to be something constrained, and shall I say malicious, at the bottom of the honey cup. . . . [H]is critical judgments . . . may be read for their pungency, but all the honesty they ever contain may be placed upon the point of a cambric needle" (*Essays and Reviews*, 1048). The irony here is obvious; less obvious is Poe's argument against the conventional claim (articulated by "Bowen") that honest judgments and fixed purposes are mutually exclusive. For Poe, honesty and fixity—ethics and aesthetics—were

neither mutually exclusive nor interdependent. Their relationship instead was anarchic.

84. Poe, *Essays and Reviews,* 1036.

85. Missing writers include the entire "New Narrative" group (Steve Abbott, Michael Amnasan, Dodie Bellamy, Bruce Boone, Robert Glück, Kevin Killian), a number of poets associated with New College (Diane Di Prima, Benjamin Hollander, Robert Kocik, Duncan McNaughton, David Meltzer, Aaron Shurin, David Levi Strauss, Susan Thackrey, John Thorpe), two members of the *HOW(ever)* circle (Susan Gevirtz, Frances Jaffer), some language writers (Alan Bernheimer, David Bromige, Jean Day, Johanna Drucker, Larry Price), and numerous unaffiliated figures such as Roberto Bedoya, Dan Davidson, Steve Dickison, Larry Eigner, Jerry Estrin, Norman Fischer, Jim Hartz, Ronald Johnson, Joanne Kyger, Laura Moriarty, Tina Rotenberg, Leslie Scalapino, and Gail Sher.

86. The portraits themselves make use of biographical and bibliographical information more or less accurate as of 1996.

87. Poe, *Essays and Reviews,* 1106.

88. The full story is too complex to tell or even summarize here, as its various strands are woven all through the fabric of Poe's final years. Moss provides the clearest discussion of the substantive issues in *Poe's Literary Battles.* For English's reply to Poe, Poe's reply to English, and English's rebuttal, see James A. Harrison's 1902 *Complete Works,* vol. 17, *Poe and His Friends: Letters Relating to Poe* (New York: AMS Press, 1965).

89. The "Benjamin Friedlander" portrait demonstrates this in two ways: concretely, by rewriting Poe's "Thomas Dunn English" portrait, and abstractly, by repeating Poe's gesture of pseudonymous self-critique. See, e.g., "A Reviewer Reviewed," cited in n. 32, supra.

90. I say "fraud" rather than "hoax." Although tempted from time to time to perpetrate a hoax, my interests ultimately led in a different direction. In hoaxes, the distinction between reality and fantasy is rendered invisible. In *Simulcast,* it is the use of fantasy to put quotation marks around reality that matters. Hoaxes also pretend toward a stability of authorship (and in their exposure simply settle into a different sort of stability). My interest here is *ambiguity* of authorship. In any event, my aim was never deception. The artifice involved in the production of these texts was never hidden (though the method of production itself might have been obscure), nor did I ever attempt to present this work as "original." This is one reason I chose to adopt such fanciful pseudonyms.

91. Another dialogue occurs between the experiments themselves, and this, too, produces a kind of "simulcast": a "multimedia" presentation of opinions whose very multiplicity makes plain the mediating force of the critical idiom. Thus, while Ron Silliman appears in the Internet-based discourse of

the *AHP* as an analogue for Madonna, he is "Evert A. Duyckinck" in the print culture of Poe's *Literati of New York City* and "Karl Jaspers" in Wahl's post-war lecture *A Short History of Existentialism*. Charles Bernstein is likewise a Madonna fan in the *AHP*, "William Cullen Bryant" in "Poe's Poetics," and "Jean Paul Sartre" in "A Short History." Taken together, then, the experiments in *Simulcast* argue for an amplified understanding of the relationship between "medium" and "message" in criticism.

92. In an essay on the *Short History*, Georges Bataille writes, "Jean Wahl spoke of philosopher-poets who would be, if I understand him correctly, philosophers by origin but only in order to liquidate a heritage. They would endlessly resolve the tension of philosophical research in poetic effusion" (quoted in Jill Robbins, *Altered Reading: Levinas and Literature* [Chicago: University of Chicago Press, 1999], 159). "Hecuba Whimsy" argues the exact opposite point: that language writing liquidates a heritage founded on poetic effusion, resolving its tensions in philosophical research. Whether this inversion of Wahl amounts to an inversion of existentialism per se remains an open question. For the purposes of translation, what mattered most was that the structure of interests remained analogous.

93. Wahl, *Short History*, 9–10.

94. Samuel R. Delany, *Longer Views: Extended Essays*, (Hanover: Wesleyan University Press, 1996) 171.

95. Charles Bernstein, *A Poetics*, (Cambridge: Harvard University Press, 1992) 151.

96. Lyn Hejinian, "Variations: A Return of Words," *In the American Tree*, ed. Ron Silliman (Orono: National Poetry Foundation, 1986), 504.

97. Bernstein, *A Poetics*, 223–24.

THE ANTI-HEGEMONY PROJECT

The AHP

by "Edgar Allen Poe"

A satire, pointedly such, at the present day, and especially by American poets, is a welcome novelty, indeed. We have really done very little in the line upon this side of the Atlantic—nothing, certainly, of importance—Kenneth Koch's cheerful poems and the doggerel verse of Ogden Nash and Dorothy Parker to the contrary notwithstanding. Some things we have produced, to be sure, which were excellent in the way of burlesque, without intending a syllable that was not utterly solemn and serious. Poems, plays, fictions, essays, epigrams, and memoirs, written by poets and possessed of this unintentional excellence, we would have no difficulty in designating by the dozen; but, in the matter of directly meant and genuine satire, especially in or concerning verse, it cannot be denied that we are sadly deficient. And yet, let it be said, while we are not, as a literary people, exactly equal to "The Dunciad"—while we have no pretensions to adopting a Popish cadence—in short, while we are no satirists ourselves, there can be no question that we answer sufficiently well as *subjects* for satire.

We repeat that we were glad to see this work of Mr. Funkhouser and company abroad on the Internet; first, because it was something new under the sun; secondly, because, in many respects, it was well executed; and, thirdly, because, in the universal corruption and rigmarole amid which we gasp for breath, it was really a pleasant thing to get even one accidental whiff of the unadulterated air of *truth*.

A brief history is sufficient to give the satire's overall dimensions. In February of 1995, a series of news briefs, modeled in style and format on those of the "clari.* news hierarchy," began to appear on Charles Bernstein's "Poetics List," which originates out of SUNY Buffalo. The contents varied, but inevitably reflected current goings-on in the "poetry world." Many of the items were surreal, but some had an almost prosaic verisimilitude. In one, the loquacious Tom Mandel became an affable retiree; in another, Ken Sherwood and Loss Glazier were called "Poetics Police"; in another, language poetry was blamed on tainted baby formula; in another, a "Save the NEA" effort was termed a cross-dressing fashion show. All of these interventions were identified as products of the "bleari.* nooz hierarchy," and further attributed to "The Anti-Hegemony Project." With surprisingly little distortion, the various jargons of politics, fashion, crime, sports, and economics were used to explain the social and aesthetic workings of the Art of the Muse—and quite adequately. The point, as soon became clear, was simple: to show that poetry's sublime particularity is no such thing at all.

More remarkable than the AHP itself, however, was the utter silence that greeted the sudden broadcast of these stories. Indeed, until an item appeared transforming Barrett Watten into a killer whale—adapted from an item on the film "Free Willy"—there was no public comment of *any* sort. And even in this instance, in the chivalrous outcry of James Sherry, response was focused on the matter of authorship, the AHP's mysterious provenance having become a focal point for counter-critique. We emphasize that authorship and not source became the focal point, for while the stories *had* been posted from identifiable "accounts," the stories themselves were unsigned, and rumors began to circulate *privately* that the true author—if such there was—kept himself hid. Chris Funkhouser, from whose account many of the stories had been sent, quickly came forward to make a public statement to the effect that the "AHP" was a cooperative project. And soon enough, discussion died down again—or at least appeared to. Inevitably, however, the rumors themselves became subjects for AHP satire. In one, a tapeworm named "Benji" was said to have burrowed deeply into Charles Bernstein's personal computer; in another, attributed to CNN (the Co-Poetry News Network), AHP activity was blamed on a sentient robot gone mad on too much literature.

For the record, the AHP's interventions originated from the following persons' accounts, at the following institutions: Carla Billitteri, Nick Lawrence, and Martin Spinelli (SUNY Buffalo), Don Byrd, Christopher Funkhouser, and Belle Gironda (SUNY Albany), Sandy Baldwin (NYU), Stephen Cope (U.C. Santa Cruz), Greg Keith (unaffiliated), Nada Gordon (unaffiliated). A few other accounts were also utilized, but as of yet we are unable to identify the owners.

But this was not the end. In a final hurrah, the AHP, after 12 days of relative silence, produced *en masse* a blitz of items of a different sort altogether. These appeared on the last day of February and the first day of March, 1995. No longer taking the form of fake news items, these final messages were modeled on the adolescent chitchat of the Internet's many Newsgroups—the Internet's discourse of choice. Presented as postings to an imaginary group called "alt.fan.silliman" (the model, we believe, was alt.fan.madonna), this later set of AHP posts used a mixture of real and superficially disguised names, and again satirized the goings-on on the Poetics List and in the poetry world. But where the "bleari" stories had adopted a sober language, and had appeared at discreet intervals, the "alt.fan.silliman" items flirted with incomprehensibility, and were so voluminous as to overwhelm altogether the Poetics List's normal flow of activity. (In a mere two days, there were 24 "alt.fan" messages. By contrast, across a period of 25 days, about 30 "bleari" messages had been generated.) This last onslaught, unlike the prior intervention, met with immediate outcry—an outcry that took two basic forms. *First,* it was said that the focus on Ron Silliman amounted to a smear campaign—in Internet lingo, "a flame"; *second,* that the sheer volume transformed the AHP's satire into a theft of the airwaves. In response, the AHP's defenders pointed out that the satires were in many ways a *tribute.* (The aggrieved poet himself weighed in with a bemused admission that he *was,* all in all, tickled by the attention—indeed, he responded to many of the "alt.fan" posts as if they had truly been the outpourings of fandom.) The second critique—that the volume of postings inherently prohibited a fair exchange of ideas—was never directly countered, but in retrospect this too seems debatable. To be sure, the swelling of traffic was sizable, but such swelling was also within the bounds of predictable occurrence. Moreover, even when such swells had drawn heated critique in the past, it was usually on account of their *content*—but this, precisely, was what the Poetics List proceeded to ignore. The real source of ire was more probably something else—something never stated directly. The "bleari" satires, for all their vehemence, treated poetry and the Poetics List as a matter of some importance. The "alt.fan" items treated these same affairs as adolescent twaddle. Could it be that the "alt.fan" postings—unlike the "bleari" items—wounded the vanity of the List as a whole, and not merely the figures named directly?

So much, in any event, for history.

As a work of the imagination and otherwise, the AHP had many defects, and though Mr. Funkhouser is a personal friend of ours, and we are happy and proud to say so, these we shall have no scruple in pointing out. However, the AHP also had many remarkable merits—merits which it will be quite useless for those aggrieved by the satire—quite useless for any *clique,* or set of *cliques,* to attempt to frown down, or to affect not to see, or to feel, or to understand.

Its prevalent blemishes were referable chiefly to the leading sin of *appropriation.* Had the work been composed professedly in paraphrase of the whole manner of our culture's self-satirizing discourse, we should have pronounced it the most ingenious and truthful thing of the kind upon record. So close is the copy, that it extends to the most trivial points—for example, the use of fancy, personalized "sig. files" in Newsgroup postings. The turns of phraseology, the forms of allusion, the use of the screen, the general conduct of the satire—everything—all—are the property of the culture as a whole. We cannot deny, it is true, that the self-satiric model of the discourse in question is unsusceptible of improvement, and that the contemporary satirist who deviates therefrom must necessarily sacrifice something of merit at the shrine of originality. Neither can we shut our eyes to the fact that the appropriation, in the present case, has conveyed, in full spirit, the subliminal critical qualities, as well as, in rigid letter, the inadvertent elegances of the journalistic and chit-chat modes of the day. We have in the AHP the bold, vigorous, and semi-lucid prose, the biting sarcasm, the pungent opinionation, and the unscrupulous directness of the world beyond poetry. Yet it will not do to forget that Mr. Funkhouser et al. have been *shown how* to achieve these virtues. They are thus only entitled to the praise of close observers and thoughtful, skilful copyists. The analyses are, to be sure, their own. They are neither clari's, nor alt.fan.madonna's—but they are molded in the identical mold used by these uncredited agencies of meaning.

Such servility of appropriation has seduced our authors into errors that their better sense should have avoided. They sometimes mistake intention; at other times they copy faults, confounding them with beauties. In the opening salvo, we find the lines: "The palace dispatched Crown Prince Gizzi and Crown Princess Willis on a Southern

California tour three days after the quake. Following oblique criticism, the pair cut short their trip and returned to Rhode Island."

The royal attributions are here adopted from a clari story about the imperial family of Japan, frequent subjects of news stories; but it should have been remembered that *Prince* and *Princess* enjoy very different meaning when applied to the ordinary citizens of a modern democracy than they do when applied to a royal family.

We are also sure that the gross vulgarity, the slander—we can use no gentler name—that disgraces the "AHP," cannot be the result of innate cruelty in the mind of the writers. It is part of the slavish and undiscriminating imitation of a culture inured to such sins. This slander has done the AHP an irreparable injury, both in a moral and intellectual view, without effecting anything whatever on the score of sarcasm, vigor or wit. "Let what is to be said, be said plainly." True; but let nothing cruel be *ever* said or conceived.

In asserting that this satire, even in its mannerism, has imbued itself with the full spirit of the polish and pungency of non- or even anti-literary language, we have already awarded it high praise. But there remains to be mentioned the far loftier merit of speaking the truth fearlessly in an epoch when truth is out of fashion and under circumstances of social position which would have deterred almost any man in our community from a similar Quixotism. For the dissemination of the AHP—an undertaking which brought under review, by name, most of our prominent *literati,* and treated them, generally, as they deserved (what treatment could be more bitter?)—for the dissemination of this attack, Mr. Funkhouser, whose subsistence lies in his pen, has little to look for apart from the silent respect of those at once honest and timid but the most malignant open or covert persecution. For this reason, and because it is the truth which he and his companions have spoken, do we say to him from the bottom of our hearts, "God speed!"

We repeat it: it is the truth that he and his committee have spoken, and who shall contradict us? They have said unscrupulously what every reasonable person among us has long known to be "as true as the tabloids"—that, as a poetic people, we are one vast perambulating humbug. They have asserted that we are *clique*-ridden, and who does not smile at the obvious truism of that assertion? They maintain that chicanery is, with us, a far surer road than talent to distinction in letters. Who gainsays this? The corrupt nature of our ordinary criticism has become notorious. Our own arm has prostrated its powers. The collusion between government funding agency and publisher, publisher and critic, critic and poet, poet and academy, academy and government agency, constitutes at once the most unbreakable ring of corruption and the most vicious circle of ideological contamination yet to become manifest in our letters. But to keep our comments focused on a single link in this *Chain:* the intercourse between publisher and author, author and critic, as it now almost universally stands, is comprised either in the paying and pocketing of blackmail, as the price of a simple forbearance, or in a direct system of petty and contemptible tit for tat, properly so called—a system even more injurious than the former to the true interests of the public, and more degrading to the buyers and sellers of good opinion, on account of the more positive character of the service here rendered for the consideration received. We laugh at the idea of any denial of our assertions upon this topic; they are infamously true. In the charge of general corruption, there are undoubtedly many noble exceptions to be made. There are, indeed, some very few magazine editors, who, maintaining an entire independence, will accept no unsolicited manuscripts at all, or who receive them with perfect understanding, on the part of these latter, that an unbiased *critique* will be given. There are even some publishers who refuse backing from the Federal government (or any other granting agency) as well. But these cases are insufficient to have much effect on the popular mistrust: a mistrust heightened by late exposure of the machinations of *coteries* in New York, San Francisco, and now all cyberspace—*coteries* which, at the bidding of leading small press publishers, manufacture, as required from time to time, a pseudo-public opinion by wholesale, for the benefit of any little hanger-on of the party, or well-"Fed" protector of the firm.

We speak of these things in the bitterness of scorn. It is unnecessary to cite instances, where one is found in almost every issue of a book. It is needless to call to mind the desperate case of Messerli—a case where the pertinacity of the effort to gull—where the obviousness of the attempt at forestalling a judgment—where the woefully overdone sun-and-mooning of that man-of-straw, together with the pitiable platitude of his production, proved a dose somewhat too potent for even the well-prepared stomach of the mob. We say it is supererogatory to dwell upon "The American Book Awards," or other similar follies, when we have, before our eyes, hourly instances of the machinations in question. The grossness of these base attempts, however, has not escaped indignant rebuke from the more honorable portions of the community; and we hail these symptoms of restiveness under the yoke of unprincipled ignorance and quackery (strong only in combination) as the harbinger of a better era for the interests of real merit, and of American poetry as a whole.

It has become, indeed, the plain duty of each individual connected with our poetry, heartily to give whatever influence he possesses to the good cause of integrity and the truth. The results attained will be worth his closest attention, for we shall thus frown down all conspiracies to foist inanity upon the public consideration at the obvious expense of every person of talent who is not a member of a *clique* in power. We may even arrive, in time, at that desirable point from which a distinct view of our persons of letters may be obtained, and their respective pretensions adjusted, by the standard of a rigorous and self-sustaining criticism alone. That their several positions are properly settled; that the positions which a vast number now hold are maintained by any better tenure than chicanery, will be asserted by none but the ignorant. We do not advance this fact as a new discovery. Its truth, on the contrary, is the subject, and has long been so, of every-day witticism and mirth.

Surely there can be few things more ridiculous than the general character and assumptions of the ordinary critical notices of new books! An editor, sometimes without the shadow of the commonest attainment—often without brains, always without time—does not scruple to give the world to understand that he is in the *daily* habit of critically reading and passing judgment over a flood of publications, one tenth of whose title-pages he may possibly have turned over, three-fourths of whose contents would be Hebrew to his most desperate efforts at comprehension, and whose entire mass and amount, as might be mathematically demonstrated, would be sufficient to occupy, in the most cursory perusal, the attention of some ten or twenty readers for a month! What he wants in plausibility, however, is made up in obsequiousness; what he lacks in time is supplied in temper. Such an editor is the most easily pleased person in the world. He admires everything, from the fat anthology of Little Boy Blue to the thinnest chapbook of How Now Brown Cow. Indeed, such editor's sole difficulty is in finding tongue to express his delight. Every saddle-stitched pamphlet is a miracle—every perfect-bound book is an epoch in letters.

Yet, in the attempt at getting definite information in regard to any one portion of our poetic literature, the merely general reader, or the foreigner, will turn in vain from print journals to cyberspace. It is not our intention here to dwell upon the radical and over-hyped hypertextual rigmarole of the Internet. Whatever virtues the Internet may hold, they are ill suited to the propagation or discussion of *poetry*, save in the satiric mode advanced by the AHP. And the demand that the AHP unmask itself rings especially hollow, resounding in the vacuous and nonindividuated depths of cyberspace. Alas, the poetic discourse found on the Internet is *virtually* anonymous. Who writes?—who causes to be written? A volley of names crisscrossing the world, with no more character than one expects of bums—drunks who seek out odd-jobs to earn the price of a bottle—*this*, we say, is the class of person who subscribes to our poetics lists. And who but a missionary could put up with such company? Who but an ass will put faith in tirades which *may* be the result of unwanted abstinence, or in panegyrics which nine times out of ten may be laid, directly or indirectly, to the charge of intoxication?

It is in the favor of these saturnine pockets of electricity that they are charged, now and again, with a good comment *de omnibus rebus et quibusdam aliis*, which may be looked into, without decided somnolent consequence, at any period not immediately subsequent to dinner. But it is useless to expect literary criticism from a "Listserv" or "Newsgroup," however useful these may be as sources of information regarding tawdrier realities. As all readers know, or should know, these venues are sadly given to naught but verbiage. It is a part of their nature, a condition of their being, a point of their faith. A veteran subscriber loves the safety of generalities, and is therefore rarely particular. "Words, words, words" are the secret of his strength. He has one or two original notions and is both wary and fussy of giving them out. Such a person's wit lies with his truth, in a well, and there is always a world of trouble in getting it up.

Should the opinions quacked by our poetic geese at large, supplemented now and then by the bubblings of fish caught in the Internet, be taken, in their wonderful aggregate, as an evidence of what American poetry absolutely is (and it may be said that, in general, they are really so taken), we shall find ourselves the most enviable set of people upon the face of the earth. Our fine writers are legion. Our very atmosphere is redolent of genius, and our nation is a huge, well-contented chameleon, grown pursy by inhaling it. We are *teretes et rotundi* —enwrapped in excellence. All our poets are Bards, good as Whitman and not yet gray; all our poetesses are "latter day Dickinsons"; nor will it do to deny that all our youthful enthusiasts are wise and talented moderns, and that everybody who takes pen in hand to attack the canon, our Republic of Letters, is as great as Caesar, or at least "great Caesar's ghost." We are thus in a glorious condition, and will remain so until forced to disgorge our ethereal honors. In truth, there is some danger that the jealousy of the rest of the world will interfere. It cannot long submit to that outrageous monopoly of all that is worth seeking "from the other side of the century," which the gentlemen and ladies of the scene betray such undoubted assurance of possessing.

But we feel angry with ourselves for the jesting tone of our observations upon this topic. The prevalence of the spirit of puffery is a subject far less for merriment than for disgust. Its truckling, yet dogmatic character—its bold, unsustained, yet self-sufficient and wholesale laudation—is becoming, more and more, an insult to the common sense of the community. Trivial as it essentially is, it has yet been made the instrument of the grossest abuse in the elevation of imbecility, to the manifest injury, to the utter ruin, of true merit. Is there any man of good feeling and of ordinary understanding—is there one single individual among all our readers—who does not feel a thrill of bitter indignation, apart from any sentiment of mirth, as he calls to mind instance after instance of the purest, of the most unadulterated quackery in letters, which has risen to a high post in the apparent popular estimation, and which still maintains it, by the sole means of a blustering arrogance, or of a busy wriggling conceit, or of the most barefaced plagiarism, or even through the simple immensity of its fawning—fawning not only unopposed by the community at large, but absolutely supported in proportion to the vociferous clamor with which it is made—in exact accordance with its utter baselessness and untenability? We should have no trouble in pointing out, today, some twenty or thirty so-called literary personages, who, if not idiots, as we half think them, or if not hardened to all sense of shame by a long course of disingenuousness, will now blush, in the perusal of these words, through conspicuousness of the shadowy nature of that purchased pedestal upon which they stand—will now tremble in thinking of the feebleness of the breath which will be adequate to the blowing it from beneath their feet. With the help of a hearty good will, even *we* may yet tumble them down.

But *a nos moutons*—to the "AHP." This satire has many faults besides those upon which we have commented. The title, for example, is not sufficiently distinctive, although otherwise good. It does not confine the attack to an *American* hegemony, while the work does. Also, the individual portions of the satire are strung together too much at random—a natural sequence is not always preserved—so that although the lights of the picture are often forcible, the whole has what, in artistic parlance, is termed an accidental and spotty appearance. In truth, the parts of the satire have evidently been composed each by each, as separate themes, and afterwards fitted into the general project, in the best manner possible.

But a more reprehensible sin than any or than all of these is yet to be mentioned—the sin of indiscriminate censure. Even here Mr. Funkhouser and friends have erred through unthinking appropriation. They have held in view the sweeping denunciations of the news media, and of the juvenile spewings of the Internet. No one in his or her senses can deny the justice of the general charges of corruption in regard to which we have just spoken from the text of our authors. But are there *no* exceptions? We should indeed blush if there were not. And is there *no* hope? Time will show. Again, it cannot be gainsaid that the greater number of those who hold high places in our poetical literature are absolute nincompoops—fellows and ladies alike innocent of reason and of rhyme. But neither are we *all* brainless. The AHP must read a little in French philosophy, for there is *some* difference between a blank page and "*carte blanche.*" It will not do in a civilized land to run amuck like a Zapatista. The NEA *has* done some good in the world. Mr. Watten is not *all* killer instinct. Mr. Silliman is not *quite* an ass. Mr. Mandel *will* babble inanely, but perhaps he cannot help it (for we have heard of such other things), and then it must not be denied that the squeaky wheel is often a cry for grease.

The fact is that our authors, in the rank exuberance of their zeal, seemed to think as little of discrimination as Jimmy Swaggart did of the Bible. Poetical "things in general" are the windmills at which they spurred their Rozinante. They as often tilted at what was true as at what was false; and thus their lines were like funhouse mirrors, which represent the fairest images as deformed. But the talent, the fearlessness, and especially the *design* of the project, will suffice to save it from that dreadful damnation of "silent contempt" to which readers throughout the country, if we are not very much mistaken, will endeavor, one and all, to consign it.

AN AHP DOSSIER

No. 1

(5 Feb 1995)

> Subject: Tough Cops Look For Trouble
> Copyright: 1999 by The Anti-Hegemony Project
> Date: 25 Dec 99 00:01:00 EST
>
> Lines: 121
>
>   BUFFALO (AHP) -- Ken Sherwood and Loss Glazier
> are trolling the desolate streets of Buffalo,
> trying to decide whose pockets to poke, whose
> socks to stretch, which kid to search.
>   Since it's snowing heavily on this particular
> night, the Poetics Program cops have few choices.
> No matter. Even the two men shoveling the sidewalk
> seem suspicious.
>   "They want this clean 'cause they've got
> something going on," says Glazier, 37.
>   Glazier and Sherwood, 26, are two members of an
> elite, 20-member unit known as the Core Reserve,
> a force with broad powers to look for proscribed
> books and papers in the possession of suspicious
> characters.
>   Their aggressive techniques are being echoed by
>

> ---More---
>
> Group bleari.rime.organized avail.: 18-25 unread: 1
>
> article 24 26-DEC-1999 12:12:12
>
> poetics programs nationwide. They stop and search
> with virtual impunity. They finger e-mail accounts
> and ask girlfriends and boyfriends to let them
> rummage through desks. They hold meetings with
> the students and faculty. They stop cars in
> the parking lot, feel under dashboards, frisk
> occupants.
>   Just what counts as proscribed materials is
> uncertain. No matter.
>   "Now, this area down here, we got a lotta
> Olson," says Glazier, tour guide in hell. "This
> next set of offices, we get a lot of performance-
> oriented stuff, screaming and such-like.
>   "There was a guy up here who people say kept his
> poetry up his rectum," he says, very matter-of-
> factly. "One day we found him strangled with his
> pants off and his legs up in the air. We assumed
> the poems had been removed."
>   The car coasts to curbs alongside earnest-
> looking youths trudging in the snow. A searchlight
> blinds them, sometimes bouncing off the glossy
> covers of university press paperbacks the police
> say are badges of ganghood.
>   "You get a guy with four or five books and he
>
> ---More---
>
> Group bleari.rime.organized avail.: 18-25 unread: 1
>
> article 24 26-DEC-1999 12:12:12
>
> starts running, he's going to cling to

> himself and hold that pile while he runs," says
> Glazier. "We call it the book run."
>   The officers check purses, disc-containers,
> sports jackets and long droopy cardigan sweaters.
> They poke fingers inside gloves. Nobody complains.
> "You know what it's about," Glazier tells a boy.
>   Sherwood gestures at a house. "We got three
> contraband books out of there. Girls let us in."
>   "Four books," corrects Glazier. "The women were
> very cooperative, but the rest of the family were
> upset the poetics police were taking their books
> and stuff. It was a nice little seizure."
>   It is 9 p.m., three hours into the shift, and
> another two-man team has found a slim volume
> during the search of a man who was wearing a ski
> mask in the falling snow.
>   The bearded, friendly man turns out to be a
> watchman at a warehouse that houses chicken wings
> and bleu cheeze for visiting poets. And he's a
>
> ---More---
>
> Group bleari.rime.organized avail.: 18-25 unread: 1
>
> article 24 26-DEC-1999 12:12:12
>
> former student of Robert Creeley's. But he doesn't
> have a permit for the book. He's under arrest.
>   The officers ask if he'll sign a release-for-
> publication form, essentially a waiver that exempts
> the police from liability. He has agreed.
>   Inside the man's clean, modest rooms, the police
> find an old John Wieners book, a dog-eared copy
> of The Colossus, a Bob Dylan biography, a lot of
> anthropology books and a powerful computer.
>   "I don't have nothing to hide," he says
> pleasantly. "I'm an ordinary person. Not too
> smart. I don't even have a modem."

> Glazier and Sherwood are hardly back on the road
> when word comes that another team has found a
> couple of kids with a manuscript as they left a
> house with a reputation for "Lang-Po" sympathies.
> The eldest, 30-year-old Nick, was carrying The
> Cultural Studies Reader and a Bob Perelman book.
> The police figure Nick's companion, 25-year-old
> Alan, has his own books at home.
> They go to Alan's house nearby. The girlfriend
> comes to the door. "Oh my God," she says to the
> three uniformed cops.
>
> ---More---
>
> Group bleari.rime.organized avail.: 18-25 unread: 1
>
> article 24 26-DEC-1999 12:12:12
>
> Sgt. Tedlock, the supervisor who's called in
> to handle this part, smoothly delivers a well-
> practiced pitch.
> "We wanted to let you know he's walking around
> with a kid who's got The Cultural Studies Reader and
> he was coming out of a known Lang-Po den," he says.
> "We're not going to arrest him," he says,
> setting up the offer. "Here's what I'm going
> to do."
> The conversation takes place as the woman walks
> back up the stairs, implicitly but not directly
> seeming to invite the officers to follow along.
> Soon, everybody is up at the top of the stairs,
> in the living room, a corner of which is the boy's
> study.
> Tedlock, eyeing the packed and wobbly bookshelf,
> tells her the police just want to look around, see
> if there's any contraband material. The woman can
> watch them. Nobody will be arrested.
> He holds out the release form. Everyone waits as
> the girlfriend anxiously ponders it.

> "I know he doesn't have a manuscript in here," she
>
> ---More---
>
> Group bleari.rime.organized avail.: 18-25 unread: 1
>
> article 24 26-DEC-1999 12:12:12
>
> stammers. "At least not a bad one." She seems to
> be weakening when her boyfriend, giving her the
> eye, interrupts with a well-placed "Kristin. . . . "
> Tedlock tells the boy not to interrupt, but it's
> too late. The woman says no. The cops get terse,
> telling her the boy is bound for trouble.
> They leave. Alan grins.
> "I'll bet the farm there's Lang-Po in that
> house," Glazier, frustrated, says outside. "He
> knows it, she knows it."
"Or that New Spirit stuff," adds Sherwood.
> "Yes, that was a suspicious looking setup,"
> reflects Tedlock, staring up at the snow. "Mighty
> suspicious."

No. 2

(5 Feb 1995)

> Subject: Poetics Program Targets Big Fish
> Copyright: 1999 by The Anti-Hegemony Project
> Date: 21 Mar 99 12:00:00 EST
> Priority: Code Blue
>
> Lines: 74
>
> AMHERST (AHP) -- Cabinet Ministers for the
> Poetics Program want the poetry "mafia" to give
> up more than 6 years of control over the bustling,
> pungent stalls of the nation's largest "fish
> market."
> Minister of Foreign Policy Robert Creeley
> announced plans for the "Wednesdays at Four Plus"

> commission to better regulate and investigate
> poets and critics doing business with the Poetics
> Program.
>   "New York mayor Rudolf Giuliani's plan for
> Fulton Fish Market gave me the idea," said
> Creeley, who declared an emergency meeting of
> the Poetics Program to unveil the plan. "The
> association was natural -- fish, Olson, poetry,
>
> ---More---
>
> Group bleari.nooz.rime.organized avail.: 50-60 unread: 5
>
> article 5050 1-APR-99 18:00:00
>
> Buffalo . . . it's your classic mob situation."
>   He and the other cabinet ministers hope to clean
> up what many say has become a dangerous place for
> those who love poetry.
>   "This has nothing to do with 'Language Poetry',"
> said Economics Minister Charles Bernstein, "despite
> what everyone has been saying."
>   "It's that damned old boys network," says
> Education Minister Susan Howe. "Not that I have
> anything against old boys. But enough's enough."
>   The size of the market has shrunk in recent
> semesters from approximately 50 people a reading
> to only 5 or 10.
>   "Students do not attend because they fear the
> readings are only payback for favors," said a
> smiling Raymond Federman, newly appointed
> Ambassador to France, a cabinet level position
> in the current administration.
>   Some poets say New York's Segue family uses its
> control over students at the university to impose
> a monopolistic "tax" on discussion driving many
> to do business at other markets on the Eastern
> Seaboard.
>

```
> ---More---
>
> Group bleari.nooz.rime.organized avail.: 50-60 unread: 5
>
> article 5050 1-APR-1999 18:00:00
>
>   The allegations have never been substantiated.
>   The "fish market," nestled among windswept
> concrete structures built on landfill in the early
> 1970s, is instrumental in the processing of some
> dozen literary events a semester. These events are
> linked to book sales and course offerings.
>   In the early 1990s it was taken over by Robert
> "Books" Bertholf, a fish handler who oversaw day-
> to-day operations in the market.
>   The market soon became a powerful center of
> rumored cronyism. Recently, the market moved to
> a new Arts Center, which some call a colder and
> grayer site.
>   Yet business is booming. This semester boasts
> more literary events than ever.
>   Under the new proposal, the market would
> be managed by the "Wednesdays at Four Plus"
> commission, which would set rates and procedures
> for the market and impose fines for rules
> violations.
>
> ---More---
>
> Group bleari.nooz.rime.organized avail.: 50-60 unread: 5
>
> article 5050 1-APR-1999 18:00:00
>
>   All poets operating in the market would have to
> be licensed and registered. The commission would
> have the power to deny licenses to anyone it deems
> unfit to do business.
>   "But what constitutes a legitimate poet?"
> wondered Charles Bernstein. Such questions remain
> to be worked out by the commission.
```

```
>   Finding answers for these questions excites some
> ministers and worries others. "Anything could
> happen," beamed Raymond Federman.
>   A dour Dennis Tedlock, Minister of Former
> Colonies, wasn't so sure. "Fish? The market is
> um, a sort of metaphor. People eat fish and study
> them . . . there might be other ways we haven't
> tried to make . . . friends with the fish."
```

No. 3

(8 Feb 1995)

```
> Subject: Fake infant formula found in California,
> library says
> Copyright: 1999 by The Anti-Hegemony Project
> Date: 15 Mar 99 50:50:00 PST
>
> Lines: 38
>
>   SAN FRANCISCO (AHP) - Fake labels and contents
> for Simulac infant formula were found on library
> shelves in northern California, Lang-Po
> Laboratories GmbH, the maker of the formula,
> announced late last night.
>   Labels have been placed on books that falsely
> say the product contains Simulac paperback infant
> formula with irony, the company said.
>   The books have been removed from library shelves
> and the origin and quality of the substance in the
> books is unknown, Lang-Po Labs, which made its
> discovery over the weekend, added.
>   The fake label reads "Simulac with irony, paper"
> with the following titles printed on the spine:
> Progress, Odes of Roba and Curve.
>
> ---More---
>
> Group bleari.biz.food_as_thought avail.: 3-9 unread: 6
>
> article 3 17-MAR-1999 19:20:21
```

```
>
>   "Parents should check the titles of any
> paperback infant formula product that they may
> have at home that was borrowed from the San
> Francisco State library or any bookstore in
> northern California," Leslie Scalapino, senior
> vice president and president of Lang-Po's Consumer
> Products Division, said in a statement.
>   Parents who discover they have fake books should
> return them to the library or bookstore from which
> they were purchased, the company said.
>   In addition to the title, the fake product can
> be identified in the following ways: it has a
> clear syntax and the powder in the book is pure
> white in color. The real product has a green-
> colored syntax and the powder is creamy yellow in
> color.
>   Lang-Po Labs said there is no need for concern
> about other Simulac infant formulas.
>   The U.S. Book and Tape Administration is
> attempting to locate the source of the unregulated
> product, the company said.
>   Anyone with information on the source of
>
> ---More---
>
> Group bleari.biz.food_as_thought avail.: 3-9 unread: 6
>
> article 3 17-MAR-1999 19:20:21
>
> tainting should immediately contact the B.T.A.
```

No. 4

(8 Feb 1995)

```
>
> Subject: Calls For Change Worry Seniors
> Copyright: 1999 by The Anti-Hegemony Project
> Date: 31 May 99 11:00:00 EST
>
> Lines: 97
```

```
>
>   WASHINGTON (AHP) -- Leaders of the Association
> of Poets in Retirement aren't quite sure what New
> Spirit Speaker Lew Daly has in mind with his call
> for rethinking Poeticare "from the ground up." But
> what they've heard worries them.
>   "The speaker's proposal left me fully
> depressed," said Rae Armantrout of San Diego,
> Calif., a member of the APR's council of outspoken
> elders. "He wants to scuttle Poeticare with some
> weasel words -- 'radical transparency'."
>   Other APR officials are more circumspect, but
> they, too, express anxiety.
>   Anselm Hollo of Boulder, Colo., a retired punster
> and part-time versifier, said, "Anytime you
> destroy something and you build from the ground
> up . . . you're in trouble because you may lose
> some of the good parts."
>
> ---More---
>
> Group bleari.nooz.aging     avail.: 55-65 unread: -1
>
> article 66 1-JUN-1999 23:59:59
>
>   "I'm not saying Poeticare shouldn't be looked at
> and modifications shouldn't be made," added Hollo,
> chairman of Numerous Adequate Poets (NAP), which
> helps shape policy for the G1-endorsed APR.
>   Poeticare is the shoe that hasn't dropped in the
> newly empowered "Spirit" majority's agenda for
> sweeping change.
>   With Small Press Publishing still accorded
> sacred cow status by both parties, the costly
> Poeticare program is among the biggest and
> most tempting targets for title-trimmers and
> word-cutters.
>   Daly called yesterday for a top-to-bottom review
> of Poeticare and its "highly centralized
```

> bureaucratic structure offering one menu for
> everybody in a monopolistic manner." He appealed
> to G1 writers to help poeticians think through
> "how we get to a better Poeticare system that
> actually works more extensively, that gives greater
> choices, and that is also socially more honest."
>   He said later that the older poets should be
>
> ---More---
>
> Group bleari.nooz.aging   avail.: 55-65 unread: -1
>
> article 66 1-JUN-1999 23:59:59
>
> able to join Happening Movements and
> Organizations (HMOs) to extend their careers,
> and use archive sales or choose other methods
> for attracting attention to their work.
>   While 10 percent of the G1 poets are enrolled
> voluntarily in HMOs, Poeticare remains a bastion
> of fee-for-service poetry. Individual arts
> organizations set fees for readings and regulate
> schedules, but the poets can utilize any series
> they wish, so long as the organization is willing
> to accept them.
>   Jean Day, a retired G1 poet who spent her career
> as top manager of Small Press Distribution, likes
> the old system. "I want fee for service (poetry).
> I want to be able to set my own agenda."
>   But most younger poets now are in some form of
> managed care. If they want unrestricted access to
> readings and publishing, they have to pay more for
> it. State-funded Poetics Programs are rushing to
> push Poeticaid recipients -- the poor and the
> socially needy -- into managed care.
>   A year ago, the APR looked to special issues of
> literary journals as a path for literary reform.
> That never materialized.

>
> ---More---
>
> Group bleari.nooz.aging   avail.: 55-65 unread: –1
>
> article 66 1-JUN-1999 23:59:59
>
>   Now it is girding for a fight just to protect
> what they have, despite President Bernstein's plea
> in last week's State of the Art address not to tap
> Poeticare to pay for G2's "Contract with America."
>   "There are things in the Poeticare system that
> clearly need work," said Jerry Rothenberg, the
> APR's executive director. "I don't think Poeticare
> is going to remain the way it is forever, or that
> HMOs are going to sweep the nation."
>   Sen. Juliana Spahr, Spir.-N.Y, reminded "Lang-Po"
> leaders that the Poeticare trust fund will go
> broke in seven years. "We can't say something
> is off the board and is untouchable," said the
> Poetics Program's Labor and Human Resources
> Committee chair.
>   She suggested that options for dealing with
> Poeticare's woes include basing Poeticare benefits
> on financial need and moving more of the G1 writers
> toward managed care.
>   Daly and the chairpersons of the Spirit Ways and
> Means and Commerce committees all support the idea
>
> ---More---
>
> Group bleari.nooz.aging   avail.: 55-65 unread: –1
>
> article 66 1-JUN-1999 23:59:59
>
> of letting people spend their words crit-free to
> help accumulate intellectual capital.
>   Bill Howe, policy director of the Center for the
> Study of Accelerated Aesthetics in Austin, said

> poetry IRAs have the potential to "lead to a
> radical restructuring of the poetry world" as
> writers gain more control over their career
> insurance dollars.
> Skeptics worry that such accounts would
> undermine the concept of intellectual fair play
> and erode the principle that those 50 and older
> are entitled to a fair hearing from their
> antecedents.

No. 5

(13 Feb 1995)

> Subject: Famous Killer Whale Set Free
> Copyright: 1999 by The Anti-Hegemony Project
> Date: 1 Mar 99 00:00:01 PST
>
> Lines: 64
>
> SAN FRANCISCO (AHP) -- This time he has a reason
> to leap.
> Watten, the killer whale made famous by the film
> "Free Barry," is heading toward a new home in
> Michigan and eventual freedom, his owners
> announced yesterday.
> The Berkeley amusement park where Watten has
> lived for the past decade signed an agreement
> donating the 3.5-ton mammal to the Free Barry
> Watten Foundation, which plans to eventually free
> him in waters off Japan after a rehabilitation
> period at the Wayne State Aquarium in Detroit.
> The amusement park said the 15-year-old whale,
> captured off the coast of Japan at age 2, has
> performed for over a hundred visitors over the
> past 10 years. Efforts to free him have been
> underway since the Poetry Flash film was released.
>
> ---More---
>

> Group bleari.poesy.animals avail.: 1-10 unread: 10
>
> article "writing degree zero" 29-FEB-1999 24:00:00
>
>   "Watten will be the only captive Langpo whale
> that doesn't have to do shows or perform," Lyn
> Hejinian, director of the foundation, said at a
> news conference yesterday.
>   The foundation plans to move him in November.
>   In many ways, Watten is like a typical human
> teen-ager -- he's got skin problems, has grown
> (to 21 feet), and now wants a girlfriend.
>   "He requires more space, different conditions and
> also a companion," said Jean Day, a spokeswoman
> for the Berkeley habitat Representations.
>   Hejinian said the park "received letters and
> proposals of aid from all over the world." She
> said it waited until receiving "an absolute
> guarantee" that conditions in the killer whale's
> new home would be adequate.
>   Hejinian said the entire project will require
> "a heck of a lot of capital" over four years and
> include Watten's "relocation, rehabilitation,
> possible mating, possible liberation and
> investigations into the whereabouts of the
> family of Watten."
>
> ---More---
>
> Group bleari.poesy.animals avail.: 1-10 unread: 10
>
> article "writing degree zero" 29-FEB-1999 24:00:00
>
>   That includes funds to build an expensive,
> 2-million-gallon tank at the Michigan aquarium.
>   Experts said Watten needs to be trained
> gradually for life at sea -- weaned, for example,
> from eating dead fish to eating live ones.
>   "Watten, who has passed all his life away from

> the sea, would encounter serious difficulties
> feeding himself, caring for himself and surviving
> by himself in a hostile environment," Hejinian
> said.
>   So far, the foundation has collected about half
> the needed funds, including a generous grant from
> Poetry Flash and George Lakoff Inc., creators of
> "Free Barry."
>   The money raised includes a small sum from
> former students at San Francisco State, who
> conducted a letter-writing campaign and saved
> pennies.
>   They began sending letters in last month to
> prominent businessmen and individuals, including
> marine sociobiologist Jacques de Certeau.
>   Certeau sent no money, but praised the children for
>
> ---More---
>
> Group bleari.poesy.animals   avail.: 1-10 unread: 10
>
> article "writing degree zero" 29-FEB-1999 24:00:00
>
> their efforts. Singer Jimmy Buffett sent $500.
>   Further fund-raising efforts will be tied to a
> Poetry Flash sequel due for release next summer.

No. 6

(14 Feb 1995)

> Subject: Home Of The Creepy-Crawlies
> Copyright: 1999 by The Anti-Hegemony Project
> Date: 20 Jun 99 05:10:15 EST
>
> Lines: 116
>
>   PROVIDENCE (AHP) -- The Poetarium is unlike most
> museums you've visited.
>   It's located in a Providence working-class

> neighborhood with bridal shops, bakeries and
> bars on every block, about 10 miles from Brown
> University.
>   When you get there, you've got to climb a flight
> of stairs.
>   Suddenly, you realize you're in the middle of
> more than 100,000 live poets, the kind that go
> "buzz" in the night.
>   Children, especially, love it.
>   More than 75,000 visitors -- mostly pre-teens --
> file into the poetry zoo each year, paying $3
> apiece to be up close and personal with the
> creepy, crawly inmates. Hundreds of school field
> trips have already been scheduled for 1999.
>
> ---More---
>
> Group bleari.poesy.animals avail.: some - unread: lots
>
> article whatever 31-JUL-1999 19:30:30
>
>   "It's not only entertaining, it's also
> educational and enlightening," says Steve Evans,
> the 30-year-old museum founder and proprietor
> of Steve's Bug-Off Poet Exterminating Co.,
> located on the building's ground floor. The
> Poetarium occupies 6,500 square feet on the
> two top floors.
>   This is the real deal, no cheesy rip-off filled
> with first editions and photographs. Evans says
> it's the largest in the country.
>   "The Smithsonian poetry exhibit in Washington
> has less square footage and I've got a million
> more poets still in storage," says Evans, proudly
> displaying a room overflowing floor-to-ceiling
> with boxes, cookie tins and Tupperware filled with
> dead poets from around the globe.
>   "I respect what they're doing. Their staff is
> extremely knowledgeable and they really do a great

> job teaching the kids," said Robert Bertholf of
> the Poetry and Rare Book Room in Buffalo, which
> has its own extensive collection. "Steve has even
> come in here and set up some wonderful exhibits,
> very professional stuff," Bertholf said.
>
> ---More---
>
> Group bleari.poesy.animals avail.: some - unread: lots
>
> article whatever 31-JUL-1999 19:30:30
>
>   The Poetarium is designed to give the illusion
> of being out in the wild. The walls are decorated
> in a bar motif, the carpets are cigarette-butt
> strewn and the soundtrack is poetry's own -- Amy
> Lowell chirping and Carl Sandburg humming. Movies,
> holograms, microscopes and professional quality
> exhibits and games keep people of all ages
> occupied.
>   There is also a real swarming beatnik read-in
> and a giant rubber-band "enjambement" for children
> to crawl through.
>   Electronic quizboards measure your poetry
> intelligence.
>   For example, did you know that New York School
> poets could survive on just the food offered at
> gallery openings? that political poets have more
> than 1,000 brothers and sisters each?
>   And yes, Language Poets really do bite, but
> maybe they're only angry about having a 12-month
> lifespan.
>   There's even a scale to weigh yourself in New
> Critics, New Formalists and other six-legged
> creatures. If you thought losing 10 pounds was
> difficult, imagine shedding a half-million
> versifiers!
>
> ---More---
>

> Group bleari.poesy.animals avail.: some - unread: lots
>
> article whatever 31-JUL-1999 19:30:30
>
>   Robert Pinsky, Eugenio Montale, Gottfried
> Benn, Edith Sitwell, Aime Cesaire, Jean Toomer,
> Ingeborg Bachmann, Rabindranath Tagore, Phyllis
> Webb, Pablo Neruda, Carl Dennis, bpNichol, Sappho,
> Jack Gilbert, Alan Gilbert, Allen Ginsberg and
> Gilbert Grape are all present.
>   "Everyone here is really nice. It's not scary,"
> said Jessica Lowenthal, 22. "I had lots of fun."
>   The centerpiece of the Poetarium is the pedants.
> Thousands and thousands of good old "poeticus
> obscurorum" -- stuffed shirts -- encased inside
> a four-foot plastic fence that surrounds a
> model library and study. The repulsive critters
> slither in and out of the cabinets and drawers
> and occasionally attempt to scale the wall.
>   "I promise you, they can't get out of there,"
> says Evans's partner, Jennifer Moxley, the curator
> and one of the tour guides. "There's a Teflon
> paint strip at the top which makes them slide back
> down. If they get past that, there's a row of
> electrical wires."
>   Numerous poetry-related items are available in the
>
> ---More---
>
> Group bleari.poesy.animals avail.: some - unread: lots
>
> article whatever 31-JUL-1999 19:30:30
>
> gift shop, including posters, T-shirts, coloring
> books, postcards and plastic Vincent Ferrinis.
>   Many of the poets are captured by Evans and his
> staff, especially service director and exhibit
> designer Peter Gizzi, a longtime poetry collector.
> Using butterfly nets and riding a mountain bike
> painted camouflage green and brown, Gizzi rolls

> into the wilds of nearby New York City and sees
> what he can snare.
>   For Evans, life's metamorphosis was a little
> more complex than word-larva-pupa-poet.
>   He began while a student, working on the side as
> a lobbyist for poetic environmentalists. This led
> to opportunities in poetry population control. But
> he still prefers collecting to killing the poets,
> and in 1997 Evans opened the museum.
>   "We used to have a smaller store, and we'd put
> whatever we caught each day in the front window --
> short story writers, translators," Evans says.
> "People were looking in the windows all the time.
>
> ---More---
>
> Group bleari.poesy.animals avail.: some - unread: lots
>
> article whatever 31-JUL-1999 19:30:30
>
> Teachers even brought their classes by. I thought
> this would be a great way to teach kids that poets
> aren't bad, once you get to know them."
>   So what's next for Evans? Would you believe a
> poetrymobile?
>   "I'm converting an old paddy wagon," he says.
> "Look for us at a school or mall or senior center
> near you."

No. 7

(21 Feb 1995)

> Subject: Basking Tapeworm
> Copyright: 1999 by The Anti-Hegemony Project
> Date: 22 Mar 99 03:22:59 EST
>
> Lines: 15
>
>   DEEP CYBERSPACE (AHP) -- A 26-foot long tapeworm
> was caught by weary computing engineers yesterday,

> who claimed the foul-smelling creature had been
> feeding off the Net. Now on display, the worm
> has turned a tiny Cyberspace village into an
> unexpected tourist attraction, the Co-Poetry
> News Network reported yesterday.
>   Engineers "netted" the basking tapeworm --
> biggest of its kind ever seen in the area -- and
> used ropes to extract it from a gaping terminal in
> Charles Bernstein's office in Clemens Hall at SUNY
> Buffalo. Bernstein, away on a reading tour, had
> left the terminal unattended and during this time
> the tapeworm -- nicknamed "Benji" by engineers --
> apparently nestled into an intractable position.
> The tapeworm drew carloads of summer vacation
>
> ---More---
>
> Group bleari.news.feeder   avail.: 1-1 unread: 0
>
> article 1   22-MAR-1999 03:22:59
>
> tourists, said CNN, which showed children
> climbing onto the giant carcass and posing for
> snapshots.

No. 8

(24 Feb 1995)

> Subject: Charles takes young prince and princess fox-
> hunting
> Copyright: 1999 by The Anti-Hegemony Project
> Date: 24 Oct 99 01:30:00 EST
>
> Lines: 25
>
>   BUFFALO (AHP) - Heir to the throne Prince
> Charles took his young son Gary and daughter Cass
> hunting yesterday, defying popular disapproval to
> initiate them into a traditional poetic pastime.
>   "I think anyone who knows anything about the

```
> history of poetry can tell you, the skills
> necessary for tracking and killing an animal
> are similar to those required for ruling the
> Imagination," said Yunte Huang, a spokesman for
> the Prince.
>   "It was . . . like shooting fish in a barrel,"
> gushed the excited princess. "I wanna go out
> again."
>   The royal trio were lashed by rain for several
> hours as they rode with the down-jacketed Poetics
> Hunt across rolling hills near Charles's country
> estate, The Fountainview Apartments, in Amherst.
>
> ---More---
>
> Group bleari.nooz.poesy  avail.: 1848-1917 unread: 0
>
> article 1917 6-NOV-1999 12:00:00
>
>   Gary, 10, and Cass, 12, have ridden at earlier
> meets but devotees of the sport said this was
> their first full-fledged hunt.
>   Charles, often accused of being out of touch
> with contemporary developments in poetry, has
> insisted his heirs should learn to hunt despite
> the anger of opponents who say the sport is
> bloodthirsty and cruel.
```

No. 9

(1 Mar 1995)

```
> ---------------------------------------------
> W = A = R = N = I = N = G
>
> A second Simulac spill has caused further
> disturbance in the downtime/cyberspace
> continuum. All messages dated Valentine's
> Day should be boiled before drinking. If
> verbal dithyrambs continue vomit drench pea
```

> bucket and spoonfeed. Repost: rapini tic
> mouse and barf the arrow. Dandy shift keys
> download Soon-Yi, Previn commensurately.
> Anti-Hemorhaging is projected bile radio.
>
> ***DONUT RED TAPERS MATCH EDGES.***
> Rasta sure by hot shots part deux con carne.
> --

No. 10

(28 Feb 1995)

> Rating: PG13
> <poetic guidance for readers over 13 suggested>
> From: djb1917@iou.albany.ahp (Donald Jaybird)
> Newsgroups: alt.fan.silliman
> Subject: Silliman in my life . . .
> Date: 14 Feb 99 22:22:22
> Organization: The Anti-Hegemony Project
> Lines: 28
>
> I just thought I'd put just my opinion of silliman
> He totally excites me and I am always looking
> forward to what he'll do next. . . . no matter
> what he does I like. Does anyone know if the
> Bay Area book awards will be broadcast on
> Pacifica and when
> ?
> I predict he will give readings in the early
> fall of 2000. I saw the Ear Inn show in New York
> City..It was increadible and unreal . . .
> I paid 85 bucks for my share of the dinner after
> . . . but it was worth it! WHAT came as a shock
> to me . . . I saw Toner in Sulfur and flipped
> out . . . I LOVE paradise . . . and lit . . . and
> ABC and hell the whole damn alphabet. . . . It
> really bugs me when people put him down . . . they
> are just jealous and ignorant. . . . .I'm looking
> forward to what he does next!

```
> --
>
> "To be a poet in this society is to become,
> however marginally, a projected (if not
> hallucinated) social object" -- R.S.
>
>    ('<      Donald Jaybird
>   ,',)         djb1917@iou.albany.ahp
>  "<<
> ---""---
```

No. 11

(28 Feb 1995)

```
> Rating: PG13
> <poetic guidance for readers over 13 suggested>
> From: kit_rubitin@bando.ahp (The Kitmeister)
> Newsgroups: alt.fan.silliman
> Subject: Re: going somewhere?
> Date: 14 Feb 1999 15:15:15
> Organization: The Anti-Hegemony Project
> Lines: 25
>
> lew@acsu.buffalo.ahp wrote:
> : All of you people who like Sillman are going
> straight to hell. How can you
> : support such filth as some kind of God? It seems
> as though you people have
> : a lot of repenting to do. burn silliman. Burn
> Silliman!!!!!
> : Lew
> : SUNY Buffalo
  -----
>
> This is the same sort of unmitigated bullshit that
> we heard last year after the L.A. earthquake where
> these pathetic bible thumpering losers stated that
> the quake was God's way of punishing a city full
> of sinners. I guess by their standards the San
```

> Fernando valley area has more sinners than, say,
> West Hollywood or other areas of the city, since
> the Valley areas were hit so much hard than the
> rest of the L.A.
>
> So you pathetic, judgemental, semi-literate
> hypocrites; get a life and get grip on something
> besides your bibles and your tiny little dicks.
> ; --)~

No. 12

(28 Feb 1995)

> Rating: PG13
> <poetic guidance for readers over 13 suggested>
> From: v21sey9@ubvms.buffalo.ahp (Juliana Spar)
> Newsgroups: alt.fan.silliman
> Subject: Re: what is this terrorism thing?
> Date: 14 Feb 1999 12:12:12
> Organization: The Anti-Hegemony Project
> Lines: 25
>
> In <??????????> ENPOPE@LSUE.ME.AHP (Erik Pope)
> writes:
>
> >
> >I am normally a Silliman fan to the max, but I
> >think I am slipping. What is the story on him
> >and Lyn Hejinian being terrorists? What was his
> >comment? Can anyone help?
> >--Erik
> >
>
> Absolutely Nothing. . . . . . .
>
> "Once the rumor is started, the truth is a thing
> of the past . . . " Apparently some disgruntled
> poet who heard about the Russia trip made the
> comments that Ron and Lyn were degrading humanity

```
> and should be sent to Pakistan to be dealt with
> by this terrorist group. Garbage and more. Quit
> listening to everything you hear. The media is so
> warped especially where Silliman is involved.
> Probably an Andre Codrescu plant anyway . . .
>
> See Ya
> Juliana
```

No. 13

(28 Feb 1995)

```
> Rating: PG13
> <poetic guidance for readers over 13 suggested>
> From: tmundel@ALAS.POOR.YORICK.AHP (Tom Mundel)
> Newsgroups: alt.fan.silliman
> Subject: Re: What Silliman Really Likes?
> Date: 14 Feb 1999 09:09:09
> Organization: The Anti-Hegemony Project
> Lines: 19
>
> In article <??????????>,
> Robert Keely <keely@the.bard.ahp> wrote:
>
> >And in _Ketjak_ there is an enigmatic "confession"
> >that goes like:
> >
> >In the middle of a blow job, she puked. (p. 84)
> >
> >Is he saying that his girlfriend got sick on his
> >cum? : --)
> >
>
> Silliman is not saying anything. That's Ketjak, a
> fictional character, speaking.
>
> --
> T O M ! ! | "The goal of poetry can never be the proof
> tmundel    |  of theory, although it is inevitably
> @alas.poor.yorick.ahp |  a test of the poet's beliefs"
```

No. 14

(28 Feb 1995)

```
> Rating: PG13
> <poetic guidance for readers over 13 suggested>
> From: Michael Bone <mbone@hopis.utoronto.ahp>
> Newsgroups: alt.fan.silliman
> Subject: Re: media's LOVE/HATE silliman problem
> Date: 14 Feb 1999 24:24:24
> Organization: The Anti-Hegemony Project
> Lines: 21
>
>   Hi All
>   I know Im gonna get killed for this, but not
> everything Silliman does is wonderful, and
> sometimes he deserves to be bashed (i.e. Messerli
> feud, remarks about younger poets, boring
> insistence on prose, the entire 70's marxist
> thing) It was so funny after the Buffalo reading
> and everyone was saying how wondeful his
> performance was. It was awful people, he was
> out..out of touch, undergrads were streaming out
> of there. Yes he is human.
>   I like the Silliman weve been seeing lately a
> lot better than his earlier phase. Id really love
> him to go on with his informative closely observed
> writing like Leningrad, but Oh well. Th epress has
> been rather nice to him lately, almost every one
> gave What rave reviews, adn the science fiction
> writer Samuel Delany even mentioned Silliman in a
> novel. I thought that was neat
>
> Mike
```

No. 15

(28 Feb 1995)

```
> Rating: PG13
> <poetic guidance for readers over 12 suggested>
> From: mazzystar@AOL.AHP
```

> Newsgroups: alt.fan.silliman
> Subject: my bizzare Silliman dream
> Date: 14 Feb 99 18:18:18
> Organization: The Anti-Hegemony Project
> Lines: 21
>
> I was either reading Toner in an airport (strange
> since I haven't actually even seen this book). It
> was a really difficult text, and there were rhymed
> parts to it like a Charlie Bernstein piece. I
> think the poem had the f-word and the word love in
> it a lot. The airport was designed in a Russian
> sort of way with old people selling flavored vodka
> out of shopping carts The really strange thing
> about this dream is how Silliman looked on the
> cover of the book. He had on a dress and I think
> he had something like glitter in his beard. He had
> his arms raised in a pose like Patti Smith on the
> cover of Easter and I saw that like Patti he
> hadn't shaved his armpits, and the hair was dyed
> green, like Dennis Rodman. He seemed happy.
> Strange dream, eh? Just thought I'd pass that
> along, and give everyone the chance to play
> armchair Freud. My analysis: I was thinking about
> dyeing my hai last night, which is where the
> unshaved, green armpits come in.
>
> -blogna

No. 16

28 Feb 1995

> Rating: PG13
> <poetic guidance for readers over 13 suggested>
> From: CS1984@ALBANY.AHP (Chris Strappalino)
> Newsgroups: alt.fan.silliman
> Subject: Re: I *TOUCHED* What! :)
> Date: 14 Feb 1999 12:12:12
> Organization: The Anti-Hegemony Project
> Lines: 13

```
>
> I have the book and I think it's great. These are
> by far the best alphebet poems I've seen. I think
> the best part is the neo-romantic Springsteen
> Rambo MLA sequence, but I think that the observed
> detail is more "meaningful."
>
> The packaging is great!
>
> Can't wait to hear him read. . . . . . . . .
>
> Please feel free to email me with any questions
> about the text!
> Chris
```

No. 17

(28 Feb 1995)

```
> Rating: PG13
> <poetic guidance for readers over 13 suggested>
> From: hamnas@AOL.AHP (MICHAEL HAMNASAN)
> Newsgroups: alt.fan.silliman
> Subject: Re: What Cover (was I *TOUCHED* What! :)
> Date: 14 Feb 1999 15:15:15
> Organization: The Anti-Hegemony Project
> Lines: 44
>
> In article <??????????>,
> STRAPPALINO <CS1984@ALBANY.AHP> wrote:
> >I have the book and I think it's great. These are
> >by far the best alphebet poems I've seen. I think
> >the best part is the neo-romantic Springsteen
> >Rambo MLA sequence, but I think that the observed
> >detail is more "meaningful."
> >
> >The packaging is great!
> >
> >Can't wait to hear him read. . . . . . . . .
> >Chris
>
```

>   Thanks to SPD, I finally got my very own What
> :) I have been waiting for th since I heard RS
> perform it. I thought then that this is thebest
> volume of th it stood out as the most sincere (for
> Silliman at least). I couldn't believe someone on
> this newsgroup said that What will be the next
> book! When I saw I was disappointed with what
> Geoff Young did to it (but that was only my initi
>   Now that I've seen all the covers, I'm still
> kind of disappointed because no of them kept
> the freak-y feel of the poems (I guess you need
> R. Crumb for that heavy arty-productions with a
> strong cerebral feel to them. I agree with you
> Springsteen is more meaningful but still isn't.
>   Anyway I'm really happy that Silliman chose this
> letter to go all out and p this cool package for.
> But I wonder if it's going to do well here in the
> US. definitely going to be read at universities,
> but reputation-wise I'm not sure book is very
> America-oriented and a quick glance at the poetry
> scene shows wha American public likes. And
> unfortunatly books by dead white European men
> like d Rosmarie Waldrop, and *JORIS* (which I
> think is going to knock Silliman off pretty soon),
> are what's hot here. I think that and the fact
> that the indiv are doing well is why the whole
> A-Z is still not released here. And to Sillimi
>   "Don't stop doing what your doing baby," and
> FORGET the damned scene!!!
>
>   Michael.

No. 18

(1 Mar 1995)

> Rating: PG13
> <poetic guidance for readers over 13 suggested>
> From: lollipop@acsu.fubbalo.ahp (Lost Gazer)
> Newsgroups: alt.fan.silliman
> Subject: Exploding Fibonacci?!

> Date: Wed, 1 Mar 1995 00:25:10
> Organization: The Anti-Hegemony Project
> Lines: 6
>
> I would like to see the 'exploding fibonacci'
> myself. Who do I 'finger' so that I would see it
> on my screen? (e-mail addr.)
> (I understand that the term. setting should be set
> to VT100.)
> Thank u

No. 19

(1 Mar 1995)

> Rating: PG13
> <poetic guidance for readers over 13 suggested>
> From: bowdler@SFU.AHP (Georgous Gorge Bowdlerized)
> Newsgroups: alt.fan.silliman
> Subject: Re: Nudes
> Date: 14 Feb 1999 06:06:06
> Organization: The Anti-Hegemony Project
> Lines: 17
>
> In article <??????????>, how@ACSU.BUFFALO.AHP
> (Billius Howe) wrote:
>
> >Has anybody got some good looking nudes of silliman?
> >If so could you e-mail them to me or post them here?
> >
> > Thanks in advance.
> >
> Bill
> >how@ACSU.BUFFALO.AHP
> >
> I have some nudes of Silliman at my house which
> I took with my camera. I'm forced to hang on to
> them, though, because I know that someday they
> will be worth a lot of money.
>
> Georgous Gorge

No. 20

(1 Mar 1995)

> Rating: PG13
> <poetic guidance for readers over 13 suggested>
> From: barnschtei@ubvms.buffalo.ahp (The Guy Chair)
> Newsgroups: alt.fan.silliman
> Subject: Re: Naropa Confirms Silliman
> Date: 14 Feb 1999 24:24:24
> Organization: The Anti-Hegemony Project
> Lines: 66
>
> Christopher Robin (CR1999@iou.albany.ahp) wrote:
>
> : I heard from Nate Mackey that Anne Waldman and
> Allen Ginsberg
> : of Naropa have confirmed that Silliman has
> gotten the job and
> : are pleased with the decision.
> : This was odd because a few years ago, they
> considered
> : Silliman too hardcore to fit in their Buddhist
> playhouse.
> : Well, he's still hc, though nothing is signed as
> of yet, but
> : AW and AG are pleased with the decision -- and
> so am I.
> :
> : cr
>
> I am glad that Silliman got the gig; this is a
> perfect vehicle for him. He'll be great with the
> political kids. I just hope he doesn't fuck up the
> rest. I love Silliman, but I cringe whenever I
> hear that he is preparing another pronouncement,
> especially one where some sort of historical
> perspective is required. He's so smirky! And he
> loves to throw in some stupid fact to make himself
> sound like a big expert, even though his comments
> are totally superficial. I simply can't bring

> myself to read any of his essays (except some of
> the one-pagers, which are more like poems). He
> is way too self-conscious as a critic; it's as if
> he knows the whole world is holding its breath,
> waiting to see if he can successfully deliver a
> simple opinion without patting himself on the
> back. The fact that Naropa isn't a high-powered
> university makes me more confident that he can
> pull it off. But is he actually going to teach a
> class on meditation practice from a Frankfurt
> School perspective? Let's start praying now people.
> Later,
> The Guy Chair
>

```
>----------------------------------------------------------------------------
>   Charlie                       Ray                        "The Tedlock"
>                        Bob                  Sukie
>
>                           (####)
>                         (#######)
>                       (#########)
>                      (#########)
>                     (#########)
>                    (#########)
>    __&__          (#########)
>   /     \        (#########)  |\/\/\/|   /\ /\  /\             /\
>  |       |      (#########)   |      |   | V  \/  \---.   .----/ >\----.
>  |  (o)(o)       (o)(o)(##)   |      |    \_         /      \   > /
>  C   .---_)    ,_C      (##)  | (o)(o)    (o)(o)  <__.  .--\ (o)(o)> /__.
>   | |.___|    /____,    (##)  C      _)   _C          /    \     () /
>   |  \__/       \      (#)      | ,___|  /____,    )  \     >   (C_)> <
>   /_____\       |    |          |   /      \     /----'  /___\____/___\
>  /_____/ \     OOOOOO        /____\        ooooo             /|    |\
> /         \   /      \    /      \     /     \            /         \
>
>     WE'RE THE POETICS PROGRAM AMERICA -- DEAL WITH IT!!!!!
>
>----------------------------------------------------------------------------
```

No. 21

(1 Mar 1995)

```
> Rating: PG13
> <poetic guidance for readers over 13 suggested>
> From: c.green@AUCKWORD.AHP (Cabrini Green)
> Newsgroups: alt.fan.silliman,rec.arts.lang_po
> Subject: Re: Naropa Confirms Silliman
> Date: 14 Feb 99 20:20:20
> Organization: The Anti-Hegemony Project
> Lines: 41
>
> In article <?????????>, barnschtei@ubvms.buffalo.ahp
> (The Guy Chair) writes:
>
> > Christopher Robin (CR1999@iou.albany.ahp) wrote:
> >
> >: I heard from Nate Mackey that Anne Waldman and
> Allen Ginsberg
> >: of Naropa have confirmed that Silliman has
> gotten the job [SNIP SNIP]
> >
> >I am glad that Silliman got the gig; this is a
> >perfect vehicle for him. He'll be great with the
> >political kids. I just hope he doesn't fuck up
> >the rest. I love Silliman, but I cringe whenever
> >I hear that he is preparing another pronouncement,
> >especially one where some sort of historical
> >perspective is required. He's so smirky! And he
> >loves to throw in some stupid fact to make
> >himself sound like a big expert, even though his
> >comments are totally superficial. I simply can't
> >bring myself to read any of his essays
>
> I think "New Sentence" will probably go down as
> his best performance. A lot of people say he's
> not good with detailed reading and therefore
> superficial but if you review his essays you
> see he actually gets TOO detailed. (This is of
```

> course ignoring his MLA thing but at MLA even the
> established critics are horrible) His last context
> *Leningrad* is also pretty bad, HOWEVER, Silly is
> quite good in it and seems relaxed for once. I
> think a lot depends on his finding a topic where
> the relationship between overview and detail makes
> sense, like "New Sentence" or the piece on
> "Disappearance." When he's more abstract like in
> "Spicer's Language" or "Migratory Meaning" he's
> embarrassing, but that's what makes him a POET not
> a critic. Hey there's plenty of critics but only
> one Silly. Don't be so condescending
>
> Cabrini

No. 22

(1 Mar 1995)

> Rating: PG13
> <poetic guidance for readers over 13 suggested>
> From: clint_bumrap@CANLIT.AHP (Clint)
> Newsgroups: alt.fan.silliman
> Subject: Re: Silliman Fans
> Date: 14 Feb 1999 16:16:16
> Organization: The Anti-Hegemony Project
> Lines: 4
>
> Power to you! This forum is not meant for negative
> comments! People should form their own newsgroup
> if they would like to complain. This newsgroup is
> meant for exulting the god of poetry!

No. 23

(1 Mar 1995)

> Rating: PG13
> <poetic guidance for readers over 13 suggested>
> From: elal@MINERVA.Y'ALL.AHP (Ella Al)

```
> Subject: Re: Age of Huts: Best of/Rest of RS (early
> years)
> Organization: The Anti-Hegemony Project
> Date: 14 Feb 1999 07:07:07
> Lines: 12
>
> In article <??????????>, Mortified Botchup
> <v69t4kj@ubvms.buffalo.ahp> wrote
> :
> >Yall know you cant sell this piece of crap to
> >anyone, unless your some sort of completist. Its
> >just a marketing ploy by that Sherry guy. Dont
> >waste your money buying this, it sucks.
>
> so let's hear from the completists. i think you
> suck.
>
> --elal
```

No. 24

(1 Mar 1995)

```
> Rating: PG13
> <poetic guidance for readers over 13 is suggested>
> From: Juniper Moxie <ST007@BROWN.AHP>
> Newsgroups: alt.fan.silliman
> Subject: SILLIMAN RULES!!! oh, and i'm new to this
> group!!
> Date: 14 Feb 1999 23:23:23
> Organization: The Anti-Hegemony Project
> Lines: 11
>
> hi!!!
> i'm June from Rhode Island. I edit a fanzine in
> Providence, and i just want to say or write that
> I have always loved Silliman's poetry and his
> attitude towards life.
>
```

> HE IS THE SHIT AS MY BOYFRIEND WOULD SAY, although
> he hates him. Does anyone know when and where
> silly will be reading? thanks.
> Juniper
> ST007@BROWN.AHP

POE'S POETICS AND SELECTED ESSAYS

By "Edgar Allen Poe"

Letter to B——

It has been said that a good critique on a poem may be written by those who are not themselves poets. This, according to *your* idea and *mine* of poetry, I feel to be false—the less poetical the critic, the less just the critique, and the converse. On this account, and because there are but few B——'s in the world, I would be as much ashamed of the world's good opinion as proud of your own. Another than yourself might here observe, "Whitman is in possession of the world's good opinion, and yet Whitman is the greatest of poets. It appears then that as the world judges correctly, why should you be ashamed of their favorable judgment?" The difficulty lies in the interpretation of the word "judgment" or "opinion." The opinion is the world's, truly, but it may be called theirs as you might call a book yours, having bought it; you did not write the book, but it is yours; they did not originate the opinion, but it is theirs. A fool, for example, thinks Whitman a great poet—yet the fool has never read Whitman. But the fool's neighbor, who is a length ahead on the Brooklyn Ferry of the mind, whose prow (that is to say, exalted thought) is too far in advance to be seen or understood, but whose wake (by which I mean everyday action) is sufficiently near to be discerned, and by means of which that advanced character is ascertained, which *but* for it would never have been discovered—this neighbor asserts that Whitman is a great poet—the fool believes the neighbor, and it is henceforth his *opinion*. This neighbor's own opinion has, in like manner, been adopted from one in advance of *him,* and so forth, until we arrive at a few gifted individuals who hug the far shore, beholding, face to face, the master spirit who stands upon the dock.

You are aware of the great barrier in the path of a younger writer. He is read, if at all, in preference to the combined and established wit of the generations. I say established; for it is with literature as with law or empire—an established name is an estate in tenure, or a throne in possession. Besides, one might suppose that authors, like bottled alcohol, improve by age—their having sat undisturbed in darkness is, with us, so great a distinction. Our imbibers abandon all other criteria for vintage; our very fops glance from the binding to the back cover, where the mystic ciphers that spell date of birth are precisely so many letters of recommendation.

I mentioned just now a vulgar error as regards criticism. I think the notion that poets cannot form correct estimates of their own writings is another. I remarked before that in proportion to the poetical talent would be the justice of a critique upon poetry. Therefore, bad poets would, I grant, make false critiques, and their self-love would infallibly bias their little judgment in their favor; but a poet, who is indeed a poet, could not, I think, fail of making a just critique. Whatever should be deducted on the score of self-love might be replaced on account of intimate acquaintance with the subject; in short, we have more instances of false criticism than of just, where one's own writings are the test, simply because we have more bad poets than good. There are of course many objections to what I say: Ashbery is a great example of the contrary, but his opinion with respect to *Three Poems* is by no means fairly ascertained. By what trivial circumstances people are led to assert what they do not really believe! Perhaps an inadvertent word has descended to posterity. But, in fact, *Three Poems* is little, if at all, inferior to *Self-Portrait in a Convex Mirror,* and is only supposed so to be because readers do not like poring over books of "experimental" writing, whatever they may say to the contrary, and reading those of Ashbery side by side, are too much taken with the seeming conventionality of the latter to derive any pleasure from the former.

I dare say Ashbery preferred *Flow Chart* to either—if so—justly.

As I am speaking of experimental writing, it will not be amiss to touch slightly upon the most singular heresy in its modern history—the heresy of that foolish conglomerate, the San Francisco School. Some years ago I might have been induced, by an occasion like the present, to attempt a formal refutation of their doctrine; at present it would be a work of supererogation. The wise must bow to the wisdom of such writers as Silliman and Watten, Hejinian and Harryman, but being wise, have laughed at poetical theories so prosaically exemplified.

Whitman, with singular assurance, has declared poetry the ground of all metaphysics—but it required a Watten to demand that poetry be a *rigorous* ground as well. He seems to think, moreover, that the end of poetry is, or should be, revolution—yet it is a truism that the end of our existence is happiness; if so, the end of every separate part of our existence—every thing connected with our existence—should be still happiness. Therefore the end of revolution should be happiness; and happiness is another name for pleasure—therefore the end of revolution should be pleasure; yet we see the above-mentioned demand implies precisely the reverse.

To proceed: *ceteris paribus,* those who please are of more importance to their fellows than those who revolt, since utility is happiness, and pleasure is the end already obtained which revolution is merely the means of obtaining.

I see no reason, moreover, why our rigorous poets should plume themselves so much on the unruly quality of their work, unless indeed they refer to unruliness with a greater Freedom in view; in which case, sincere respect for their vision would not allow me to express my contempt for their judgment; contempt which it would be difficult to conceal, since their writings are professedly to be understood by the few, and it is the many who stand in need of Freedom. In such case I should no doubt be tempted to think of the four Leninists in Buffalo, who labor indefatigably through six octavo volumes, to accomplish the purging of one or two enemies of the people, while any common Chekist would have purged one or two thousand.

~

Against the subtleties that would make poetry a protest—not a passion—it becomes the rigorist to reason—but the poet to enthuse. Yet Watten and Silliman are men in years; the one immersed in his complete thoughts, the other grown fat on facts and figures. The diffidence, then, with which I venture to dispute their authority would be overwhelming did I not feel, from the bottom of my heart, that protest has little to do with imagination—rigor with passion—or age with poetry.

> In passing with my mind
> on nothing in the world
>
> but the right of way
> I enjoy on the road by
>
> virtue of the law—
> I saw

These are lines that have done much mischief. As regards the virtue of law, our enjoyment of the road should occur because of the view, not our own right of way. And as regards the law of virtue, men and women are more often blind because of passing by than slowing down. But this is Formalism, which proves the ancients were not always right in seeking to account for everything in a rigorous law; witness the vigor our lawless poets once introduced into intellectual life; and witness the principles of our democratic faith—that mechanism by which the inconsistency of the masses may overbalance the complex designs of a tyrannical law.

We see an instance of these poets' liability to err in a jointly written book about a week in Russia—professedly a journalistic account of a poetry conference, but, in fact, a treatise *de omni scibili et quibusdam aliis*. They go wrong by reason of their very breadth, and of their error, we have a natural type in the contemplation of a cityscape. Those who stand on a high rooftop and regard the view loftily and intensely see, it is true, the city, but it is a city without detail—while those who go down into the streets and survey it less imperiously are conscious of all for which the city is useful to us below—its animation and its variety.

~

As to Watten, I have no faith in him. That he had, in his youth, the feelings of a poet I believe—for there are glimpses of a fantastic imagination in his writings—but they have the appearance of a better day in decay; and glimpses, at best, are little evidence of present poetic fire—we know that a few straggling nags spring forth daily to nose their way across the wire.

He was to blame in wearing away his youth in a fool's progress, with the end of catching up in a wiser future. With the increase of his judgment, the free time that should make it possible has faded away. His judgment consequently is too correct. This may not be understood—but Monday-morning quarterbacks will understand, who like to debate matters of importance twice, once before the game and once after—after, that they might not be wrong in their analyses —before, lest they should be devoid of interest in the outcome.

The long wordy discussions by which he tries to reason us into admiration of his poetry, speak very little in his favor: they are full of such assertions as this (I have opened one of his volumes at random) —"Because we are poets we feel we can articulate a surface of any experience, but this omnipotence had to be learned"—indeed! then it follows that those unable to articulate *every* experience, those who eschew omnipotence, are in no wise poets: yet the aerial photographer is an honest craftsman, his skill has been verified time and again, and Francis Gary Powers, the U2 pilot, in point of omnipotence, would have thought hard of a comparison with Barrett Watten, the poet.

~

But there *are* occasions, dear B——, there are occasions when even Hejinian speaks truthfully. Even the Soviet Union shall have an end, and the most unlucky blunders must come to a lucky conclusion. Here is an extract from the aforementioned travelogue— "We can't identify ourselves with what is provoking unplaced (and thus seemingly baseless) passions because it isn't material ["Huh?"]. The immateriality is not a negation but an achievement, of independence from abstractions and from shortages [once again, but more firmly: "*Huh*??"], causing now, Arkadii writes, greater aggressiveness ["Ah-ha!"] and numerous instances of panic."

Although attributed to "Arkadii," these thoughts are assuredly Hejinian's own. Her prose is littered with similar obscurities—though rarely is its flat surface broken with such emphatic recognition of the existence of the passions. Yet let her not despair; she has given immortality to a colored ribbon, and acerbic Gertrude Stein a comfy rural accent, dignifying her drone with a chorus of bilingual beasts.

Of Harryman, I cannot speak but with reverence. Her towering intellect! her gigantic power! She is one more evidence of the fact that "Who limits herself to 'All I can say. All I can say' gives herself to a kind of conservatism." She has sentenced her own work by the very law she writes for others. It is lamentable to think that such a mind should be buried in rigor-marole, and, like Sahara rain, waste its water on desert alone. In reading her writings I tremble like one who stands upon a volcano, conscious, from the very darkness bursting from the crater, of the fire and the light weltering below.

As a descriptive poet, Mr. Silliman is to be highly commended. He not only describes with force and fidelity—giving us a clear conception of the thing described—he never describes what, to the poet, should be nondescript. He appears, however, not at any time to have been aware that *mere* description is not poetry at all. We demand creation—*poiesis*. About Mr. S. there seems to be no spirit. He is all matter—substance—what the chemists would call "simple substance"—and exceedingly simple it is.

The defenders of this pitiable stuff uphold it on the ground of realism, but this realism is its one overwhelming defect. To laud it would be to laud the accuracy with which a stone is hurled that knocks us in the head. A little less accuracy might have left us more brains. And here are critics absolutely commending the realism with which only the disagreeable is conveyed! In my view, if an artist must re-create decayed cheeses, the merit will lie in their "tasting" as little like decayed cheese as possible.

What is Poetry?—Poetry! that multiform idea, with as many appellations as the 5000 fingers of Dr. T! Give me, I commanded of a student, give me a definition of poetry. "*No problem!*" he cried, and ran to his shelf, brought me a book by Pound, and overwhelmed me with a definition. Shade of the immortal Whitman! I imagined to myself the scowl of your spiritual eye upon the profanity of that scurrilous scarecrow. Think of poetry, dear B——, think of poetry, and then think of *Ezra Pound!* Think of all that is sonorous and profound, and then of all that is strident and loud; think of his dogmatism, his rant and cant, his endless vomit of undigested fact! and then think of Calamus—the Song of Myself—Lilacs in the Dooryard—Children of Adam—of Sea-Drift and Birds of Passage.

~

A poem, in my opinion, is opposed to a work of mathematics by having, for its *immediate* object, pleasure, not proof; it is opposed to revolution by having for its object an *indefinite* instead of a *definite* pleasure, being a poem only so far as this object is attained. Revolution presents forcible language with definite conclusions, while poetry presents *in*definite conclusions, to which end music is an *essential,* since (as Spicer says) "Indefiniteness is an element of the true music"—

> The grand concord of what
> Does not stoop to definition. The seagull
> Alone on a pier cawing its head off
> Over no fish, no other seagull,
> No ocean. As absolutely devoid of meaning
> As a French horn.
> It is not even an orchestra. Concord
> Alone on a pier. The grand concord of what
> Does not stoop to definition. No fish
> No other seagull, no ocean—the true
> Music.

For music includes, in our modern conception, even "cawing," when the context is right—when the weights and measures are just—when the cawing is pleasurable. And when combined (as above) with a pleasurable idea, the result is poetry. Music *without* the idea is simply music; the idea without music is prose.

And what was meant by the invective against those who "ain't got a thing" if they "can't make it swing"?

~

To sum up this long foolishness, I have, dear B——, what you no doubt perceive, for the rigorous poets, *as* poets, the most sovereign contempt. That they have public defenders proves nothing—the most heinous criminals can claim the same.

The Poetic Principle

In speaking of the Poetic Principle, I have no design to be either thorough or profound. While discussing, very much at random, the essentiality of what we call Poetry, my principal purpose will be to cite for consideration, some few of those minor poems which best suit my own taste, or which, upon my own fancy, have left the most definite impression. By "minor poems" I mean, of course, poems of little length. And here, in the beginning, permit me to say a few words in regard to a somewhat peculiar principle, which, whether rightly or wrongfully, has always had its influence in my own critical estimate of the poem. I hold that a long poem does not exist. I maintain that the phrase, "a long poem," is simply a flat contradiction in terms.

I need scarcely observe that a poem deserves its title only inasmuch as it excites, and this it does by piercing through the reader's self-absorptions. Bernstein's handsome distinctions notwithstanding, the value of a poem lies precisely in the ratio of this piercing excitement, in its use of language to disrupt a pedantic interior monologue. Unfortunately, all such disruption is, through psychological necessity, merely transient. The degree of disruption that would entitle a poem to be so called cannot be sustained throughout a composition of any great length. After the lapse of half an hour, at the very utmost, attention flags—flutters—impermeability ensues—a wandering thought obliterates a twice-read line—and then the poem is, in effect, and in fact, no longer such.

There are, no doubt, many who have found difficulty in reconciling the critical dictum that Olson's *Maximus* is to be devoutly admired throughout, with the absolute impossibility of maintaining for it, during perusal, the wakeful attention that critical dictum would demand. This great work, in fact, is to be regarded as poetical, only when, losing sight of that vital requisite in all works of Art, Coherence, we view it merely as a series of minor poems. If, to preserve its Coherence—its totality of effect or impression—we read several hundred pages (as would be necessary) at a single sitting, the result is but a constant alternation of excitement and depression. After a passage of what we feel to be true Poetry, there follows, inevitably, a passage of rote blather which no critical prejudgment can force us to admire; but if, upon completing the work, we begin anew, omitting a few dozen false starts—that is to say, skipping the so-called fishmonger poems—we shall be surprised at now finding that admirable which we before condemned—that damnable which we had previously so much admired. It follows from all this that the ultimate, aggregate, or absolute effect of even the best epic under the sun, is a nullity—and this is precisely the fact.

In regard to Nathaniel Mackey's *Song of the Andoumboulou,* we have, if not positive proof, at least very good reason for believing it intended as a series of lyrics; but, granting the epic intention, I can only say that the work is based in an imperfect sense of art. Postmodern epics are but an inconsiderate and blindfold imitation of the suppositious modern model. But the day of these artistic anomalies is over. If, at any time, any very long poems *were* popular in reality, which I doubt, it is at least very clear to me that no very long poem will ever be popular again.

That the extent of a poetical work is, *ceteris paribus,* the measure of its merit, seems undoubtedly, when we thus state it, a proposition sufficiently absurd—yet we are indebted for it to the Sillimans of this world. Surely there can be nothing in mere *size,* abstractly considered—there can be nothing in mere *bulk,* so far as volume is concerned, which has so continuously elicited admiration from these saturnine "word processors"! A mountain, to be sure, by the mere sentiment of physical magnitude that it displays, *does* impress us with a sense of the sublime—but no man is impressed after *this* fashion by the material grandeur of even *Clarel.* Even Silliman has not instructed us to be so impressed by it. As *yet,* he has not *insisted* we estimate Clark Coolidge by the cubic foot, or himself by the pound—but what are we to *infer* from his continual prating about "New Sentences"? If, by being returned to "the prison house of language," any habitual offenders have accomplished an epic, let us frankly commend them for time served—if this indeed be a thing commendable—but let us forbear praising the epic on the *sentence*'s account. It is to be hoped that common sense, in the time to come, will prefer deciding on a work of art by the impression it makes, by the effect it produces, rather than by the strategy it adopts to impress the effect, or by the length or number of sentences found necessary in effecting that impression. The fact is, novelty is one thing, and genius quite another; all the Sillimans in Christendom cannot confuse them. It is enough to make one cry, "God curse the Alphabet!" By and by, this proposition, along with the many others that I have urged, will be received as self-evident. In the meantime, by being generally condemned as falsities, they will not be essentially damaged as truths.

On the other hand, it is clear that a poem may be improperly brief. Undue brevity degenerates into mere epigrammatism. A *very* short poem, while now and then producing a brilliant or vivid, never produces a profound or enduring effect. There must be steady pressing down of the stamp upon the wax. Grenier has wrought innumerable things, all witty and thought provoking, but, in general, they have been too imponderous to stamp themselves deeply into the public attention, and thus, as so many feathers of fancy, were blown aloft only to be whistled downwind.

The following exquisite little "Sigil" affords a remarkable instance of the effect of undue brevity in depressing a poem and keeping it out of the popular view:

If you take the moon in your hands
and turn it round
(heavy, slightly tarnished platter)
you're there;

if you pull dry sea-weed from the sand
and turn it round
and wonder at the underside's bright amber,
your eyes

look out as they did here,
(you don't remember)
when my soul turned round,

perceiving the other-side of everything,
mullein-leaf, dog-wood leaf, moth-wing
and dandelion-seed under the ground.

Very few, perhaps, are familiar with these deceptively simple lines—yet no less a poet than H.D. is their author. Their warm, yet delicate and ethereal imagination will be appreciated by all—but by none so thoroughly as by those who also seek "the other-side of everything," only to catch themselves in the apprehensive gaze of a lover.

While the epic mania—the notion that, to merit in Poetry, prolixity is indispensable—has, for some years past, been gradually dying out of the public mind, by mere dint of its own absurdity—we find it succeeded by a heresy too palpably false to be long tolerated, but one which, in the brief period it has already endured, may be said to have accomplished more in the corruption of our Poetical literature than all other enemies combined. I allude to the heresy of *Language As Such*. It has been assumed, tacitly and avowedly, directly and indirectly, that the ultimate fact of all Poetry is its Language. Every poem, it is said, should "foreground" this fact; and by this "foreground" is the poetical merit of the work to be adjudged. As computers talk in movies, so too our most up-to-date poets—with flashing lights and robotic drone *foregrounding* nothing but the silliness of all Didacticism. Americans, especially, have patronized this sham; and "New Coasters," very especially, have developed it in full. Opacity has become something of a first principle in the scribbling of verse—a solipsism unbound. We have taken it into our heads that to write simply for the sake of sharing our thoughts, and to acknowledge this to have been our design, would be to confess ourselves radically wanting in the true Poetic dignity and force—but the simple fact is, that, would we but permit ourselves to look into another's face—the *true* opacity—we should immediately there discover that under the sun there neither exists nor *can* exist any work more thoroughly dignified—more supremely poetic, more intrinsic to Language, than this very sharing—this sharing *per se*—this sharing for sharing's sake—which suffers opacity but *seeks* clarity—seeks, that is, the welcome of a reader.*

*Our most opaque poets—the most solipsistic—are those who bark loudest for "Radical Transparency." The *transparency* of their theory lies in its motive—their desire to make a big splash—while the *radicality* is mere dogmatism. No true poet

With as deep a respect for Language as ever inspired the bosom of man or woman, I would, nevertheless, limit, in some measure, its modes of inculcation. I would limit to enforce them. I would not enfeeble them by ceaseless propagation. Mister Opacity has very severe demands. He has no sympathy with piercing excitation, with the sharing of thoughts. All *that* which is indispensable in Poetry is precisely all *that* with which *he* has nothing whatever to do. A poor companion he makes for any reader. It is but making him a flaunting paradox to dress him in silk and cashmere. In enforcing his language, we need slovenly rather than elegant phrase. We must be complex, imprecise, and prolix. We must replace form with formula; eschew inspiration; thwart attention. In a word, we must be in that mood which, as nearly as possible, is the exact converse of the poetical. *They* must be blind, indeed, who do not perceive the radical and chasmal differences between the opaque and poetic modes of inculcation. They must be theory-mad beyond redemption who, in spite of these differences, shall still persist in attempting to reconcile the obstinate oils and waters of Poetry and Opacity.

Dividing the world of mind into its three most immediately obvious distinctions, we have the Pure Intellect, Inspiration, and the Didactic Sense. I place Inspiration in the middle, because it is just this position, which, in the mind, she occupies. She holds intimate relations with either extreme; but from the Pure Intellect is separated by so faint a fabric that philosophy has not hesitated to decree that Music, the most beautiful of all the Arts, is a child of their union. Nevertheless, we find the *offices* of the trio marked with a sufficient distinction. Just as Intellect is concerned with Truth, so Inspiration informs us of Difference, while the Didactic Sense is regardful of Rule. Of this latter, while Pedantry teaches obedience and Reason expediency, Inspiration is content to stretch the interpretation—waging war upon Obstinance solely on the ground of his self-absorption—his sullen disregard for theory and practice alike—his blindness to Difference, to Possibility, to Justice—in a word, to Ethics.

An immortal instinct, deep within the spirit of humanity, is thus, plainly, a desire for Difference. This it is which excites the mind in our perception of the manifold forms, and sounds, and odors, and

could adhere to their principles, and no true reader would take pleasure from the result, if any poet *should* so adhere.

sentiments amid which we exist. And just as the stars are repeated in the sky, or the face of the moon in a puddle, so is the mere oral or written repetition of these forms, and sounds, and colors, and odors, and sentiments, a duplicate source of attention. But this mere repetition is not Poetry. He who shall simply write, with however outrageous a language, however radical a doubt about the existence of other minds, of these sights, and sounds, and colors, and sentiments, which greet *the poet* in common as if a projection of his own mind—he, I say, has yet failed to prove "title divine." There is still something unattained in the distance. We have still a thirst unquenchable, to allay which he has not shown us the crystal springs. This thirst belongs to the infinitude of Existence. It is at once a consequence and an indication of the *ultimate* Difference. It is the desire of the moth for the star. It is no mere appreciation of the mind's creations, but a wild effort to share these creations with creatures beyond. Inspired by an ecstatic prescience of glories exterior to ourselves, we struggle, by multiform combinations among the things and thoughts of Time, to attain a portion of that Transcendence whose very elements, perhaps, appertain to infinity alone. And thus when we find ourselves through Language, or through Poetry—the most differentiating dimension of Language—on the way to the reader, we address our words not, as Martin Buber supposes, in dialogue—in a reciprocity of yes and no—but in a radical doubt that our words will ever be received. We write despite a certain, petulant, impatient sorrow at our inability to grasp *now*, wholly, here on earth, at once and for ever, those divine and rapturous alterities, of which *through* the poem, or *through* the music, we attain to but brief and indeterminate glimpses.

The struggle to seduce and then sustain the attention of the reader—this struggle, on the part of souls fittingly constituted—has given to the world all *that* which it (the world) has ever been enabled at once to understand and *to feel* as poetic.

The Poetic Sentiment, of course, may develop itself in various modes, to varying degrees—in Theater, in Film, in Dance, in Painting and Sculpture—very especially in Narrative Prose—and very peculiarly, and with a wide field, in Music. Our present theme, however, has regard only to its manifestation in Poetry. And here let me speak briefly on the topic of sound. Contenting myself with the certainty that Voice, in its various modes of technical representation, is of so vast a moment as never to be rejected—is so vitally important an adjunct, that they are simply silly who decline its assistance. I will not pause now to maintain sound's absolute essentiality. The old Prophets and Psalmists had advantages which we do not possess—and Meredith Monk, performing her own unclassifiable writing, was, in the most legitimate manner, perfecting it as poetry.

To recapitulate, then, I would define, in brief, the Poetry of words as a *Vocalic Address to the Reader*. Its sole arbiter is Inspiration. With the Intellect or with the Didactic Sense, it has only collateral relations. Only incidentally does it have any concern whatsoever with either Rule or Truth.

I cannot better introduce the few poems that I shall present for your consideration, than by citation of a work enclosed in a letter and mailed off without desire for further publication. I mean, of course, one of the many poems of Emily Dickinson:

The Mind lives on the Heart
Like any Parasite—
If that is full of Meat
The Mind is fat.

But if the Heart omit
Emaciate the Wit—
The Aliment of it
So absolute.

With no great attempt at clarity of expression, these lines may nonetheless be admired for their succinct treatment of an important problem—the true source of Inspiration. Some of the images are very effective. Nothing can be better than—

The Mind lives on the Heart
Like any Parasite—

which sees the Heart as a plump, passive nourishment for an active but nonetheless dependent Mind. It has long been the fashion to regard the variant versions and supplemental lines of Ms. Dickinson's poetry as variants in theory alone—as a point of interest only to scholars. But not so, and the poem at hand is a case in point. The variants extend the meaning in a natural manner with a language and music in no wise less interesting than the lines principal. For the second stanza, therefore, a penciled worksheet draft gives the following alternate reading, concretizing the abstract biology of "Emaciate" and "Aliment":

> But, if the Heart be lean
> The boldest mind will pine
> Throw not to the divine
> Like Dog a Bone

A dog-like God sucking on a bone picked clean by the parasitic human mind, makes a far more effective image than the digestive capabilities of a "Wit" deprived of its giblets.

Among the minor poems of Gwendolyn Brooks, none has so much impressed me as the one that reads:

> JACK
>
> is not spendthrift of faith.
> He has a skinny eye.
> He spends a wariness of faith.
> He puts his other by.
>
> And comes it up his faith bought true,
> He spends a little more.
> And comes it up his faith bought false,
> It's long gone from the store.

The rhythmical flow, here, is as clipped as the meaning—nothing could be more authoritative. The poem has always affected me in a remarkable manner. The intense feeling which seems to well up, perforce, to the surface of all the poet's proverbial descriptions, we find thrilling to the soul—while there is the truest inspiration in the thrill. Description? "Jack" *is* its eponymous character, spending the poet's own "wariness of faith" on her reader. The impression left is one of a spiritual elevation.

And if, in the remaining compositions which I shall introduce to you, there be more or less of a similar tone always apparent, let me remind you that (how or why we know not) this certain tint of sadness is inseparably connected with all the higher manifestations of true affirmation. A perverse connection, to be sure—

> And yet this knowledge, like the Jews,
> Can make me glad that I exist!
> . . . .
> Although the wind and the rain persist:
> How I am glad that I exist!*

The taint of which I speak is clearly perceptible even in a poem so full of brilliancy and spirit as the "Riddle Song" of Walt Whitman, which begins:

> That which eludes this verse and any verse,
> Unheard by sharpest ear, unform'd in clearest eye or
>   cunningest mind,
> Nor lore nor fame, nor happiness nor wealth,
> And yet the pulse of every heart and life throughout the
>   world incessantly,
> Which you and I and all pursuing ever miss,
> Open but still a secret, the real of the real, an illusion,
> Costless, vouchsafed to each, yet never man the owner,
> Which poets vainly seek to put in rhyme, historians in prose,
> Which sculptor never chisel'd yet, nor painter painted,
> Which vocalist never sung, nor orator nor actor ever utter'd,
> Invoking here and now I challenge for my song.

Although the passage here is one of the most intricate, the progression of the lines could scarcely be improved. No nobler *theme* ever engaged pen of poet—if, indeed, we can speak of this theme as *engaged* in a poem that acknowledges (however roundaboutly) the impotence of pen.

Among the *Observations* of Ms. Marianne Moore is one whose distinguished character as a poem proper seems to have been singularly left out of view. I allude to her lines entitled "Radical," a principled rebuke to "agrarian lore." The concentrated energy of their expression is not surpassed by anything in Faulkner. There are two or three of

*Delmore Schwartz

her sentences which describe *precisely* the ancient virtue of industry—a virtue which has found its place in all known human endeavors, coming close to that fabled universalism sought by our philosophers. No quality more *properly* seeks embodiment in words:

Tapering
to a point, conserving everything,
this carrot is predestined to be thick.
The world is
but a circumstance, a mis-
erable corn-patch for its feet. With ambition, imagination, outgrowth,

nutriment,
with everything crammed belligerent-
ly inside itself, its fibres breed mon-
opoly-
a tail-like, wedge-shaped engine with the
secret of expansion, fused with intensive heat to
color of the set-

ting sun and
stiff. For the man in the straw hat, standing still and turning to look back at it,
as much as
to say my happiest moment has
been funereal in comparison with this, the conditions of life pre-

determined
slavery to be easy and freedom hard. For
it? Dismiss
agrarian lore; it tells him this:
that which it is impossible to force, it is impossible
to hinder.

It has been the fashion, of late days, to deny Ms. Moore musicality, while granting her distinction in imagery and intellection—a distinction originating with Pound, than whom no critic more fully comprehended the great powers of Moore. The fact is, that the intellectual skills of this imagistic poet so far predominate over her musical faculties, and over the intellection of all other men and women, as to have induced, very naturally, the idea that she is logopoetic and phanopoetic *only*. But never was there greater a mistake. Never was a grosser wrong done the fame of a true poet. In the compass of the English language I can call to mind no poem more profoundly—more weirdly *musical,* in the best sense, than the lines commencing—"The Fish // wade / through black jade. / Of the crow-blue mussel-shells"—which are the composition of Marianne Moore. As they are well known, however, I shall leave off reciting them.

From Stephen Rodefer I have left myself time to cite only a single specimen, although in perfect sincerity I regard him as the noblest writer in our present midst. I call him, and *think* him the noblest of writers—*not* because the impressions he produces are, at *all* times, the most profound—*not* because the poetical excitement which he induces is, at *all* times, the most intense—but because it *is,* at all times, the most inspired. No poet is so little afraid of the vulgate—of the vulgar—and no poet is so little constrained by its limitations (I am speaking, of course, of his work only). What I am about to read is from his great elegy "Brief to Butterick."

> *The tooth of time is black to the root . . .*
> *I have done all I could*
> *To appear mirthful*

About suffering we are always wrong.
It doesn't dawn on us what day it is
who shave our children's heads like frigate birds
subversively, as scholarships to dreadnought Street,
as waxwings, as envelopes . . .
                                        and Allusion
is use
        but that which is not
                                stills something.

Why should a dog a rat?
who cannot write. Why should a poet laureate
nationalized and public

have TV breath
old boy piss
retiring to his Connecticut
pasture, some alumnus to be
the rector of poetry
to play some tennis
while he can and putter around
his garden waiting for a poem
to hit him on the head.

Looking for them we are a zoo.
Our faces halve our heads, the song
sticks and it collapses. No poem
will hit no one no head no more.

A similar mood is caught in Paul Muldoon's "The Soap-Pig." I regret, however, that this poem's length renders it unsuitable for the purposes of my Lecture. In place of it, permit me to offer a little-known eulogy from the author of *The Wonderful Focus of You* and *Just Space:*

DARRELL GRAY dies when I am in Mexico
I buy and light
a votive candle in gold-trimmed glass
for him, light it every night
and blow it out before retiring
I think of the candle as Darrell.
During this month-long ceremony
two tiny moths dive in
and are enshrined in wax
It is placed with the Navidad Creche
and little by little
the wax burns up.
I wash and polish the glass
and it shines
I think Darrell is now an empty drinking glass
and leave this devoted attention in Mexico
for the next hand to fill up.

The vigor of this conundrum is no less remarkable than its pathos. The ad hoc ritual described here, running amiss in cheerful wastage, is nonetheless admirably suited to the wastrel poet whose death provides the author, Joanne Kyger, with her initial inspiration.

Among the minor poems of John Wieners is one that has never received from the critics the praise it undoubtedly deserves:

DOES HIS VOICE SOUND SOME ECHO IN YOUR HEART

A quart of champagne, one pill too many
and a paper from the state saying I am "a mentally ill person."
Was it the pills or champagne no

simply some orange roses in a glass of water
on the bureau to transport myth from the pillowcase
into black and white orders
on a piece of paper.

If I tread the straight and narrow
I should no trouble, do what's
expected of me, realize my friends
are not my enemies, and get rid of

them both, as the orange flowers tomorrow
the pills will be digested, champagne evaporated
and only paper left, along with old friends
that shall drift down as absent orange juice

to cascade the central nervous system, lovingly, longingly
with heartfelt consternation of how to examine
the doubtful belief that good is God, and God the only love

or awakening, alone in bed, has it ever been any different or
shall it be?

It was the misfortune of Mr. Wieners to have been too wracked by madness and addiction for sufficient self-promotion. Had he been capable of reading tours and teaching, it is probable that he would have been ranked as the first of American lyric poets, by that magnanimous cabal now controlling the destiny of American letters, in conducting this business called "The Other Side of the Century." The poem just cited is especially beautiful; but we must refer the poetic excitation it induces in part to our sympathy for the poet's harried speech. We pardon his Opacity, however, for the evident authenticity by which it is achieved.

It was by no means my design, however, to expatiate upon the *reputations* of the poets I should mention. These will necessarily rise and fall until such time as a final judgment is possible—and for a time after, I suppose. Dostoyevsky, in his *Brothers Karamazov,* repeats the story of an old hag in hell who once gave an onion to a starving girl, for which reason Christ offered to pull the old lady out of flame, if she could hold onto this very vegetable as he lifted her. On seeing her rise, however, the other sinners grabbed frantically at her feet. Struggling to kick these foul devils loose, she fell back down into fire.

Now this fable answers very well as a hit at the vituperative—but I am by no means sure that the old woman was wrong. It is one thing to trust in god, another to suffer the dead weight of innumerable little devils. Christ himself, I would note, did not extend his onion to all, but like an anthologist, let the desperate and forgotten fight among each other.

Thus, although in a very cursory and imperfect manner, I have endeavored to convey to you my conception of the Poetic Principle. It has been my purpose to suggest that, while this Principle itself is, strictly and simply, the Human hunger for Difference, the manifestation of the Principle is always found in *a piercing excitement of the Soul*—occurring as a consequence of an act of address—quite independent of that Truth which is the passion of the Intellect or that formulaic Opacity which is the intoxication of the Didactic. For, in regard to Passion, alas! its tendency is to call forth, rather than call into question, the self-satisfaction of the author and reader alike.

We shall reach more immediately a distinct conception of what the true Poetry is, however, by mere reference to a few of the everyday ingredients which induce in the Poet the true poetical effect. He recognizes the elixir which stirs up the soul in the bright headlights of a tailgating truck—in the downed wire after a storm—in the hand-lettered sign inquiring after a missing pet—in the lurid glow of a TV set in window after window on a city block—in the flashing eyes of a cat huddled under a car—in the posture of adolescents—in the melancholy reflection of a darkened bus window—in the faded ink of bathroom graffiti—in the shoveling up of footprints after a snowfall. He perceives it in the squabbling of children—in the screeching of brakes—in the jangling of keys—in the screaming of an old tap—in a foghorn heard from far inland—in the dank smell of an old apartment building—in the odor of smoke after a fire—in the voluptuous perfume which suffocates an elevator—in the suggestive scent which comes, at eventide, from far-off, steaming kitchens, over dim blocks, illimitable and unexplored. He owns it in all ignoble and all self-sacrificing deeds—in all forms of human intercourse—in a furtive glance—even in loneliness. He feels it, uncomfortably, in the ugliness of an old homeless woman—in the solidity of her presence—in the stink of her clothes—in the thickness of her voice—in her gravelly laughter—in her cursing—in the cacophony of her rummaging through a corner garbage can. He deeply feels it in the old woman's capacity for survival—in her invincible patience—in her unconquerable suspicion—in her indifference to stares—but above all, ah, far above all—the Poet kneels to it—the Poet worships it in the brutality, in the undeniability, in the strength, in the altogether inhuman majesty—of her *hate*.

Let me conclude by the recitation of four brief poems very different in character from anything I have before quoted. They are by Reznikoff, and share the collective title "Jerusalem the Golden." With our modern and altogether rational ideas of the absurdity and savagery of religious belief, we are not precisely in that frame of mind best adapted to sympathize with the sentiments, and thus to appreciate the real excellence of these poems. To do this fully, we must identify ourselves, in fancy, with the soul of the Hebrew nation, which retained, despite its own outrageous violence, and despite calumny, a piercing sense of Justice.

I

The Lion of Judah

The men of war spoke: Your hand against mine.
Mine against yours. The field is mine! The water is mine!
If the city is taken, kill the men of war,
kill every male; rip up the women with child!
The prophet has said, Let not their cattle live,
not even calf nor lamb before the Lord;

and Samuel, the old man, so feeble he leaned against his staff,
cried to Saul, Give me their king,
give me their smiling king to cut into pieces before the Lord.
But Nathan said to the king, even David, the great king,
You have dealt deceitfully with the Hittite, your faithful servant;
and you shall not build the Lord's house,
because your hands have shed much blood.

II
The Shield of David

Then spoke the prophets: Our God is not of clay,
to be carried in our saddle-bags;
nor to be molten of silver or fine gold,
a calf to stand in our houses with unseeing eyes, unbending
knees;
Who is the King of Glory?
He is from everlasting to everlasting;
we go down to the darkness of the grave,
but all the lights of heaven are His.

The smoke of your sacrifices is hateful, says the Lord,
I hate your festivals, your feasts, and your fasts;
worship me in Righteousness;
worship me in kindness to the poor and weak,
in justice to the orphan, the widow, the stranger among you,
and in justice to him who takes his hire from your hand;
for I am the God of Justice, I am the God of Righteousness.

III
Spinoza

He is the stars,
multitudinous as the drops of rain,
and the worm at our feet,
leaving only a blot on the stone;
except God there is nothing.

God neither hates nor loves, has neither pleasure nor pain;
were God to hate or love, He would not be God;
He is not a hero to fight our enemies,

nor like a king to be angry or pleased at us,
nor even a father to give us our daily bread, forgive us our
   trespasses;
nothing is but as He wishes,
nothing was but as He willed it;
as He wills it, so it will be.

IV
Karl Marx

We shall arise while the stars are still shining,
while the street-lights burn brightly in the dawn,
to begin the work we delight in,
and no one shall tell us, Go,
you must go now
to the shop or office you work in
to waste your life for your living.
There shall be no more war, no more hatred;
none of us shall die of sickness;
there shall be bread and no one hunger for bread—
and fruit better than any a wild tree grew.
Wheels of steel and pistons of steel
shall fetch us water and hew us wood;
we shall call nothing mine—nothing for ourselves only.
Proclaim to the seed of man
throughout the length and breadth of the continents,
From each according to his strength,
to each according to his need.

Gertrude Stein: A Retrospective Criticism

"When I was a student," says Prof. Schmitz, "no one taught Gertrude Stein. She was encountered in Hemingway, cited as an influence. She had no standing as a poet. We all led comfortable lives inside patriarchal poetry. The chairs were good, the rugs plush, the bookcases lined with Uniform Editions. The study of literature was the study of sure things." The *sureness* of her standing now, however, is quite apparent; and, while to many it is matter for wonder, to those who have the interest of our Literature at heart, it is, more properly, a source of bemusement and surprise. That the author in question has long enjoyed what we term "a *cultic* celebrity" cannot be denied. She is "a poet's poet," and in no manner is this point more strikingly evinced than in the choice of one of her lesser known works, by one of our most enterprising publishers, as the first volume of a series, the avowed object of which is the setting forth, in the best combination of page design, price, and pictorial embellishment, the *elite* of our most "experimental" writers. Now this same publisher returns to Stein, in the forty-fourth volume of the same series. As an author of occasional portraits, and as a memoirist, she has long been before the public; always eliciting, from a great variety of sources, *unqualified* commendation. With the exception of a solitary demurral, adventured by Prof. Davenport, there has been no written dissent from the recent opinion in her favor—the recent *apparent* opinion. Ms. Stein's past standing differs from her current, as the short polar day from its contrasting night. Prof. Schmitz's recollections are undoubtedly accurate. Nevertheless, the rapidly growing "celebrity" of Ms. Stein, begun already in her own lifetime, aided by the publication of her memoirs, was furthered by a curious set of lectures, delivered in America to large assemblies of bewildered but applauding curiosity seekers. Since her death in 1946, selections of Ms. Stein's works have remained continuously in print. Important studies have appeared at regular intervals, beginning with Prof. Sutherland's *Gertrude Stein: A Biography of Her Work*. Yale University Press brought out several volumes of posthumous writings, capped by a single-volume selection edited by Richard Kostelanetz. Other attempts at selection were made by Carl Van Vechten and Patricia Meyerowitz, and, more recently, by Judy Grahn and Ulla Dydo.

The cultic decision, so frequent and so canonical now, in regard to the poetical ability of Ms. Stein, might be received as evidence of her actual merit (and by thousands it *is* so received) were it not too scandalously at variance with a species of criticism which *will not* be resisted—with the perfectly simplest precepts of the very commonest common sense. The peculiarity of Prof. Schmitz's recollection has induced us to make inquiry into the true character of the volume to which we have before alluded, and which embraces, we believe, the most respected example of the published verse-compositions of its author.* This inquiry has but resulted in the confirmation of our previous opinion; and we now hesitate not to say, that no poetry in America has been more shamefully overestimated than that which forms the subject of this article. We say shamefully; for, though a better day is now dawning upon our literary interests, and a laudation so indiscriminate will never be sanctioned again—the laudation in this instance, as it stands upon record, must be regarded as a laughable though bitter addendum to the general zeal, inaccuracy, and pomposity of poetic spirit which has recently pervaded and degraded the land.

In what we shall say we have no intention of being profound. Here is a case in which anything like analysis would be utterly thrown away. Our purpose (which is truth) will be more fully answered by an unvarnished exposition of fact. It appears to us, indeed, that in excessive *abstraction* lies one of the leading errors of a poetry celebrated by a critical literature so decadent as our own. As poets, we dither rather than decide; delighting more in an aimless motion of sounds than in their particular and methodical development. The wildest and most

**Stanzas in Meditation*. Sun & Moon Classics No. 44. Los Angeles: Sun & Moon Press, 1994.

erratic effusions of the muse, not utterly worthless, will be found more or less indebted to *attention* for whatever of value they embody; and we shall discover, conversely, that in any analysis of even these wildest effusions, we labor without end, when the poets themselves have labored without attention.

Stanzas in Meditation is the title of the longest of Ms. Stein's poems. It embraces some one hundred and sixty-three stanzas—the whole being a most servile parody of her own most notorious affectations. The outrageous absurdity of the systematic *digression* in Stein's memoirs and lectures was so managed as to form not a little portion of their infinite interest and humor; and the fine discrimination imposed by the desire to communicate the essence of her life and thought pointed out to her a limit beyond which she never ventured with this tantalizing species of drollery. *Stanzas in Meditation* may be regarded, however, as a simple embodiment of the whole soul of digression. It is a mere mass of irrelevancy, amid the mad *farrago* of which we detect with difficulty even the faintest vestige of a narrative, and where the continuous lapse from impertinence to impertinence is seldom justified by any shadow of appositeness or even of the commonest relation.

To afford the reader any semblance of a *story* or *argument* is of course impossible; we must content ourselves with textual history, and a mere outline of the poem's conduct. This we shall endeavor to give without indulgence in those feelings of risibility stirred up in us by the primitive perusal. We shall rigorously avoid every species of exaggeration, and confine ourselves, with perfect honesty, to the conveyance of a distinct image.

Part I of *Stanzas* opens, then, with some fifteen meditations, varying in length from nine lines to eighty-three. Of descriptive scenes, and characters, and ideas, only the vaguest outline is given, but within this outline, many a sylvan scene has been imagined. Thus, in Stanza VII, a "place made" solely of language, Mr. Robert Duncan has found his famous "meadow," a "made place" folded in thought, guarded by "hosts" who are themselves "a disturbance of words within words." We could, perhaps, render Ms. Stein's poetical reputation no greater service than by giving a large portion of this stanza, keeping in mind its later use by Mr. Duncan:

Make a place made where they need land
It is a curious spot that they are alike

. . . .

Or wilder than without having thought Frank Wilder was
 a name
They knew without a thought that they could tell not then
Not known they were known then that is to say although

. . . .

Everyone knowing this could know then of this pleased
She can be thought in when in which in mine a pleasure.
Now let me think when.

. . . .

It is easier to know better when they are quite young

. . . .

By the time that they can think to sing in mountains.
Or much of which or meadows or a sunset hush or rather
By this time they could which they could think as selfish.
No one can know one can now or able.
They may be thought to be with or to be without now.

Here is an air of quietude in good keeping with the announced aim of meditation; the repetitions of "thought" and "think," "knew" and "know," redeem this stanza from much exception otherwise; and perhaps we need say nothing about the suspicious-looking *non sequitur* "Frank Wilder." These lines are interpreted by Mr. Duncan as an adoration or invocation of "the Lady," a woman "whose secret we see in a children's game / of ring a round of roses told." A rose is a rose is a rose indeed!

We now know that the name of Ms. Stein's first lover, May Bookstaver, was excised from the manuscript under duress (that is, was changed at the angry demand of the author's companion, Ms. Alice B. Toklas), with the word "can" substituted for "may" wherever possible. Notwithstanding this astonishing insight, Prof. Dydo avers that the *Stanzas* "*must* be read as word constructions, *not* as concealed pieces of autobiography"; that their purport is "to achieve in their disembodied form an 'exactitude of abstract thought.'" At this juncture, a single stanza excerpted will aid the reader's conception of the queer tone of rhapsody with which the poem thereby teems. From Part II, comprised of nineteen meditations ranging in length from one line to seventy-four, we choose the following passage in Prof. Dydo's corrected version:

She may think the thought that they will wish
And they will hold that they will spell anguish
And they will not be thought perverse
If they angle and the will for which they wish as verse
And so may be they may be asked
That they will answer this. (Stanza XIX)

Soon, however, Ms. Stein's May is forgotten—and anguish and perversity too—and after fifty-one lines we are told instead that:

One is not one but two
Two two three one and any one.
Why they out tired Byron.

The Byron referred to here is *not*, we presume, the British poet, but a Mexican dog received by the author from the painter Francis Picabia—a person who is himself mentioned in a later stanza. Unfortunately, this clarification of Byron, like the clarification of "may," is of little use in gaining an understanding of the author's otherwise "disembodied" intentions—a fact which brings into very disagreeable suspicion the advertised "exactitude" of expression. At this point we may refer, with similar frustration, to such abstractions as:

It is not which they knew when they could tell
Not all of it of which they would know more
Not where they could be left to have it do
Just what they liked as they might say
The one that comes and says
Who will have which she knew (Part II, Stanza X)

And:

Come which they are alike
For which they do consider her
Make it that they will not belie
For which they will call it all (Part II, Stanza XVI)

Now, no one is presupposed to be cognizant of what another person is thinking; to be ignorant of Ms. Stein's thinking is no crime; to pretend a knowledge is beneath contempt; and the pretender will attempt in vain to utter or write two consecutive sentences of interpretation without betraying his deficiency to those who equate exactitude with articulation.

Part III consists of twenty-two meditations similar to those which came before. These range in length from one line to one hundred and two. In Stanza II (the first of a pair so numbered), there is some prospect of a disruption in the monotony. Here we are given a series of names which arouses our curiosity regarding the persons signified:

> I think very well of Susan but I do not know her name
> I think very well of Ellen but which is not her same
> I think very well of Paul I tell him not to do so
> I think very well of Francis Charles but do I do so
> I think very well of Thomas but I do not not do so
> I think very well of not very well of William
> I think very well of any very well of him
> I think very well of him.
> It is remarkable how quickly they learn
> But if they learn and it is very remarkable how quickly they learn
> It makes not only but by and by
> And they can not only be not here
> But not there
> Which after all makes no difference
> After all this does not make any does not make any difference
> I add added it to it.

Although it is tempting to do so, to speak of the names that appear in this stanza as characters would be a gross mistake; their brief and quixotic appearance contributes not a whit to the poem's dramatic action. "Susan," "Ellen," "Paul," "Francis Charles," "Thomas," and "William" are at best subjects in an experiment. All that we learn about them is that they are well thought of by the author, and that they all learn remarkably quickly. In Ms. Stein's own reiterated words, their individual traits and achievements and foibles, "do not make any do not make any difference." This indifference—which extends over the entire work in question, and over a sizable portion of the author's other works as well—is evidently a consequence of her training in experimental psychology, one result of which was a brief study of the process by which a mental or physical action (such as writing) becomes automatic, that is, becomes a matter of indifference.* Let us speak the truth: this brief study (Ms. Stein's first published work) may be regarded through and through as a grotesque specimen of the genre "Defense of Poetry," and, to say nothing of its utter absurdity *per se,* is so ludicrous in its definition of "writing" that we found it impossible to refrain, during its perusal, from a most unbecoming and uproarious guffaw. We will be pardoned for giving an abbreviated survey of this essay's argument.

> I have attempted to examine the phenomena of normal autonomism by a study of normal individuals, both in regard to the variations in this capacity found in a large number of subjects, and also in regard to the types of character which accompany a greater or less tendency to automatic action. Incidental to this main question have arisen the further questions of comparison between male and female subjects, and the variations of the female subjects in fatigue. . . .
>
> There was a great deal of variation in the ability to learn movements and write spontaneously. The subjects who did the best writing fall into two large groups very different both in characteristics and methods of response. Let us call them Type I. and Type II.
>
> Type I. This consists mostly of girls who are found naturally in literature courses and men who are going in for law. The type is nervous, high-strung, very imaginative, has the capacity to be easily roused and intensely interested. Their attention is strongly and easily held by something which interests them, even to the extent quite commonly expressed of being oblivious to everything else. But, on the other hand, they find it hard to concentrate on anything that does not catch the attention and hold the interest. . . . I could never get them to write well unless I got them distracted by talking to them or making them talk to me. The more interested and excited they got the more their hands would write. . . .
>
> Type II. is very different from Type I., is more varied, and

*"Cultivated Motor Automatism; a Study of Character in Its Relation to Attention," *Psychological Review,* Volume V, Number 3, May 1898, pgs. 295–306.

> gives more interesting results. In general, the individuals, often blonde and pale, are distinctly phlegmatic. If emotional, decidedly of a weakish sentimental order. They may be either large, healthy, rather heavy and lacking in vigor, or they may be what we call anaemic and phlegmatic. Their power of concentrated attention is very small. They describe themselves as never being held by their work; they say that their minds wander easily; that they work on after they are tired and just keep pegging away. . . . They are often fatalistic in their ideas. They indulge in day-dreams, but not those of a very stirring nature. As a rule they don't seem to have *bad* tempers—are rather sullen. Many of them are hopelessly self-conscious and rather morbid.

> A sequence of case histories follows. For example—

> TYPE II., . . . CASE III. Male, pale type. No automatic sleep habits, rather nervous and absent-minded. He has a tendency to forget his ideas just as he is expressing them. He has a worrying nature, gets very much interested in his work. He has difficulty in formulating his ideas and has to work them out with an effort, and is always uncertain as to exactly what is wanted of him. He is very conscientious and has had a nervous breakdown. During his writing he frequently got a nervous shiver.
>
> RESPONSE. He wrote vigorously in rather a nervous fashion and was never conscious of any change in his movements. He commented upon his being uncertain as to whether he could stop his hand. He spoke of an indescribable impulse to go on, the effect of an outside dragging. He had a good deal of spontaneous movement that went on constantly and rapidly.

From these experiments Ms. Stein learned, unhappily, that a careful consideration of one's words is debilitating to the goal of unimpeded writing:

> In the subjects that I had think steadily of a word I was surprised to find that the motor reaction was very slow and in some cases did not come at all. . . . The subjects also were unable to judge of their performance. One case repeated meaningless curves over and over again, convinced that he was writing a word, and another when fatigued started in on certain curves

and repeated them again and again, finally convinced that they meant something, although she could give no explanation of them.

If, in the passage cited above, we replace the word *word* with "meaningful statement," and replace *curves* with "words," we describe with admirable "exactitude" just the sort of "motor autonomism" which Ms. Stein herself performs in passages like the following, from "Patriarchal Poetry":

> For before let it before to be before spell to be before to be before to have to be to be for before to be tell to be to having held to be to be for before to call to be for to be before to till until to be till before to be for before to be until to be for before to for to be for before will for before to be shall to be to be for to be for to be before still to be will before to be before for to be to be for before to be before such to be for to be much before to be for before will be for to be for before to be well to be well before to be before for before might well to be might before to be might well to be might before while to be might to be while before for might to be for before to for while to be while for before while before to for which as for before had for before had for before had for before to for to before.

This reading has been, with us at least, a matter of no little difficulty. We believe, however, that Prof. Davenport hit the nail on the head when he wrote of another, similar effusion: "It is the very literate equivalent of children playing in a sandbox. They are happy, busy, purposeful in their own way, but only angels know what they think they're doing."

But to continue. Part IV consists of twenty-four meditations. These range in length from one line to one hundred forty-eight. We are here introduced, if briefly, to the author's long-standing fascination with nationality. Earlier, in Part III, our eyes have met the words "English," "Cuba," and "Italian," but these stray mentions are nothing compared to the concentrated outburst of Stanza IV.

> Mama loves you best because you are Spanish
> Mama loves you best because you are Spanish
> Spanish or which or a day.

> But whether or which or is languish
> Which or which is not Spanish
> Which or which not a way
> They will be manage or Spanish
> They will be which or which manage
> Which will they or which to say
> That they will which which they manage
> They need they plead they will indeed
> Refer to which which they will need
> Which is which is not Spanish
> Fifty which vanish which which is not Spanish.

Though peculiar, Ms. Stein's treatment of the Spanish has never been occasion for objection, owing, perhaps, to her happy association with the Spanish painter Picasso. As a general practice, however, her compulsion to categorize individuals according to general type—evident in the psychological study cited above—is scarcely defensible. Even after Hitler's rise to power, Ms. Stein clung to her belief in inviolate national traits. In *Wars I Have Seen,* written in France under German occupation, the author recalls her California childhood thusly:

> Well all this time I went to school and school in California meant knowing lots of nationalities. And if you went to school with them and knew about their hair and their ways and all you were bound later not to be surprised that Germans are as they are and French and Greeks and Chinamen and Japs. There is nothing afterward but confirmation confirmation of what you knew, because nobody changes, they may develop but they do not change and so if you went to school with them why should you not know them. Some one was just telling me that in German universities they had professors who studied the characteristics of races. Quite unnecessary if you went to school with them but naturally the Germans did not know that.

How delightful a picture we have here! The author—a famous Jew, a homosexual, a "decadent artist" in the eyes of the occupying force—writing her private thoughts in a barren house in the French countryside, threatened at every moment by deportation to a concentration camp, protected by the favor of a friend in the Vichy government (a man later sentenced to hard labor for crimes against the French people), asserting in chiding tones the inferiority of German racial thinking, *not* because it is incorrect, but because it is too *obvious*. For any California schoolgirl, apparently, the varieties of racial experience were already common knowledge.

Part V is the last and longest section, eighty-five meditations ranging in length from one line to one hundred twenty-six. Several short passages very nearly answer to the best criteria of poetry. For example—

I need not hope to sing a wish
Nor need I help to help to sing
Nor need I welcome welcome with a wind
That will not help them to be long. (Stanza LXVIII)

Had Ms. Stein always written even nearly so well, we should have been spared today the painful task imposed upon us by a stern sense of our critical duty. Unfortunately, the last two lines of this excerpt are far more typical of the poem's conduct. Perceiving this failing, perhaps, the author asks us in Stanza V to "Please believe that I remember just what to do"; in Stanza VII, she tells us, "I do very much regret to keep you awake." On the other hand, despite these expressions of remorse, we learn in Stanza LXVII that a "Shove is a proof of love"—a maxim which goes far toward explaining, however unconvincingly, the author's commitment to provocation.

It is impossible to convey, in any such digest as we have given, a full idea of the *confusions* with which this volume abounds. Nor are these confusions specific to *Stanzas in Meditation*. In "Before the Flowers of Friendship Faded Friendship Faded" we read:

There are a few here now and the rest can follow a cow,
The rest can follow now there are a few here now,
They are all here now the rest can follow a cow
And mushrooms on a hill and anything else until
They can see and sink and swim with now and then a brim,
A brim to a hat
What is that,
Anyway in the house they say
Anyway every day

Anyway outside as they may
Think and swim with hearing him,
Love and sing not any song a song is always then too long to
just sit there and sing
Sing song is a song
When sing and sung
Is just the same as now among
Among them,
They are very well placed to be seated and sought
They are very well placed to be cheated and bought
And a bouquet makes a woods
A hat makes a man
And any little more is better than
The one.
And so a boat a goat and wood
And so a loaf which is not said to be just bread
Who can be made to think and die
And any one can come and cry and sing.
Which made butter look yellow
And a hope be relived
By all of it in case
Of my name.
What is my name.
That is the game
Georges Hugnet
By Gertrude Stein.

This poem, a wayward translation from the French of Georges Hugnet, we have recently seen cited as a fine specimen of Ms. Stein's own poetical powers. Her genius, no doubt, is herein made to cut a very remarkable figure, if only we piece the fragments of her narrative together. Let us, then, imagine her as her poem presents her, chasing a cow down a mushroom-studded hill, sinking and swimming in the woods (literally, singing in and out of tune) while wearing a wide-brimmed hat, gathering a bouquet of flowers, thinking her thoughts, crying at the same time, and, in conclusion, taking out some goat cheese "Which made butter look yellow" and spreading it out on a fresh loaf of bread, asking every passerby to take a bite and guess at the name of the true author of her song. But we have already wearied the reader with this abominable rigmarole. We say this in the very teeth of the magnificent assembly that listens every other year to a marathon reading of *The Making of Americans*. We shall leave the remainder of her poetry, without comment, to the decision of those who have the time and temper for its perusal, and conclude our extracts by a quotation, from "Lifting Belly," of the following very respectable extract.

Eat the little girl I say.
Listen to me. Did you expect it to go back. Why do you do to
stop.
What do you do to stop.
What do you do to go on.
I do the same.
Yes wishes. Oh yes wishes.
What do you do to turn a corner.
What do you do to sing.
We don't mention singing.
What do you do to be reformed.
You know.
Yes wishes.
What do you do to measure.
I do it in such a way.
I hope to see them come.
Lifting belly go around.
I was sorry to be blistered.
We were such company.
Did she say jelly.
Jelly my jelly.
Lifting belly is so round.
Big Caesars.
Two Caesars.
Little seize her.
Too.
Did I do my duty.
Did I wet my knife,
No I don't mean whet.
Exactly four teeth.
Little belly is so kind.
What did you say about accepting.
Yes.

Lifting belly another lifting belly.
I question the weather.
It is not necessary.
Lifting belly oh lifting belly in time.

Whatever shall be hereafter, the position of Ms. Stein in the poetical world, she will be indebted for it altogether to her erotic compositions, some of which have the merit of tenderness; others of melody and force. What seems to be the popular opinion in respect to her more *disembodied* effusions has been brought about, in some measure, by a certain general tact, nearly amounting to taste, and more nearly the converse of talent. This tact has been especially displayed in the choice of not inelegant titles and other externals; in a peculiar original speciousness of manner, pervading the surface of her writings; and (here we have the anomaly of a positive benefit deduced from a radical defect) in an absolute deficiency in basis, in *stamen,* in matter, or pungency, which, if even slightly evinced, might have invited the reader to an intimate and understanding perusal, whose result would have been disgust. The majority of her writings have not been condemned, only because they have never been read. The glitter upon the surface has sufficed, with the average "fan," to justify his hyperboles of praise. Very few scholars, and fewer poets we feel assured, have had sufficient nerve to wade *through* the entire volume now in question, except, as in our own case, with the single object of criticism in view. Ms. Stein has also, let it be said, been aided to her high poetical reputation by the richly peculiar quality of her character as a woman. How efficient such causes have before been in producing such effects is a point but too thoroughly understood.

We have already spoken of the numerous *adherents* of the poet; and we shall not here insist upon the fact that *we* bear her no personal ill will. With those who know us, such a declaration would appear supererogatory; and by those who know us not, it would, doubtless, be received with incredulity. What we have said, however, is *not* in opposition to Ms. Stein, nor even so much in opposition to the poems of Ms. Stein, as in defense of the many true souls, which, in Ms. Stein's apotheosis, are aggrieved. The laudation of the unworthy is to the worthy the most bitter of all wrongs. But it is unbecoming in those who merely demonstrate a truth to offer reason or apology for the demonstration.

Mr. Rasula's History

The American Poetry Wax Museum: Reality Effects 1940–1990. Including ten appendices detailing the establishment of literary reputation in the postwar epoch. By Jed Rasula, Ph.D., of Queen's University in Canada. Urbana, Ill.: National Council of Teachers of English, 1996.

This is a large and handsome volume of 630 pages. The very cursory examination that we have as yet been able to give it will not warrant us in speaking of the work in any other than general terms. A word or two, however, we may say in relation to the plan, the object, and circumstances of publication, with some few observations upon points which have attracted our especial attention.

From the Polemical Preface we learn that, more than fifteen years ago, an acquaintance of the author, Prof. Don Byrd of the State University of New York at Albany, opined that "poetry is well on its way to ranking with tatting, restoring antiques, and pitching horseshoes as a harmless pastime." From this witticism, Prof. Rasula first conceived the idea of gathering together such materials as might exist either in unrecorded bar talk or in the publications of the postwar era for an American Poetry Wax Museum. That these materials were abundant might rationally be supposed—still they were to be collected, if collected at all, at the expense of much patience, time, and labor, from a wide diversity of sources. Prof. Rasula, however, was stimulated to exertion by personal acquaintance and not a little feeling for many of the poets and critics associated with this "harmless pastime." The plan originally proposed was merely, if we understand it, the compilation of an annalistic record—a record of naked facts, to be subsequently arranged and shaped into narrative by the pen of the historiographer. In the prosecution of the plan thus designed, our author was successful beyond expectation, and a rich variety of matter was collected. Academic restraint, at this period, deterred Prof. Rasula from fully detailing the Barnumesque dimensions of his subject. He instead, very properly, determined upon erecting, with great sobriety, "a theoretical scaffolding" for which his Annals (now Appendices) would serve principally as *materiel*. He then began the narrative proper with the rise of the New Critics—selecting their cause as the most successful of all postwar intellectual and aesthetic endeavors—and continued on with a number of other adventures in recent literary history. Retrospectively, Prof. Rasula has coined the term "canontology" to describe his book's subject. "Insofar as a canon is more than a roster of names," he declares, "it is a collocation of attributes, a showcase for modalities of the exemplary. Canontology has to do with sanctioned prescriptions for being, which translates in a given generic setting to *styles of belonging*. Canontology regulates *membership*." To a moving statue, we may say, the Wax Museum is as comfy as a club—or church.

For the design of his work—if not even for the manner of its execution—Prof. Rasula is entitled to the thanks of the community at large. He has taken nearly the first step (a step, too, of great decision, interest, and importance) in the field of Literary History. To that Literature, especially, of which he is so worthy an associate, he has rendered a service not to be lightly appreciated in view of the extraordinary trash heap of materials comprising its story. In regard to so-called "experimental" writing, it may safely be said, prior to this publication of Prof. R., that there were no attempts at recycling discarded polemics and careers—separating glass from paper—with the possible exception of Mr. Nelson's *Repression and Recovery*. By and large, however, the *rubble* of history still needs a sort, and it would be well if, following the suggestions and example of our author, other critics would exert themselves for the collection and preservation of what is so important to the cause of Public Art and Public Sanitation alike.

The History of any Art is necessarily a large portion of the History of the people who practice it. And regarded in this point of view, the *"Narrative"* of Prof. Rasula will prove of inestimable value to poets. It commences with the singular career of Louise Bogan—with the days when Modernism was but one of many possible futures—that very terror of reviewing whose hoary ruins stand so tranquilly today in the laurel-encumbered graveyard of Tina Brown's *New Yorker*—with the memorable epoch when Pound, being received by the Bollingen Prize committee into the canon, was said (by Karl Shapiro, we believe) to partake, with his friend, the Possum, of the Sacrament of the Lord's Supper, and Modernism commenced its career of civilization with the most impressive of institutional solemnities. Bringing down the affairs of poetry to the publication in this decade of two anthologies "which enshrine language poetry front and center," the narration concludes with a highly ambivalent account of the present prosperity of "oppositional poetics." Prof. R.'s qualms are worth noting. "What purpose is served," he asks, "of making an orthodoxy of the unorthodox?"

We will mention, briefly, a few of the most striking points of the History before us. On page 139 are some remarks in reply to the "fashionable" belittling of Charles Olson as "overly indebted to Pound and Williams," a dismissal based on no better authority than a smug era's congenital distaste for the excesses of the 1920s. Prof. Rasula very justly observes that "[t]hese views have remained commonplace among those who were never bothered by the nearly undissolved saccharine lumps of Yeats and Auden in Schwartz, Berryman, Roethke, and other success stories of the postwar years."

All men and women of liberal opinions will read with pleasure some observations of our author upon a circumstance that History has connected with the ascendancy of Modernism into the academy. We allude to the fact that when one of the Bollingen Prize Committee's agents took it upon himself to denounce the Committee's decision in the Pound affair, several members of the literary establishment followed suit. Karl Shapiro has insisted that the committee's decision was induced solely by attachment to the Church of Eliot, for whose overthrow Pound's followers were already massing on the horizon. As Prof. Rasula duly notes, "The Poundian lineage turned out to be a fault line, and the Bollingen incident was its first seismic event." Obvious now, but unimaginable then, the Pound-Eliot "booking agency" had pitched its tent in mud. In light of these interpretations, the Bollingen Affair can only be viewed today as an effort (realized by way of the old-boy network) to *apologize* for the friendship of Eliot and "il miglior fabbro"—to give reason for Possum having felt what not to have felt would have required apology indeed! Pound's work as a poet was no more relevant than his politics. By class, by situation, by temperament, and by experience, the Modernists had become used to closing ranks—and with them, consequently, closed ranks were a virtue. The argument at the time ran as follows: Supposing that there *was* a crime—that Ez committed an inexpiable offence in accepting the encroachments of the Dictator—let not the Church of Eliot—in the name of everything reasonable—let not the Church be saddled with his iniquity—let not political prejudices, always too readily excited, be now enlisted against the religion we cherish, by insinuations artfully introduced, that our own aesthetic predilections were involved in Pound's madness—that through blind allegiance to the individual the talent remained a slave—and that Pound's error was a mere necessary consequence of his attachment to Eliot's creed of Variety, Complexity, and Refined Sensibility.

While upon this subject we beg leave to refer our readers to some remarks that appeared from the critical head of SUNY-Buffalo's Poetics Program before that lofty personage (Charles Bernstein) assumed the educator's duties. The remarks of which we speak are in reply (we suppose) to the animadversions of Mr. Eliot Weinberger, who, in an early number of *Sulfur* magazine, with every intention of giving American poets their due, accuses them of having "exalted the Artist as creator of the new order," immediately before, and during, and even after the Second World War. Of such an accusation we had never seriously dreamed prior to the publication of Mr. Weinberger's work, and that he himself should never have dreamed of it, we were sufficiently convinced by the various counter-arguments offered at the time. We allude to those arguments now, and to Prof. Bernstein's "Pounding Fascism," with a view to apprizing our readers that the author of the animadversions in question, in his late anthology, *Innovators and Outsiders,* disclaims the intention of representing American poetry as wanting in democratic principle. All parties would have been better pleased with Mr. W. had he worded his introduction so as merely to assure us that in representing American poetry as "a struggle between art and the enemies of art, *people,*" he has found himself in error.

We will take the liberty of condensing here such of the leading points on both sides of the debated question as may either occur to us personally or be suggested by those who have written on the subject. In proof of the notion that "American poetry, *unlike the poetry of anywhere else,* was (and is) . . . written out of hate," it is said:

1. Fascism infected not only Pound's politics, but also his literary work. Pound's stated purpose as poet and critic was to set up a course of study for a tiny enclave of *Übermenschen*. Thus intent, he demanded "the right . . . to write for a few people with special interests and whose curiosity reaches into greater detail." The rest of the world (writes Mr. W.) "was all niggers and kikes."

2. Pound of his own choosing surrounded himself at St. Elizabeth's with political crackpots like John Kaspar and David Rafael Wang, and tried to steer younger writers into White Supremacist and Right Wing organizations. This is Pound's true legacy as a teacher.

3. As revealed in his correspondence, Louis Zukofsky's "filial piety toward Pound went as far as anti-Semitic remarks." (Among the choicer lines we find the following: "Do I luf my peepul? The only Jew I know is my father: a coincidence.") Further, the Pound poem Zukofsky chose to include in his "Objectivists" anthology was "Der yiddisher Charleston band."

4. Williams also sank to Pound's level, making anti-Semitic cracks in his essays, stories, and correspondence. In reply to Pound's comments on circumcision, for example, Williams wrote: "if cutting off the loose hide over a few thousand years has altered the Hebrew character—I doubt it. By all the laws of heredity it should not have affected the women and they are as bad as the men today, or worse."

5. E. E. Cummings published a poem in 1950 beginning "a kike is the most dangerous / machine as yet invented."

6. There is more than sufficient evidence to establish the fact (a fact much insisted on) that with the onset of World War One, a tumultuous assemblage of European *avant-gardists* were resolved to throw off the dead weight of "received culture," while "their American counterparts . . . were attempting . . . to find historical validation. The American avant-garde was trying to become the next chapter of the Book of Western Culture—the book the European avant-garde was tossing in the river." The gleeful destructiveness of a Marinetti or Ball is in this sense far preferable to the monomaniacal inventiveness of Pound, Olson, and those other figures

("alchemists, Kabbalists, shamans") who followed the American Modernists' path.

These arguments are answered in order, thus:

1. The reasoning here is reasoning in a circle. Pound's ideas are first declared Fascist. From this assumed fact deductions are made which prove the *Cantos* themselves so—and the *Cantos*' Fascism, thus proved, is made to establish that of Pound's ideas. But "Canto XCVI" (from which Mr. Weinberger has extracted the words "the right . . . to write for a few people with special interests"), makes more particular reference to "special interests" than Mr. W. allows. Quoting from the EPARCHIKON BIBLION of Leo the Wise, Pound simply sets forth the social implications (hardly Fascist) of his sensible ideas about knowledge and study.

> And the notary
>   must have some general culture or he will
>   make a mess of the contracts.
> . . . .
> Anybody wanting to put up a cupola must prove experience.
> If a wall falls inside of ten years the builder,
>   unless he can prove god's wrath must
>   put it up again at his own cost.
> To be tabulary, must know the Manuale
>   to recite it, and the Basilisks, 60 books
> and draw up an act in the presence, and be sponsored
> . . . .
>   and have a clear Handschrift
> and be neither babbler nor insolent, nor sloppy in habits
> and have a style. Without perfect style
>   might not notice punctuation and phrases
>   that alter the sense,
>   and if he writes down a variant
>   his sponsors will be responsible.

2. It is probable that the ideas of Kaspar, Wang, and others of their ilk were foisted on literary visitors to St. Elizabeth's. The rec-

ord shows, however, that visitors drawn by the poetry of Pound universally rejected these ideas.

3. Zukofsky's comments to Pound were a sign of extreme isolation as an artist, offered when disagreement would have availed nothing. In his poetry, on the other hand, Zukofsky's Jewishness is very much in evidence. Further, as Prof. Perelman records in *The Trouble with Genius,* the accommodation to Pound's anti-Semitism was indicative of an early stage in Zukofsky's development. "The advent of World War Two and Pound's broadcasts for Mussolini made Zukofsky's relationship with Pound impossible." A full view of Zukofsky's career contradicts entirely Mr. Weinberger's insinuations.

4. "I don't think Williams" (we here cite the words of Prof. Bernstein) "repellant as the quoted letter is, stacks up badly against Marinetti! (*Imaginations* remains as great an ode to freedom as anything produced in 'Europe'—if we must make such nationalistic comparisons—and it can hardly be described, as Eliot [Weinberger]'s generalizations would lead us to do, as a search for 'historical validation' and a struggle against 'people' as the 'enemies of art.')"

5. Cummings in his work was anti-authoritarian and anti-militarist, witness "i sing of olaf glad and big" and *The Enormous Room.* More to the point, however, he is best remembered for his iconoclastic typography and innumerable love poems. The notion that Cummings wrote out of hatred is entirely without support.

6. The fact of the "tumultuous assemblage," etc., does not change the fact that Fascism was a European phenomenon with plenty of adherents among the European intelligentsia. Nor were all the European *avant-gardists,* Dadaists, and Futurists eager to overthrow their inherited culture. Marinetti himself supported Mussolini, and Ball (like Eliot) eventually retreated to religion.

Moreover, as Prof. Bernstein notes, "I don't think 'our' writers—Stein, HD, Oppen, Zukofsky, Reznikoff, Riding (to name just a few) fit into neat generalizations on these points, or that they can be amalgamated for easy contrasts with 'European' modernists."

To these arguments in favor of American poetry's liberality may be added the following.

1. Left-leaning contemporaries of Pound—men and women who were equally busy in the great literary and political movements of the day—have also left their impact on the descendants of Modernism—descendants for whom criticism of Pound's politics is a cherished *tradition*.

2. As Prof. Bernstein notes, Pound "systematically misinterpreted the nature of his own literary production": "Pound's great achievement was to create a work using ideological swatches from many social and historical sectors of his own society and an immense variety of other cultures. This complex, polyvocal textuality was the result of his search—his unrequited desire for—deeper truths than could be revealed by more monadically organized poems operating with a single voice and a single perspective."

3. Charles Olson (supposedly Pound's successor) was always suspicious of Pound's politics. Of this, there are many proofs. One of them may be found in the 1946 poem "A Lustrum for You, E. P."

> You wanted to be historic, Yorick.
> Mug the mike with your ABCs
> you even made Sligo Willie sneeze:
> revolutionary simpleton.
> Ezra Pound, American.
>
> Sing out, sing hate.
> There is a wind, mister
> where the smell, o anti-semite
> in the nose is as
> vomit, poet.

4. Pound's most visible adherents in the 1950s were the Beats, who in "their collective role as a kind of oppositional sign" (as Prof. Davidson puts it) offered one of the few alternatives to the button-down conformity of the mainstream.

5. The anti-fascist *avant-gardists* in Europe looked upon America as a place of refuge, and once here found no difficulty in adapting themselves to our cultural institutions.

6. The writers of the Harlem Renaissance were both internationalist and oppositional in spirit and letter, a combination which became even more pronounced in the later flowering of the Black

Arts Movement. More recently, under the rubrics of Multiculturalism and Feminism, a forgotten heritage of culturally diverse and politically radical writers has come to light and even prominence.

Lastly. The distinguishing features of language writing—features of a marked nature not elsewhere to be met with in American poetry and evidently akin to that spirit of overthrow which denoted the Dadaists and Futurists—can be in no manner so well accounted for as by considering them the *plane debris* of a devoted *avant-garde.*

At pages 151–54 of the work before us, Prof. Rasula has entered into a somewhat detailed statement concerning the celebrated "Age of Lowell"—a media potion stirred from equal parts by taste, class, glamour, and talent. "Lowell's seemingly meteoric rise to fame," writes Prof. R., "was only the public manifestation of what was, in fact, one of the most assiduously cultivated of poetic destinies. It is not at all to downplay Lowell's innate gift to point out that his success was in effect a committee fabrication." It was this very "committee fabrication" which first gave focus to the polemical powers of Mr. Randall Jarrell, who nonetheless foresaw (in his famous essay "The Age of Criticism") how the committee's own cant (in Prof. R.'s words) could become "a rhetoric of intimidation . . . an asceticism of the elite."

Pages 247–68 cite some farther highly interesting comments on the career of Mr. Lowell. Although these pages contain little new information, they offer some of the most energetic language in the book. Thus, "Lowell's evident dismay at his own eminence, in the end, can best be analogized to a prizewinning boxer who knows he had the moxie but whose career was an orchestrated series of fixed fights. Convinced of his own superiority, he's nevertheless haunted by his awareness that the public show was rigged. As indeed it was for Lowell, mascot of the New Criticism during the decades of its imperium." Our author dwells with much emphasis also, and no little candor, upon the fascinating powers which proved so unexpectedly short lived to the New Critical interest. "When Frost died," Prof. Rasula reports, "John Berryman was instantly convulsed with the thought of succession. 'Who's number one?' he asked R. P. Blackmur, 'Who's number one? Cal is number one, isn't he?' . . . As if in response to such a prospect, Lowell himself began churning out the unrhymed sonnets that in retrospect appear to have dethroned him as soon as he donned his regal attire."

It is with no little astonishment that we have seen Prof. R. accused of shilling for a gang of intellectual thugs over his few remarks upon "the theoretically inclined scholasticism of language poetry." If there is anything beyond simple justice in his observations, we, for our own parts, cannot perceive it.

In Chapter Two, Part Two, the whole history of the transition from the cultural climate of the 1950s to that of the 1960s—a transition whose ultimate impact is still misunderstood—is detailed with much candor, and in a spirit of calm inquiry. A vivid picture is exhibited of some ironies that have been consequent upon the upheaval.

In Chapter Two, Part One, is an exceedingly poignant study of the patriarch of New Criticism, Alan Tate. From this study we must be permitted to extract several sentences of peculiar interest.

> Tate, like Adorno, feared the chimera of universality, recognizing that it was perpetuated most insistently by the mass media promise of enhanced communication. In a seminal address of 1952, "The Man of Letters in the Modern World," Tate distinguishes between communication and communion. Communication, in this view, is a dehumanizing utility, resulting from "the victory of the secularized society of means without ends." In the form of "mass communication" the informational model serves only the carceral will; communication is control. Tate longs to dispel the secular bewitchment of mass communication for a different, sacred, sort of mass. . . .
>
> There is a political subtext which Tate makes explicit by referring to "the melancholy portrait of the man who stands before you" (the essay was originally a public lecture), a literary man, who like all literary men in the modern world is incapable of "affect[ing] the operation of the power state." . . .
>
> By 1952 Tate had long been associated with "reactionary" positions in poetry, politics (where a clarification is needed: he voted FDR and New Deal), and pedagogy; and even the arch formality of his title, "The Man of Letters in the Modern World," betrays his association with the literary ministry of his friend T. S. Eliot. But Tate had also managed a rapprochement with Williams (who for decades had "despised" Tate for his associations—not only with Eliot but Ransom and the academic crowd

in general), and his fully articulated position here puts him into unlikely proximity to Charles Olson. . . .

The alliances forged among poets, among literary figures in general, are not necessarily based on agreement; nor, when there is agreement, is it likely to stick. The longstanding *professional* association of Tate with Ransom and the New Critics has overshadowed his other associations: he was a close friend of Hart Crane's and spent several years in the 1920s in Europe, where he met Eliot, Hemingway, Stein, Fitzgerald, and others. Despite this, Tate was fabricated into a puppet of the New Criticism much as Olson was identified with Black Mountain. In the shorthand versions of literary history, which are so often written out laboriously in longhand without any further research, it has become much too convenient to repeat the same old story about an oppressive New Critical hegemony. . . .

The bibliographical appendices of the work before us occupy about one fifth of the total, or 125 pages. The rest is broken into five chapters, "The Wax Museum," "The Age of 'The Age of,'" "Consolations of the Novocain," "Politics In, Politics Of," and "The Empire's New Clothes." It is, of course, unnecessary to dwell on the great value to readers of this book of such a compilation. Very few, if any, social histories of postwar American poetry are in existence. We will conclude our notice by heartily recommending the entire volume as an important addition to Literary Criticism as well as History.

Blockage, Breakdown, Baffle

Dark City. By Charles Bernstein. Sun & Moon Classics 48. Los Angeles: Sun & Moon Press, 1994.

Mr. Bernstein's position in the poetical world is, perhaps, better settled than that of any American of his generation. There is less difference of opinion about his rank; but, as used to be more usual, the agreement is more decided in private literary circles than in what appears to be the public expression of sentiment as gleaned from the critical literature. I may as well observe here, too, that this coincidence of opinion in private circles used to be in all cases very noticeable when compared with the discrepancies of the apparent public opinion. In private it was quite a rare thing to find any strongly marked disagreement—I mean, of course, about mere authorial merit. The author accustomed to seclusion, and mingling for the first time freely with the literary people about him, was invariably startled and delighted to find that the decisions of his own unbiased judgment—decisions to which he had refrained from giving voice on account of their broad contradiction to the decision of the critics—were sustained quite as matters of course by almost every person with whom he conversed. The fact is, that when brought face to face with each other we were constrained to a certain amount of honesty by the sheer trouble it would cause to mould the countenance to a lie. We put on paper with a grave air what we could not for our lives assert personally to a friend without blushing or laughing outright. That the opinion of critics is not honest, that a *purely* honest criticism is impossible, has never been denied by the practitioners of that art themselves. Individual critics, of course, are now and then honest, but I speak of the combined effect. Indeed, it would be difficult for those conversant with the *modus operandi* of public journals to deny the general falsity of impression conveyed. Let in America a book be published of an unknown, careless, or uninfluential author; if he publishes it "on his own account," he will be confounded at finding that no notice of it is taken at all (except, perhaps, in freebie tabloids or anarchist rags as this one). If it has been entrusted to a publisher of *caste,* there will appear forthwith in each of the leading *literary* journals a variously phrased *critique* to the extent of a paragraph or two, and to the effect that "we have received, from the fertile press of So and So, a volume entitled This and That, which appears to be well worthy perusal, and which is 'got up' in the customary neat style of the enterprising firm of So and So." On the other hand, let our author have acquired influence, experience, or (what will stand him in good stead of either) effrontery, on the issue of his book, he will receive from his publisher a hundred copies (or more, as the case may be) "for distribution among friends connected with the press." Armed with these, he will write personally either at the office or (if he understands the game) at the private residence of every editor within reach, enter into correspondence, compliment the fellow, interest him, as if incidentally, in the subject of the book, and finally, watching an opportunity, beg leave to send "a volume which, quite opportunely, is on the very matter now under discussion." If the editor seems sufficiently interested, the rest is left to fate; but if there is any lukewarmness (usually indicated by a polite regret on the editor's part that he "really has no time to render the work that justice which its importance demands"), then our author is prepared to understand and to sympathize; has, luckily, a friend thoroughly conversant with the topic; and who (perhaps) could be persuaded to write some account of the volume—provided that the editor would be kind enough just to glance over the *critique* and amend it in accordance with his own particular views. Glad to fill half a column or so of editorial space, and still more glad to draw the time-consuming correspondence to a close, the editor assents. The author consults the friend, offering instruction touching the strong points of the volume, and insinuating in *some* shape a *quid pro quo,* gets an elaborate *critique* written (or, what is more usual and far more simple, writes it himself), and the business in this individual quarter is accomplished. Nothing more than sheer impudence is required to accomplish it in all. The machinations of this system show most crudely in that odious form of journalism called *the blurb,* where the sole point of the notice is to sell books. Increasingly, the blurb is the model for all other species of *critique*. Indeed, a reputable critic in a reputable biannual recently averred, without the slightest sense of shame, "Of course it is well-known that reviews don't necessarily make for readers, but, to speak informally, it's also good to know that something's 'getting through.' Ah, for a publicity machine to project us into middle America."

Now the effect of this system (for it has really grown to be such) is obvious. In ninety-nine cases out of a hundred, men of genius, too indolent and careless about worldly concerns to bestir themselves after this fashion, have also that pride of intellect which would prevent them, under any circumstance, from even insinuating, by the presentation of a book to a member of the press, a desire to have that book reviewed. They, consequently, and their works, are utterly overwhelmed and extinguished in the flood of *apparent* public adulation upon which in gilded barges are borne triumphant the ingenious toady and diligent quack.

In general, the books of the toadies and quacks, not being read at all, are safe from any contradiction of this self-bestowed praise; but now and then it happens that the excess of the laudation works out in part its own remedy. Men of leisure, hearing one of the toady works commended, look at it, read it, read its preface (if there be such) and a few pages of the body, and throw it aside in disgust, wondering at the ill taste of the *blurbists* who extol it. But there is an iteration, and then a continuous reiteration of the panegyric, till these men of leisure begin to suspect themselves in the wrong, to fancy that there may really be something good lying *perdu* in the volume. In a fit of desperate curiosity they read it through critically, their indignation growing hotter at each succeeding page until it gets the better even of contempt. The result is that reviews and, worse yet, blurbs now appear in various quarters entirely at variance with the opinion so generally expressed, and which, but for these indignation reviews, would have passed universally current as the opinion of the public. It is in this manner that those gross *seeming* discrepancies arise which so often astonish us, but which vanish instantaneously in private society. For this reason, the gradual erosion of the distinction between poet and critic is greatly to be lamented, if only for the coeval erosion of private honesty. I would not confuse, however, the honesty of whispered opinion with the affectations of mere negativity—the habitual jealousy which *also* afflicts us, and which I consider even more pernicious than critical hyperbole.

But although it may be said, in general, that Mr. Bernstein's position is *comparatively* well settled, still for some time past there has been a growing tendency to underestimate him. The new licentious "schools" of poetry—I do not now speak of the language poets, who are the merest nobodies, fatiguing even themselves—but the survivors of the Beat and Black Mountain and New York schools, have, in their rashness of spirit, much in accordance with the whole spirit of the age, thrown into the shade necessarily all which seems akin to the Modernism of three score years ago, even when produced by one of their own. The verities, even the most justifiable *decora* of Modernist composition, are regarded, *per se,* with a suspicious eye. I mean that, from finding them so long in connection with an old world way of thinking (call it European, whether expatriate or immigrant in character), we have come at last to dislike them, not merely as the outward visible signs of that sensibility, but as things evil in themselves. It is very clear that those accuracies and elegancies of style, and of general manner, which in the time of Stevens were considered as *prima facie* and indispensable indications of genius, are now conversely regarded. How few are willing to admit the possibility of reconciling genius with artistic skill! Yet this reconciliation is not only possible, but also an absolute necessity. It is mere prejudice that has hitherto prevented the union, by studiously insisting upon a natural repulsion which not only does not exist, but which is at war with all the analogies of nature. The greatest poems will not be written until this prejudice is annihilated; and I mean to express a very exalted opinion of Mr. Bernstein when I say that his works in time to come will do much towards the annihilation.

I have never disbelieved in the perfect consistency, and even congeniality, of the highest genius and the profoundest art; but in the case of the author of "The Lives of the Toll Takers," I *have* fallen into the general error of undervaluing his poetic ability on account of the mere "elegancies and accuracies" to which allusion has already been made. I confess that, with an absolute abstraction from all personal feelings, and with the most sincere intention to do justice, I was at one period beguiled into this popular error; there can be no difficulty, therefore, on my part, in excusing the inadvertence in others.

It will never do to claim for Bernstein a genius of the loftiest order, but there has been latterly, since the ascendancy of Ms. Susan Howe and certain others of lesser ability, a growing disposition to deny him *genius* in *any* respect. He is now commonly spoken of as "a man of high poetical *talent,* very '*correct,*' with an eclectic appreciation of his fellow poets and great critical powers, but rather too much of the old-school manner of Zukofsky, Riding, and Stein." This is the truth, but not the whole truth. Mr. Bernstein has genius, and that of a marked character, but it has been overlooked by the recent schools, because deficient in those externals which have become in a measure symbolical of those schools.

Prof. Perelman, in summing up his comments on Bernstein, has the following *apparent* objection: "This is the opposite of wit, nothing is pointed, there's a lot of blockage, breakdown, baffles. This would seem to be in accordance with a pronounced strain of language writing theory." Prof. McGann, writing under the *nom de plume* Anne Mack, makes a related observation. "For to Bernstein 'signification' is a system of feedback loops, a generative intercourse; and—paradoxically—it functions most richly through its resistances, particularities, and 'impermeable' features. His ideology of language is that everything signifies, but it is an ideology which, in its own enactment, reveals its inherent contradictions." This view is further corroborated by Mr. Silliman, who has said of an earlier work (I delete the interposed citation), "Bernstein is rejecting analysis, intersubjectivity, and memory as roads out of the vicious circle of ideology's solipsism."

Now, in courting "blockage, breakdown, baffle," in allowing *neither* simple escape *nor* straightforward access, the poet has merely shown himself the profound artist, has merely evinced a proper consciousness that simple reassurances are not the legitimate aims of poetry. That they are not, I have repeatedly shown, or attempted to show, and to go over the demonstration now would be foreign to the gossiping and desultory nature of the present article. What Prof. McGann means by "ideology of language" is, I presume, not very clear to him; but it is possible he employs the phrase in consequence of the ideological *and* linguistic focus of the work he discusses. It is, however, precisely the difference *between* ideology and language that opens a space for the true poetical art. Ideology proper and poesy are discordant. Poetry, in its "resistances," explores the possibilities *of language.* With *ideology* it has nothing to do; or rather, poetic "signification" occurs only as an extrication—or attempted extrication—from ideology's "vicious circle," rightly called (by Mr. Silliman) solipsistic. The "intersubjective," *if* it exists in verse, exists solely in this very process of extrication, in "signification," *not* because persons are mere constructs of verbiage, but because verbiage, language-as-extrication, is how the personal becomes known. Blockage, breakdown, baffle: these are our Roads to Emmaus.

The author of *Social Values and Poetic Acts* thinks the "extreme playfulness" of Bernstein significant. "Not least significant," he says, "is the understanding that poetry always speaks in a contemporary idiom—that its dialect(s), like everything else about it, are time and place specific." *The Nude Formalism* appeared in 1989, and the poet was born in 1950; he was more than thirty-eight, then, when this volume was printed—although the poems were reportedly written earlier. I quote a few verses from "Gosh."

When fled I found my love defamed in clang
Of riotous bed she came, along the flues
I harbored there, scarce chance upon harangue
By labors grant the fig of latched amus

This is a fair specimen of the book as a whole, both as regards its satirical and rhythmical power. A satire is, of course, no *poem.* I have known boys of an earlier age to do better things, although the case is rare. All depends upon the course of education. Bernstein, for his part, is familiar with the best English and American literature; perceiving in himself, when twentysomething, indications of superior genius, he attended carefully to his own instruction, teaching himself the art of literary composition, and honing his literary taste. This being understood, the marvel of such verse as I have quoted ceases at once, even admitting it to be a product of the recent decade, and not an earlier; but it is difficult to make any such admission. Some literary father *must* have suggested, revised, retouched.

At sixteen pages, "Emotions of Normal People" is one of the longer poems of *Dark City.* It is also the one improper theme of the author.

The design is, from a survey of various specimens of language, and from the juxtaposition of mercantile and sociological data, to satirize the notion that feelings and desires are in any way natural. All this would have been more rationally, because more effectually, accomplished in prose. Dismissing it as a poem (which, in its general tendency, it is not), one might commend the programmatic force of the argument but for the hackneyed conflation of *person* and *machine*. Messrs. Deleuze and Guattari in *Anti-Oedipus* explore a similar conflation with far greater profundity.

The final six pages are a textbook example of carefully sequenced statement (within the narrow limits of *bricolage*).

The opening three pages are a good specimen of nonsense verse:

Enter the

Digitalizing oscilloscope with 20

GHz bandwidth, 10 ps resolution &

Floating-point primitives upwardly

Compatible with target-embedded

Resident assemblers & wet-wet

Compilers.

Found language? Lineation alone permits us to read these words as poetry. As in "R. Mutt's" famous toilet, the art lies in the tilt, and in the context.

The poem, in general, has a unity of intention. Its tone of cheerful derision is well sustained throughout. There is, as well, an occasional quaint grace of self-derision, as in:

The
only thing nicer
than a letter from a friend
is taking the time to read it
over a warm cup of Orange
Cappucino

Or better:

In any case, sarcasm

is evidence of a sadistic trend in one's

personality.

But we look in vain for anything more worthy commendation.

"Sunsickness" is the poem from this collection by which Mr. Bernstein is best known, but is by no means his best poem. It owes the *extent* of its celebrity to its nearly absolute freedom from *defect,* in the ordinary understanding of the term. I mean to say that its negative merit recommends it to the public attention. It is a thoughtful, well-phrased, well-constructed, well-versified poem. The conclusion is exceedingly noble, and has done wonders for the success of the whole composition.

"Desalination" is very clever, but like "Sunsickness" owes a great deal to its completeness and pointed termination.

"How I Painted Certain of My Pictures" will strike every poet as the truest *poem* written by Bernstein. It is richly ideal.

"Debris of Shock / Shock of Debris" is sweet and perfectly well modulated in its rhythm and inexpressibly pathetic. It serves well to illustrate my previous remarks about language-as-extrication in relation to ideology. In "Shock" there is, very properly, nothing of the intense *politicizing* of this ideological "Debris"; but the subdued sorrow which comes up, as if perforce, to the surface of the poet's *sayings* about this "plain" material, we find thrilling to the soul, while there is yet a political *inspiration* in the thrill.

Looking for society

in a lamppost will not necessarily eliminate

need for empirical

evidence. There are the

below-the-surface conduits

to consider. As a rule, I keep

my mittens in the drawer. Structure

is metaphorical, function metonymic. Meaning

my aim is to blur

the distinction between logic and normalization.

("Though I still don't get how confusion
is supposed to be positive?") Are they literally
bricks or are they literal steps? The infernal

machinery of missing harness, by the bus,

gates close to malediction, as in

get off my bunt, churning

in make-work flirtation, shocked to find a bandit

loosened

The thoughts expressed here belong to a high class of poetry: language stripping itself of reassuring meaning in a dance of paradox and ambiguity.

I copy at random a few passages of similar cast.

The things I

write are

not about me

though they

become me.

You look so bec

   oming, she said, attending the flower pots.

*   *   *

            Ratiocination cops

plea to lesser offense. Curls dwindle

in the high-pressure dome. The dreidl

begins to wobble wildly before tumbling to

ground. Emanations suffuse the body.

Sound permeates the *schul*. Young man

with horn can't hit imaginary note.

*   *   *

Stalled among the pantomimes,

obsolete rimes.

There is a fine echo of sound to sense in this; and in the same poem from which these lines are taken ("How I Painted Certain of My Pictures") may be found two other equally happy examples, e.g.:

Still waters run about as deep

as you can blow them.

And again—

The silencers click onto

the muzzles.

I resume the imaginative extracts:

The thing then to watch the spectacle

without being sucked up

in

it—for there is

a danger in finding yourself dictating

defenses to crimes not only not committed

but really just the opposite

of crimes

* * *

Rue or be ruled or take a ruler
to wind to measure the gravity
that locates

* * *

Love's no more than that
a straw against the wind
that blows us to the ground
without submission.

This latter passage is especially beautiful. To endow inanimate nature happily with sentience and a capability of action is one of the severest tests of the poet.

This is the difference between truth
and reality: the one advertises itself
in the court of brute circumstance
the other is framed by its own
insistences. Truth's religious, reality
cultural, or rather

truth is the ground of reality's
appearance but reality intervenes
against all odds.

In a poem "*for Susan,*" ("Virtual Reality,") are some richly imaginative lines.

So sway the
swivels, corpusculate the
dilations.
For I've
learned that relations
are a small
twig in the blizzard
of projections
& expectations.

The happiest *finale* to these brief extracts will be the magnificent conclusion of "Sunsickness."

For what

you may learn is that by going

down into the secrets of your

own crimes you descend

into the streets of all

mimes (minds). Anyway:

some other. Worlds

hourly changing

sparring with cause to an

unknowable end. Asking

no less, demanding no

more.

In the minor morals of the muse, Mr. Bernstein excels. In versification (*as far as he* goes), he is unsurpassed in America—unless, indeed, by Mr. Ashbery. Mr. Mackey is not so thorough a versifier within Mr. Bernstein's limits, but a far better one upon the whole, on account of his greater range. Mr. B., however, is by no means always accurate—or defensible, for accurate is not the term. His lines are occasionally ridiculous through a punning which bites more than it chews, as in:

Funny, you don't look

gluish.

Now and then, in attempting a nearly sentimental address, he gets out of his depth, as in:

Come
love, come, take this
shadow I call me: cast
it against stone, lest the gloom
become us.

Not infrequently, too, even his slapstick is inexcusably rough, as in:

Whadda you *mean* you're

Going to the next poem? *This is the best*

Part! Oh, I'm sorry, I guess I misunderstood

You.

Mr. Bernstein is not devoid of mannerisms, of which one of the most noticeable is his resolution of a statement by means of *non sequitur,* sometimes justified by a pun, as in:

Michael writes of sun, but all I can think

of is sunsickness, too much in the sun

never a daughter.

Sometimes not, as with:

Our jailors
are our constipating sense of self—
not that madmen claim many kin.

Of merely grammatical errors, the poet is rarely guilty. Faulty constructions are more frequently chargeable to him, though these faults are almost certainly intentional. In "Heart in My Eye," we read—

gumption gum drilled or
guttered, the contraption
is delinquent must fly
trap or elevate

It will be understood that I pick these flaws only with difficulty from the poems of Bernstein. He is, in the "minor morals," the most generally correct of our recent poets.

He is now 45 years of age. In height, he is, perhaps five feet seven. His frame is rather robust. His countenance is pale, bordering on gray. His eyes are watchful; his lips, full and perpetually in motion, even when he is silent; the expression of the smile hard, cold—even sardonic. The forehead is broad, with prominent organs of ideality; a good deal bald; the hair curly and grayish. His bearing is quite unpretentious, yet full of the Jew's expressive intellectuality. In general, he looks in worse health since he began the commute back and forth between New York City and Buffalo. He seems active—physically and morally—energetic. His dress is plain to the extreme of simplicity, although of late there is a certain degree of rumpled academicism about it.

In character, no man stands more loftily than Bernstein. The peculiar melancholy expression of his countenance has caused him to be accused of an abiding sarcasm, or wishy-washiness of heart. Never was there a greater mistake. His soul is charity itself, in all respects generous and noble. His deepest opinions are undoubtedly reserved.

Of late, Mr. Bernstein has nearly, if not altogether abandoned "making the scene," although he still writes with unabated vigor, and remains one of *Sulfur* magazine's contributing editors. He is increasingly identified with the ill-starred Poetics Program of SUNY Buffalo, where in 1990 he became the David Gray Professor of Poetry and Letters. He is married (to Susan Bee, the painter), has two children (Emma and Felix), and divides residence between the Fountainview Apartments of Western New York, and the Upper West Side of Manhattan. I have thought that these brief personal details of one of the most justly celebrated men in America might not prove uninteresting to some readers.

Mr. Daly's Polemic

Swallowing the Scroll: Late in a Prophetic Tradition with the Poetry of Susan Howe and John Taggart. By Lew Daly. Buffalo, N.Y.: apex of the M supplement #1.

Of Mr. Daly we know nothing—although we believe that he is a student in SUNY Buffalo's Poetics Program—or perhaps a graduate, or perhaps a Professor of that Institution. Of his book, lately, we have heard a great deal—that is to say, we have heard it announced in every possible variation of phrase, as "forthcoming." For several months past, indeed, much amusement has been occasioned in the various literary coteries in New York by the pertinacity and obviousness of an attempt made by the poet's friends to get up an anticipatory excitement in his favor. There were multitudinous dark rumors of something *in posse*—whispered insinuations that the sun had at length arisen or would certainly arise—that a book was really in press which would revolutionize the poetical world—that the MS. had been submitted to the inspection of a junto of critics, whose fiat was well understood to be Fate (Mr. Robert Creeley, if we remember aright, forming one of the junto)—that the work had by them been approved, and its successful reception and illimitable glorification assured. Ms. Rosmarie Waldrop, in consequence, countermanding an order given her publishers (New Directions) to issue forthwith a new paperback edition of her dissertation on Wittgenstein. Suggestions of this nature, busily circulated in private, were, in good time, insinuated through the press, until at length the public expectation was as much on tiptoes as public expectation, in America, can ever be expected to be about so small a matter as the issue of a volume of American poetry or poetics. The climax of this whole effort, however, at forestalling the critical opinion, and by far the most injudicious portion of the procedure, was the publisher's announcement of the forthcoming book as "a very remarkable example of poetic criticism."

The fact is that the only remarkable thing about Mr. Daly's writing is its remarkable conceit, ignorance, impudence, obscurity, pedantry, and bombast—we are sorry to say all this, but there is an old adage about the falling of the Heavens. Nor must we be misunderstood. We intend to wrong neither Mr. Daly nor our own conscience by denying him particular merits—such as they are. His book is *not* altogether contemptible—although the conduct of his friends has inoculated nine-tenths of the community with the opinion that it is—but what we wish to say is that "remarkable" is by no means the epithet to be applied, in the way of commendation, either to anything that he has yet done or to anything he may hereafter accomplish. In a word, while he has undoubtedly given proof of a very ordinary species of talent, no man or woman whose opinion is entitled to the slightest respect will admit in him any indication of genius.

The "particular merits" to which, in the case of Mr. Daly, we have allusion, are merely the accidental merits of particular passages. We say *accidental* because poetical merit that is not simply an accident is very sure to be found more or less in a state of *diffusion* throughout even a work of criticism. No man or woman is entitled to the sacred name of poet because a few sentences of worth may be culled from 95 pages of claptrap; nor would the case be in any respect altered if these few sentences, or even if a few passages of length, were of an excellence even supreme. For a poet is necessarily a person of genius, and with the spirit of true genius even its veriest commonplaces are intertwined and inexplicably intertangled. When, therefore, amid a Sahara of obscurity, we discover an occasional Oasis, we must not so far forget ourselves as to fancy any latent fertility in the sands. It is our purpose, however, to do the fullest justice to Mr. Daly, and we proceed at once to cull from his book whatever, in our opinion, will put in the fairest light his poetical pretensions.

And first we extract the *one* brief passage that aroused in us what we recognized as the Poetical Sentiment. It occurs, at page 41, in a subsection called "The Gospel According to Mary," which, although excessively obscure at all points, is, upon the whole, the least reprehensible portion of the volume. The heroine of this subsection—not

Mary Magdalene but Susan Howe—is here exorbitantly praised, with Wallace Stevens's name strangely substituted for the more suitable example of H.D.:

> On what other scale than that of the path from the Easter Tomb in Palestine to the poet's desk past two millenia [sic] of silencing by the apostles; on what other scale than that of the path from Passion to the poet's tomb before which history rolled its wheelstones of both church and state, forcing night onto the page on which she 'weeps to wake,' as Percy Shelley said, the light and writes *I am;* on what other scale than that of Prophets and Gospels reconceptualized in this way are we to witness this—one of the most truly radical returns of the spirit of prophecy in American poetry, if not since the 19th century, then since the final poems of Wallace Stevens.

At page 65, in a subsection of much general *eloquence,* there occur a few lines of which we should not hesitate to speak enthusiastically were we not perfectly well aware of the purpose of Mr. Daly's argument:

> In the promissory economy of the departure of faith, the son, as a sign not of God, but of woman and man, is an emphasis placed on the Fall. That the child must, both in theory and practice, improve upon the paternity of God—the principle of creation—to become a father, marks in the course of what is therefore only an appropriative repetition of that primal day, the pursuit of an insuperable homogeneity: the patriarchal line.

At page 10, in the preface, we meet, also, a passage of high merit, though sadly disfigured:

> I will provisionally describe by the word "prophecy" here a poetry that might be said to permit—on a stage of public hierarchy, and under the full weight of our disgrace as citizens on such a stage—enunciation in an encounter with the supra-hierarchical, the power of God.

The disfiguration to which we allude lies in making poetry's "stage" less solid than the emotions of those who would ascend to speak. Concrete froth on a pitcher of beer could not effect a more ridiculous image. Moreover, by giving less weight to history's "stage" than the actor's "disgrace," our author betrays an overweening aestheticism. In Mr. Daly's scenario, the Poet does not so much bear witness to the Age as the Age to the Poet. "Enunciation" occurs less as an encounter with God than as the aftertaste of God's "power." (This "power," alas, has little to do with revelation, but is merely the bombast of any competent preacher.) The poetry in question is not *really* prophecy, but only allows itself to be *described* as such.

At page 11, still in the same preface, we find some lines that are very quotable, and will serve to make our readers understand what we mean by the eloquence of the book:

> Reinscribed as avant-garde, to be a heart cut-out and made the variable, and not the iconoclasm, of a body of seditions from which the poem—thus severed by discourse—is therefore relativized out of range and bathed in light, the work of Howe and, even more marginally, that of Taggart, lives on inimitably in our minds, and as it is intended to live: as material testimony to an encounter with the heteronomous, or to encounter as such, in terms of what is in the first instance a criteriology of the divine.

We extract this *not* because we like it ourselves, but because we take it for granted that there are many who will, and that Mr. Daly himself would desire us to extract it, to hold in our minds as a beating specimen of his *power*. The "heart" is poetry, cut from society's "body" and "[r]einscribed" in the mind of the reader. We disapprove, however, the butchering method by which this operation is performed. The "material testimony" should be understood, we fancy, as an expression of approval on the part of Mr. Daly for the fine idea that immediately precedes—the metaphorical organ transplant. It is, in fact, by no means destitute of force—but if the heart is *intended* to live in the reader's mind, why disparage discourse, which removes the organ preparatory for transplant?

At page 83, there are two sentences put under the heading "die Entzauberung der Welt." We cite these sentences as the best thing of equal length to be found in the book. The compaction of Olson and Nietzsche is especially noble.

> Lost with the language of God is the illegibility of descent in those who live, that they might gather irresistibly in what the language gives. Lost though it may be to internecine legibility—and to a war between the Cosmos and the Occident—the exteriority of a human, all too human universe may still exist: but as a language of the loss as such, considered as a call for which the language is, as prophecy, the unresolved sensorium that comes across.

We give the lines as they are: abstraction weakens the sense, and the blanket use of "language" to describe all of Mr. Daly's terms—his descent, gift, war, loss, prophecy, and sensorium—blunts the impact of the argument.

Of that species of composition that comes most appropriately under the head, *Drivel,* we should have no trouble in selecting as many specimens as our readers could desire. We will afflict them with one or two:

> Shards of the law now ground-down to and convergent in a single point, or, the tip of a shard in the heart heteronomously dislodged, and impolitic all too idolatrously to the point (of bringing annihilation upon itself), must now be offered-up before enormous crowds. (Pg. 19)

And of a poet:

> The appellative sedimentation from the depths of which those who populate her work—all perhaps Lazaruses—are resurrected, is in the first instance informed by, and therefore confirmation of a sometimes fierce, and sometimes pure experiment in the communicative and the absurd. (Pg. 36)

In "The Passion," we are entertained after this fashion:

> Whereas Marx's revolutionary teleology contains within itself the seeds of factory-built totalitarianism, Kierkegaard's encompassing religiosity in *Fear and Trembling* sustains a pitch of paradox that, if followed openly, would lead to potlatch in a social

> sphere abandoned by Enlightenment to reflection and bureaucracy. (Pg. 71)

In "For Robert Duncan," we have it thus:

> In the wings from which such a stage, the stage of symbolic order, might be spied and rightly sacrificed in the face to face relation that the very fact of language gives a name—a fact that only poetry corroborates—language is itself understood to have a meaning.

Just above this there is a passage where Mr. Daly grotesquely confuses the two meanings of "wing":

> This is a gospel resistance that keeps us together in the off-stage of the outside—the threat to all theater in the understudy's cry—or under wings not ever spent by winds, but spread before us as though through a force of verisimilitude to Benjamin's Angel's vision—depicting as it does the process of history as wind that, under the shelter of progress, blows between paradise and annihilation. (Pg. 87)

But in mercy to our readers, we forbear.

Mr. Daly is never elevated beyond the dead level of his habitual opacity by even the simplest theme in the world. That any man could, at one and the same time, fancy himself a poet and string together as many pitiable inanities as we see here, on so truly suggestive a theme as Mark Rothko's paintings, is to our apprehension a miracle of miracles. The topic would seem to be, of itself, sufficient to elicit fire from ice—to breathe animation into the most stolid of stone. Mr. Daly winds up a dissertation on "blood and ash"—

> Thus having faced the expectation of "The Rothko Chapel Poem," perhaps as the Israelites in the wilderness did the flames of revelation in the face of Moses—through a veil of mercy, I have been unable to fully countenance the sorrows I perceive within the poem without a measure, however extreme, of con-

> textualization in terms of the late medieval and Renaissance traditions of Passion mysticism (pg. 67)

The whole of which would read better if it were:

> Thus having tried to read "The Rothko Chapel Poem," perhaps as a tourist in Paris would labor to understand a menu—through tears of hunger, I have been unable to accept the unappetizing quality of the poem, though an afternoon with the cook would probably explain everything.

Even with the great theme, Mary, our poet fails in his obvious effort to work himself into a fit of inspiration. One of his goals is to write a hymn to religious verse—but from beginning to end it is nothing more than a silly hymn to a great line of literary "D's":

> Expanding on DUNCAN's "line is in itself metaphor," each *page* is aligned as but a pentecost of itself, renouncing parity between the lines. Each page being like a site-specific but self-disengraving graph of articulations hitherto merely consubstantial with, and therefore, ultimately, indivisible from, inscrutability—that archimedean point to all prophetic cataloging and litany; each page as such affords us a view of, approach to, or consequence of, the Magdalenian gospel from behind eyes of prophets from DEBORAH to DICKINSON, in light hiding the poet from our own eyes but shining on God. (Pg. 43)

The suggestion is obvious. We might earlier have wondered what Mr. Daly meant by "immodesty," when on the opening page of his treatise he declared, "I take . . . as a model for the immodesty of my claims for them, the immodesty of the poems themselves" —but no longer (pg. 7).

At one point, the poet directs himself, as Youth's representative, to issue a proclamation as follows:

> Toward an aftermath of Romantic desire . . . we, being the young, have been forced at this time to mislead ourselves even further —brought as never before to the point of being led headlong,

> and in hordes, into a divide on every side of which a silence has begun to reign. In this divide resides the ethical relation. Unearthed asymmetries shadowing immanence, and in fact capacitating the very disgrace that we must make of it, take shape in magnanimity and abasement at this time. (Pgs. 47–48)

The "*hordes*" has reference to Mr. Daly's contemporaries, who are not fellow actors, but part of the scenery. They appear in this production as a grand backdrop for Mr. Daly's "disgrace," "magnanimity," and "debasement." The silence, however, must be an awful burden for our poet, who thinks it necessary to issue a proclamation to those leading Youth toward the divide—lest any should chance to be unaware of the fact that he (Mr. Daly) has discovered the divide to be a fine place after all (for there "resides the ethical relation")—but whether "Romantic desire," for having inspired an "aftermath," or "[u]nearthed asymmetries," for their "shadowing" of "immanence," are objects of devotion or despisal—that, for the life of us, we cannot tell.

Of the "divide" in question—the present moment in poetry—Mr. Daly says:

> On the basis of a profound distrust of instrumental models of language, and in coincidence with the entrenchment of such models in the university-centered mainstream poetry renaissance of the seventies, remarkable strides—of theoretical resistance to, and aesthetic liberty from, the mainstream sensibility—have been taken by avant-garde poets during the last twenty years. Yet, as is the case with all bourgeois transformations, the moment of discovery—of the discovery of resistance—has passed. When the tenets of resistance become presumptions, they necessarily overdetermine that resistance, with the consequence of one-dimensionality at the level of practice.

And:

> In a moment of despair I would characterize what is at this point required of the avant-garde, then, as a vast expiation—involving years of completely re-oriented study and practice—for its betrayal of the radical historical traditions of the sacred and the creative word. (Pg. 84)

That so clever a personage as Mr. Daly should not be elated by the avant-garde's "remarkable strides," but feel "despair" instead—and active anger too—is certainly nothing more than reasonable and proper—but then he should have left the task of demanding expiation to some other uninterested individual—even Cicero has been held to blame for a want of modesty—and although, to be sure, Cicero was not Mr. Daly, still Mr. Daly may be in danger of blame. He may have enemies (*very* little men!) who will pretend to deny that "the radical and historical traditions of the sacred and the creative word" (if *this* is their study) bear, at all points, more than a partial resemblance to "bourgeois transformations" and "one-dimensionality at the level of practice."

We have said that the "remarkable" feature, or at least one of the "remarkable" features of this volume, is its obscurity—its opacity. Whenever the reader meets anything not decidedly obscure, he may take it for granted, at once, that it is stolen. When the poet speaks, for example, at page 27, of a "radical, rather than general, skepticism," he is borrowing without acknowledgment—or proper explanation—an idea that derives from the work of Emmanuel Levinas. The grossest allusions and appropriations abound. We would have no trouble in pointing out a score from this obscure source alone. On page 40, Mr. Daly says, "that which is otherwise than Being, or beyond essence, does not exist apart from self-destruction," and just after, "only in this less limited sense . . . can the Good beyond being . . . eventuate in a rectitude of which we cannot dream." In another passage, also beholden to Levinas, a curious pun suggests that our author should like nothing *better* than to forget the obligation, the literary debt: "We will write with the ardor of a lower life-form, reserving for exteriority the higher. We are DAILY brought to bear against the profane by a face in the square, by a hand in the gears." At page 15, our author applies a Levinasian code word to a redaction of our own "Tell-Tale Heart," describing certain poems as being "diachronic like the recondite stroke of a clock soaked in blood." Discussing Susan Howe's "complex, almost formidable" reading of 19th century literature, he credits to *Typee*'s author an idea whose articulation recalls our most unimportant self:

> Melville tells us that there will be a conflict between consciousness, the availability of self, and conscience, the overcoming of

> our self-sufficiency, forever registering its pendulum swings like battle-cries in the deepest recesses of our mortality. (Pg. 49)

And on page 55:

> In a pendulum swing of pure hierarchy between dirge-like prosodic grapplings and breakthroughs of inarticulable affection, Howe goes about the task of registering counterhistory in typeface and singing.

But it is folly to pursue these thefts. As to any property of our own, Mr. Daly is very cordially welcome to whatever use he can make of it. But others may not be so pacifically disposed, and the book before us might be very materially thinned and reduced in cost by discarding from it all that belongs to Levinas, Derrida, Blanchot, Bataille, Benjamin, Foucault—the very class of thinkers, by the way, whom Mr. Lew Daly, in his "Contextual Imperative" (*apex of the M*, no. 2) most especially effects to contemn.

It has been rumored, we say, or rather it has been *announced* that Mr. Daly is a graduate or perhaps a Professor in the Poetics Program—but we have had much difficulty in believing anything of the kind. The pages before us are not only utterly devoid of that classicism of tone and manner—that better species of classicism which a liberal education never fails to impart—but they abound in the most outrageously vulgar violations of usage—of style in its most extended sense.

Of felicitous phrasing, and all that appertains to it, Mr. Daly is ignorant in the extreme. We doubt if he can tell the difference between qualification and peroration. In long sentences he continuously begins with an involuted construction:

> Felled as we one day must be by a call to which language as we know it has deafened us . . . (pg. 27)

> Serpentine and self-begotten as the temptation of structure may be in an age enamored more with the absence of God than the victims of paradise . . . (pgs. 42–43)

> While some of us, like Susan Howe, may certainly harbor in our work an implicit, and even an ongoing, consideration of the Bible . . . (pg. 46)

> However different hymnody and discant [sic] may be from litany, permutation from glossolalia . . . (pg. 55)

> Following Psalm 22, to which Jesus remains most fully connected in the icons and altarpieces of Northerners, both Catholic and Quietist, before the Enlightenment . . . (pg. 59)

> Though repressed during the time between the return from the Babylonian exile and the birth of John the Baptist—repressed, that is, by priestly reforms under Ezra to make way for the Canon and the Law of the Scribes . . . (pgs. 61–62)

We encounter the passive voice at every step, searching in vain for many a sentence's subject. Whenever possible, moreover, Mr. Daly places his cart before the horse and begins his sentence with an aside. Sentences? They are merely wind-up toys with feet that tromp up and down until the tension in the crank is completely depleted. In a word, judging from his powers of articulation, we might suppose that the poet could neither speak, hear, nor make use of his fingers. We do not know, in America, a stylist so utterly wretched and contemptible.

His most extraordinary sins, however, are in point of meaning. Here is his first sentence:

> Having taken into account certain of the most explicit demands of context in their work, I could not continue to write within the limits of what began here as a more formal review of recent publications by the poets Susan Howe and John Taggart; the type of articulation to which I was initially reconciled did not accommodate what had inspired me to speak.

What is any body to make of all this? What is meant by the context *in* their work? And is the "type of articulation" to which Mr. Daly was "initially reconciled" irreconcilable with "the most explicit demands of context," or only with inspiration?

At page 20, in 58 words, we have one of the grossest blunders:

> Once the flesh around the bullet the penetration of which is without end, swallows by analogy the phallus of the assassin and centers our rage, sentences hitherto handed down by us now des-

> tine us to fulfill a judgment that we cannot make—as though in preparation for our coming to face, and be disgraced by, what we've made.

At page 24, we read:

> A gesture that is in the last instance still a premise of the language, and even the poem, in which it is represented necessarily shatters opacity, but is itself outshone by light on the absurd.

At page 29, is something even grosser than this:

> For Simone Weil the abyss of revelation was the space of her experience with the point of a nail the head of which is the entire universe between the individual and God.

At page 89, is a combination of several species of error:

> Far from being that which distinguishes us from animals, language is that which degrades us in their eyes, for by "their eyes" I mean the eyes are watching God.

And just after—

> Notwithstanding the political correctness of the rejection of the Pauline spirit/letter dualism, the time has come for us to flush from the thickets of post-Modern formalist anti-transcendentalism the lame-duck theology still underlying it.

Invariably Mr. Daly mixes his metaphor—if he has not already *mashed* it. The fact is, he is absurdly ignorant of the commonest principles of composition—and the only excuse we can make to our readers for annoying them with specifications in this respect is that, without the specifications, we should never have been believed.

But enough of this folly. We are heartily tired of the book, and thoroughly disgusted with the impudence of the parties who have been aiding and abetting in thrusting it before the public. To the poet himself we have only to say—from any farther specimens of your stupidity, God give us daily deliverance!

THE LITERATI OF SAN FRANCISCO

By "Edgar Allen Poe"

The Literati of San Francisco

And Neighboring Environs
Some Honest Opinions at Random Respecting Their Authorial Merits, with Occasional Words of Personality

In a criticism on Bernstein published elsewhere, I was at some pains in pointing out the distinction between the popular "opinion" of the merits of contemporary authors and the opinions held and expressed of them in private literary society.* The former species of "opinion" can be called "opinion" only by courtesy. It is the public's own, just as we consider a book our own when we have bought it. In general, this opinion is adopted from the journals of the day, and I have endeavored to show that the cases are rare indeed in which these journals express any other sentiment about books than such as may be attributed directly to the authors of the books. The most "popular," the most "successful" writers among us (for a brief period, at least) are, ninety-nine times out of a hundred, persons of mere address, perseverance, effrontery—in a word, busybodies, toadies, quacks. These people easily succeed in *boring* editors (whose attention is too often entirely engrossed by politics or other "business" matter) into the admission of favorable notices written or caused to be written by interested parties—or, at least, into the admission of *some* notice where, under ordinary circumstances, *no* notice would be given at all. In this way ephemeral "reputations" are manufactured which, for the most part, serve all the purposes designed—that is to say, the putting of money into the purse of the quack and the quack's publisher, invariably in the form of a government subsidy; for there never was a quack who could be brought to comprehend the value of mere fame. Now, men and women of genius will not resort to these maneuvers, because

*See "Blockage, Breakdown, Baffle," pp. 170–84, above.

genius involves in its very essence a scorn of chicanery; and thus for a time the quacks always get the advantage of them, both in respect to pecuniary profit and what *appears* to be public esteem.

There is another point of view, too. Your literary quacks court, in especial, the personal acquaintance of those "connected with the magazines." Now these latter, even when penning a voluntary, that is to say, an unmotivated notice of the book of an acquaintance, feel as if writing not so much for the eye of the public as for the eye of the acquaintance, and the notice is fashioned accordingly. Through a feeling akin to the impulse that makes it unpleasant to speak ill of one to one's face, the bad points of the work are slurred over and the good ones brought out into the best light. In the case of men and women of genius, editors, as a general rule, tend to have little to no acquaintance with these persons of genius, a class proverbial for shunning society.

But the very critics who hesitate at saying in print an ill word of authors personally known are usually the most frank in private. In literary society, they seem bent upon avenging the wrongs self-inflicted upon their own consciences. Here, accordingly, the quacks are treated as they deserve—even a little more harshly than they deserve—by way of striking a balance. True merit, on the same principle, is apt to be slightly overrated; but, upon the whole, there is a close approximation to absolute honesty of opinion; and this honesty is further secured by the mere trouble to which it puts one in conversation to model one's countenance to a falsehood. We place on paper without hesitation a tissue of flatteries, to which in society we could not give utterance, for our lives, without either blushing or laughing outright.

For these reasons there exists a very remarkable discrepancy between the apparent public opinion of any given author's merits and the opinion which is expressed of him or her orally by those who are best qualified to judge. For example, Mr. Rodefer, the author of *Four Lectures,* is scarcely recognized by the journals or by the public, and when noticed at all, is noticed merely to be damned by faint praise. Now, my own opinion of him is that although his walk is limited and he is fairly to be charged with mannerism, for he treats all subjects in a similar tone of dreamy *innuendo,* yet in this walk he evinces extraordinary genius, having no rival either in America or elsewhere. This opinion I have never heard gainsaid by any literary person in the country. That this opinion, however, is a spoken and not a written one, is referable to the facts, first, that Mr. Rodefer *is* a poor companion in polite society, and, second, that he is *not* an ubiquitous quack.

Again, of Mr. and Mrs. Waldrop, who, although they evince little quackery *per se,* have, through their social and literary position—she as a publisher, he a professor—a whole legion of active quacks at their control—of *them,* what is the apparent popular opinion? Of course, that they are poetical phenomena, as entirely without fault as the luxurious paper upon which their poems are borne to the public eye. However, in private society, although they are regarded with one voice as poets of far more than usual ability, as well-read persons and skillful artists, they are more esteemed as determined imitators and dexterous translators of the ideas of other people. For years I have conversed with no literary person who did not entertain precisely these ideas of Mr. and Mrs. W. This is only one example of how, on literary topics, there exists in society a seemingly wonderful coincidence of opinion. Authors accustomed to seclusion, and mingling for the first time in literary society, are astonished and delighted at finding common to all whom they meet conclusions which they had blindly fancied were attained by themselves alone, conclusions that run, in fact, in opposition to the judgment of mankind.

In the series of papers which I now propose, my design is, in giving my own unbiased opinion of the *literati* (male and female) of the San Francisco Bay Area, to give at the same time, very closely if not with absolute accuracy, that of conversational society in avant-garde literary circles. It must be expected, of course, that, in innumerable particulars, I shall differ from the voice, that is to say, from what appears to be the voice of the public—but this is a matter of no consequence whatever.

San Francisco literature may be taken as a fair representation of that of the country at large. The city itself, including various environs, is the focus of American letters. Its poets include, perhaps, one-fourth of all in America, and the influence they exert on their brethren and sistren, if seemingly silent, is not the less extensive and decisive. As I shall have to speak of many individuals, my limits will not permit me to speak of them other than in brief; but this brevity will be merely consistent with the design, which is that of simple *opinion,* with little of either argument or detail. With one or two exceptions, I am well acquainted with every author to be introduced, and I shall avail myself of the acquaintance to convey, generally, some idea of the personal appearance of all who, in this regard, would be likely to interest the readers of the magazine. As any precise order or arrangement seems unnecessary and may be inconvenient, I shall maintain none. It will be understood that, without reference to supposed merit or demerit, each individual is introduced absolutely at random. It is with great regret that I could not, at the present time, incorporate in this group portrait *every* practitioner of the art of poetry currently or recently in residence in the Bay Area. Of necessity, then, I have limited my scrutiny to a mere twenty-two poets.

BOB PERELMAN

One of the founders of the language school in San Francisco, Bob Perelman is now a Professor of English Literature at the University of Pennsylvania. He has long been distinguished for the extent and variety of his attainments in poetry and poetics; indeed, as an expostulator on these subjects it is probable that he has no equal among us. He has published a great deal, both poetry and prose, and his books have always the good fortune to attract attention throughout the civilized world. Of late, he has created a singular commotion in the realm of verse by his *Marginalization of Poetry*. This work has been zealously attacked and as zealously defended by the professor and his friends. There can be no doubt that, up to this period, the Perelmanites have had the best of the battle. *The Marginalization* is lucidly, succinctly, rigorously, and logically written, and proves, in my opinion, everything that it attempts—provided we admit the dubious assumptions from which it starts; and this is as much as can be well said of any disquisition on poetics under the sun. It might be hinted, too, in reference as well to Prof. Perelman as to his opponents, "Who limits himself to 'All I can say. All I can say' gives himself to a kind of conservatism." An earlier work in the same genre, *The Trouble with Genius,* made less noise.

Professor Perelman was also, at one time, the editor of *Hills,* a magazine which had the misfortune of falling between two stools, never having been able to make up its mind whether to be popular with the poetry journals or dignified with the poetics journals. It was a "happy *medium*" between the two classes, and met the fate of all happy *media* in dying, as well through lack of foes as of friends. *In media tutissimus ibi* is the worst advice in the world for an editor of a magazine. Its observance proved the downfall of Mr. Amnasan and his really meritorious *Ottotole. Hills* is best remembered for a collection of transcribed "talks" by poets delivered in Prof. Perelman's San Francisco loft before he embarked upon his academic career. This issue of his magazine was the prototype for a more substantial and entirely different collection brought out by Southern Illinois University Press, called *Writing/Talks,* whose contributors included Charles Bernstein, Beverly Dahlen, Michael Palmer, and Lyn Hejinian.

The titles of these publications deceive us. They are by no means "talks" as men and women usually understand the term—not that true talk of which Andy Warhol has been the best historiographer. In a word it is not *gossip,* which has never been better defined than by Zora Neale Hurston, who speaks of people "passing this world and the next one through their mouths," nor more thoroughly comprehended than by Gertrude Stein, Jack Kerouac, and David Antin, who made it their profession and purpose. Embracing all things, it has neither beginning, nor middle, nor end. Thus, it was not properly said of gossips that "they commence their discourse by jumping *in media res.*" For clearly gossips commence not at all, but are commenced by their material, which has indeterminate beginnings and ends. As for laws, true talkers recognize but one, the invariable absence of all. And for their roads, were they as straight as the one "paved with good intentions," nevertheless would they be malcontent without a frequent hop, skip, and a jump over the fences which make good neighbors, into the tempting pastures of digression beyond. Such are gossips, and of such alone is the true *talk*. One of Prof. Perelman's contributors (a gentleman) asked a fellow poet, in my presence, if she had ever heard him *lecture*. She answered very slyly, "I've never heard you do anything else." The truth is that "*Written* Talks" *might* have answered as a title for these collections, but their character can be fully conveyed only in "Pre-Recorded Essays" or even "Well-Rehearsed Harangues."

Professor Perelman's best-known poem is probably "China," which received some words of commendation from the author of *The Prison House of Language,* and I am ashamed to say, owes most of its literary significance to this circumstance. Prof. Jameson's remarks (in an essay in *New Left Review*) were scarcely concerned with poetic value, being much more focused on matters of history, theory, and politics; he is, nonetheless, entitled to our respect for the breadth of his interests and curiosity. "China," casually compared with other poems of the same epoch, is a good poem—indeed, an excellent one, but, considered more closely, its merits are very inconsiderable. It has many of the traits of Watten's *Plasma/Parallels/"X,"* to which, in its mode of construction, its themes, and several other points, it bears as close a resemblance as, in the nature of things, it could very well bear. It is no means, improbable, however, that Watten received some advice from Prof. Perelman in the composition of his chapbook, or at least was guided by his advice in many particulars of poetic form.

His subsequent works are more startling and more original. "Chaim Soutine," a series of meditations on the life of the well-known Jewish painter, is, I think, the best work in verse of its author, and evinces a fine sense of allegory, with keen appreciation of the lyrical in historical detail. Prof. Perelman is fond of political poems, and writes them with verve, investing his rhetoric with equal measures of intelligence and humor. "Seduced by Analogy" and "The Broken Mirror" were chosen by Douglas Messerli for his anthology, but are by no means so good as the less poetic compositions "Picture," "Life Forms," "Sex," and "A Literal Translation of Virgil's Fourth Eclogue."

Captive Audience is a long satirical poem, with many intricate and clever passages, well wrought. For example—

To keep the storyboards
true to life, and to maintain
a minimum of decorum, an outhouse
in every firefight, the CIA
was thoroughly and truly unleashed
in an orchestration
of chance that even John Cage
would have to call deliberate.
Beneath the archaic torso
of voting patterns and viewing habits
the present has left a blank.
It reads: "Moderation for the few
(who must—one at a time—
change their lives),
termination for those chickens
who try to cross the road

without a good reason."
If that leaves out human agency,
like they—inhuman non-agents—say,
just call it realism's
protective coloring.
But a syntax that bombs its own debris
Is a syntax that has got to go.

There is something of the "exquisite corpse" throughout this poem, and, indeed, throughout all the political poems of Prof. Perelman—perhaps a little *too much*.

He is one of the most amiable men in the world, universally respected and beloved. His frank, unpretending simplicity of demeanor is especially winning.

In person he is over six feet tall, but stooped. His countenance expresses rather benevolence and profound earnestness than high intelligence. The eyes are sensitive, but watchful; the other features, in general, massive. The forehead, phrenologically, indicates causality and compassion, with deficient ideality—the organization that induces strict logicality from insufficient premises. His dress is neat and proper. His speech indicates, in the most striking manner, the sympathetic attentiveness, directness, and especially, the *unpretentiousness* of his mental character, but bears about it a species of hesitation and inconsequence, which betray the fact that Prof. Perelman has not altogether succeeded in convincing himself of those important truths which he is so anxious to impress upon his auditors.

ANDREW SCHELLING

Mr. Andrew Schelling aided Mr. Norman Fischer, I believe, some years ago in the conduct of a conference on meditation and poetry, and he has been elsewhere connected with the spiritual community of the Bay Area. He is more recently known, however, as the author of a neat volume entitled *The India Book*—a simple title for a good collection of essays and translations. The endeavor to convey India only by those impressions that would naturally be made upon an obsessive Yankee gives the work a certain air of originality—the rarest of all qualities in descriptions of this exotic land. The style is pure and sparkling, although occasionally slick and *dilettantesque*. The love of remark is much in the usual way—*selon les règles* never very exceptionable, and never very profound. An example suffices:

> The thigh-bone trumpets, as well as the abbot's magic drum, devised of two human craniums set together like an hourglass, stretched over by skin and rattled by a small bead swung from a shred of skin—these are spiritually complex items. Magically dangerous, such instruments are sounded only by trained and qualified lamas who have traveled the demonic worlds and know their way through the pavilions of Death.

Mr. Schelling, in connection with Mr. Benjamin Friedlander, was one of the editors and originators of *Jimmy & Lucy's House of "K,"* decidedly the very best journal of critical comment ever published in the Bay Area. A large number of its most interesting papers were the work of Mr. S. The magazine was, upon the whole, a little *too poor* to enjoy extensive popularity—although here I am using an equivocal phrase, for a *poorer* journal with greater resources might have been far more acceptable to the public. I must be understood, then, as first employing the epithet "poor" in the economic sense. The general demeanor of *Jimmy & Lucy's* was *excessively impoverished,* but this character applies more to its external or mechanical appearance than to its essential qualities. Unhappily, magazines and other similar publications are in the beginning judged chiefly by externals. Although admitted as *arbitri elegantiarum* in all points of what is called program or project, people believed *Jimmy & Lucy's* looked very much like other works that had failed through cheapness of thought; and they, the people, had no patience to examine any farther. Caesar's wife was required not only to *be* virtuous but to seem so, and in criticism it is demanded not only that we not be mean, but that we not array ourselves in mean habiliments.

It cannot be said of *Jimmy & Lucy's* exactly that it wanted *force.* It was deficient in power of impression, and this deficiency is to be attributed in part to the exceeding brevity of its articles—brevity that degenerated into mere paragraphism, precluding dissertation or argument, and thus all permanent effect. The magazine had, in fact, some of the worst or most inconvenient features without any of the compensating advantages of an in-house document. The mannerism to which I refer seemed to have its source in undue admiration and consequent imitation of *L=A=N=G=U=A=G=E*.

Mr. Schelling is not unaccomplished, converses readily on many topics, and has a reasonable knowledge of American literature; his proficiency in Buddhist philosophy and Sanskrit has obtained for him a professorship at the Naropa Institute in Boulder, Colorado.

In character he has much general amiability. He is warmhearted, curious, and not easily agitated. His address is somewhat awkward, but "insinuating" from its warmth and vivacity. He speaks continuously and slowly, with a tendency to hold forth which, at times, is by no means unpleasing; he is well postured, and happiest when in motion, or out of doors. In the street he walks with a quick gait, straight-backed, his glance cast about inquisitively.

In person he is six feet tall or so, thin and angularly proportioned, with hair dark and curling. The lines around his eyes give a sense of contentedness; he has, as well, a small, perfect nose, fine teeth, a neatly kept beard, and a smile of peculiar sweetness. The general expression of the countenance when in repose is rather stern, but animation much alters its character. He is probably forty years of age. Recently separated from his wife, Mr. Schelling lives now with the poet Anne Waldman. He has one child, a daughter.

ROBERT GRENIER

Robert Grenier, of Bolinas, is at the same time one of the best and one of the worst poets in America. His productions affect one as a random tuning of the radio: strange, incongruous statements of more than peculiar juxtaposition and snatches of harsh unsustained music. Even his worst nonsense (and some of it is horrible) has an indefinite charm of weirdness and song. We can never be sure that there is *any* meaning in his words—nor is there meaning in many of our catchiest musical phrases—but the effect is very similar in both. His figures of speech are literalness run aground, and his grammar is often nothing at all. Yet there are as fine individual passages in the poems of Grenier, as in those of any poet whatsoever.

In recent years he has abandoned print for calligraphy. Unfortunately, Mr. Grenier's manuscripts are exceedingly illegible for the uninitiated. It is necessary to read one half of them and guess at the balance. The handwriting itself is bold, large, sprawling, and irregular. It is more angular than round, which gives the work an odd appearance if held upside down or in any position other than the proper one. Many of the words are run together so that what is actually a sentence is frequently mistaken for a single word. Some suppose the work to be written in a violent hurry. In fact, each letter is formed with a thorough distinctness and individuality—to the point that readability is compromised. The poems themselves are composed in multicolored layers of overlapping "scrawl"—the color enhancing the work's overall clarity, while at the same time impeding the work's publication by raising the costs of reproduction.

It is in the chirography of such men as Mr. Grenier that we look with certainty for indications of poetic temperament. The life of an artist is incessantly disturbed by those adventitious events testing the natural disposition of a man of the world, allowing his real nature to manifest itself in MS. The poet, who, pressed for time, is often forced to embody a world of heterogeneous perceptions, on scraps of paper, with the stumps of all variety of pencil, will soon find the indoctrinated characters of his psyche crystallize into a substance which would fascinate Watson or Crick; and from chirography so disturbed, it is possible, in theory, to understand everything. In a similar manner, poets who pass through many striking phases of development acquire in each change of style a temporary inflection of the handwriting; the whole resulting, after many years, in a MS. as legible as any topographical map. We see, accordingly, in Mr. Grenier's scrawl each and all of the known idiosyncrasies of his taste and intellect. We recognize at once the scrupulous precision and literality of his style—the love of detail that prompts him to lay out the contents of a book on a Ping-Pong table, so as to comprehend visually the inter-relationships between individual poems. We perceive, too, the disdain of superfluous embellishment which distinguishes his writing, and which leads him to treat the most contingent aspects of language as carriers of meaning. Anyone, from Mr. Grenier's penmanship, might suppose his mind to be what it really is—excessively fixed on minutiae, but active and good-humored.

In person he is short and slender, probably five feet eight inches, with a runner's build, but his limbs are of surprising muscularity and strength, the whole frame indicating prodigious vitality and energy—the latter is, in fact, the leading trait in his character. His head is small, compact—the features in keeping; complexion fair; eyes piercingly bright, lips thin; hair gray, and closely cropped. His age is about fifty-five. His address is the most genial that can be conceived, its *bonhomie* irresistible. He speaks in a loud, clear voice, idiosyncratically, with a constant modulation of tone; his staccato rhythm gives the sense of moment-by-moment thought, as if he were picking a way with bare feet through broken glass. When excited, he speaks with greater speed, though still in clipped rhythm, and lifts up his voice an octave to become, even, squeaky at times. His conversation proper is a peculiar form of performance art, made up of tragedy, comedy, and the broadest of all possible farce. He has an organic, uninhibited flow of talk, always swelling over its boundaries and sweeping everything before it right and left. He is very earnest, intense, emphatic; thumps the table with his fist; shocks the nerves of the fastidious. He was for many years the caretaker of the poet Larry Eigner in Berkeley, but presently lives in Bolinas. His daughter, Amy, well known to readers of Mr. Grenier's early poetry, is now grown. He is unmarried.

EILEEN CORDER

Ms. Corder is in some respects a remarkable woman, and has undoubtedly wrought a deeper impression upon *literary society* than any one of her peers in the Bay Area.

She became first known through her dramatic works, direction of Poet's Theater, and acting. To her performances, she drew large and discriminating audiences in San Francisco, and from elsewhere to the north and east. Her subjects were much in the usual way of these exhibitions, including comic as well as serious pieces, chiefly in verse. Her principal collaborators were the language poets (she was married at the time to Nick Robinson, younger brother of Kit), and that group's particular brand of wit was well stocked in her theater, as a quick perusal of Ms. Corder's first book, *Busy Wrong*, reveals. In her earliest stage work she evinced no *very* refined taste, but was probably influenced by the physical rather than verbal possibilities of her *programmes*. She spoke well; her voice was melodious; her youth and general appearance excited interest, but, upon the whole, she produced no great result, and the enterprise may be termed unsuccessful, although the language poets, as was their wont, spoke in the most sonorous tone of her achievement.

It was during this period of stage work that her name, prefixed to an occasional play or review in the magazines, first attracted an attention that, but for the acquaintance with her quackier advocates, it might not have attracted.

These early plays may be said to be *cleverly* written. They are lively, nonsensical, *avant-garde,* and scintillate with a species of sarcastic wit that might be termed good were it in any respect original. In point of style—that is to say, of mere American English, her plays are very respectable. Her scant attempts at prose showed promise also. One of the best of these, written with Mr. Nick Robinson, is entitled "Skeletons in the Dressing Room," published in *Jimmy & Lucy's House of "K"* for November 1985. The subject, Luis Valdez, is exceedingly interesting, and prefigures the later development of her work.

In one of her last productions as director of Poet's Theater, she mounted a performance of Leslie Scalapino's *Leg,* a play that she presented in Los Angeles as well as San Francisco, with a cast that included many of the younger poets on the scene. Shortly after this tour, her life took a sharp turn in another direction. Her marriage ended and she became the companion of Jeff Gburek, an actor in her company. She also quit her long-time association with Small Press Distribution to join a collective bakery. (She has since earned her license to teach in the public schools.) During this time, Ms. Corder made her first attempts at writing verse.

In looking carefully over her first poems, I find no one work entitled to commendation as a whole; in very few of them do I observe even noticeable passages, and I confess that I am surprised and disappointed at this result of my inquiry; nor can I make up my mind that there is not much latent poetical power in Ms. Corder. From a sequence published in Mr. Gburek's magazine, *'Aql,* I copy a single section as the most favorable specimen which I have seen of her early verse:

lights come on every 30 seconds then every 15 they
are unbearably bright I have to close my eyes

blinded after several assaults and in a fit I wheel
around the children cry my eyes pop open as if I
can't breathe

then I look I look
light blares from behind me I see clearly the strain
in their faces pulled in afraid to afraid of being
caught

up in the dish the sun burns another world at
poverty

each step quick and you jump

black suns appear to us they fall below the upper horizon
black suns wide open again pulsing
heart-barking men stand outside the plastic barriers
bright yellow which cut
they cut flesh
cut as we freeze whatever pose we had hoped to forget
black suns that are
wax
and then the long falling away
long no longer falling away

In this there is much force, and the idea in the italicized lines is so well *put* as to have the air of originality. Indeed, I am not sure that the thought of "heart-barking men" is *not* original—in any event, it is exceedingly *natural* and impressive. I say "natural" because, in any unfriendly encounter with the police, when official barriers, no matter how frangible, keep the crowd at a far remove—in other words, when the outcry of the populace is rendered irrelevant to all proceedings—then does its heart-felt anger become a kind of "barking." The whole poem is of higher merit than any other I find with her name attached. In general, she is sentimental through excess of empathy. This is even truer of a later sequence of poems (gathered in a special issue of Mr. Gburek's magazine, under the title *unazonasacra*) written after an extended visit to Italy.

Her first return to the stage after the dissolution of Poet's Theater was her political play, "I Can See What You're Thinking." Much of this play's success is referable to the interest felt in her subject matter: the history of prisons.

The play is not without fault. It may be commended especially for the variety of its perspectives. The worst acting dramas in the world are what activists call *Guerilla Theater;* the intellect of an audience can never safely be harassed by dogmatism. The numerous recitations from history books and sociological studies are, in this regard, a serious defect. A political play should in all cases be concerned with *action*—with nothing else. Whatever cannot be explained by such action should be communicated in a pamphlet handed out at the door.

Since separating from Mr. Gburek, Ms. Corder has published on her own a pamphlet of remarkable poems, sent others to the magazines, and written several more which remain in manuscript. These poems, naive in form but forceful in their sympathies, afford glimpses (I cannot help thinking) of a genius as yet unrevealed, except in her capacity of actress.

In this capacity, if she be true to herself, she will assuredly win a very enviable distinction. She has done well, wonderfully well, in lyric poetry and dramatic monologue; but if she knew her own strength, she would confine herself nearly altogether to the depicting (in poetry not less than on stage) of the more gentle tendencies and more harsh sufferings of the poor. Her empathy for the latter is intense. In the utterance of the truly generous, of the really noble, of the unaffectedly committed utterance, we see her bosom heave, her cheek grow pale, her limbs tremble, her lip quiver, and nature's own tear rush impetuously to the eye.

Indeed, the great charm of her manner is naturalness. She looks, speaks, and moves with a well-controlled impulsiveness, as different as can be conceived from the customary rant and cant, the hack conventionality of the spoken-word claque. Her voice is rich and voluminous, and although by no means powerful, it is so well managed as to seem so. Her utterance is singularly distinct, warm with its Ohio inflections, the sole blemish being an occasional loftiness of tone, adopted probably from her former companion, Mr. Gburek. Her reading could scarcely be improved. Her action is distinguished by an ease and self-possession that would do credit to a veteran. Her step is the perfection of grace. Often have I watched her for hours with the closest scrutiny, yet never for an instant did I observe her in an attitude of the least awkwardness or even constraint, while many of her seemingly impulsive gestures spoke in loud terms of the woman of genius, of the poet imbued with the profoundest sentiment of the beautiful in motion.

Her figure appears slight, even fragile, but years of labor have lent an iron to her muscle. Her face is remarkably fine and of that precise character best adapted to the stage. The forehead is, perhaps, the least prepossessing feature, although it is by no means an unintellectual one. Her hair is long and straight, a light auburn (when not dyed red), often tied back in a braided ponytail. The eyes are brown, with flecks of green and yellow, and lively like a child's. The nose is somewhat bulbous, pierced with a gold stud, and indicative of earthy dignity. This quality is also shown in the somewhat excessive roundness of the cheeks. The mouth is small, with flexible lips, capable of the most instantaneous and surprising of expressions. It is quite impossible to conceive a more radiantly beautiful smile. Her daughter Columbine is a constant companion at all public events, exhibiting a spirited brashness that many a poet has attempted without success to emulate.

MICHAEL PALMER

Michael Palmer was a well-known teacher of Poetics at the New College of California. If not absolutely the best, he is at least considered the best purely lyrical poet in America. In Paris, his poetic acquirements are more sincerely respected than those of any of our countrymen. His additions to the tradition of Baudelaire, Mallarmé, and Jabès are there justly regarded as evincing a nice perception of method and an accurate as well as extensive taste, but his *Sun* has superseded the work of the younger of the post-war Frenchmen altogether. Many of Palmer's publications have been adopted as textbooks by our own aspiring writers—an honor to be properly understood only by those acquainted with the many high requisites for attaining it. Under the name "Analytic Lyric," the poet's project has enjoyed as wide an influence as any save those of Professors Bernstein and Howe. As a commentator (if not exactly critic), he may rank with any of his day, and has evinced powers very unusual in men who devote their lives to poetical lore. His propriety with regard to aesthetic matters is very remarkable—in this particular he is always to be relied on. The trait manifests itself even in his dress, which is a model of neatness and symmetry, exceeding in these respects anything of the kind with which I am acquainted. (Indeed, the photograph given on the back cover of Mr. Palmer's collection *First Figure* made a stir at the time of publication, for showing how neatly ironed he kept the crease in his denim trousers.) In poetry, perhaps, the propriety is somewhat *too* neat and *too* regular, as well as too diminutive, to be called sublime; it might be mistaken at any time, however, for a very elaborate copper-plate engraving of the sublime.

But his poetics, although fully in keeping—so far as precision is concerned—with his mental character, is, in its entire freedom from flourish or superfluity, as much *out* of keeping with his verbal style. In his interviews, he is singularly Creeleyesque—except in those places where he is, instead, Duncanian.

An attempt was made not long ago to prepossess the public against his three North Point books, the most important of his works, by getting up a hue and cry of imitation—in the case of all similar books, this is the most preposterous accusation in the world, although, from its very preposterousness, one not easily rebutted. Obviously, the design in any volume of verse is, in the first place, to make an appealing collection of successful effects, and the poet who should be weak enough to ignore indisputable success for the mere purpose of winning credit with a few bookish men and women for originality deserves to be dubbed, by the public at least, an incompetent. There are very few points of poetical craftsmanship which are not the common property of "the learned" throughout the world, and in composing any poetry of any sort at all, recourse is unscrupulously and even necessarily had in all cases to similar works which have preceded. In availing themselves of these latter, however, it is the practice of quacks to assemble page after page by mixing and matching the qualities of several different authors, making a havoc of their disparate styles, or entering a grotesque alteration in this or that particular, but preserving throughout the achievement of these prior models, their vocabulary, structures of feeling, etc. etc., while everything is so completely *confused* or *repackaged* as to leave no room for a direct charge of imitation; and this is considered and lauded as originality. Now, those who, in availing themselves of the labors of their predecessors (and it is clear that all poets *must* avail themselves of such labors)—they who shall ape *faithfully* the effects to be desired without attempt at palming off the achievement as original are certainly not imitators, even if they fail to make *direct* acknowledgement of indebtedness. They are unquestionably *less* imitative than the disingenuous and contemptible quacks who wriggle themselves, as above explained, into a reputation for originality, a reputation quite out of place in a case of this kind—the public, of course, never caring a straw whether a poet be original or derivative. These attacks upon the San Francisco aesthete are to be attributed to a *clique* of pedants across the Bay, gentlemen and ladies envious of his success, and whose own "collections" are noticeable only for the singular patience and ingenuity with which their dovetailing chicanery is concealed from the *public* eye.

Mr. Palmer is, perhaps, fifty-two years of age; about five feet ten inches in height; average build; hair brown and tousled; eyes dark and passive; mouth mal-formed—the lips thin and asymmetrically twisted, having a certain stiffness; the smile particularly Quixotic. His address in general is slow, reasoned, cordial, full of circumspect intelligence. His whole air is *distingue* in the best understanding of the term—that is, he would impress anyone at first sight with the idea of his being no ordinary man. He has qualities, indeed, which would have insured him eminent success in any pursuit; and there are times when his friends are half disposed to regret his exclusive devotion to literature. He was one of the originators of the well-remembered journal *Joglars,* his associate in the conduct and proprietorship being Clark Coolidge. His wife is an architect and the two share a daughter. New writings are eagerly awaited.

NATHANIEL MACKEY

I am not sure that Mackey is not the greatest of poets. The uncertainty attending the public conception of the term "poet" alone prevents me from demonstrating that he is. Other bards produce effects that are, now and then, otherwise produced than by what we call poems, but Mackey produces an effect that only a poem does. His alone are idiosyncratic poems. By the enjoyment or non-enjoyment of his "Song of the Andoumboulou," or of the various parts of "Mu," I would test anyone's ideal sense.

There are passages in his works that rivet a conviction I have taken from Spicer, that the *indefinite* is an element in the true *poiesis*. Why do some persons fatigue themselves in attempts to unravel such fantasy-pieces as "Ohnedaruth's Day Begun"? It would better avail one to unweave the "*ventum textilem.*" If the author did not deliberately propose to himself a suggestive indefiniteness of meaning, with the view of bringing about a definitiveness of vague and therefore of spiritual *effect*—this work, at least, arose from the silent analytical promptings of a poetic genius which, in its supreme development, embodies all orders of intellectual capacity.

I *know* that indefiniteness is an element of the true music—I mean of the true musical expression. Give to it any undue decision—imbue it with any very real determinate tone—and you deprive it, at once, of its ethereal, its ideal, its intrinsic and essential character. You dispel its luxury of dream. You dissolve the atmosphere of the mystic upon which it floats. You exhaust it of its breath of faery. It now becomes a tangible and easy appreciable idea—a thing of the earth, earthy. It has not, indeed, lost its power to please, but all the distinctiveness of that power has vanished. And to the uncultivated talent, or to the unimaginative apprehension, this deprivation of its most delicate grace will be, not infrequently, a recommendation. A determinateness of music is sought—and often by writers who should know better—as a means to wisdom rather than rejected as foolishness. Thus we have even from a high authority like Prof. Mackey attempts at a *stipulation* of music. Who can forget the silliness of certain portions of his *Bedouin Hornbook?* What man or woman of taste must but laugh at the interminable drums, trumpets, blunderbusses, and cowry shells? "The insensate rhythm," writes Mackey's musician N., "into whose order we'd been inducted maintained neither a directly dialectical nor a directly diametrical but an oblique centrifugal relation to the metronomic center whose initiatic split between 'bottom' and 'top' now seemed so remote." The word "initiatic" describes well a quality of music Mackey's fiction *strains* to attain, but which his verse quite carries easily, as a boat does its wake.

Mackey's prose abounds in minute tonal lapses sufficient to assure me that—in common with all poets living and dead—he has neglected to make precise investigation of the principles of rhetoric; but on the other hand, so perfect is his instinct for the rhythms of speech that, like the late Rahsaan Roland Kirk, he seems *to see with his ear*.

Professor Mackey is nearing fifty; he is of slender build and medium height, skin a warm brown; hair short and eyes cat-like, alert. He moves with a princely gait and his countenance expresses sensibility and benevolence. He converses slowly and with perfect deliberation. He teaches at U.C. Santa Cruz, where he is well known for his radio show, Tanganyika Strut. Mr. Mackey never appears in public without donning a characteristic little cap, no small number of which he appears to have collected. His magazine *Hambone* is scrupulously edited, a rare occurrence these days. He is a fine critic. He is married to the French scholar Pascal Gaitet.

BEVERLY DAHLEN

Beverly Dahlen is known chiefly as the author of *A Reading*. The publication of this work, however, was never *completed*. Only three volumes of this "interminable" poem (as the author herself defines it) have appeared, and we have yet to see a collection of her remarkable essays. It is to be hoped that we shall yet have the latter.

Of the volumes of poems issued, one, entitled *Out of the Third*, includes a sequence of so many peculiar excellencies that I copied the whole of it, although quite long, into my notebook. Entitled "Tree," it will remind many a reader of Tchelitchew's fine picture, "Hide-and-Seek," although between poem and painting there is no more than a very admissible resemblance.

I quote a section from "Tree" (the fifth) by way of bringing the piece to the attention of any one who may have overlooked it.

my mother is a foreigner
her mother spoke nothing
but Finn
        she died
        strangled

of fishbones
cancer
and salt

            (crossed over
            oceans
            years ago

      the old country: what is it?

      somebody told me
      Finn is a language
      that has no root

The vein of nostalgia opened here should be, so far as a single sequence is concerned, defended as a legitimate subject for art, conferring high pleasure on a numerous and cultivated class of minds. Less gifted writers, in their continuous and uniform insistence on this subject, have exceeded the proper limits of nostalgia and impinged upon the bathetic. Skirting this risk, Ms. Dahlen's early writings abound, nevertheless, in lofty merit, and have, in especial, some passages of rich imagination and exquisite pathos. In this endeavor, she is aided by a high order of historical consciousness. For example:

The Great Plains a burial mound
The ditched bodies of women
and Indians

You creaked over the Divide.
Tons of books in foreign languages
heaped in the backs of wagons.
Corinthian columns lashed on pack-mules
split in the snow.
Oxen in the salt deserts
collapsing under the weight
of Egyptian pyramids.

The late west

Abbeys and cathedrals on the swarming backs
of Chinese slaves. Hordes of Irish
dragging the Tower of London
towards the cascades. Rafted down
the Columbia through the red snow.
At the mouth a pot of boiling salt
and the clocks and compasses of Lewis and Clark.
Sacajawea a bewildered pillar pointing
at the sea.

It must be confessed, however, that this last passage reminds us forcibly of the *Catalpa* of Kenneth Irby.

With *A Reading,* Ms. Dahlen began an open-ended work in poetry and prose, diaristic in part, which took as its method of composition the Freudian technique of free association. This method, we have heard, "specifically requires a non-judgmental attitude toward thought," its avowed purpose being the evasion of inhibitions, resistances, censorship, and taboos. Thus, according to Norman O. Brown, "To experience Freud is to partake a second time of forbidden fruit." Notwithstanding a resistance to certain conclusions of Freud's (in particular, those tainted by misogyny), Ms. Dahlen has accepted Prof. Brown's comment and even amplified its meaning, declaring, "Even in my apostasy I had to admit that knowledge is forbidden, not just some knowledge, but all of it."

The comments cited here are taken from Ms. Dahlen's 80 Langton Street Talk, "Forbidden Knowledge." This Talk is, at many points, well reasoned, and, as a clear *résumé* of psychoanalytic thinking, it may be considered commendable. Its premises, however (shared by all who write on this vexed topic, whether Freudian, Lacanian, or Kristevan), are admitted only very partially by the world at large—a fact of which the author affects to be unconcerned. Neither does she make the slightest attempt at bringing forward one persuasive argument in their favor. Any one of ordinary self-consciousness would have adduced and maintained a dozen.

"A Reading 7" is the concluding section of the first volume, and itself concludes with an exceedingly vigorous stanza, putting me not a little in mind of a scattered, but more intellectual, Spicer:

> haunted certain core words
> decentered
> at the shifting boundary
> where in a starburst in a silver dollar in a candybar
> where stalagmites a word associated with caves winter
> the redcross the weather blue
> his hand on my crotch these were loaded words I told you so
> birda flying out of the mill in the desert spots on the picture
> picture birds a particular
> he looked down, he walked out, he cut the fish bait.
> beet beet
> then made over a package wrapped
> signifier to signifier the signifier buried

in the backyard a bottle of white rum he dug it up
and on top of that this
happened

I fully agree with Prof. DuPlessis (Rachel Blau) that the ancient scribes had, in their habit of writing over imperfectly erased text, no term more appropriate than "palimpsest" for those "incisions of memory and event, little traces and fleetings which may recede, may suddenly rear up." We discover a similar occurrence in *A Reading*.

Passages like this one are worthy of the author of *A Blue Fire:*

there is a mark-up, it is difficult to resist it, the filth and
greed. some made gold from that shit, the squeamish bottom.
an archaic word preserved here, *dross,* a euphemism. shit is
fine for everybody else. speaking of one's own, we say *dross*.
thereby preserved from it, the veiling over. the displacement
from below upward, all symbol systems point in another
direction.

And this, in reference to the psychic toll of life in the city, is natural and forcible:

arrested. stopped right there. she had been coming up the
street in a car without the proper license. he had been
following her. there was nothing but to go on alone. she
turned the corner. he was nowhere in sight. the world was
not transformed. there was no use in it. the exchange was
meaningless. it was the desire for meaning itself.

This again is exceedingly spirited:

in a fell swoop
these rocks these bands

in which voice breaks paper
paper covers rock
rock smashes hand scissors
regardless

one thing over another
in a climbing power

By the way, how happens it that in the intricate sequence that follows (taken from section eight), the "object of all this learning to be undone," the unravelling of the mind's "glowing thread," is named by the poet *aphasia* rather than *a reading?*

when retyping it was found out there was no standard text
but errors crept in which drifted changing the meaning
ultimately and there was no way in which comparing notes
the original could be discerned. there was no ideal text. there
was nothing to check it against. there were not corrections to
be made. no authority to whom regressing, reverting.

. . . she had her
comeuppance but she chose that way. she wanted to stay
there inside that and who could not say better not to have made
that compromise. . . .

. . . one would have thought
why bother. what possible meaning inhabiting that chaos. a
desire for meaning itself.

. . . that stanza
deliberately broken up. walls and headstones. a resting
place. finally.

she who is not anyone, anonymous, animas, she would not be
learned any other way, not as a name, but entirely. how she
would have a name now that names were away and settling.
she wanted to diddle that. . . .

the object of all this learning to be undone. there is a glowing
thread, twined, aphasia would undo it.

When in the lines of an earlier section, number five (partly a letter to DuPlessis), aphasia is taken up, Dahlen states:

an other is so
much an hallucination it's scary. I don't know what I speak to.

here, because you are not here, looking back I see it. . . .
that X which was laid over it ages ago. no wonder I am a
woman. now.
impossible. woman, that impossibility. that it takes place at all
in any of us.
"takes place." take it. there's a word for you. by god, it makes
me angry to
think that "take" appears here so easily, or any word, upon
the 'mystic writing pad.'

. . . it is heartless. I had no heart for it. it
is what is lost that must be claimed. not found (impossibility)
but claimed
as loss. to say it.

In section fifteen, a similar exception is taken to the notion of a simple, instantaneous undoing through aphasia. Here Ms. Dahlen puts her point forth with even greater force, if that is possible, than before:

if the word
does not arise it will fall back, the thing itself, it will fall again
into that ocean where it is not biodegradable. it is not truly
broken
up into its constituent parts. it is a hunk of something
indigestible.

Ms. Dahlen has all the imagination of Ms. Scalapino, but with more refined taste; she has all the curiosity of Mr. Silliman, but with more discernment, and (surprisingly) equal ambition. She comes closer than any other writer, living or dead, to composing a poem in "open form."

My extracts are already extended to a greater length than I had designed or than comports with the plan of these papers, or I would make several others. *The Egyptian Poems* have hieratic power. "Of the

Origin of the Gods: A Catechism," in particular, will touch a chord in the hearts of all who read it.

Ms. Dahlen is about fifty years of age, of medium height, with pale complexion, round cheeks, and her head a bowl of silver hair cut straight at the neck. Her countenance expresses sensibility and benevolence. She converses slowly and with perfect deliberation. In no respect can she be termed beautiful (as the world understands the epithet), but the question, "Is it really possible that she is not so?" is very frequently asked, and *most* frequently by those who most intimately know her.

TED PEARSON

Ted Pearson is the author of *Evidence* and two subsequent works, *Planetary Gear* and *Acoustic Masks,* as well as two or three pieces of prose. Although not a language poet himself, he has made common cause with that claque, sharing in particular their strong predilection for Zukofsky. This predilection stems in the case of the language poets to the poet's scientific method; however, with Mr. Pearson, it stems from Zukofsky's style.

The language poets were decidedly luckier in their emphasis. If ever a mortal "wreaked his thoughts upon expression," it was Zukofsky. If ever a poet sang—as mechanical bird sings—perfectly—but without feeling and with utter disregard for the end result—that poet was the author of *80 Flowers*. Of Art—beyond that which is instinctive with Genius—he either had little or disdained all. He loved, on the other hand, that Rule which is an emanation of science, because his own soul was mathematics in itself. His rhapsodies are but the rough notes—the stenographic memoranda of controlled experiments—memoranda which, because they were all-sufficient for his own intelligence, he cared not to be at the trouble of writing out in full for humankind. In all his works, we find no conception thoroughly wrought—for this reason he is the most fatiguing of poets. Yet he wearies in saying too little rather than too much. What, in him, seems the diffuseness of one idea is the conglomerate concision of many: and it is this species of concision that renders him obscure. With such a man, to imitate was out of the question. It would have served no purpose, for he spoke to his own inclination alone, which would have comprehended no alien tongue. Thus he was profoundly original. His quaintness arose from intuitive perception of that truth to which Bacon alone has given distinct utterance: "there is no exquisite Beauty which has not some strangeness in its proportions." But whether obscure, original, or quaint, Zukofsky had no *affectations*. He was at all times serious and sincere.

From his *ruins,* there sprang into existence, affronting the Heavens, a tottering and fantastic *pagoda,* in which the salient angels, tipped with mad jangling bells, were the idiosyncratic *faults* of the original—faults which cannot be considered such in view of his purposes, but which are monstrous when we regard his works as addressed to mankind. In large part through the labors of Cid Corman, a "school" arose—if that absurd term must still be employed—a mere *style*—upon the basis of the Zukofsky who had none, properly so called. Innumerable young men, dazzled with the glare and bewildered by the *bizarrerie* of the lightning that flickered through the clouds of *"A,"* had no trouble whatever in heaping up imitative vapors, but, for the lightning, were forced to be content with its *spectrum,* in which the *bizarrerie* appeared without the fire. Nor were mature minds unimpressed by the contemplation of a greater and more mature; and thus, gradually, into a methodical school of all stylelessness—of obscurity, quaintness, and concision—were interwoven the out of place exoticism of Bunting, and the more anomalous metaphysics of Oppen. Matters were now verging to their worse; at length, in *Ted Pearson,* poetic inconsistency attained its extreme. But it was precisely this extreme (for the greatest truth and the greatest error are scarcely two points in a circle) which, following the style of all extremes, wrought in him (Pearson) a natural and inevitable misgiving; leading him first to shrink wholly into, and secondly to investigate, this schoolish manner, and finally to winnow, from its best elements, a truer and purer style. His later books transform as wholly as cocoons do caterpillars the tinkling sentimentality of the early work. From *Acoustic Masks:*

Carrier waves
    in holophrase

        redact the hymnal
            from its hymns

a wanton por nada
          ebbs and flows

                    in a tango of
                              phantom limbs

But the process is not yet complete; and partly for this reason, but chiefly on account of the mere fortuitousness of the mental and moral combination that shall unite in one person (if *ever* it shall) the Zukofskyan *mechanical* and Pearsonian *poetic* sense with the most profound Understanding (based both in *Experience* and *Analysis*) and the sternest Will that will properly blend and rigorously control all—chiefly, I say, because such combination of seeming antagonisms will be only a "happy chance"—the world has never yet seen the noblest poem which, possibly, *can* be composed.

In person Mr. Pearson stands about five feet ten inches; hair long and black with traces of gray, usually tied tightly back in ponytail, but sometimes loose, and wild looking, in a manner very reminiscent of William Everson. His beard is neatly trimmed. In dress he is apt to affect a down to earth elegance, priding himself especially on personal acquaintance with both artists and workingmen. He walks softly and slowly. His address is quite good, carefully considered and insinuating. His conversation has now and then the merit of humor, but he has a perfect mania for gaining the last word, and it is impossible to utter a sentence in his presence without feeling the pressure of Mr. Pearson's own point of view—whether he agrees or disagrees. He has much warmth of feeling, and is not a person to be disliked, although very apt to irritate and annoy. From Menlo Park Mr. Pearson departed some time hence to Ithaca, N.Y. He is now resident in Buffalo.

DAVID MELNICK

During his long public silence, Melnick composed a number of poetical works, most of which were consigned to the wastebasket, others kept for want of bother. Since breaking his silence, he has published one section of a work called *Men in Aida*. The entire work circulated for a while among the small presses but found no takers.

Melnick's silence followed self-publication of a work called *Pcoet*, an extreme species of nonsense that contained (in Melnick's own conception) a queer form of Projective Verse. In *Men in Aida,* Melnick has contrived an equally extreme epic—a transliteration (*not* translation) of Books 1–3 of Homer's *Iliad.* In this latter work of Melnick's, there is at least some scholarship and subject matter to be had, if equally queer and nonsensical. Melnick regards this exercise as the best of his compositions. A first book, *Eclogs,* is also worth seeking out, as are the surviving chapters of an unfinished dissertation, published long ago in the magazines.

Melnick is now nearing sixty years old, if he has not yet reached that age, and bears on his person the marks of long suffering; he has lost a lover to AIDS; his hair and beard became gray many years ago; just now he is suffering from severe obscurity, and from this it can scarcely be expected he will recover.

In figure he is short and round. His forehead is rather low, but broad. His eyes are large but weak; the nose flat; the mouth large. His features in general have all the Mediterranean mobility of the *Sephardim;* their expression is animated and full of intelligence. He speaks slowly, with a voice that bubbles warmly from deep within a melancholy solitude. He is sweet, frank, generous, chivalrous, warmly attached to his friends, and self-effacing to a fault. His *Graecophilia* is unbounded, and he is quite enthusiastic in his defense of the language poets as well.

STEPHEN RODEFER

We shall address ourselves to *Rodefer*'s poetical achievement elsewhere, and so confine ourselves to the author's critical work. We note in passing, however, that Mr. Messerli has neglected to include Rodefer's poetry in the massive anthology *From the Other Side of the Century,* selecting in his place Mr. Rodefer's own former pupil, Jean Day, as well as such lesser worthies as Carl Rakosi, Joseph Ceravolo, Ron Padgett, Michael Brownstein, Lewis Warsh, Marjorie Welish, John Godfrey, and Joan Retallack—we will desist from listing any further, though we might rattle off half the occupants of Mr. Messerli's "zoo" before finding reason to hold our tongue. That each of the men and women listed above has written a work of real wit and intelligence none will gainsay; that each of these men and women has written an entire *book* of wit and intelligence is open to question; that their work, taken as a whole, excels Mr. Rodefer's in either of these two qualities, *or any other,* only a dunderhead, or a person with a grudge, would dare to claim. *The man* Rodefer is admittedly peculiar; his qualities are *not* entirely admirable. That he is given to churlish behavior is a commonly held opinion; that a postmodern Palgrave, as Mr. Messerli styles himself, would exact retribution from Rodefer *the poet* is contemptible —a dereliction of aesthetic duty—the one crime of which Rodefer remains assuredly innocent. In Palgrave's own era the prig who so attempted would be hounded forever from office, and put in the stocks to boot, like any other transgressor of professional duty or social rank (for anthologists are, in matters of art, the writer's acknowledged inferior). From François Villon to Gregory Corso, from Richard Savage to Etheridge Knight, the ne'er-do-wells of poetry have suffered *personally* while prospering (as Blake would put it) *in eternity.* No more, it would seem; our decorous era will permit only team players into the annals of Art. Criminals, cads, and drunks are not to be considered.

But to return to the task at hand.

Mr. Rodefer is little known as a critic *by his writings,* either to the public or in literary society, but he has made a great many "sensations" *personally.* I am not sure that his published interviews give an accurate sense of this aspect of his address. His published correspondence, privately circulated by the author himself in photocopy, is more revealing.

One of his earliest substantial critical works—if not the earliest— was "Prologue to Language Doubling," published in one of the Bay Area's many "little" magazines. It is a dashing, reckless Thesis, brimful of talent and audacity. Of course it was covertly admired by the few and loudly condemned by all of the many who can fairly be said to have seen it at all. It had no great circulation. There was something wrong, I fancy, in the mode of its issue.

"Language Doubling" was followed in a later issue of the same magazine by a lengthy essay on the work of Ron Silliman, published under the *nom de plume* of Thomas White. It made much noise in the literary world, and no little curiosity was excited in regard to its author, who was generally supposed to be Leslie Scalapino's husband. There were some grounds for this supposition, the gentleman's name being "Thomas White," but the name was taken, in fact, from Robert Creeley, who used it on occasion in the *Black Mountain Review.* The title of the essay, "What I See in the Silliman Project," recalls a well-known work by Edward Dorn, though the piece itself is in the Mary McCarthy or Randall Jarrell way. The argument is an attempt to reconcile his simultaneous amazement and boredom with the "relentless *indication*" that Mr. Silliman has taken as his style. "The work is isotropic without variation. It is fractal, but there is no long shot. The style flirts with the stereotype of itself. . . . Because everything is equal, nothing is distinct. Because no subordination is allowed, no emphasis is possible." The validity of this reading is assumed on the somewhat unphilosophical ground that "what Nietzsche termed 'the strength to forget' " is an essential element of the true poesy. "Innovation based on repetition," we are told, "is a kind of mind control. What is missing in this writing is interruption and rest—and a barbaric intuition for change." The author himself supposes that this argument justifies the intuitions of his own barbarism, and thus he strives to reach beyond his grasp, for if "the ultimate difficulty for a writer now is to be writing in a culture no longer interested in literacy," it must be agreed that the critic's task is equally difficult for a similar reason—and with a similar conclusion. In other words, the only thing proved is the rather bullish proposition that the best warnings may go unheeded, that "there may be nothing to be done . . . except to make the record." Presumably, Mr. R.'s own "relentless *indication*" is bound to suffer the same fate as Mr. S.'s.

Partly on account of what most persons would term their provocativeness, partly also on account of the prevalent idea that Mr. Rodefer had breached decorum by siding with Mr. Duncan, and *against* General Watten, in an argument played out in the pages of *Poetry Flash*, "Prologue to Language Doubling" and "What I See in the Silliman Project" were, by the San Francisco literati, most unscrupulously misrepresented and abused. The literati of New York were, it appears, quick to follow in condemnation, and Mr. Rodefer thought proper to avenge his wrongs by the composition of a broadside leveled at the cliquishness of the poetry world in general, but more especially at Mr. Bernstein, already a professor of poetry in Buffalo, and a man to whom the author bore something of a grudge. This broadside, though intended for a symposium in the journal *Tyuonyi*, was subsequently titled "Dupe Check," and contained such platitudes as, "The only reason for a poet to live is to write," and, "In many ways poetry is for the rich." Owing to the piece's rejection by the editors, no great many copies were read, but the few that got into circulation made quite a hubbub, and with reason, for the broadside was not only bitter but also personal in the last degree. It was, moreover, very threateningly obscure—*paranoid* is, perhaps, the more appropriate word. This trait was exacerbated, no doubt, by the fact that the language poets, without exception, or nearly so, had begun to shun Mr. Rodefer whenever possible, without taking pains to grant him his due as a poet—a fact already mentioned in my introductory paragraph.

"Dupe Check" belongs to a species of allegory at which Mr. Rodefer surpasses all other poets. He has a knack for transmuting grievance into gold—or, if not gold, then a reasonable facsimile. Even in a piece like "Dupe Check" one can find lines of real merit. Here, for example, is a snub raised to the status of universal truth:

> Someone will give what was supposed to be your copy to someone else. Then you will be given someone else's copy. It will all be inscribed. And this is what is called context or society.

A similar work, "Automatic Toll of Criticism," is more casual. I do not think it especially meritorious. It contains, however, a few truth-telling and discriminative statements, and its epigraph (from Kristeva) is well worthy citation:

> All criticism is doomed to analyze only its own perceptions. What the critic is finally saying is, this is my fantasy when faced with the work. What is essential for the interpreter is an ethics of modesty: that he not consider his own perception is the only one.

Mr. Rodefer would do well to take these sentiments to heart.

The author's best effort in this type of prose is "The Library of Label," a remembrance of his unhappy employment at the Archive of New Poetry in San Diego, written for a collection of statements by librarian poets:

> The universe, which others call the Library, is composed of an indefinite and perhaps infinite number of hexes, where one may sleep standing up and satisfy necessity. Paranoia is the logical exaggeration of what is called "being careful." You can slip a disc, and the record is erased completely. Strindberg thought he

> had enemies trying to subdue him with electromagnetic fields, yet he was the Shakespeare of Sweden. I was once the Shakespeare of the local collapsible hexagon labeled the Library, the synergetic ranch. It is a name loved from birth, but married now to the inaccessible circumference.

I am not aware that, since removing to England, Mr. Rodefer has written anything more in prose, apart from *Chateau d'If,* an unpublished novelette. This work is highly spoken of by those who have seen it, but is, I believe, principally a compendium or compilation of his experiences in Cambridge. An extended notation on Ted Greenwald was printed in the catalogue for 80 Langton Street.

In personal character Mr. R. is one of the most remarkable men I have yet had the pleasure of meeting. He is undoubtedly one of "Nature's own noblemen," full of generosity, courage, ardor—chivalrous in every respect, but, unhappily, carrying his ideas of chivalry, or rather of independence, to the point of Quixotism, if not of absolute insanity. He has no doubt been misapprehended, and therefore wronged by the world; but he should not fail to remember that the source of the wrong lay in his own idiosyncrasy—one altogether unintelligible and unappreciable by the mass of mankind.

He has been a hanger-on of some of the strangest and most influential, and some of the most strife-ridden scenes in the history of our letters. His talent for turning up unexpectedly is a matter of legend. His travels are extensive, and at various times he has made his home in New York, New Mexico, California, England and France. His aesthetic sense is to be highly respected, although he is apt to swear somewhat too roundly by "systematic derangement of the senses." Discretion is not Mr. Rodefer's *forte.*

He is about fifty-two or three—certainly not more than fifty-five years of age. As a husband, a father, a friend, he has met with nearly equal disappointment, and has absolutely disappointed in each capacity. Two of his most marked characteristics are fixity of purpose and a passion for being mysterious. His most intimate friends seem to know nothing of his movements, and it is folly to expect from him a direct answer about anything. He has, apparently, taught; pretends to knowledge of French (of which he is profoundly ignorant); has been engaged in an infinite variety of affairs and occupations, and now, I believe, lives by shuttling between artist colonies. In person he is well made, or was until recently, when years of drinking began to show in a jowlier face and thicker middle. He is probably six feet tall, or six feet one, muscular and active; hair blonde and complexion ruddy; fine teeth; blues eyes often damp with feeling, even velvety; the whole expression of the countenance manly, frank, and prepossessing in the highest degree. Mr. Rodefer's recitations are among the very best of their kind—a strong voice, shaken with emotion or nervousness, declaiming melodious but nonsensical lines as if they were the most obvious things to say in the world.

ROBERT DUNCAN

The name of Duncan is at least as well established in the poetical world as that of any American since World War II. Our principal postwar poets are, perhaps, most frequently named in this order—Ginsberg, Rich, Ashbery, Plath, Creeley, Lowell, O'Hara, Bishop, Merrill, Baraka, Brooks, Olson, Duncan, and so on—Duncan coming last in the series, but holding, in fact, a rank in the public opinion quite equal to that of Brooks. The accuracy of the arrangement made above may, indeed, be questioned. For my own part, I should have it thus—Creeley, O'Hara, Olson, Baraka, Merrill, Brooks, Ashbery, Duncan, Ginsberg, Plath, Lowell, Bishop, Rich; and, estimating rather the poetic capacity than the poems actually accomplished, there are about two dozen comparatively unread poets whom I would place in the series between Merrill and Ashbery, while there are about a dozen whom I should assign a position between Ashbery and Plath. Two dozen at least might find room between Plath and Rich—this latter poet, I fear, owing a very large portion of her reputation to her attainments in prose. One or two poets now in my mind's eye I should have no hesitation in posting even above Merrill—still not intending this as very extravagant praise.

It is noticeable, however, that in the arrangement I attribute to the popular understanding, the order observed is nearly, if not exactly, that of the appeal—the personal appeal—of the individual poets. Those most read own the most readily idealized public personae, and this is not to be accounted for by mere reference to the old saw—that it is better to lead by example than precept. Intellectual fashion, aversion to taint, and a species of quasi-religious devotion to celebrity have blended and finally confounded with admiration or appreciation the *personalities* of American literature, among whom there is not one whose accomplishments have not been grossly overrated by his or her readers. Hitherto we have been in no mood to view with calmness and discuss with discrimination the real claims of the few who were most adept at convincing the public that our nation's poets are not all prigs, professors, aristocrats, and fascists, as at one period it half affected and wholly wished to believe. Is there any one so blind as not to see that Mr. Snyder, for example, owes much, and Mr. Cage nearly all, of his reputation as a poet to his undeniably charming manner of living? Is there any one so dull as not to know that poems that neither of these gentlemen could have written are written daily by praiseworthy authors, without attracting much more of a commendation than can be included in a dust-jacket blurb? And, again, is there anyone so prejudiced as not to acknowledge that all this happens because the public is desirous only of poets, not poetry?

I mean to say, of course, that Mr. Duncan, in the *apparent* public estimate, maintains a somewhat lower position than that to which, on absolute grounds, he is entitled. There is something, too, in the *pretension* of certain of his compositions—something altogether distinct from poetic fraud—which has helped disestablish him in the public's regard; and much, also, must be admitted on the score of his unabashed narcissism, which was deservedly resented. With all these demerits, however, there will still be found a large amount of poetical fame to which he is fairly entitled, and which he does, in fact, grudgingly receive.

He has written much more than the casual reader is likely to find, having begun at an early age—when quite a boy, indeed. His "juvenile" works, however, have been kept very judiciously out of print. Attention was first called to him by his essay "The Homosexual in Society," published in Dwight MacDonald's *Politics* in 1944. The personal revelation incorporated in this essay led John Crowe Ransom to return Duncan's 1942 poem "An African Elegy," already accepted for publication in *The Kenyon Review*—an action that gave this poem a consequence and notoriety to which it is entitled on no other account. This and other poems written at the same time were later gathered in *The Years as Catches*. They are not without a species of drollery, but are facile imitations of Mr. Duncan's earliest literary models.

Likewise, "The Venice Poem," composed in 1948, was not a product of any great originality. "The whole poem moves toward affirming a

Dionysiac anti-art," says Mr. Duncan's biographer, "[b]ut the movement itself occurs within a musically defined form complete with 'Recorso' and 'Coda'"; truth be told, however, these contradictory impulses are only signs that Mr. Duncan had not reconciled his various influences. If we except a certain rhythmic ease and delicacy, with some fancy of sentiment, there is really very little about this poem to be admired. He, unfortunately, esteemed it very highly, and gave its composition a prominent place in his own development as an artist. It is an artful hybrid of Eliot's *Four Quartets* and Pound's *Cantos*—the former a series of melodic pomposities, the latter a vehicle for squibs at a random collection of persons and things.

Our poet, indeed, seems to have been much impressed by the *Cantos,* and attempted throughout his career to engraft its bookishness even upon the grace and delicacy of his *Passages,* a sequence of poems included in several later volumes. A good example of this Poundianism occurs in the fourteenth poem in the series, called "Chords":

> What does it mean that the Tritopatores, *"doorkeepers and*
> *guardians of the winds,"* carry the human Psyche to Night's
> invisible palace,   to the Egg
>
> where Eros sleeps,
> the Protoegregorikos, the First Awakend?

These things may lay claim to oddity, but no more. They are totally out of keeping with the tone of the sweet sequence into which they are thus clumsily introduced, and serve no other purpose than to deprive it of all unity of effect. If a poet *must* be a pedagogue, let him be just that; he can be nothing better at the same moment. To be fancifully didactic, or didactically fanciful, is intolerable to language poets and beasts and children.

Passages is distinguished, in general, by that air of learnedness and grace, which is the prevailing feature of the muse of Duncan. "The Torso" (*Passages* 18) is a good specimen of this manner. "In Blood's Domaine [*Passages*]" belongs to a very high order of poetry.

> Link by link I can disown no link of this chain from my
> conscience.

> Would you forget the furnaces of burning meat purity demands?
> There is no ecstasy of Beauty in which I will not remember Man's misery.
>
> Jesus, in this passage —He is like a man coming forward in a hospital theater—
> Cries out: I come not to heal but to tear the scab from the wound you wanted to forget.
> May the grass no longer spread out to cover the works of man in the ruin of earth.
>
> What Angel, what Gift of the Poem, has brought into my body
>
> this sickness of living?

This is exquisitely decadent, and the effect is singularly increased by the conjunction of concentration camps and Christ. Inspired by Baudelaire, these lines are, I think, the most hyperbolic to be found in Duncan's *oeuvre*. I would be at a loss to discover their parallel in all American poetry.

The series of *Passages* called *Of the War* have much political, without any great amount of *poetic* power. Force is its prevailing feature—force resulting rather from outrage, erudition, and a judicious disposal of the circumstances of the poem, than from any truly lyrical momentum. I should do my conscience great wrong were I to speak of "Up Rising" as it is fashionable to speak of it, at least in print. Even as political oratory, many American and a multitude of foreign compositions of a similar character surpass it.

A second sequence, *The Structure of Rhyme,* has numerous lines exemplifying its author's felicity of *expression;* as, for instance, "The eyes that are horns of the moon feast on the leaves of trampled sentences." And, again:

> My spirit is like a mountain deprived of the sky. I worry the
> showing forth by Day, craving truth to break from obscurity
> the old scales, the stars of my crown.

But to the *sentiment* involved in this last passage, I feel disposed to yield an assent more thorough than might be expected. His spirit, indeed, was like a mountain deprived of sky. As a man of wisdom, no person on the face of the earth has been more extravagantly, more absurdly overrated.

"A Seventeenth Century Suite in Homage to the Metaphysical Genius in English Poetry (1590–1690)," first published in a special issue of John Taggart's journal *Maps,* is one of the most characteristic works of Duncan, abounding in his most distinguished traits: grace, learnedness, loftiness, power, *pretension*. The pomposity of:

> This is not a baby on fire but a babe of fire,
> flesh burning with its own flame,   not toward death
>   but alive with flame,   suffering its *self*
> the heat of the heart the rose was hearth of

has, I regret to see, been retained in the book publication. The last line is certainly not English as it stands, and, besides, is quite ridiculous. What is the meaning of this:

> All the doors of Life's wounds I have long closed in me
> break open from His body and pour forth
> therefrom fire that is his blood

Duncan's *Sonnets* are, as a whole, one of his best sequences. Their simplicity and delicacy of sentiment will recommend them to all readers. They are, however, unabashedly imitative, and the final conceit of the first sonnet,

> Sharpening their vision, Dante says, like a man
>   seeking to thread a needle,
> They try the eyes of other men

although clever, suffers by comparison to the still more clever conceit of Jack Spicer:

> Poetry, almost blind like a camera
> Is alive in sight only for a second. Click,

Snap goes the eyelid of the eye before movement
Almost as the word happens.

In his ear, Mr. Duncan is usual, although in this regard Mr. Ginsberg has paid him numerous compliments. "Often I Am Permitted to Return to a Meadow" has certainly some vigor of music, but its author, in short, writes ponderously, with excessive mannerism, and, as a matter of course, seldom effectively, so far as the giving of pleasure is concerned.

Personally, he was a man to be appreciated, even respected, but not especially beloved, though he had his chosen few who held him dear. His courage and commitment in matters of principle or art were beyond reproach, but he was not the most loyal of friends, and his vanity was easily roused to anger by the talents and accomplishments of real or imagined poetic rivals. When pampered within his own circle of associates, he was all ardor, enthusiasm, and cordiality, but to the world at large, he was reserved, shunning society, into which he was seduced only with difficulty, and upon rare occasion. The love of private study seemed to become with him a passion.

He was a good amateur linguist, and an excellent *belles lettres* scholar; in general, his essays were meticulously conceived and beautifully written, although more discursive than erudite. He was what the world calls *ultra* in most of his opinions, particularly about myth and ritual, and was fond of broaching and supporting what the world calls heresies. He was choice and accurate in his language, and held forth without exhaustion on a wide variety of topics, although a soft stutter invariably entered his voice when he spoke with excitement. His manners were dignified, like a cat's, with grace and a little tincture of cruelty. He affected a velvet cape at one time, but in later years favored a plain brown suit with wide orange tie. His forehead was a noble one, broad, massive, and intellectual; his hair thick and gray about the temples; eyes dark and brilliant, but with a tendency to cross; nose Grecian; chin prominent; mouth finely chiseled and full of expression, although the lips were thin; his smile was peculiarly ambiguous.

On the cover of *Ironwood* magazine for Fall 1983, there appeared a likeness of Mr. Duncan from a painting by the poet's longtime companion, Jess Collins. The image conveys a good general idea of the man, especially of his *soul,* for he is fixed there like a bust upon a grand piano, surrounded by the bric-a-brac of his art.

For many years before his death in 1988, he was superintendent of the Poetics Program at the New College of California, where he assembled a staff that included the poets Diane Di Prima, David Meltzer, Duncan McNaughton, and Michael Palmer.

CARLA HARRYMAN

Ms. Harryman has made several collections of her work, and written much for the stage. Her earliest compositions were contributed to Ms. Hejinian's Tuumba Press, which brought out two of Ms. Harryman's chapbooks. The second in particular attracted very positive attention and helped to enhance the reputation of the series at a time when its success was far from assured. These two chapbooks were subsequently, with some other pieces, published in volume form, with the title *Animal Instincts*.

She has subsequently written several better things—*Memory Play,* for example, and *There Never Was a Rose without a Thorn*. These are on domestic and psychological subjects; in social and political ones, she has comparatively failed. She is fond of the bold, striking, disjunctive—in a word, of the postmodern gothic; she has a quick appreciation of picturesque, and is not unskilled in delineations of relationships. She seizes adroitly on salient incidents and presents them with vividness to the eye, but in their combinations or ramifications, she is by no means so thoroughly at home—that is to say, her plots are not so good as their individual items. Her style is what the critics usually term "powerful," but lacks real power through its verboseness and floridity. It is, in fact, generally diffuse—even anarchic—involved, needlessly digressive, and superabundant in *non-sequiturs,* although these latter features are frequently witty. She has much in common with Kathy Acker—the characteristic trait of each being a clipped, caustic, erotic authority that keeps clear of mere slickness by never bothering to hide the artifice involved in its creation. The personas adopted by the two writers are very close. Ms. Harryman has the more talent of the two, but is somewhat the less adventurous. She has occasional flashes of a far higher order of merit than appertains to her ordinary style.

Of Ms. Harryman's plays, I have seen so very little performed that I feel myself scarcely in condition to speak of them, save as writing. Their described action has a *fidgety* effect, and would seem to indicate a mind without settled aims—restless and full of activity. Few of the characters are presented twice in the same manner, and their manner of *speaking* varies continually. Sometimes the dialogue is conversational, with lines neatly fitting together—other times the spoken words are like a monologue splintered into pieces, then picked up at random by innocent bystanders—still other times, the spoken lines fly off, with a jerk, in several competing directions. The tone, also, of the plays is changeable—sometimes the language is very light and playful, sometimes excessively heavy.

She is about the medium height; hair and eyes dark, the latter large and expressive; the mouth a fine one and indicative of firmness; the whole countenance pleasing, intellectual, always in motion. Married to General Watten, with one child, a son, she is a distant relation of the immortal author of *The Telling*.

RON SILLIMAN

Mr. Silliman is one of the most influential of the San Francisco *littérateurs*, and has done a great deal for the interests of American letters. Not the least important service tendered by him was the conception and editorship of *In the American Tree*, published after some few years delay by the National Poetry Foundation. This hefty collection of language poetry brought to public notice many valuable fugitive works that had previously suffered neglect, and at the same time afforded unwanted encouragement to several lesser-known authors by publishing their writing, in good style and in good company, without trouble or expense to the authors themselves, and in the very teeth of the disadvantages arising from the want of critical response. At one time it seemed that this happy scheme was to be overwhelmed by the competition of a rival publisher—taken, in fact, quite out of the hands of those who, by "right of first discovery," were entitled at least to its first fruits. A less-generous but better-distributed "Anthology" in imitation was set on foot, but whatever might have been the temporary success of this latter, the original one had already too well established itself in the public favor to be overthrown, and thus was not prevented from proving of great benefit to our literature at large.

His earliest published work of any length was *Ketjak*, a geometrically plotted prose poem designed in the first place as a freestanding work, but enfolded afterwards into a larger structure (*The Age of Huts*).

Tjanting next appeared—also a geometrically plotted prose poem—and was more favorably received even than its predecessor. Its success—partially owing, perhaps, to the influence of Mr. Silliman's public agitation for "The New Sentence"—encouraged him to attempt a poem of somewhat greater elaborateness as well as length, and *The Alphabet* was soon announced, establishing him at once as the foremost prose poet of his generation. Several sections of this poem have already been published, although the entire work remains unfinished. The first three sections ("Albany," "Blue," "Carbon") were also the first to appear, Ms. Hejinian's Tuumba Press having swiftly brought them out as a handsome chapbook under the title *ABC*. Afterwards came *Paradise* (the "P" section), which won the San Francisco State Poetry Center Book Award, and then *Lit,* not nearly so successful, and then *What,* which took rank in the public esteem with *Tjanting* and *Paradise*. The other sections I have seen are *Demo to Ink, Jones, Manifest, N/O,* ®, *Toner,* and *Xing*. These portions of the poem are no less meritorious than the portions that preceded them, although they have not attracted nearly as much attention. Public interest in the series has no doubt begun to wane—a purposeful lack of development makes this all but inevitable—and yet Mr. Silliman's most cynical readers continue to admire his industriousness, and continue to cheer for his poem's ultimate completion.

In addition to his more obvious literary engagements, Mr. Silliman participates a great deal, editorially and otherwise, in the publication of *Socialist Review*. His political activities, although abated in recent years, stretch back to the 1960s and include, most notably, a struggle to defeat the new sentencing guidelines for California prisons in the 1970s.

In character he is remarkable, distinguished for the doggedness of his manner, his love of minutia and fixity of purpose, his active intellect, his mistrust of all power, and especially for an almost Quixotic fidelity to his poetic and political allies. He seems perpetually alert to small slights and misrepresentations, and I have no doubt that in his secret heart he is oppressed by an unknown fate.

In person he is equally simple as in character—the one is a *pendant* of the other. He is about five feet nine inches high, somewhat husky. Neither his nose nor his forehead can be defended; the latter would puzzle phrenology. His eyes and hair are light; his beard trimmed to preserve the general roundness of the head. The whole expression of his face is one of alertness and consideration, contributing to give the sensation of a bulldog. He is probably forty-five, but seems already in his fifties. His dress, also, is in full keeping with his character, loose fitting and plain, far from fashionable, and conveying an instantaneous conviction of the working class gentleman dressed for a Sunday in the park.

BENJAMIN FRIEDLANDER

I have seen one or two brief poems of considerable merit with the signature of *Benjamin Friedlander* appended. For example:

INSOMNIA

Walking in the rainfinite.
  Is it permitted—am I?
—to lag along the fennel track,
episodic?

We, the drenched combines of yore,
depleted,
  gather up the war *repeated* in the clenched kiss
proffered at the door.

He—blemishes—our souls
replenishing the stream
whose icy crystal pours across
a broken length of dream.

I must confess, however, that I do not appreciate the "clenched kiss" of such a word as "rainfinite," and, perhaps, there is a little taint of self-dramatization in the passage about "drenched combines of yore." Let us be charitable, however, and set all this down under the head of dreaminess—one of the first of poetical requisites. The *inexcusable* sin of Mr. F. is mimicry—if this be not too mild a term. Emily Dickinson is his especial favorite. He has taken, too, most unwarrantable liberties, in the way of downright plagiarism, from a German poet whose works are not fully available in English—this lack Mr. Friedlander takes as his license. I refer, of course, to the poems of Paul Celan —a favorite of the neo-post-romanticals.

I place Mr. Friedlander, however, on my list of San Francisco *literati* not on account of his poetry (which I presume he is not weak enough to estimate very highly), but on the score of his having edited for several years, with the aid of Andrew Schelling, two magazines, the first called *Jimmy & Lucy's House of "K,"* and the second *Dark Ages Clasp the Daisy Root*. These works, though professedly "available," were issued at irregular intervals, and were unfortunate, I fear, in not attaining at any period very extensive circulations.

I learn that Mr. F. is not without talent; but the fate of his magazines should indicate to him the necessity of applying himself to study. No spectacle can be more pitiable than that of a man without the commonest school education busying himself in attempts to instruct humankind on topics of polite literature. The absurdity in such cases does not lie merely in the ignorance displayed by the would-be instructor, but in the transparency of the shifts by which he endeavors to keep this ignorance concealed. The co-editor of *Jimmy & Lucy's House of "K"* and *Dark Ages Clasp the Daisy Root,* for example, was not laughed at so much on account of mixing essays on punk rock with reviews of books of language poetry, and ending poems with corny rhymes—poems, mind you, that are not intended as light or comical verses—as where he rhymes, above, "stream" with "dream"—he was not, I say, laughed at *so much* for his excusable deficiencies in taste as when, in the hope of disguising such deficiency, he perpetually lamented the "typographical blunders" that "in the most unaccountable manner" *crept* into his publications. Nobody was so stupid as to suppose that there existed in San Francisco a single proofreader—or even a single typist—who would permit *such* errors to escape. By the excuses offered, the errors were only the more obviously nailed to the counter as Mr. Friedlander's own.

I make these remarks in no spirit of unkindness. Mr. F. is yet young —certainly not more than thirty-five—and might, with his talents, readily improve himself at points where he is most defective. No one of any generosity would think the worse of him for getting private instruction. Some recent tracts produced by him in association with Jeff Gburek show a glint of promise.

I do not personally know Mr. Friedlander. He lived for many years,

I believe, in the East Bay, where he was involved with a claque which included Michael Amnasan, Michael Anderson, Steve Farmer, Nada Gordon, Jessica Grim, Andrea Hollowell, Pat Reed, David Sheidlower, and others; he subsequently left town for the East Coast. About his personal appearance there is nothing very observable. I cannot say whether he is married or not.

TOM MANDEL

Douglas Messerli neglects to include Mr. Mandel in his massive anthology *From the Other Side of the Century,* including in Mr. Mandel's stead the likes of Dennis Phillips, Charles North, Diane Ward, James Sherry, and Abigail Child. That Mr. Mandel's verse, of which no little has seen print, is superior to these says very little. His *EncY,* praised by Bruce Andrews in *L=A=N=G=U=A=G=E* magazine, is a period piece, dating from an era when "nonreferential" was a byword among poets. Mr. Mandel's later work shows a change in direction—toward nostalgic evocations of the Old World, peppered with the vocabulary of mysticism. In *Central Europe* and *Four Strange Books* and *Letters of the Law,* he appears to yearn for a species of profundity utterly beyond the grasp of his superficial insight and workmanlike craft. That Mr. Mandel has the *ability* to write profound verse none has ever doubted. But Mr. Mandel's restiveness is proverbial. To devote himself to a single text, in the manner of the Rabbis, to worry the meaning of a single line, goes utterly contrary to the poet's nature.

The truth seems to be that Mr. Mandel is a vivacious, fanciful, entertaining talker—a first rate one—with a literary style that, considering our times—in view of such stylists as fill Mr. Messerli's anthology, for example—may be termed respectable, and no more. Mr. Silliman has suggested that Mandel's professed interest in religion is an important influence on the New Spirit crowd. It is scarcely worthwhile to inquire what the architect of the "New *Sentence*" wishes us to understand by "influence," since it is generally supposed that the younger writers are utterly ignorant of the work that has preceded them; but if Mr. Silliman wants to place the blame for this work at Mr. Mandel's feet, we will not contest the point.

A two-page poem from *Letters of the Law,* called "Feelings, Foreign," gives adequate testimony to Mr. Mandel's poetic activity. The first stanza runs thus:

I'm singing along with you,
                              but more originally.
Will a saint sound
contradiction and the righteous
not suffer?

The clumsy rhythm of line two makes laborious a thought already too questionable for the opening of a poem; the clever statement that follows is nonetheless neat. Is the statement true? No matter. The stanza as a whole describes perfectly the twin domains (dare I say? the a: and b: drives) of Mr. Mandel's *ars poetica: first,* an act of imitation full of feeling, which the poet thinks it witty to call original; *second,* an overdramatization of the simple task of making sense. He says:

Continuity bought at a price
of invented faith, bare illusion
that makes no sense without
                              the cheap toys
that come free in the box . . .

To which we say, *Indeed?* Then sing on, bright poet, without continuity, and join the dim chorus to which you lend your art.

Mr. Mandel is what one used to call a gentleman scholar. For a short time he was the director of the Poetry Center at San Francisco State, but the principal part of his life has been devoted to business. He has dark curly hair and an impish grin, and enjoys good food and drink. A lover of jazz and cars, philosophy and women, he currently resides in Washington, D.C., where he is married to the poet Beth Josselow.

STEVE BENSON

Steve Benson is one of the least intolerable of the school of Bay Area language poets—and, in fact, I believe that he has at last "come out from among them," abandoned their doctrines (whatever they are) and given up their company in disgust. He was at one time one of the most noted, and undoubtedly one of the least pretentious contributors, to Mr. Perelman's Talk series (which helped establish that infamous claque in San Francisco), but he has reformed his habits of thought and speech, domiciled himself on the East Coast, and set up the shingle of a psychotherapist.

About ten years ago, two memorable chapbooks by Mr. Benson, *Dominance* and *Briarcombe Paragraphs,* were published in California and France. Both of these works demonstrate Mr. Benson's fine ear for prose—for *true* prose, and not the New Sentence (whatever that might be) of Mr. Silliman. Critics and lay readers alike most unmercifully neglected these books, and much injustice, in my opinion, was done to the poet. He seems to me to possess unusual vivacity of fancy and dexterity of expression, while his phraseology is remarkable for its accuracy, vigor, and even for its originality of effect. I might say, perhaps, rather more than all this, and maintain that he has imagination if he would only condescend to employ it, which he will not, or *would* not until lately—the word compounders and quibble concoctors of Frogpondium having inoculated him with a preference for Imagination's half sister, the Cinderella, Experiment. Mr. Benson has seldom contented himself with harmonious combinations of thought. There must always be, to afford him perfect satisfaction, a certain amount of the odd, of the whimsical, of the affected, of the *bizarre.* He is as full of absurd improvisations as H. D. Moe or Jim Brody, with this difference, that the improvisations of these latter are banalities beyond redemption—whimsical, irremediable, self-contented nonsensicalities, and insomuch are good for their kind; but the improvisations of Mr. Benson are, for the most part, experiments intentionally manufactured, for experiment's sake, out of the material for properly imaginative, harmonious, proportionate, or poetical ideas. We see every moment that he has been at uncommon *pains* to make a spectacle of himself. In this respect, Mr. Benson's *Blue Books* is his most representative production.

But perhaps I am wrong in supposing that I am at all in condition to decide on the merits of Mr. B.'s poetry, which is professedly incomprehensible. "I scarcely apprehend what I'm saying to myself," says the poet in *Reverse Order:*

> My unrealized enmity explodes at this moment, at my fantasy.
>   At myself.
>
> Or at what I know. I refuse to echo anything I understand.

Changing the subject, do animal noises, supposed to express
the body's functions,

Actually betray the mind? Listen in an ostrich's yellow crevices

Reflecting lunar expansiveness. A glimmer doesn't remind me
of its origins. And

Light is dying, changing, somehow, something else.

My look wanders, drifts and splits into fractured thought,

which I imagine funky, like oatmeal stuck on the insides of
the bowl.

The camera in the circus tent tastes thick.

Fanciful, pretty, and neatly turned, this is all very well—all with the exception of the last line, and it is a pity it was not left out. It is laughable to see that the language poets, if beguiled for a minute or two into respectable English and self-reflection, are always sure to remember their cue just as they get to the end of their song, which, by way of *salvo,* they then round off with a bit of antipoetic BS about thick tasting cameras. It is especially observable that, in adopting the cant of nonsense, the cant of vagueness soon follows. Can Mr. Benson, or anybody else, inform me why it is that, in the really sensible passages of what I have here quoted, he employs a plainness of address, and only in the final line of goosetherumfoodle employs a pleonasm? The point, well articulated, required no such ugly exemplification.

One of the best known of Mr. Benson's compositions is undoubtedly "The Busses," first published by Ms. Hejinian's Tuumba Press and reproduced in facsimile in *Blue Books*. It has some quotidian observations, and piquant ones, suiting the subject; but they are more than half divested of their quotely quality by the attempt at enhancing them through *oddity* of composition. *Eccentricity* is an admissible and important aspect of phenomenological study—an adjunct whose value has long been misapprehended—but in picturing the everyday operations of the mind, it is altogether out of place. What idea of consciousness, of thought, for example, can any human being connect with the discontinuities of a metaphorical bus ride when the ride is reproduced in language so trippingly fantastical, so palpably adapted to a purpose, as that which follows:

democratic neighbors would be enough siastical communion
  ballyhooing the longevitus
    distance like wiseacres
      on a country squaredance.
                  The time is shot out of line
                  The time is shot from a line
  and we're caring for grandmothers who are out of synch
with the age of dimensions we know nothing of.
    As I would be the first to admit   sadness melts.
    duration is not in power—   gives drinks away.

It is more difficult to conceive anything more ludicrously out of keeping than the thoughts of these lines and the *petit-matre,* fidgety, hop, skip, and a jump air of the words and the Lilliputian parts of this passage.

A somewhat similar kind of investigation is attempted by Mr. B. in his "Dialogues," but as the method of composition is essentially different, the effect is by no means so displeasing. I copy a few of the lines as the most self-illuminating passage that I can find among all the writings of its author.

It fades away.
What?
It fades away easily enough.
What?
Oh—the music.
I ground you in the situation.
These words aren't enough.
We're talking to each other.
What I'm not interested in is our talking to each other as
    though for the sense of some reader or writer. We need
    to talk to each other for the situation we're responsible
    to our*selves,* and that is not elucidating something out-
    side of our own concerns for the sake of someone who,

by our book, isn't really there.
"By our book." "By our book." I like that situation, that expression, that shared ambiguity and doubt.
Your reading over my shoulder is almost like reading it backwards.

Mr. Benson is well educated and quite accomplished. Like his friend Ms. Harryman, he is an improviser, dramatist, and stylist in prose, being in each capacity very respectably successful.

He is about forty-five years of age; in height, perhaps six feet one; athletic, with a runner's body, lanky and flexible; front face not unhandsome—the forehead evincing intellect, the smile sheepish and broad all at once; but the effect is marred by a slightly bowed quality in the posture, which Mr. Benson adopts when engaged in conversation. At these times, a curious mixture of nervous boredom and wide-eyed attentiveness is evinced, to disagreeable effect. His eyes and hair are dark brown—the latter worn short. A serious and sad expression comes over the face when Mr. Benson believes himself unobserved. He dresses with marked preppiness. He is recently married.

LYN HEJINIAN

Ms. Hejinian was at one time editor, or one of the editors of Tuumba Press, to which she contributed many of the most emphatic, and certainly some of the most peculiar papers. She is known, too, by *My Life,* a remarkable assemblage of sketches, issued in 1980 by Burning Deck, and reissued in expanded form some years after by Sun & Moon. She is intellectually associated with General Barrett Watten, an author who has occasioned much discussion, having had the good fortune to be warmly abused and chivalrously defended in the pages of *Poetry Flash,* and she has lately written a poetic collaboration with General Watten's wife, Ms. Carla Harryman. More recently, she has published *The Cold of Poetry, The Cell,* and *Oxota: A Short Russian Novel.* At present, she is co-editor of *Poetics Journal,* for which she has furnished a great deal of matter, all falling under the general heading Criticism. Two of the best examples of this are her review of a biography of William Carlos Williams, and an appeal to the public against the concept of "Closure." The review did her infinite credit; it was frank, candid, independent, and, in ludicrous contrast to the usual mere glorifications of the day, gave honor *only* where honor was due, yet evinced the most thorough capacity to appreciate and the most sincere intention to place in the fairest light the real and idiosyncratic merits of the poet.

In my opinion it is one of the very few reviews of Williams's career, ever published in America, of which the critics have not had abundant reason to be ashamed. Mr. Williams is entitled to a certain and very distinguished rank among the poets of his country, but our country is disgraced by the evident toadyism which would award to his aesthetic position and influence, to his everydayness and likeability, to the acuity of his line as seen through the eye of Mr. Robert Creeley, an amount of indiscriminate approbation that neither could nor would have been given to the poems themselves.

Her "Quest for Knowledge in the Western Poem," or rather her Philippic against those who would *situate* knowledge in the West, was one of the most eloquent and well-argued essays I have read in some time.

"The Rejection of Closure" is an essay that few poets in the country could have written, and no poet in the country *would* have written, with the exception of Ms. Hejinian. In the way of independence, of unmitigated radicalism, it is the production of one of America's most perspicuous "Native Agents," and Semiotext(e) would do well to include the essay in their series. I need scarcely say that the essay is searching, emphatic, thoughtful, suggestive, brilliant, and to a certain extent scholarly—for all that Ms. Hejinian produces is entitled to these epithets—but I must say that the conclusions reached are only partly my own. Not that they are by any means too bold, too novel, too startling, or too dangerous in their consequences; in their attainment, however, too many premises have been distorted and too many analogical inferences left altogether out of sight. Ms. Hejinian has erred, too, through her own excessive ambition. She judges the capacities of language by the heart and intellect of Ms. Hejinian, but there are not more than one or two dozen Ms. Hejinians on the whole face of the earth.

The most favorable notice of Ms. Hejinian's genius (for high genius she unquestionably possesses) is to be obtained, perhaps, from her contributions to Tuumba Press, and from her *My Life* and *Oxota*. Many of the *descriptions* in this last volume are unrivaled for their *graphicality* (why is there not such a word?), for the force through which they convey the true by the novel or unexpected, by the introduction of touches that other artists would be sure to omit as irrelevant to the subject. This faculty, too, springs from her subjectiveness, which leads her to paint a scene less by its features than its effects.

Here, for example, is a portion of her account of a meeting with Russian writers:

> Observations that days come, arrive, approach, are blots,
> hangovers, reactionary reactions, said the doorkeeper at
> the Writers Union on Voinova
> The future can't be made out with such metaphors, he added,
> tapping a new tabloid
> So, it is my right to present this to an American
> Plumbers' beauties are plumbers' proofs
> And so, our new poets in leather jackets won't get wet
> Only our cheerful tongues
> Upstairs I met with Evgenii Ivanovich, who has translating the
> American metaphorist Raymond Chandler
> A pale man with tiny pad
> He turned away and lifted its page
> What does it mean, please, "The woman had rubber lips with
> no tread"
> She's lost her grip on the truth
> Or maybe what she says goes by him
> We have no such metaphors, he said, but maybe I'll find one
> Maybe something like, "The circle she made with her mouth
> was warped."

The truthfulness of the passage will be felt by all. Perhaps every (imaginative) writer who dreams of escaping the past, whether such past be understood as metaphor or tradition, confronts issues similar to those raised by this passage. But most persons, through wishful overexcitement, would never think of describing *how* the dream is pursued, even though this alone conveys the difficulty and necessity of the task. Hence, we find so many desperate attempts on the part of ordinary critics and poets to describe the future of literature as if it had already been achieved. Mr. David Antin, to be sure, in his many "Talk" poems, is sufficiently sober in his attention; he describes neither the future of poetry nor its means of achievement, but rather the need for such a future as felt by *him*. This need makes him think of his *own* antipathies, of his *own* interests, and so forth, and so forth;

and it is only when we come to think that the thought of Mr. Antin's antipathies and interests are quite idiosyncratic, confined exclusively to Mr. Antin, that we are in a condition to understand how, in despite of his sobriety, he has failed to convey an idea of anything beyond one Mr. David Antin.

From the essay entitled "Variations: A Return of Words," I copy a paragraph which will serve at once to exemplify Ms. Hejinian's more earnest (declamatory) style, and to show the tenor of her prospective speculations:

> Probably all feeling are cliches—which is not to say that they are invalid, or stupid, or even absurd (though like anything else, they may be). Feelings are common to us all, never new, stunning only to the person feeling them at the time, and foolish (or boring) to everyone else. Thoughts, however, can be affective whether one shares them at the moment or not, and they can be original.

From what I have quoted, a *general* conception of the prose style of the authoress may be gathered. Her manner, however, is infinitely varied. It is always emphatic—but I am not sure that it is always anything else, unless I say picturesque. It rather indicates than evinces scholarship. Perhaps only the scholastic, or, more properly, those accustomed to look narrowly at the intention of a phrase, would be willing to acquit her of grammatical ignorance, to attribute her slovenliness to an anxiety for the kernel in disregard for the shell or to waywardness, affectation, or blind reverence for Gertrude Stein. Perhaps only persons such as these would be able to detect in her strange and continual inaccuracies a capacity for the accurate.

> My old aunt entertained us with her lie, a story about an event in her girlhood, a catastrophe *in a sailboat that never occurred,* but she was blameless, unaccountable, since, in the course of the telling she had come to believe the lie herself.
>
> *   *   *
>
> Ultimately, conditions are incomprehensible without the use of analytical conceptual structures, but an initial, essential recognition of difference—of strangeness—develops only with at-

tention to single objects, while others are temporarily held in abeyance.

* * *

I think of you English, so frequent, and deserved, and thereby desired, their common practice and continually think of it, who, since the Elizabethans, save Sterne and Joyce, have so troubled language to the imagination, and Melville, of whose *Mardi* the critics wrote, in 1849, "a tedious, floundering work of uncertain meaning or no meaning at all."

These are merely a few, a very few instances, taken at random from among a multitude of *willful* murders committed by Ms. Hejinian on the American Idiom. Such tidbits as used to fill out the *New Yorker*'s rear pages could easily be discovered in surplus in the pages of her books.

In spite of these things, however, and her frequent unjustifiable Steinisms (such as writing sentences that are not sentences, since, to be parsed, reference must be had to preceding sentences), the style of Ms. Hejinian is one of the very best with which I am acquainted. In general effect, I know no style that surpasses it. It is singularly piquant, vivid, terse, bold, luminous—leaving details out of sight, it is everything that a style need be.

I believe that Ms. Hejinian has written much poetry, although only a portion has been published and remains in print. That portion is tainted with the affectation of the *language poets* (I use this term, of course, in the sense that the public of late seems resolved to give it), but is brimful of poetic *sentiment*. Here, for example, is something in Clark Coolidge's manner, of which the author of *Quartz Hearts* might have had no reason to be ashamed:

The inanimate are *rocks,* desks, bubble,
mineral, ramps. *It is the concrete being*
that reasons. The baseboard weighing
its wall span. The clouds never form regiments
and don't march. The gap in my education
needn't be filled. Stubbornness is provocative.

The pessimist suppresses a generous anger. A Trace
linked to a fence of forgetting. *Lying awake*
may serve the purpose that dreams do. In the dark
opaque disposal of the missing past. Canned laughter
is white noise. Comparable repositories freight dust
into the shadows. Anger the animate of stubbornness.

To show the evident ponderousness with which this poem was constructed, I have italicized a superfluous reiteration and two locutionary improprieties. The final line of the first stanza is difficult of pronunciation through excess of consonants. Indeed, the force of the poem is not musical but propositional—in this Ms. Hejinian differs most markedly from her model.

The supposition that the book of an author is a thing apart from the author's self is, I think, ill founded. The soul is a cypher, in the sense of a cryptograph; and the shorter a cryptograph is, the more difficulty there is in comprehension—at a certain point of brevity it would bid defiance to an army of Watsons and Cricks. And thus he who has written very little may in that little either conceal his spirit or convey quite an erroneous idea of it—of his acquirements, talents, temper, manner, tenor, and depth (or shallowness) of thought—in a word, of his character, of himself. But this is impossible with him who has written much. Of such a person we get, from his books, not merely a just, but the most just representation. Ron, the individual, personal man, in tweed jacket and sneakers, is not by any means the veritable Mr. Silliman, who is discoverable only in *What,* where his soul is deliberately and nakedly set forth. And who would ever know Susan Howe by looking at her or talking with her, or doing anything with her at all except reading her *Emily Dickinson?* What poet, in especial, but must feel—at least the better portion of him or herself—more fairly represented in even the most common verse (earnestly written) than in the most elaborate or most intimate personalities?

I put all this as a general proposition, to which Ms. Hejinian affords a marked exception—to this extent, that her personal character and her printed books are merely one and the same thing. We get access to her soul *as* directly from the one as from the other—no *more* readily from this than from that—easily from either. Her acts are bookish, and her books are less thoughts than acts. Her literary and her conversational manner are identical. Here is a passage from *Redo:*

Nostalgia is the elixir drained
from guilt . . . I've been writing
with the fingers of my non-writing hand
I patted the dashboard. "Hi, car."
It responded "Hello Mommy."

Now all this is precisely as Ms. Hejinian would *speak* it. She is perpetually saying just such things in just such words. To get the *conversational* woman in the mind's eye, all that is needed is to imagine her reciting the lines just quoted; but first let us have the *personal* woman. She is of the medium height; nothing remarkable about the figure; a profusion of frizzy blonde-gray hair; eyes palish blue, full of water, and widely set apart, like a reptile's; capacious forehead; the mouth when in repose indicates profound sensibility, capacity for affection, even love—when moved by a slight smile, it becomes even beautiful in the intensity of this expression; but the upper lip, as if impelled by the action of involuntary muscles, habitually uplifts itself, conveying the impression of a sneer. Imagine, now, a person of this description looking you at one moment earnestly in the face, at the next seeming to look only within her own spirit or at the wall; moving nervously every now and then in her chair; speaking in a high key, but emphatically, carefully (not hurriedly or loudly), with a delicious distinctness of enunciation—speaking, I say, the lines in question, and emphasizing certain words unpredictably, not by impulsion of the breath (as is usual), but by drawing them out as long as possible, nearly closing her eyes the while—imagine all this, and we have both the woman and the authoress before us.

BARRETT WATTEN

General Watten occupied some ten years ago quite a conspicuous position among the *littérateurs* of the Bay Area. His name was seen very frequently in *Poetry Flash* and other similar papers in connection with his military campaigns and occasional public speeches. His only study of logistics, I believe, is *Total Syntax*, a work of considerable ingenuity, though one that met a very mixed reception from the press.

Much of this reception, however, is attributable to the personal popularity of the man in his own *camp*, as it were—his facility in making acquaintances and his tact in converting them into unwavering allies. Those disposed *against* the General have found him an equally popular opponent.

General Watten has an exhaustless fund of *vitality*. His energy, activity, and indefatigability are proverbial, not less than his peculiar sociability. These qualities give him unusual influence among his fellow citizens and have constituted him (as precisely the same traits have *not* constituted Mr. Silliman) one of a standing committee for the regulation of certain affairs—such as, for instance, the getting up a complimentary benefit, or a public demonstration of respect for some deceased worthy, or a ball and dinner to Mr. Creeley or Mr. Dragomoschenko.

It is the curse of a certain order of mind that it can never rest satisfied with the consciousness of its ability to do a thing. Still less is it content with doing it. It must both know and show all the steps taken to arrive at its accomplishment. Such a mind belongs to General Watten. His poetic style is noticeable for its concision, luminousness, completeness—each quality in its proper place. He has that *method* so generally characteristic of the scientist proper. Everything he writes is a model in its peculiar way, serving just the purposes intended and nothing to spare. As a consequence, it has been the fate of this gentleman to see his work condemned *ad infinitum,* and lauded *ad nauseam*—a fact that speaks much in its praise. We know of no American author who has evinced greater ingenuity of mind in writing, and we know of none who has more narrowly missed placing himself at the head of our letters.

Mr. Watten is not only a General, but co-editor of *Poetics Journal,* a Member of the Board of Directors of New Langton Arts, a contributing editor to *Artweek,* a Managing Editor of *Representations,* and now serving at a new post in Detroit; his other accomplishments are more than I can now enumerate. His manners are *recherche,* courteous—a little in the old school way. He is sensitive, punctilious; speaks well, roundly, fluently, plausibly, and is skilled in pouring oil upon the waters of stormy debate.

An accurate representation of Mr. Watten can be found on the back of his book *Progress*. He is, perhaps, fifty years of age, but has a boyish look; he is about five feet eleven in height, slender, neat, with an air of military compactness; he is married to the writer Carla Harryman, with whom he has a son; he looks especially well on horseback.

NORMA COLE

Norma Cole, for the last five or six years, has been rapidly attaining distinction—and this, evidently, with no effort at attaining it. She seems, in fact, to have no object in view beyond that of giving voice to intuitions or to fancies of the moment. "Necessity," says the proverb, "is the mother of Invention" and the invention of Ms. C., at least, springs plainly from necessity—from the necessity of invention. *Not* to write poetry—not to think it, type it, cut it up, and be it, is entirely out of her power.

It may be questioned whether, with more "binding energy" (as DuPlessis put it), more industry, more definite purpose, more ambition, Ms. Cole would have made a more decided impression on the public mind. She might, upon the whole, have written "better" poems, but the chances are that she would have failed in conveying so vivid and so just an idea of her powers as a poet. The cool *opacité* of her style—that mystery which now so captivates—is but a portion and consequence of her unworldly nature, of her disregard of mere popularity, but it affords us glimpses (which we could not otherwise have obtained) of a capacity for accomplishing what she has not accomplished and in all probability never will. But in the world of poetry, there is already more than enough of this uncongenial ambition and pretence.

Her first volume, *Mace Hill Remap,* was published, I believe, by Joseph Simas, of Paris, a city where the poet has often resided and where she is most warmly regarded by her fellow poets. I have now lying before me my own copy of this volume, well-thumbed and wine stained—a most strangely conceived book, dedicated in its own obscure fashion to her former tutor, Michael Palmer. The book contains a number of what academics call "juvenile" poems, written when Ms. C. could not have been writing for more than a few years, and evincing a very unusual precocity. She was in this period almost exclusively associated with the magazine *Acts,* a magazine co-edited by David Levi Strauss and Benjamin Hollander. *Acts* at that time was the house organ of New College, where Robert Duncan, David Meltzer, and Diane Di Prima, among others, were then teaching, and an institution which saw itself as offering an alternative to language poetry, which was already at this time the dominant force in the Bay Area. So many hopes did the New College poets pin on Ms. Cole's career that the title of her first book inspired another, less successful magazine, called *Remap,* which was co-edited by Carolyn Kemp and Todd Barron.

A second volume, *Metamorphopsia,* followed shortly thereafter, produced in Connecticut by Potes & Poets Press. The book contains five sequences, the longest of which is "Paper House." Its alphabetical structure is well known to all children, though only twenty-four poems are included (the "y" and "z" having been excluded). The title sequence, "Metamorphopsia," is written in double column. Like shredded posters in a subway station, they are pleasing to the eye, but defy all attempts at comprehension. The "Itinerary" of another sequence is an uncontrolled meandering from subject to subject. "Letters of Discipline" is the airiest section of the book, recalling the fragments of Sappho and Archillochos. A mystical faith in the power of language is the volume's bright point. Its intelligence, even in code, and its ability to effect effortless transformation are each represented with mysteriousness and grace.

This, in a sequence called "The Provinces," is a forcible redaction of Ovid:

> Transform me, said Caenis, into an invulnerable fighter
> I am weary of being blind
> as much as painters cover their own stuff
> emerging with things intersection their savage looking
> far murmur real walls illustrating clearness
> millions of strange shadows a carpet
> 's coded pattern turns when exposed to air
> dreams rose applied to attention unguarded
> old baggage passed naturally drawn upon borders.

The story is a minor one from Book XII of the *Metamorphosis,* a volume which Ms. Cole might fairly be said to worship. Caenis, though born a woman, was made into a man at her own request by Neptune, who seized and raped the maiden while she was walking alone along the sea. So pleased was Neptune in the pleasure he took of Caenis that the God enlarged upon the maiden's request of manhood by making her invulnerable to wounds in combat, declaring aloud that she "should not dye of steele." This incident is especially well suited to contemporary use, and with more of that art which Ms. C. does *not* possess, she might have woven it into a poem that the world would not willingly let die. As it is, she has merely succeeded in showing what she might, should, and *could* have done, but unhappily did not.

A third volume, entitled *My Bird Book,* published in Los Angeles by Littoral Books (Todd Barron being one of the editors), met with a *really* cordial reception in Vancouver, where Ms. Cole, Canadian by birth, has frequently been a visitor. Despite their disagreements on other matters, the poets associated with the town's leading magazines (*Writing, Motel,* and *Raddle Moon*) all greeted this work with enthusiasm. Even Mr. Blaser became a devotee of Ms. C. Her merits as a poet and translator had already introduced her name into the local discourse (she was petted in especial by Susan Clark and Steven Forth), but her "Destitution: A Tale" (a poetical *essay,* notwithstanding its title) had at once an evidently favorable effect upon her fortunes. Her achievements as a poet were all placed in a more advantageous light by its assured, if mysterious, polemic.

As her books have received comparatively little critical comment, I may be pardoned for making one or two other extracts. "Gannet," although by no means one of her best poems, will very well serve to show the characteristic manner of the poetess. I quote the second of seven brief sections.

a wonder tale
told in bends and
folds like certain words
unbraided clarity
that granite triangle really a painted sail
the old south church, the corporate reading program
    expressway
for these things alter the prospect
stroll down the aisle of any supermarket
yoghurt faces you

Every true poet must here appreciate the exceeding richness of detail, the attenuated allusion to Ginsberg's "Supermarket in California," the braided obscurity of overt and insinuated meaning (as in the "hurt" of "yoghurt"). The lines I have italicized describe the *sensation* of meaning in a manner that has seldom, in its peculiar and very *mysterious* manner, been equaled.

I cannot speak of the poems of Ms. Cole without a strong propensity to ring the changes upon the evocative word "*mystery*" and its derivatives. It seems, indeed, the one-key phrase unlocking the cryptograph of her power—of the effect she produces. And yet, the effect is scarcely more a secret than the key. Mystery, perhaps, may be most satisfactorily defined as a term applied, in despair, to that class of the impressions of thought which admit neither of analysis nor of comprehension. It is in this penetralium of opacity—in *mystery*—that Ms. Cole excels any poet of her chosen community—or indeed, of any community under the sun. She is not, however, more mysterious herself than appreciative of the mysterious, under whatever guise it is presented to her consideration. The sentiment, the perception, and the keenest enjoyment of mystery, render themselves manifest in innumerable instances, as well throughout her prose as her poetry. A fine example is to be found in "Raven," included in *My Bird Book*. Ravens have often sounded in poetry—their mournful tones have been recorded, I mean—but assuredly never have they been brought so fully to the ear of the mind as in the verses that follow:

Says I am invisible in my feathers

World knot
young beyond half casual theme
courtoisie & turbulence a few more slowly now
we read little gold suns over the airstrip
no medical treatment for civilians
expeditions *speaking like through a screen door*
peaches for eyes

How faint the spot harmonates unbarred by time, wit and the
shape memory bolted
unobtainable until we learn it

Come up now onto the roof of my mouth and *see* this
shadow that has driven people mad

Common denominators this papers generosity
water's constancy emptied field

what we know passed to the back
mirrors open up another front

"Thou wilt never see that raven again, for I am that raven."

Mr. Steve Dickison of Berkeley has lately initiated a new press, Listening Chamber, with another, but still very imperfect collection of Ms. Cole's writings, entitled *Mars*, a book that bears on its cover an ingenious and beautiful collage by the artist Jess, the companion of the late Robert Duncan. In general, this volume embraces by no means the best of her works, although some of her best works ("Ruth," for example) are included. "Rosetta," one of her longest compositions, a very complex poem—quite as hermetic as anything written by Zukofsky—is omitted. The volume contains a number of the least explicable poems in Ms. Scalapino's Gulf War anthology, and also more than enough with alchemical or astrological allusion—a kind of writing which, through an odd perversity, the fair authoress deliberately chose to affect, but which no poet can admit to being poetical at all. These *jeux d'esprit* (for what else shall we call them?) afforded her, however, a fine opportunity for the display of ingenuity and an *intricacy* in which she especially excels.

Of this latter quality, in its better phase—that is to say, existing apart from the alchemy—I must be permitted to give two worthwhile specimens:

On the anniversary of fact we marched into bed with
them and paid with extraordinary rage

A grazing field masking the toxic canal, capped and causal,
removing the deaf signs

How they treated objects without arms, an admirable ideal

Where to place the stops grew out of a sensible idea, a
sequence of notes

* * *

Book, think of something, astral projection stuck to the wall

The name of arcing across, making distinctions with unholy certainty

Barely given
and then its anagram

Overrun house and cuts in return for blood

"On the anniversary of fact," independently of its mere intricacy, well exemplifies the poet's unusual turn of thought, her exactitude and facility in compacting details into an unassimilable *sensation* of meaning. The phraseology (except in the last stanza, which puts me in mind of Pound) is defective. The subject of the sentence in the second stanza is obscure, and very nearly effaced in the third. The grammar is intuitive, but the intuitions come to naught—e.g. "How they treated objects without arms, an admirable ideal."

Here the comma should be a colon, and comprehension falters because it is not. "Book, think of something" is the better poem in every respect—the encapsulation of H.D. is exquisite. Both these pieces are from a sequence called "What Others Had Told Me." Another, called "Probation," offers itself as a species of "foreplay." "Ruth" is a reading of Levinas. The other sequences ("Mars," "Mercury," and "Saturn") are characteristically mysterious responses to the Gulf War.

Ms. Cole's character is daguerreotyped in her works—reading the one, we know the other. She is ardent, sensitive, attentive; the very soul of seriousness and honor; a student of poetic mysteries, with a heart so radically artless as to seem abundant in art—universally respected, admired, and beloved. In person she is about the medium height, broad shouldered, proper in both dress and posture, but with an aura of sadness, whether in action or repose; complexion dark, hair very black and glossy; lips thin; cheekbones pronounced; eyes of a warm, puddling brown, and large, with a singular capacity of expression. She has a son, Jesse, but devotes nearly as much attention to her friends, who stand a little in awe of her. Recently married to Prof. Robert Kaufman, Ms. Cole is also known for her painting.

KATHLEEN FRASER

Ms. Fraser has acquired a just celebrity by many compositions of high merit, the most noticeable of which are *What I Want, Each Next, Something (even human voices) in the foreground, a lake, Notes preceding trust,* and *when new time folds*. Her essay "Partial Local Coherence" is still the most *coherent* account of the language poets, of whose work Ms. Fraser was an early champion. Her mimeo mag *(How)ever,* which attempted to fuse feminism and experimentalism, had a welcome effect. Formed in collaboration with Frances Jaffer, Rachel Blau DuPlessis, Beverly Dahlen, and Susan Howe, *(How)ever*'s itinerary remains relevant more than a decade later. "Medusa's hair was snakes. Was thought, split inward," in especial, which dates from the same period as essay and magazine, is written with great vigor, and, as a feminist use of classical myth, is not far inferior to the "Laugh" of Cixous. Some of her prose poems are distinguished for graceful and brilliant *introspection*—a quality rarely noted in our experimenters. Although not prolific, she continues to write both poetry and prose, and invariably writes well. She has not often attempted translation, but I make no doubt that in this she would excel. It seems, indeed, the legitimate province of her fervid and fanciful nature. I quote one of her versifications from Italian to instance her intense appreciation of genius in others and exemplify the force of her poetic expression:

> Silent in the extreme, you've stopped critiquing,
> except for this looming cross, your master. I've become mystic
> it shows in my empty pockets.
>
> O man o man o man without whom there is
> no mercy for woman o woman her tense fear:
> be my god then or make an excuse for your escape.
>
> His run for it? Mine—it's no sin
> to run away from love of others' happiness, or races
> between the heart's frailties, their falling tears.
> You mystery man, take me, but then don't come back: your bitter
>
> moan isn't worth my rebel life. Has he left you, really,
> leaving you on your cloud? Delight, then,

is the liberty I take with dogs, trains, the dull-witted
or the trajectory of my own mind.

Ms. Fraser, casually observed, has nothing particularly striking in her personal appearance. One would pass her in the street a dozen times without notice. She is low in stature and thickly framed. Her complexion is florid; eyes round and hair soft and brown, usually worn in a light perm; features in general large. The expression of her countenance, when animated, is highly sensual. Her dress is casual but fashionable—understated, expensive. Her bearing needs excitement, however, to impress it with life and dignity. She is of that order of beings who are themselves only on "great occasions." I need scarcely add that she has always been distinguished for her energetic and active philanthropy.

PAT REED

Ms. Pat Reed has written much but published little. All her books of poetry are full of interest. *Sea Asleep* and *More Awesome* are especially so, but upon the whole I am best pleased with her long poem *Kismet.* To plot it has little pretension. The scene moves from America to Spain to Morocco, propelled by fate, as the title indicates. Yet it is a noble composition throughout—imaginative, eloquent, full of dignity, and well sustained. It abounds in detached passages of high merit—for example:

I tried to write this

in the dark—fearing

light would

scare it back

but it's fallen in

with light

is the lantern

done?

logs and their hot shadows

and lake

warm at the shore

Their hands inside

the sun

and another kind of dove

sits in the rays

streaming out

& everyone bows

near the lit bench

in another room

with a painting

& the angel's coming in

from the garden

that we're escaping,

stepping on fruit

fallen, shocked

---

it's all

cracked atlantic

atop the lightlock

a tower

sheds its mirror eye

out walking across

the end of land

and the moon hits

on a bird of a girl

bobbing & singing

in a white gazebo

Ms. Reed has taken no care whatever for her literary fame. A great number of her finest compositions, both in poetry and prose, have been distributed to friends as keepsakes or sent as letters, and are now lying *perdus* about the country in out-of-the-way nooks and corners. Many a goodly reputation has been reared upon a far more unstable basis than her unclaimed and uncollected "fugitive pieces." She has, upon the whole, no equal among her generation—certainly no superior. She is not so vigorous as Mr. Farmer, nor so assured as Ms. Moriarty, nor so caustic as Mr. Price, nor so dignified as Ms. Ward, nor so graceful, fanciful and *dreamlike* as Mr. Hollander, but she is *deficient* in none of the qualities for which these poets are noted, and in certain respects surpasses them all. Her subjects are *fresh*, if not always vividly original, and she manages them with more skill than is usually exhibited by our experimentalists. She also has much imagination and sensibility, while her style is pure, earnest, and devoid of verbiage and exaggeration. I make a point of reading all works to which I see the name of Ms. Reed appended.

Ms. Reed has done almost as much in prose as in poetry, but then her prose is merely poetry in disguise. Of pure prose, of prose proper, she has, perhaps, never written a line in her life. Her epistolary and other narratives are in a class by themselves. She begins with a desperate effort at being sedate—that is to say, sufficiently prosaic and matter-of-fact for the purpose of an explanation or recitation of fact, but in a few sentences, we behold uprising the leaven of an unrighteousness of the muse; then, after some flourishes and futile attempts at repression, a scrap of verse renders itself manifest; then another and another; then comes a poem outright, and then another and another and another, with little odd batches of prose in between, until at length the mask is thrown fairly off and far away, and the whole story *sings*.

I shall say nothing farther, then, of Ms. Reed's prose.

In character she is independent, adventurous, courageous, "equal to any Fate," capable of even foolish risks in whatever should seem to her a holy cause. She has her hobbies, however (of which a very indefinite idea of "duty" is one), and is, of course, readily imposed upon by any artful person who perceives and takes advantage of this amiable failing. She is equally at home in the high reaches of the Sierras and industrial wastes of Oakland, in the sea and on the highway—a most exemplary Californian.

She is about the medium height, perhaps a little below it, and brittle in appearance, but strong. Her face is strongly lined by the sun, and, perhaps, from the same cause, there is a marked sense of distance in the eyes; a certain calm, clear *luminousness*, however, about these latter, amply compensates for the harshness of the effect, and the forehead is truly beautiful in its intellectuality. The hair is straight and blond; the mouth well formed and remarkably sharp in its expression. Her manners are those of a highbred woman, but her ordinary *manner* vacillates, in a singular way, between cordiality and a reserve amounting to *hauteur*. Unmarried, she is about forty years of age.

KIT ROBINSON

Mr. Robinson has become entirely known through his contributions to our small press literature. I am not familiar with his scant forays into critical prose, but Mr. Robinson's poems have been numerous and often excellent. His first collection, *Chinatown of Chayenne,* was published twenty years ago in an exquisitely tasteful form by Whale Cloth Press of Iowa City. Since then he has published some dozen books, the most recent, if I am not mistaken, being *Balance Sheet*—apparently a companion to an earlier volume, *Ice Cubes,* brought out by the same press—Roof Books of New York City. The opening section of *Balance Sheet,* entitled "Counter-Meditation," is by no means the most meritorious, although Mr. Robinson has seen fit to republish this piece in its entirety from a chapbook brought out in the Canary Islands by Zasterle Press. In general, these "Counter-Meditations" evince the author's poetic fervor, classicism of taste and keen appreciation of found and ordinary language. None of these verses can be judiciously commended as a whole, but none of them lacks merit, and there are several that would do credit to any poet in the land. Still, even these latter verses are rather particularly than generally commendable, for even though they abound in forcible passages, they lack unity, totality, and ultimate effect. For example:

> The limitations of
> a brown notebook
> are three inches
>
> by five inches
> by a person
> unable to escape
>
> from a shadow
> of fluctuating dimensions
> even in a hundred thousand million eternities.

The opening stanza of the title poem, "Balance Sheet," puts me in mind of the rich spirit of O'Hara's noble epic, "Second Avenue."

> Pieced lines and lined pieces lead to the blind shed, its light
> green finish peeled off before the eyes can catch hold. Stasis
> has become a way to get the job done, an unlikely reminder
> blessed with the virtues inherent in a peach pit, part of
>   something
> much longer, but remaining, for the time being, a cradle to
>   stillness.

The phrases are well balanced, and the idea of the peach pit as a cradle to stillness is one of the happiest imaginable; neither can anything be more fanciful nor more appropriately expressed than "Stasis / has become a way to get the job done."

The final section of *Balance Sheet* continues the earlier exercise in one-word-per-line pieces (called "Ice Cubes") begun in the earlier book—a book also divided into three parts. That these pieces *are* exercises does not detract from the minor pleasures they afford.

Among the most surrealist in spirit and altogether the best of Mr. Robinson's poems, I consider his admirable anthology piece "In the American Tree," unaccountably excluded from Mr. Messerli's book—perhaps out of lingering resentment toward Mr. Silliman, who took Mr. Robinson's title as his own when editing the big treasury of language writing. Mr. Robinson's "Tree" is noticeable for the vigor of its transformations. A more recent instance of Mr. Robinson's transformative imagination, simpler than "Tree" but no less delightful, is "Nursery Rhyme," whose concluding couplets run:

> A sky can open, but a ditch can't rise.
> *An edge can cut, but a pill can't spill.*
>
> A beach can stretch, but a body can't believe.
> *A wall can stand, but a reason can't complain.*
>
> A room can contain, but a switch can't stay the same
> A place can evoke, but a visit can't last forever.

A sea can swell, but a blank can't be read.
A surface can recede, but a tense can't be nonsense.

I italicize what I think the effective points. In the line,

"A beach can stretch,"

the two components of the preceding line appear to have happily suggested the image of a shoreline, a spilling edge as it were. The effect of this subtle continuity is to recall the prose opening of the poem, where the terms of the verses are first laid out—a psycho-mnemonic pedagogy wholly appropriate to a "Nursery Rhyme." I must not be understood as citing these passages or giving their analysis in illustration of some pedagogical *intent* of Mr. Robinson, but of an occasional happiness to which he is led by a logical mind. Upon the whole, he has a keen sense of poetic excellencies, and gives every indication of that great ability which sustains, beyond verse or book, a whole *career* in poetry. With more earnest promotion, he might accomplish much in the way of example to the young, who too eagerly imitate the ill-disciplined quacks who now dominate the scene.

In character Mr. R. is sincere, fervent, benevolent, with a mind given to the truest wit—inured to praise and blame by a solid sense of self-worth; in temperament, haughty (although this is not precisely the term); in manner, subdued, stern, yet with grace and dignity; converses impressively, earnestly, and with a powerful voice. In person he is tall and slender, with short hair and powerful eyes—reminiscent to a great degree of Anthony Perkins.

A SHORT HISTORY OF LANGUAGE POETRY

By "Hecuba Whimsy"

A Short History of Language Poetry

One day not long ago, as I was leaving the Ear Inn in New York, I passed a ragtag group of poets, one of whom stepped up to me and said: "You, lady, are a language poet!"

I denied that I was. Why? I had not stopped to consider, but doubtless I felt that the names of literary schools conceal vague generalities.

The subject of language writing, or of poetries of "the material text," now receives as much attention in Tuscaloosa and Manoa as in New York City or San Francisco. Bob Perelman has published a book of essays on the subject with Princeton University Press; a friend informs me that *Diacritics,* a rarified journal of Critical Theory, has featured a roundtable discussion involving language writing; and even attacks are widespread now in academia, witness the charge made by Mutlu Konuk Blasing that the movement "mystifies its own techniques" and is, in the end, "totalitarian." Language writing has become not only a small press industry, but also an industry for the universities.

Industry is certainly required to define this poetics satisfactorily. The word "materials" was first used by Clark Coolidge as a way of describing poetic language, but may we credit Coolidge with creating a poetics of the "material text"—or even with creating "language poetry"? He has scarcely expressed a desire to justify his methods, and even less, to be a poet with fixed doctrine. Among those younger than Coolidge, even among those who speak freely of dialectical materialism and of writing as "made thought," mixed feelings have been expressed. Barrett Watten has opposed what he terms *L=A=N=G=U=A=G=E* magazine's "over-all equivalence of activity . . . in which particular motives are effaced." Ron Silliman, for his part, has asserted that the designation "language writing" is at best an occasion for "negative solidarity"! So it seems only right to restrict our application of the term "language poetry" to those who willingly accept it: to the editors of *L=A=N=G=U=A=G=E* in New York, i.e., Charles Bernstein and Bruce Andrews, and those others (like Rae Armantrout, Alan Davies, Steve McCaffery, and Bob Perelman) who employ terms like "language-centered" and "language writing" in their criticism. But we still have not found a definition of the terms.

We face another difficulty in the paradox that the manner in which most of us characterize poetries of the material text partakes of what Bernstein calls "concrete forms of stabilization." We CHARACTERIZE the poetics—this is precisely what Bernstein, and Silliman as well, would like to avoid, since we are concerned with work that, strictly speaking, belonged to a moment of provisional and strategic formulation, and cannot be subject to strict definition or rigorous critique. And yet we are gathered here today to discuss this work.*

To begin with, we must contrast poetics of the material text to previous conceptions of the poem, as found, say, in Williams, Zukofsky, and Creeley. Williams sought a local idiom that could serve as the seed for a new literary flowering. Generally speaking, the American poet has wished, since Poe and Emerson, to rise above the realm of contingency and find a language universal and eternal. She has generally operated—or so she believed—solely by common sense. For Zukofsky, poetry became the search for an arithmetical precision, since numbers alone (in Zukofsky's estimation) are immutable. One might say that the last poet of this kind was Creeley, who carried farthest this effort to record the mind's experience as knowledge. On the other hand, Creeley differed from his predecessors in his insistence upon the contingency of language and the importance that he assigned to this notion. Already, in this sense, he had diverged from the tradition of Williams, Pound, Zukofsky, and other modernists, even from such romantic moderns as Stevens or Crane. Nevertheless, Creeley maintained Williams's "dream of a common language." He tells us that

*The substance of the text was originally delivered as a virtual lecture organized by the Center for the Study of Accelerated Aesthetics. The author prepared the slightly revised transcript offered here. The discussion that follows is based on an on-line chat session staged one week after the original webcast.

form is only an "extension" of content; that our thoughts and feelings have form solely because each thought, each feeling, is bound to experience, which itself has form only because it takes shape in history and as a habit of speech, at a specific moment in the evolution of language. To understand anything that happens in a poem we must refer from the form to the social content which is the self, extended from the more general social form which is our speech, which itself is a content, extending in like fashion from the most general social form of all, which is the totality of our language. This is the conception that Coolidge, whom we may call the founder of language poetry, came forward to contradict.

Opposing the pursuit of objectivity and the passion for socially constructed forms that he found in Creeley, Coolidge proposed a notion that true poetry lies in "obduration"; that true poetry is achieved at *risk* of comprehension. To consider the poem as a form of knowledge would be self-negating. "It has always puzzled me," he confides in a notebook, "when a poet, who must / primarily expend so much energy transforming / the common language into an irreducible variation, / then immediately wants to break down what / he has made into the common tongue again. / As if fear of the unknown were / the mother of discourse." By dint of knowledge, Coolidge says, we have forgotten what it means to write poems. His principal enemy is the expositor of a system, i.e., the critic or professor.

The poet, as Coolidge defines her, is first of all she who enters into an unlimited relationship with her work and has an unlimited interest in herself and her materials. Secondly, the poet is only a poet in the act of writing, with the work literally before her; and, applying this idea to music, Coolidge says (in conversation with Watten): "It's a constant use of discrete and changing melodies, . . . there's no sonata form, no theme and variation . . . in fact the only thing that brings it all close to traditional form is a kind of rhythmic, crescendos and silences, that gives it a kind of structure." It is a matter of improvisation, and sustained effort is required in order for anything of use to be accomplished. Thirdly, then, the poet is involved in an exploration of words and forms; she follows her interests with purpose, remaining open to accidents; she is a digger, a rock hound, a spelunker in Plato's Cave. This passion for exploration is what Coolidge calls "sufferance of thought."

The notions of structure and material have an importance of the first order in the poetics of Coolidge. Each structure is a vain attempt at including the flux of life, for the poet feels herself surrounded by and filled with her materials; nevertheless, she structures. Note that what we have just said concerning the poet's commitment to exploration and improvisation discloses the object of her writing: the unknown—for when engaged in research, one can only predict those conclusions that are not subject to experiment. Thus, the *how* of the quest gives the goal; and, since the writer who truly engages in a quest is never certain of success, her discoveries will always include a certain number of dead ends and banalities, like those of Jack Kerouac's bop prosody. Under the influence of her materials and structures, the poet will ceaselessly strive to document her efforts at articulation, to uncover an original and authentic experience of language. As Coolidge writes in *Quartz Hearts*, "I would like for writing to do what it only could. / I would like my mind to be there."

But so far we have dwelt only on the procedural aspect of Coolidge's poetics. For him, as for the other poets whom we will consider, there is no procedure without a certain negative capability also. The poet must always feel herself in the presence of sense and nonsense alike, and be committed to one no more than the other. "Sometimes it strikes me," writes Coolidge, in a letter to Paul Metcalf, "that poets are the most limited of people in the various areas of external feed-in they allow, they tend to get 'stuck with themselves,' trapped in a needlessly single mode of language/thought. . . . Open the sluices. O poets, you have nothing to lose." To feel oneself open in this way to nonsense no less than sense is to feel only partially engaged with the referential task of writing. Thus, it is by the gaps in knowledge, and particularly by consciousness of those gaps, that one enters the poem. But once in the poem, one still has to progress, by a sort of intellectual voyage, from a practice of composition that stays close to reference, to the highest stage of pure sound. In the highest state of poetry, reason is scandalized, for we meet with the celebration of nonsense in the idea of "language as material," discovered at a certain place and a certain moment in history.

The poet, then, will be she who has this intensity of engagement because she is no longer "stuck" with herself, but is instead in contact with something outside, an "external feed-in." She will undergo a kind of subversion of the understanding. She will be a mere participant in the activity of making meaning, and yet completely invested in respect to her writing because a lifetime of interest or a lifetime of boredom hangs upon the result. Thus, she will be in relation with what Coolidge enigmatically describes as "A tune of / such device it could collect all the chords," with a language that, though sounded, is absolutely heterogeneous to speech, with a verbal music that, no doubt, embraces all communication, but which we feel to be other than our own usage because, in our petty day-to-day rationality, we neglect to keep track of its "ultimate changes."

We have noted two ways by which Coolidge opposed Creeley: by the emphasis laid upon improvisation and exploration, and by the importance assigned to "sound as thought." We must add to these distinctions Coolidge's insistence upon the idea of "arrangement," which he called (in its grammatical context) "axial armature." For Creeley, the poem is the necessary unfolding of experience, and arrangement (syntax) is necessity understood. For Coolidge, on the contrary, syntax is possibility, and any poetics that limits his playful mode of composition would be oppressive, suffocating. Moreover, the idea of arrangement is linked to the idea of objects, and we may contrast Coolidge's fabled collection of rocks, with all their jumble of fissures and markings, to the logical unwinding of Creeley's *Words* and *Pieces,* just as the musical and linguistic travelogue of Coolidge has been contrasted to Creeley's search for an absolute location in the social totality.

Naturally, the ideas of Coolidge pose many problems. On the one hand, is there not a tendency in Coolidge to rationalize and explain away the difficulty of "obduration" by presenting it as the just expression of an experience that eludes straightforward articulation? And although he purports to present us with music as a freer form of articulation, does he not thereby mute the very musicality of music by defining it in linguistic terms? On the other hand, Coolidge himself realized that sound as thought did not constitute the supreme solution to the problem of articulating experience, which would have been reached in music only if thought's measure had no other means of expression. Let us add that the problem exists only for those who dwell in language; for the lucky, that is to say, for those who truly express themselves musically, the difficulty vanishes. In short, this entire construction exists only from a "logocentric" point of view. But perhaps this does not constitute a genuine objection. In a general way, it is very difficult to determine whether such observations are objections or whether, by accentuating the difficulty, they reinforce Coolidge's conception. We could say the same in regard to questions brought out by the relation between material and structure (the intensity of the material's impact being paradoxically dependent upon the apparent transparency of the structure), and by the relation between structure and meaning (for if the structure is essential to the material, the paradox threatens to vanish).

Without a doubt we could trace the history of the material text back to John Ashbery, a writer whom Coolidge much admires, and to Ashbery's shadow boxing in recent years with critics and professors. To academicism Ashbery opposes what he calls the "gesture which is neither embrace nor warning / But which holds something of both in pure / Affirmation that doesn't affirm anything." We may even find in Frank O'Hara's "Second Avenue" or "Biotherm" certain stylistic features that are not dissimilar to Coolidge's; but we must be wary of attributing too much historical importance to the New York School. Moreover, even those aspects of Ashbery and O'Hara that did slip into Coolidge's work of the 1970s lost in transit their character of aestheticism and nostalgia.

We could even trace these poetics back to Charles Olson, who argued that "The Advantage of Literacy Is That Words Can Be on the Page," which demonstrated on historical grounds that written language developed as a consequence of the non-identity of sound and meaning ("About the only way the character of the pun—and rhyme which has struck me now for some time as a most interesting crazy business of writing right now—makes sense"). Language ceased to be magic, and became instead object. Alternatively, we could go back to Stein, who replaced Joyce's historicism with a kind of writing that conceived of language as an autonomous system of signs. It remains no less true, however, that we are able to recognize and understand these early prefigurations of language poetry only because a Coolidge composed his poems.

~

The second major phase in the development of language poetry occurred when three San Francisco poets, Silliman, Watten, and Lyn Hejinian, perceiving in Coolidge's materiality a new approach to the problem of the subject, translated the reflections of Coolidge into more intellectual terms.

We may consider the poetics of Silliman as a sort of politicizing and generalizing of the poetics of Coolidge. In the poetics of Silliman, we are no longer referred to music, but rather, to deep structures of our experience of which we may glimpse only scattered regions. Language has multiple functions, and each utterance has multiple possibilities of meaning. But we respond to one, we ignore another, and we never attain to that absolute physical location in words that Creeley hoped to reach through the unwinding of the mind to its necessary conclusion. The absolute, in Silliman's poetics, is instead the social totality, which reveals itself only partly—in bits of torn paper, in scattered flashes, like intermittent strokes of a pen. We have the sensation of a tunnel into which our thought plunges like a subway. Consequently, we are doomed to "ideological entanglement"; individual identity is refracted utterly by language, yet fulfills itself in this very fragmentation by sensing the background of form from which everything we can know or feel emerges.

We know that this background is something real; we derive our reality from it; yet we cannot construe it from within, and as social subjects we cannot even express ourselves completely. But in this awareness of objective social forces, which comes most vividly to us in situations in which the referential functions of language are strained to the utmost, we fully realize our condition. Whether it be an official government statement or an avant-garde poem, we sense that there is something more pressing at issue than sense, something that evades or undermines our conventions of comprehension—we open ourselves to reality precisely by virtue of our relation to this incomprehension. In this respect, we find in Coolidge and Silliman the same connections between openness and incomprehension. But Silliman, unlike Coolidge, recognizes, even in the face of pure nonsense, the durability of convention. To account for this durability, he has taken over from linguistics the concept of a "Parsimony Principle," a means of "insinuating unity and closure" even in texts that aspire to antithetical qualities. Crediting this mechanism entirely to "*the mind of the reader,*" Silliman rejects any definition of meaning that would limit articulation to authorial intention or treat it as a consequence of the text as such.

Silliman senses deeply the social values that frame all acts of interpretation, and the crises resident in our experience of incomprehension. He also endeavors to complement Coolidge's intuitions—his refusal "to carve connotative domains from words"—with a profound feeling for human communication and human history. For Silliman, we are not isolated soloists, as Coolidge would have us be isolated, practicing in the basement with drum kit and headphones. Communication, a struggling for collective action with other persons, is at the core of his system.

Communication has consistently been one of the major problems for poetics of the material text. Indirect in Coolidge, direct and even crude in Silliman, divided into message and structure in Watten, posed as a matter of epistemology by Hejinian, clumsy and failing in Bernstein, communication is always there—at least as a problem. Even in the absence of communication, the idea obstinately persists.

Now let us turn to Watten. His problem is the scientific problem of meaning formation. It has been said, unjustly perhaps, that he is not a language poet, but a poet of linguistics, and that his eventual aims are theoretical. Watten considers the problems of poetry primarily as a mode of critical theory, turning to poetry as a framing mechanism because critical thinking can only occur (according to Watten) as a conscious attention to the formal and social parameters within which all communicative acts are staged. To be sure, there are other forms of critical framing for Watten: there is the analogous example of conceptual art and its innovative use of gallery space; there is the presentation of examples in philosophy; there is the use of case study in the social and natural sciences; but only in poetry is framing itself framed and thus made truly subject to scrutiny. Galleries are pitched in permanent struggle with the forces of commerce; science is compromised by its institutional commitments; philosophy remains chained to a traditional mode of argumentation; none of these areas of research can claim the intellectual and social independence—the marginality—of poetry.

In order that we may truly recognize the ubiquity of the frame, and not remain unwitting consumers of language-as-ideology, we must overcome the lures of direct address and Imagism ("direct treatment of the thing"). Ordinarily, due to our own laziness and the pressure of "subjective aesthetic principles," we remain caught in the snares of personality study, where we are not really able to perceive the workings of ideology. Only by attending to technique, declares Watten, are we able to wrest poetic language free from these snares. And an awareness of writing as technique is attainable only by undergoing what the Russian Formalists called a "semantic shift," which opens up a domain of negativity from which the world erupts as if anew, putting "An end to sleepwalking." This negativity is the power that Watten also calls *Total Syntax*—the domain of text understood as a re-presentation of context—where we discover a kind of agency in the work's articulation of its "intrinsic and extrinsic dimensions." As a consequence of this twofold articulation—"the work in the world" and "the world in the work"—our entanglement in ideology becomes recognizable as material fact.

Coolidge insisted upon an agency immanent in language, which he describes in *The Crystal Text* as "active possibilities." He conceived of this agency in natural terms, using the model of climatology and geology. Agency for Watten, however, is essentially a product of social conditions and does not lead to unlimited possibility, to a world that is (in Wittgenstein's definition) "all that is the case." His total syntax is rather an active *im*possibility. Through technique, the poet probes this impossibility, from which erupts "everything that is *not* the case," and into which every sign or frame threatens to crumble and collapse. This attempt to articulate a productive negativity (even if we were to consider it mistaken) is one of Watten's most interesting ventures.

Naturally, this negativity is difficult to describe. Strictly speaking, we cannot even say that it is an agency. Provisionally, however, Watten has invented a formula, "The world is structured on its own displacement," to characterize its action. Negativity structures itself and everything else. It is an active negativity that causes the world that erupts from it to tremble to the foundations. One might say that it is the negative foundation of the world, from which poetic language displaces itself by a process of defamiliarization. Let us remark parenthetically that in the title poem of *Conduit,* the book in which Watten discloses his theory of negativity, he suggests that this displacement, indifferent to each and every particular sign, each and every individual frame, can be, none other, at bottom, than signification as such—for what is there, he argues, indifferent to each speech *act,* if not the destabilizing mechanism of the real, "a sequence of linguistic artifacts at zero degree," characterized poetically as "a mirror of containers" in which "experience is access to language only." Thus, we reach by a different route the identification that Creeley had sought between language and experience. And this is so, in Watten's work, notwithstanding a certain "nonfunctional relation" between material social conditions, on one hand, and poetic technique, on the other.

In any case, the experience of negativity reveals us to ourselves as entangled in language, displaced in ideology, without recourse or refuge. How we are entangled in language, we do not know. This brings us to one of the fundamental assertions of language poetry: we write, without discovering any sure basis for our language external to language itself; hence, we are, for all practical purposes, constructs of language.

Obviously, we have abandoned any humanist scheme, any free negotiation of competing ideologies, at the center of which would be identity, the one nonnegotiable content of every separate ideology. Now we see only language, displaced in a myriad of structures; here, identity becomes merely a formal possibility of language. No doubt, one may seek out the identities of material things and zoological or botanical species, but there can be no essential identity of an individual person or social class. Here we see most clearly the "subject matter"—if we may so speak!—of the poetics of the material text, as contrasted to nearly all other modernist and postmodernist poetics, from Williams to Creeley, in which form always derives from content, and especially from the content of a poet's experience.

The identity of a social subject—this construct of ideology displaced into the world—is essentially, then, a function of language. Buffeted by social conditions, identity becomes a form of "evidence," as for Coolidge, the artist, engaged in her projects, discovers the world as "a baffle that shows through to / you, everywhere." Nonetheless, although we generally experience our subjectivity as a distending of possibilities into a largely unexplored world, the moment invariably comes when the world appears to contract in on us, defining subjectivity as an experience of *im*possibility. This is, of course, the moment of historical crisis or trauma, when social conditions become determinate, a moment that Watten characterizes allegorically in *Bad History* as the execution of a "General Will," an ideology whose constituent subjects ("beneficiaries") remain beholden, however divergent their competing claims or discrepant stakes, to the fixed fact of power as actually constituted ("the law of inheritance"). It is this fact of our contraction within and to the horizon of a "General Will" that accounts for the determinate character of social conditions.

Nevertheless, within this contraction, bound by this social contract, we do accomplish a movement—or rather, movements—of transformation; not beyond ideology (since, as Watten notes, quoting Žižek, "the idea of the possible *end* of ideology is an ideological idea *par excellence*"), and certainly not towards a perfect State ("failure" being a constituent element of "the real"—the principle teaching that Watten confirmed with his trip to Russia). Instead, we accomplish our transformations for a known community of readers, within a given world, and towards a concrete future. Conceived in this way, the idea of transformation loses its utopian character, acquiring instead a semantic and performative one; it is a transformation through everyday language. Let us note immediately, however, in reply to any possible objections from those who might insist that transformation implies in common parlance an affirmation of revolutionary hopes, that Watten introduces the word "transformation" so as to distinguish language poetry from Surrealism, which declared itself a revolutionary movement in explicitly Leninist terms. Properly speaking, to transform is to alter the form (and thus the content) of some person, place, or thing. For this reason, a *perfect* State or *perfected* methodology could no longer stake credible claim to transformation as its goal; only "the perception of mind in control of its language" is capable of effecting transformation in perpetuity. For Watten, the object of transformation is thus no longer "a specially valued" social or aesthetic system, but instead the power to manipulate and indeed embody the frame; that is, "the ability not simply to control information but to be the literal point where information issues forth."

Let us examine more closely these various transformations. First, there is transformation (or, for those who still shy away from this term: "formal experiment") within a community of readers—readers who are, often enough, also writers. In a manifesto written by Watten with five other Bay Area poets, we read, "If there has been one premise of our group that approaches the status of a first principle, its has been not the 'self-sufficiency of language' or the 'materiality of the sign' but *the reciprocity of practice implied by a community of writers who read each other's work*." Here, a poetics that first presented itself as a critique of normative models of communication becomes an affirmation of the power and efficacy of intellectual exchange. Curiously enough, few poets have insisted upon the poet's participation or relationship with a community of other writers. Although Robin Blaser speaks of his "Great Companions," and Creeley of "The Company," most poets are uncomfortable with explicit membership in a group formation. Even Stein, center of the avant-garde in Paris, emphasizes her isolation as a writer of American English. Watten and his colleagues are unique in their admission of "being primarily interested in [their] own work" as an "Aesthetic Tendency," in their insistence that "Collectivity . . . is as much a source of value as the individual author." In a brilliant elaboration on Creeley, Watten declares art "a process set in motion by a group of people" and not "an object made by one person." For Creeley, process is individual act; its purpose, in art, is "a manifest directly of the *energy* inherent in the materials literally, and their physical manipulation" by the artist. According to Watten, communities are likewise a manifestation of energy, but this is true not because communities are "energetic," but because they are engaged directly with the materials of their world, in direct relation with language—language in the street, so to speak. Even in their most isolated activity, even when they think themselves most opaque and private, writers remain products of a "social process."

Second, not only is the work always, as a matter of course, in natural relation with a community of readers, but the work is in immediate relation with a given world. We are elements in a composition, so to speak. We are naturally enclosed by "all that is the case": this is the significance of the word *Frame,* which implies a location in actual, physical space. By way of suggesting the same notion, Watten speaks of Robert Smithson's "sculptural syntax" as "articulated on a linguistic axis of which the central terms are *space* and *time.*"

Third, then, we transform language in a temporal dimension, with an eye toward the future. And thus it is that our political and aesthetic programs are inevitably teleological. We are always concerned with something yet to be realized; and language, insofar as we ourselves are its construction, is teleological precisely because it is offered to posterity. In fact, what Watten calls *Progress* (however ironically) is always and essentially a practice of language distended toward a concrete, if unknown, context.

It is clear that these three transforming movements are not quite analogous to transformation as conceived by Coolidge and Silliman, since they are not primarily transformations in consciousness (conceived in Romantic terms by Coolidge, and in Frankfurt School terms by Silliman), but instead in the structures of language (the structures of address included). We take control of language, but always under the aegis of an ordering mind.

We have been at pains to examine three modes of transformation that enter into Watten's poetics. Two other aspects of transformation complete the list: transformation of language into literature (through technique), and transformation of technique into social act (through method). In summary, time, space, community, technique, and method are the five uses of the idea of transformation to be found in Watten. We may feel that in this multiplicity of meanings there are sources of confusion.

We turn now to Lyn Hejinian. Her concerns are epistemological and psychological rather than sociopolitical, and her work affords a more sympathetic account of subjectivity than does either Silliman's or Watten's. In places—for instance, in her personification of knowledge as a female Faust, as "La Faustienne," or in her spirited defense of "cogitation"—there is even a recuperation of the subject as traditionally conceived.

We have noticed, in reading Watten, that the subject always has an eye on the future. On the other hand, like the repeated lines of Hejinian's *My Life,* this future is always in part a recapitulation of the past. Hejinian's earliest work took cognizance of this condition of temporality, describing the subject as a "mask of motion"—the word "motion" implying a free movement toward the future, and the word "mask" implying the fixity of an inescapable past. For Hejinian, despite the emphasis on deep structures of language and larger social forms, the poet necessarily finds herself defined in her actions by such-and-such an upbringing and such-and-such a community, in such-and-such a time and place. This means that she is not only a function of her culture in general, but she is also a product of her own particular biography. We might also note that the poet's future is limited by the fact that death occurs at such-and-such a date as the terminus of her creations. Thus, the telos of Hejinian's work is qualified by the fact that her own authorial possibilities are not abstract ones; instead, they are embedded in specific conditions she herself has not chosen.

Thus, the subject moves ceaselessly from her future to her past, from her anticipations and plans to her memories, regrets, and remorses. This fact of being constantly in touch with both the future and the past constitutes a key concept in the poetics of Hejinian: the rejection (or better: postponement) of closure. Being both before and behind herself, she exists in the same time as herself. Consequently, for Hejinian the "Rejection of Closure," i.e., the continuous present, is in some sense a juncture of her future and her past. We may fix upon this idea as the starting point of Hejinian's poetics, from which she conceives of writing as an aid to memory, by which the poet takes upon herself her past, her future, and her present, and affirms the continuity of her consciousness. Here, we may note, in passing, the possibility of comparing the poetics of Hejinian with the notational poetics of Robert Grenier. We may also compare it, as always, with the poetics of Coolidge. We may perceive the influence of Coolidge on Hejinian's view of consciousness; on her treatment of person, place, and thing; on the pre-eminence accorded to thought (a pre-eminence, to be sure, which also appears in the poetry of Creeley); and even on the notion of a rejection of closure.

It is important for a proper understanding of Hejinian that we do not consider these notions as a series of poetical dogmas. According to Hejinian, the poet, more actively than other social subjects, creates herself. In fact, the poet *is* that social subject who creates herself, who shapes, plays with, or draws into visibility the very structure of her subjectivity. We noted, in discussing Watten, that the poetics of the material text is essentially the affirmation that subjectivity has no essential substratum of reality. (This affirmation goes beyond merely stating, after Creeley, that its content comes after its form.) We may add, now, as a second characteristic, that subjectivity, because it is without fixed reality, is the mutability of reality itself. Inasmuch as the subject is a construct of language, and language-as-material an exposure of language-as-illusion, the language poet comes in contact, when she frees herself from the logic of representation, with the very materiality of the illusions within which her subjectivity operates. Only at this point is it possible to speak of a "true" knowledge of the world, or of subjectivity in any kind of meaningful sense as a locus for such knowledge.

If we take Hejinian's definition of poetry to be the recovery of the world by a social subject conscious of the material basis of her illusions, the second definition, proposed by the poet at the end of her long poem *The Guard,* is "construction worker" (and not, as is often said, a worker in deconstruction). If we understand by construction the discovery of subjectivity as a construct of language, poetry becomes for us the acknowledgement of self as one object among others in the world, that is, as a noun. Self-awareness in poetry becomes a knowledge of nounal relations, not only in their syntactic possibilities (their "arrangement," as Coolidge would have it), but also in their power to constitute the world. From this point of view, the poetics of Hejinian are an expansion, and in a certain sense, a negation of Coolidge's emphasis on exploration. We must recognize the injustice of reproaching this poetics for doubting reality and abandoning self-expression in favor of language games. On the contrary, Hejinian's poetics declares that there is no dichotomy between language and world or language and the self, and that the very distinction between a language game and reportage or self-expression, residual in Coolidge, must be exploded to reveal the poet as amassing experience. In other words, according to Hejinian, the poet becomes conscious of herself as a locus of knowledge precisely insofar as she apprehends herself and the world in which she operates as a construct of language. Indeed, without a verifiable *moment* of construction—consciousness coming into existence in the same manner and at the same time as the self and the world it apprehends—the phrase "construct of language" ceases to have any meaning.

In putting the notion of a direct experience of reality into question, the language poet unsettles the very structure of the subjectivity to which she is bound. In her every poetical work, the linguistic substratum of subjectivity is brought into focus at the same time as the reality of her consciousness of that substratum is placed in doubt and cast into a supreme gamble. Thus, we see the ideas of subjectivity and reality, and we may even add, subjectivity and world, constantly reuniting. Thus, when Hejinian speaks of "The Person," her focus is not any particular individual. She is describing personhood as such. Her poetry's specific perceptions are doubtless derived from her own experience. Through this perception, she arrives at the general conditions of existence in the world, or what Hejinian calls poetically "a whole / landscape of undivided situations," and in her account of a trip to Russia, "a continuum of options." In this respect, the poetics of Hejinian claim a further distinction from the poetics of Watten, in that Watten always remains in the social, whereas Hejinian attains sociality, that is to say, the general characteristics of individual experience. One may well ask if the notion of identity is not surreptitiously reinscribed in such a project, and if Watten is not more consistent in his banishment of this notion. One may ask further if her interest in the construction of personhood and memory is compatible with affirmations of the materiality of language.

Perhaps the most important question of all concerns the kind of political conclusions that may be drawn from these conceptions of Hejinian. Simply stated, we may say that, finding ourselves constructs of language and objects in a field of social forces, we must assert the fact of consciousness and—as has already been intimated in our discussion of Watten—shoulder the responsibilities of individual action. The poet is not to remain in a stage of self-reflexivity or in a stage of self and world creation, as exemplified by the work of Juliana Spahr and Lisa Robertson, two writers whose reflections are linked in origin to the ideas of Hejinian. According to each of these writers, the poet must also submit such postures to critique. In Hejinian's case, the poet may begin to take action through a process of description "that restores realness to things in the world and separates things from ideology," through a "poetics of scrutiny" whose positive result is "strangeness." This concept is comparable to the notion of "obduration" in Coolidge and to the play of "nonsense" in the "poethical" practice of Joan Retallack.

Hejinian has not systematized her thought in these matters. "The Quest for Knowledge in the Western Poem" is the name of one of her most searching works as a critic, and, in fact, one sees that for Hejinian, the very nature of knowledge constitutes a quest, and that she strives to situate her own explorations within the context of what is often called "the western box," i.e., a tradition of thought stretching from Socrates to Francis Bacon to William James. Nevertheless, one cannot say that her interest in epistemology is systematic. One may even raise the question of why it is unsystematic, and whether there may not be for Hejinian an irreducible difference between knowledge and epistemology, that is, between a poetic project and poetics. "Writing," she tells us, is an "unsystematized accumulation of statements and findings." But can one found a poetics upon such a project? This, it seems, is Hejinian's problem.

Prior to the publication of "The Quest for Knowledge," Hejinian attempted, in certain lectures and essays, to erect a poetics more involved with phenomenological than epistemological questioning. In these works, she enjoins us to attend "The wanton consciousness of consciousness" which occurs in the acts of reading and writing. To this end, she invokes the thought of Gertrude Stein, who shows that "things take place inside the writing, are perceived there, not elsewhere, outside it." Coextensive with this work, Hejinian has made a painstaking study of the idea of realism; but here, it seems, she is confronted with antinomies and wavers between a language-centered solipsism indebted to pre-Freudian psychology (especially that of Stein's teacher, William James) and a fascination with material and social conditions consistent with her readings in Zola, Dickens, Jack London, and the like.

Recalling her description of poetry's task "to provoke and sustain in both writer and readers an experience of experience," one may well ask after the reasons for her specific choices of subject matter. This question brings to the foreground the whole problem of idealism in Hejinian. No doubt, she would like to pass beyond the antinomy of idealism—realism. Nevertheless, it seems (save in certain poems of particular intensity) that she is pushed now towards idealism, now towards realism, and that, despite all her desire to do so, she does not succeed in passing beyond the domain in which these two doctrines stand in opposition. One might say that one of the attractions of her work derives in good part from the fact that she carries far each of these two great intellectual tendencies: the idealistic tendency, so recurrent in experimental writing, to define experience entirely as a condition of language; and the realistic tendency to insist upon persons, places, and things as irreducible to their linguistic apprehension. Thus, Hejinian says on the one hand that "[b]ecause we have language we find ourselves in a peculiar relationship to the objects, events, and situations which constitute what we imagine of the world," that "the limits of language are the limits of what we might know." On the other hand, she says that "[w]e delight in our sensuous involvement with the materials of language, we long to join words to the world—to close the gap between ourselves and things, and we suffer from doubt and anxiety as to our capacity to do so because of the limits of language itself." At times, it seems that this doubt and anxiety, in turn, should be defined as the desire to surrender to things. In the latter case, the realistic element seeks preeminence. But the problem remains, essentially, unresolved.

We can see that the poetics of Hejinian contain a number of heterogeneous elements. The importance in her work of self-reflexivity —the image of herself "as a spectator of the spectating," a marked influence of Gertrude Stein—leads to a definition of poetry as spectacle, and recognition that "Western curiosity is addicted to the theatricality of seeing and being seen." On the other hand, Hejinian's "spectating" always occurs in a particular locale, an idea that is foreign to Stein and may have come in part from Williams, a rarely remarked influence, and from her fascination with the nineteenth-century novel. And we must not forget her interest in "Strangeness," the "defamiliarization" of Russian Formalism, which Hejinian has also discovered in detective stories, travel literature, and in her translations of her friend Arkadii Dragomoshenko. It is the fusion of elements borrowed from the American avant-garde, realist fiction, and Russian Formalism that gives to the poetry of Hejinian its particular tonality.

Before embarking on a critical exploration of the poetics of Silliman, Watten, and Hejinian, we may point out that the first two elements in this fusion are linked. The language experiments of the avant-garde are central, not only because they bring new forms of creation into existence, but because they extend the work of realism into a description of consciousness; and the authenticity and authority of the realist novel is due in large part to "the autonomy of the writing—the high visibility of its devices and even its intrusive strangeness." We sense in her poetics both a tendency towards an extreme subjectivity and a tendency towards a deeply felt objectivity.

This sketch of the poetics of Hejinian, Watten, and Silliman leads to some further considerations. Taken as a whole, does not their project imply a worldview that is negated by the poetry itself? There is no place for self-expression, it seems, and yet, when they depict themselves as subjects of history, and even as agents of social change, is there not—at least, in these expressions—an echo of the personalist poetics which characterize their earliest writings and the sense of personal mission which marks them as children who came of age in the 1960s? Could it be, moreover, that if the language poets were completely free of their humanist presuppositions, they would cease to be language poets? Midway between Noam Chomsky and Michel Foucault, they are in the world of Foucault with the feelings of Chomsky, and in the world of Chomsky with the feelings of Foucault.

In the second place, could we not conceive of a poetics of the material text linked, not solely to experiences of ideological entanglement, socially constructed meaning, and psychological realism, but also to feelings of transcendence and spirituality? The students of Robert Duncan have often voiced this objection to the language poets. The language poets would doubtless reply that, language being a human creation and ourselves its sole users, there is no basis for such a linkage. But does the power of language extend only so far as its intended functions would take it? Certain passages in Bernstein's *A Poetics* challenge the Bay Area language writers on this very point by according a special status to *dys*function. Minimizing the necessity of theoretical "seriousness"—an idea of the first importance for Silliman, Watten, and Hejinian—he develops a notion of "critical excess" in which "the inadequacy of our / explanatory paradigms is neither ignored / nor regretted but brought into fruitful play."

Lastly, our assessment brings us to these poets' political aims. Their paratactic methods of composition, by which they aimed to take upon themselves the full weight of a revolutionary vanguard, constitute a sort of act of faith. In Olson, this act of faith is understandable as a concrete act of the creative will, but it is less clearly substantiated in Silliman, Watten, and Hejinian. Moreover, the parataxis of these latter writers remains extremely formal. How does one proceed from theory to practice, and from language practice to social action? Silliman, the most politically engaged of these three writers, describes this movement in terms too general to permit a concrete application. Moreover, we cannot set aside the fact that at the time of his trip to the Soviet Union—arguably, the ultimate and most applicable subject for Silliman's work—his paratactic jottings became indistinguishable from the diaristic notes of a journalist or tourist. This does not detract in the slightest from the literary merit of Silliman's writing, or from the intellectual force of his ideas. We may, however, conclude from this evidence that the political dimension of Silliman's project remains purely formal, admits of several interpretations, and is, finally, not a politics at all.

We come now to the third stage in this brief history of language poetry.

Several young and able New York poets have found in the ideas of Coolidge something fresh and significant that answers to their own ideas of what is possible in poetry. There was already in New York—particularly in the writing of Jackson Mac Low—something that could be compared to the poetics of Silliman, Watten, and Hejinian. Furthermore, the influence of the San Francisco poets was directly felt in New York through the circulation of magazines and pamphlets—though, to be sure, in a small circle of writers.

The poetics of Bernstein, although containing much that is original with him, is linked in part with the poetics of Stein and in part with that of Zukofsky. The latter leads him into a kind of intellectuality that may not be completely consonant with the elements he may have derived from Stein. In common with Zukofsky, Bernstein views style as a problem of philosophy—of ethics rather than aesthetics—and defines language as a continuum of possibilities ranging between two limits, though for Bernstein this continuum is often rendered in a sense more indebted to the divergence opened up between Creeley and Coolidge (two readers of Zukofsky) than the old Objectivist himself. Bernstein characterizes poetic language as having two forms: "*absorption,*" which at its highest level "can be achieved without transparency, causal / unity, or traditional metrics," and which corresponds to the experiential "poetics of duration" of Creeley; and "*impermeability,*" a form of "obduration" construed in Coolidge-fashion as a function of "doubt, noise, resistance."

For Bernstein, the privileged term is "*absorption*"; but what, then, is the status of "*impermeability*"? This is one of the most difficult problems to resolve in his poetics. When he argues for absorption, he classifies himself as a pragmatist. When he defines impermeability as a form of "physicality," of "foreignness," of "nonsocial 'identity' / at odds with its social 'selves,' " and even of "group particularization" asserting its "antiabsorptive autonomism," he calls this pragmatism into question. When he speaks against absorptive writing, describing it as a form of "syntactic ideality" and calling its "dilemma" one "of belief," he classifies himself as a skeptic. This dynamic of opposition is not dissimilar to the split in Hejinian between realism and idealism. For Bernstein, however, the irresolution is a conscious stance, one which he adopts for reasons hinted at in the analogical definition of impermeability and made crystal clear in an early essay on Stanley Cavell: "At the basis of the human socius is the ceding of skepticism so that society can take place. And the retreat from the monstrousness of society is the abrogation of this ceding."

Inasmuch as Bernstein adopts "antiabsorptive / techniques . . . toward absorptive ends" and "absorptive means . . . / toward anti-absorptive ends"—that is, inasmuch as "the / distinction / between the two / terms / breaks / down"—one is tempted to ask if it is still proper to speak of "*absorption*" and "*impermeability*" as defining the "upper" and "lower" or "inner" and "outer" limits on a continuum of values. If the value of a continuum is its calibration of distinctions, what value can there be, in the end, in Bernstein's?

Second, one may question whether or not there is something concrete in language called "absorption" as Bernstein defines it; one may question whether there exists an essential property of a given text that does not depend for its corroboration upon the subjective responses of a reader. On this point, Silliman's poetics, in which meaning is the province of the reader—as a consequence of which, even "impermeable" writing can have meaning—seems far more rigorous. No doubt, Bernstein's affirmation of the "absorptive" qualities of writing responds to a political concern on his part, and answers a need to affirm poetry as attaining a sociality independent of its status as cultural artifact. But does one have the right to pass from this assertion to the notion that this sociality is a determinate quality of writing, and is objectively so—that it is, in fact, something governed by the author's intentions?

On a good number of occasions, as we have said, Bernstein makes a forceful case for the skeptic. But by his insistence on the intentionality of artifice, by his definition of poetry as "the continuation of politics by other means," by his conception of comedy as a destabilization of "authoritative/controlling discourse," by his affirmation of "the possibility of truthfulness or good faith or communication," and by his insistence on the failure inherent in all attempts to safeguard art from critical and commercial appropriation, he seems to summarize the frequently justifiable grounds for the liberal intellectual's animadversions to skepticism.

Perhaps the duality of Bernstein's work is one of its intrinsic characteristics, and thus should not be cast aside. A search for justification and the impossibility of justification are recurrent *motifs* in both his poetry and criticism. His writing is one of the incarnations of a project in which the ideas are of less importance than their style of deployment. Bernstein is akin in this respect to Walter Benjamin, who wrote in his *Arcades Project:* "To be a dialectician means to have the wind of history in one's sails. The sails are the concepts. It isn't enough, though, to have sails at one's disposal. The art of setting them is the decisive factor."

This is not to say that an effort by Bernstein to reconcile his contradictory tendencies is either inadvisable or improbable. There is the absorptive Bernstein of *The Nude Formalism,* "Of Time and the Line," "Emotions of Normal People," and "Dear Mr. Fanelli." There is the antiabsorptive Bernstein of *Disfrutes,* "Asylum," and "The Rudder of Inexorability." And there is the Bernstein of "Standing Target," "Dysraphism," "Blow-Me-Down-Etude," and "Lives of the Toll Takers," works which combine divergent and contrary aspects of Bernstein. There may yet be a Bernstein who will find a way beyond this oscillation.

A few summary remarks are suggested by this brief survey of the language poets. Coolidge is not at all interested in theory, and in this respect, he is more "purely" poetic than Silliman, Watten, and Bernstein, or even, to a lesser extent, Hejinian. Thus, in the history of language poetry, one goes from a consideration of poetry proper to a study of language with the help of the idea of poetry. The latter method is that of Watten and Bernstein in particular. Nevertheless, Watten and Bernstein differ considerably, and Bernstein is closer than Watten to Hejinian and Coolidge. (For example, Bernstein criticizes the pre-eminence that Watten assigns to the theoretical over the poetic.) Silliman's position is more conflicted.

We might further mention, without discussing, writers such as Tina Darragh, Kit Robinson, Stephen Rodefer, and Hannah Weiner, whose ideas are similar to the poets under discussion here (and to others already cited), though applied according to different scales of literary value. We must omit discussion of those who, like Susan Howe, Michael Palmer, and Rosmarie Waldrop, are often classed as language poets, but who would refuse to accept the appellation.

Let us construct a few rules-of-thumb for distinguishing between language poets and non-language poets. If we say: *Subjectivity is a vector of social forces; desire, a function of ideology; freedom, a matter of conscious critique and transformation;* then we are speaking in the manner of Watten and Silliman. If we say: *The individual, self-aware as a consequence of language, strives in language to apprehend "the real," seeking thereby to con-*

nect with "other minds"; then we recognize the accents of Hejinian or Bernstein. If we say: "A poem can't free us from the struggle for existence, but it can uncover desires and appetites buried under the accumulating emergencies of our lives," as Adrienne Rich says; or, "No poet is ever quite sure what she's going to say next, if she's doing it right—in any poem," as Alice Notley says; or, "The unrealizable ideal is to write as if the earth opened and spoke," as Frank Bidart says; then we are moving in a sphere which is no longer that of the material text.

~

The language poets remind us, but in a new way, of what a number of poets and critics have tried to teach us: that there are forms of language that cannot be completely understood under the rubric of subjectivity. Naturally, those who are of a contrary opinion will still try to explain the material text in personalizing terms—for example, by psychology or biography. Such explanations often have some validity, but they are never completely satisfactory.

Thanks to language poetry, "Unconfusion" once again "submits / its confusion to proof." And this reminds us that there are many language poets—or, as Coolidge would say, many poets. We have just intimated that Marianne Moore was a language poet. We could say the same of Schwitters, Khlebnikov, and Césaire; of Ezra Pound, the fascist writer from whom Bruce Andrews—an avowed leftist—has taken over the dictum: "*make it new*"; of Rimbaud, cummings, and Cage—even of Christopher Smart. We could make the same claim for Williams's great enemy, T. S. Eliot, whose *Waste Land* is said to have "made poetry and criticism one and the same thing." We could show that the best of our mainstream poets—Anne Carson, Paul Muldoon—derive their greatness by placing questions of language in the foreground.

There is, however, a question that may trouble the poetics, and even the poetry, of the language poet. Does she not risk rendering illegible the very language that she wishes above all to foreground? In the words of Jean Baudrillard: "*[T]he medium is the message* not only signifies the end of the message, but also the end of the medium. There are no more media in the literal sense of the word . . . —that is, of a mediating power between one reality and another, between one state of the real and another." With this dilemma in view, Bob

Perelman has called for a return to "narrative" and "intelligibility." Bruce Andrews, for his part, has declared, "[We] can take our well-developed attention to signs & our desire for their dishevelment & expose it to a social dialogue." One may trace this retreat from "obduration" even further, for not only has Andrews shifted his work's emphasis from "critique" to "explanation," but in his development he has modified his famously destructive poetics so as to allow for the "positive power" of a "social productivity of meaning," "an address *to* the context." Language poetry thus affirms its heretofore hidden link with Whitman, that is, affirms the materiality not only of texts, but also of the "social method . . . that places and positions texts within the horizon of some outer social world." And this suggests a major problem confronting the language poet, i.e., is it possible for a writer to place and position her texts within the horizon of some "outer social world" without surrendering control to the very processes she would controvert? Bruce Boone, among others, has suggested no, arguing for an insuperable gap between the role of language in poetry and the role of "language poetry" in the world. In this regard, the language poets' fruitless attempt to police public response to their work—most notably, their early attempt to ban use of the term "language poetry"—may reveal something essential about the writing itself.

At any rate, it is clear that one of the consequences of the language poetry movement and of the poetics of material text is that we have to abandon the majority of the ideas of so-called "creative writing," and of what has been called "confessional" verse. In particular, we have to abandon the ideas of self-expression and authorial voice. Poetry—so goes the new affirmation—must cease to be a poetry of feelings and must become a poetry of words. We are observing a whole poetic movement which dislodges previous poetic concepts, and which tends to make more acute our objective understanding at the same time as it makes us feel more strongly than ever the social construction of experience. In this we are witnessing and participating in the beginning of a new mode of writing.

We see that the negations advanced by the poets of the material text imply some affirmations—in Silliman, for example, the negations affirm our inseparability from the world at large. Doubtless we have also noticed, in reviewing rapidly the various poetics of material text, that we find ourselves time and again before impasses. In Hejinian, for example, we do not know if her interest in the problem of knowledge is idealism or realism. There is a similar impasse in Bernstein, where his pragmatist faith in the sufficiency of language opposes his fascination with insufficiency. In Watten, we see an attempt to overcome this impasse through the productive negativity of his various acts of transformation, but, on certain points, we also see a return, perhaps even a recoil, from the conceptions of Coolidge towards those of Creeley. But these impasses need not turn us back. The permanence of the dogma under whose banners language writing is attacked is itself a reason for reaffirming the importance and the leading role of poetics of the material text. All great poetries have encountered such impasses, but art has somehow gone ahead and somehow found a solution. Perhaps, in order to facilitate an egress from these difficulties, it will be necessary to distinguish more carefully among the different elements that we have enumerated, e.g., the insistence upon materiality, and the insistence upon a critique of the subject. No doubt there are different problems, levels of achievement, and resources to be found in these poetics; but it is only by distinguishing the various problems, levels, and resources, and assessing their relative importance, that we will be able to gain an insight into their difficulties and possibly pass beyond them.

DISCUSSION

Guantanamo Bey:

In my opinion, your description of the poetics of Watten was astoundingly clear; for it is not an easy topic. However, although you have made some important points, I am not entirely satisfied with the way in which you have treated the question of the relationship between Coolidge and Watten. I find the difference between Watten and Coolidge colossal, and perhaps the influence of Coolidge exaggerated. Despite his emphasis on language as material, Coolidge's "materialism" is essentially a mode of play—so much so that his recent tendency toward lyrical effusion might well be described as a shift from playing with the materials of language to playing with the material called "Coolidge." Here, any hint of the Marxism that clings to readings of Coolidge's earlier work falls away. He does not wish to defend his writing on the grounds of necessity, and he does not believe in the usefulness of retrospective explanations; he believes only in the decisiveness of playing. I think that Bernstein is much closer to Coolidge than Watten. And yet, he parts from Coolidge in his desire to write a defense of poetry, which is, in my opinion, absolutely inconsistent: defending a position is *anti*poetic from the point of view of play. Bernstein was certainly nearer the truth when he defined poetry as "a heat-seeking missile that finds its target but refuses to detonate." Yet Watten and Bernstein want their poems to detonate—Watten more so than Bernstein.

Why are defenses of poetry antipoetic? Because they are always focused on contingencies while claiming to address essentials. In a defense of poetry, the possibilities of meaning generated in play are hypostatized. The poem's "meaning," a mere contingency, becomes the focus of attention, while "possibility," the essential element, grows more abstract; and this is so even when the meaning that becomes hypostatized is the meaning of possibility itself. In defenses of poetry —in every defense of poetry—the play of language is minimized. Play is minimized because its purposelessness is indefensible, except when fitted into a pragmatic frame. It is precisely in this respect that I feel myself rather close to Coolidge. In my opinion, the central element has vanished in the poetry of Watten.

Of the San Francisco poets, Silliman, through his emphasis on the sheer accumulation of language, remains closer to the spirit of play. I thus have greater sympathy for the practice of Silliman, though you assign much more importance to the work of Watten and Hejinian.

Winnie Nelson:

First of all, I would like to congratulate Hecuba on having been able to say *No* to the stranger who asked her if she was a language poet. I would even like to hope that this *No* will eventually grow into complete non-acceptance.

The term "material" introduced by Coolidge and the poetics of the material text—of which Coolidge's first serious reader, Watten, was the promoter—had a definite historical significance as weapons against the ritual and romance of the New American Poetry. Moreover, there is no doubt about the fact that "material" for Coolidge was primarily that of the visual artist—truth incarnated in paint rather than image, formal decisions which initiate a series of physical acts, which inscribe the work with content by the very fact of physicality. Like most doctrines, the poetics of material signs is right in what it denies and wrong in what it affirms.

In Bernstein—who is not an honest thinker, but an able constructor and calculator bereft of ethics and intellectual scruples—the poetics of the material text has lost its negative sincerity: it has become a mere means dexterously used to pass from the vanguard postures with which he began to an academic counter-canon.

Bernstein's essays proclaim a possible liaison between the romantic materialism of Creeley and Coolidge, and the anti-romantic materialism of the Frankfurt school. To become "language poetry," poetry first passes through the purgatories of "language as such" and "ideology critique" to rediscover itself—impoverished to the limit. If one could accept the work of Bernstein, I believe one could purely and simply accept just as easily, and with far more sensibleness, J. H. Prynne or Susan Howe, neither of whom is bereft, as is Bernstein, of consequences and a sense of history.

And if one attaches some importance to the notion of poetry, at least as a battle against "ideology" and all the traditional and acquired habits of mind, one must note that in no poetics is poetry found to be more impoverished or lax than precisely in "language poetry." In Zukofsky and Coolidge, it was artificially reduced to pure music. In Bernstein, it becomes white noise, which nullifies itself; only tangentially does Bernstein arrive at "real material relations." One affirms poetry after one has carefully emptied it of all its richness, all its powers of articulation, and all its collective and historical aspects! The call to poetry becomes an evasion, a replacement of wisdom with random ambiguities and punning.

History repeats itself. As the New American Poetry amounted to a total destruction or transformation of experience into a chaos of sensation, so language poetry applies itself to the task of reducing experience to zero. This is the impotence of attenuated thought.

Hecuba Whimsy:

I could not let pass, without registering a protest, the remarks of my friend Winnie, whose vehement words were perhaps more forceful than premeditated.

Wyman Jennings:

To begin with, I was a little surprised that in her brilliant exposition, Hecuba spoke so little of a poet—essential, so I believe—to understanding language writers: Robert Grenier. Writing, according to Grenier, is an embodiment of perception—not a commentary on perception or an account of things that occur amid daily life, but perception as such. Writing is dominated in its entirety by the fact of perception, for the very simple reason that writing is by nature an act of attention. Grenier says somewhere that attention, in poetry, is the "invention & enactment of various 'syntaxes.'" This syntax, in simple terms, means narration. Narration determines the form of reality we confront in writing. When Grenier speaks of language, it is of reality that he is speaking. He says so himself in his fragmentary notes on Coolidge and Zukofsky: "Words are as real as anything else & deserve to be treated primarily as facts (not signs) in a physical force field." There is the core of his poetics.

Or consider Hannah Weiner. The poet exists as a receiver of language and is the only one who receives—who can receive—the transmission. It is the inexorable influx of language—instructions, chatter, nonsense—which determines and characterizes her poetry, not to mention the fact that she brings her particular skill to the task of arrangement. Her situation is bizarre, but a general truth emerges: as we perceive, as we register our perceptions, *so* must our reality be. Which is to say, the poet must be "clairvoyant" (Grenier speaks of a "symbiosis" between language and mind) and reveal what language itself says, without letting the artifices and masks of the poet as individual dissimulate some interfering fantasy.

It is this awareness of perception as an acquirement of language that constitutes attention. The emphasis on clairvoyance (or symbiosis) merely indicates the poet's suspicion of understanding, which Grenier and Wiener regard as a secondary order of perception. Both poets, having no interest in the problem of ideology, echo Emerson's acceptance of perception's sufficiency: "Whether nature enjoy a substantial existence without, or is only in the apocalypse of the mind, it is alike useful and venerable to me." And there you see how the notion of authenticity survives in language writing. If we give in to the necessity of language—if in registering our perceptions we give in to this necessity—then we arrive at that authenticity that reveals the world to us and, at the same time, permits us to reveal the world. If I treat language as something wholly separate from perception, I fall into the inauthentic. Only if I am truly "in" language can I reveal the world as I perceive it. Grenier, in his handwritten poems, pushes this idea to an extreme limit, attempting to "write nature," not simply in his choice of words or syntax, but in the singularity of his work's graphic iteration.

To say to Grenier: "One must not focus on language, but nature; as Gary Snyder said, on the wild, the wild edges of nature which *resist* language" is all very well. But Snyder's "nature," like Thoreau's, rests upon a mysticism and romanticism. Grenier wants neither; and in his notes on Coolidge and Zukofsky, he says very succinctly (in a short passage that contains what is perhaps most important in the essay) that the problem of language is not its ability to grasp nature, but what happens when nature is grasped. His dissent from Coolidge lies just here, for the work of Coolidge represents for Grenier the "last ditch effort of romanticism to establish itself via total control over a verbal universe." I do not think that the common reading of Grenier's slogan "I HATE SPEECH" catches his thought very well. The poet writes his world into existence. But the poet must also inhabit his world—he is not in a position to destroy or even control it, nor has he any natural right to impose his will on that world, which is to say, on language. Grenier accords language the same respect that Snyder accords nature. His hatred of speech is in fact a hatred of imposed control. I do not see the problems that have been found with this doctrine.

Nils Ya:

There may still be a grave obscurity. Although you distinguish between Grenier's "nature" and Snyder's, you still employ the phrase "by nature" in a manner that is not entirely happy. In other words, you suggest that Grenier discovers something like an "essence," an essence of which he cannot gain an unmediated perception, since there is an explicit rejection of mysticism and romanticism. Nevertheless, he discovers without a doubt that his acts of attention bring him into the presence of nature. But is this a fact relevant to writing or simply an axiom Grenier adopts so as to avoid solipsism? What does it mean when he says that writing is "by nature" an act of attention? And can he argue without slippage that the "nature" of this attention is not nature but *writing?* It seems to me that he remains entangled in the very presupposition he wants to avoid, which is precisely that nature is anterior to any representation of nature.

Wyman Jennings:

In my opinion, that is mostly a terminological dispute. The terms "nature" and "essence" are vague enough, but if you define "nature" after the fashion of Snyder, as a process of unimaginable complexity, then poetry becomes essentially an expression of overflow—of awe sustained amid partial awareness—of myth attempting to conjure understanding. It is clear that, in this sense, Grenier's *Sentences* and even his later handwritten poems aspire to something different, and are neither "natural" nor "essential" in the Snyder sense. It is true, nevertheless, as Bob Perelman has suggested, that *Sentences* does become at times an experience of "too much," of "amazement amid confusion," and that it also at times inspires the conjuring of understanding in what Roland Barthes, if not Edith Hamilton, would call a myth. One might say, for example, that poetry is essentially a complex process of signification without thereby going beyond Grenier's poetics. Writing is, by nature, a sequence of signs unfolding in time; that is the foundation of Grenier's thought. Poetry is always a temporal experience, and always informs experience. Moreover, poetry is always experienced through an act of perception. Language is an essential, not a contingent, aspect of perception, and in that sense, I would use the term "nature" or "essence" without discomfiture. Language is something essential to perception. I might even say that it forms its nature.

Nils Ya:

My objection certainly went beyond the question of vocabulary. Here is exactly what I mean: Can Grenier maintain that language is sufficient to reveal the world if he does not first posit a reality beyond perception or a perception prior to language? Is it not in an essentially romantic perspective, which posits an absolute reality, that attention (or "symbiosis," god help us) takes on its character . . . ? And does not the relinquishment of control constitute a sort of stoicism idiosyncratic to the practice of Grenier?

Wyman Jennings:

That is a very difficult question and one may answer it in a number of different ways. One may maintain (as has been held, and as I am inclined to believe) that the effort of communication would be absurd if one had no belief in the concept of a shared reality. One cannot have language, for instance, without a shared understanding of its rules. But you know that is an opinion not shared by everyone; it is a pragmatic argument.

You say that language's sufficiency *depends* upon the reality of the world we apprehend. I don't know. It may be, on the contrary, that the reality of the world is *founded* on the sufficiency of language, the capacity of our senses, the breadth of our imaginations. Evidently that is the viewpoint of Grenier. I believe that this viewpoint is perfectly tenable. One does not need to believe in gods, eternal truths, or unimpeachable evidence to make sense of one's experience. Moreover, the constructive value of language—the fact of its materiality and intersubjectivity—remains, despite all the critiques, a reassuring fact. This is what Grenier tries to express, or make us feel, in his transcriptions of bird songs or of his daughter's conversation. Through indecipherables, it seems to him, we discover the foundation of language on which we are perched or from which we attempt to emerge—we find an ocean of language out of which we struggle to leap, but which is always there to catch us, and in which we are always about to sink.

Dirk Jefferson:

I wanted to say a word during the preceding discussion in regard to what Wyman said. I am convinced that Hejinian is right on the question of realism. Moreover, I am always struck by the profound confusion of Grenier's poetics. Slogans like "I HATE SPEECH" cannot be translated into coherent doctrine. You have said that he doesn't reject speech as voice, but as self-assertion. This is a reasonable interpretation, but what does it mean? Does "I HATE SPEECH" really mean "I hate self-assertion," or does it perhaps mean "I hate *listening* to self-assertion"? Therein lies a far-reaching distinction, and consequently I am not at all in agreement with Wyman. The underlying seriousness of Grenier's position is far from self-evident.

Furthermore, one does not know just how to account for this kind of rejection which, in any case, is in no way axiomatic, but which follows more quixotically from a desire for personal probity. I wonder, for this reason, if one doesn't have to speak in terms of morality, and, as in Hejinian's rejection of closure, put the accent on psychology, on the status of our relationships "to the objects, events, and situations that constitute what we imagine of the world." This would enormously reduce the importance of the natural, but would accentuate the moral character of Grenier's thought. But that would absolutely not permit us to arrive, as Wyman seemed to be suggesting, at an "authentic" perception of the real—because, if it is perception at all, it is perception at the "inauthentic" level, the level of individual psychology or "autobiography."

And now I come to a final question. To recapitulate what Wyman said: he who takes refuge in mysticism or romanticism lives in the inauthentic sphere. But I ask: can this refuge of mysticism be adequately conflated with self-assertion or subjectivity? It seems to me that these are two different modes of inauthentic perception, and if Grenier means to treat them as one and the same, he is guilty of a great confusion. What he rejects is a certain contemptible blindness, a certain juvenility, if you like, about common existence which, in effect, consists of dissimulating the fact of "things as they are" and taking refuge in illusions. But may we really, in the name of any sound analysis, identify that with the experience of the devout Buddhist or wise ascetic? That is an absurdity. So that, in reality, all this condemnation of subjectivity which has the air of being central and cogent seems to me extraordinarily hyperbolic, and (to repeat) I, who can not be suspected of an excessive sympathy for the thought of Hejinian in this manner, find her comments on psychology more honest and more sound.

Kimberly Filbee:

I would like to go back to two questions raised by Hecuba's lecture. The first concerns the definition of language poetry. The second is relative to the notion of equivalence encoded in the movement's very name: why should the arbitrariness of the sign be more generative for poetry than other theories of language? This question carries a criticism of Bernstein which we often hear, in different forms—a criticism which I do not wish to refute as Bernstein's follower, but which I would like to consider in order to explain him.

You have even raised a third question: who are the language poets? And you were able to find language poetry everywhere. There are language poets farther back than Coolidge and Ashbery, in Zukofsky and Stein; and nowhere: because everyone evinces boredom with it. This is what Baraka refers to, vis-à-vis jazz, as the second stage of a cultural lag. During the lag time, everyone cries, "That's not music, it's noise!" Later, these same people say indignantly, "But why are you playing that way, it's old hat?!" There is even a later stage, when the music is celebrated in its true originality.

This multiplication of a singular doctrine down through the past and horizontally across the field of present-day endeavor fortunately will end in its own erasure. Then, perhaps, we will come to realize that there is only one "L=A=N=G=U=A=G=E Poet," and that this one and only language poet is neither Silliman, nor Watten, nor Hejinian, nor even—despite his impressive contributions to *L=A=N=G=U=A=G=E* magazine—Bruce Andrews. The only language poet is Bernstein himself, who now shies away from the term.

Why Bernstein? Because the poetic accomplishments of Bernstein have furnished the light by which we are able to discern language writing in a variety of dark corners where, it seems, it was swept out of view. This is even true in respect to Stein. It is possible that behind each maneuver of Bernstein, there is some Steinian habit of mind—certainly, Stein's writing was well known among poets—Robert Duncan and John Cage, for example, read her carefully at the beginning of the 1950s—but it is thanks to Bernstein that her turns of phrase have sounded their note of cultural critique. I mean that, prior to Bernstein, interest in Stein was confined to the areas of style, psychology, linguistic abstraction, or intellectual fashion, and that after Bernstein, she came into the purview of poetics.

In what did it consist—this transformation, which was the achievement of Bernstein?

What he did is retrieve works that may be called "nonsensical," disseminated over the length and breadth of literary history, and relate them to those monuments, frames of reference, that—despite all the discredit their official status assigns them—are endowed with an exceptional degree of explanatory power: namely, the obsessions of professors—canon formation, standard usage, power, resistance, ideology, etc. Bernstein drew a connection between nonsensical writing and the interests of the professors.

To enter into Bernstein's thought, it is not enough to trace his gestures toward systematic thinking, or the manner in which he links the techniques—puns, part words, found language, the comedy of incorrect grammar, etc.—that begin to trail through the magazines and scenes. In ascending towards the academy—towards the ever-renewed light that emanates from the mythical abode of higher education—one must ask: Which essential insight of Bernstein's casts its particular illumination over all the insights whereby the language poets discovered a project, transforming old writing into a new poetics?

Well, I think that the new "twist" originated by Bernstein consists in distinguishing between poetic language and poetic form, and in giving to the latter the complexity, the transformative power, the meaningful content, which until then resided in the former. To read or write language poetry means to experience language—the very measure of thought—as form, a form that itself produces meaning, and that acts on the reader in a meaningful way whenever language is consumed. Form is thus the essential element of any utterance, its true meaning. Until recently, the meaning of an utterance has been a reality independent of its form. This meaning, which, in the Wittgensteinian notion of meaning as use, remains quite serene and equal to the rigors of communication among all the mishaps that befall an intention, appears in language poetry as the mishap itself, as form's adventure.

When Bernstein speaks of "absorption" and "impermeability," of compliance and resistance, what he adds that is new to our millenary knowledge of our thoughts and feelings, our social nature, and our experience of the world, is that these "mind-texture determinants" (in Armand Schwerner's phrase)—*compliance* and *resistance* being descriptions of the moods which accompany communication, not the act of communication itself—that these characteristics of poetic language are not qualities that arise from determinate conditions of speech; that they are not even formally contained, as in the talk pieces of David Antin, in the nature or essence of poetry understood as a particular kind of public act; that they are neither contingent nor necessary attributes of specific kinds of writing; and finally, that they *are* consequences of the instability of *meaning*, heretofore considered to be communicable, comprehensible, reproducible. One may say that language poetry consists in feeling and thinking that meaning is an unfixed, unfixable artifice.

When in his essays (I have not yet read *My Way*) Bernstein utilizes poetic techniques such as line breaks, alliteration, and rhyme, it is this artificiality of utterance that he is trying to accentuate.

Thus, in language poetry there are no longer any fixed meanings; absorption and impermeability alike become expressions of meaning's mutability.

I think that a certain use of clear statement—which does not mean that I see clarity as a purely verbal phenomenon—placed in the service of this notion of artificiality is more illuminating of the essence of language poetry than explorations of materiality, subjectivity, and ideology, projects which are in themselves as Marxist or Structuralist as they are poetic.

But do not the notions of "production" and "consumption" suffice to fix the meaning of this poetry both socially and historically? Is not language given over for consumption at the stage where its production of meaning has come to a stop?

I do not think so—and here I have an opportunity to reply to the second question raised for me by Hecuba's lecture: why did Bernstein choose arbitrariness rather than, for example, deep structure or etymological development, to characterize poetic language?

A form of production given over to the reader for consumption: this describes a poem which least resembles a finished product, self-contained within a particular social context and history. By this very emphasis on process, the product consumed becomes an afterthought. The realization of the process is not the poem's primary concern.

In order that form may inevitably constitute meaning, in order that meaning may inevitably be a process rather than product, it is necessary that language be defined other than by reference to an external reality, and that it function independently of a pre-existing intention. The essence of language must be other than the communication of a fixed meaning. So, Bernstein says: arbitrariness is such an essence; the substitutability of signs in a system of differential relations is what constitutes language prior to its use in any particular act of communication. At the same time, to recognize the stability of the system as a whole is to recognize the instability of any particular sign-signified relation—it is to read the sign as such and not the sign as a "reference to external reality." One may also say that Bernstein gives a graphic illustration of this stability that inheres in the system with the equal signs of the name *L=A=N=G=U=A=G=E*. These "equal signs" are indications of equal value, not meaning. They show that one sign is *as good* as another, though they all are different. They illustrate how language operates precisely by breaking with the illusion of transparent meaning.

Needing a poetic language that is neither the consequence nor the precursor of the act of communication, Bernstein detaches the notion of poetic language from the notion of communication. This permits poetic language ever to remain poetic, so much so that the moment in which it is epitomized is: nonsense. The notion of nonsense allows poetic language to be thought and seized as poetry: it is part of this fundamental intuition; it is the enactment of a process. I do not know if you agree with me.

The material text is produced in such a manner that each word's meaning is already undermined by the poem's overall tendency toward nonsense, and this tendency is, for Bernstein, the process of poetry *par excellence,* because all other forms of language fulfill themselves in the act of communication, whereas nonsense remains inexhaustible. This is the sense in which Bernstein suggests that nonsense is the poetry of communication.

Hecuba Whimsy:

In my opinion, Stein sheds, in her *Stanzas in Meditation,* all possible light on this notion of arbitrariness, which, more so than Duchamp, she places at the center of her work. It is not through Bernstein that one discovers Stein, even if, historically speaking, many have done so (some people would not have cared to read H.D. if Robert Duncan had not been so strong an advocate). It is not from Bernstein that literary historians like Neil Schmitz and Ulla Dydo (and a good many painters and musicians) found out about Stein. Moreover, many discovered her not through Bernstein but through William Gass or Judy Grahn, whom Kim has not mentioned—or through Hejinian's response to Stein, which is earlier and more thorough than Bernstein's. But no matter. . . . It is not because of Bernstein that the writings of Stein sound a note as poetics—that is, unless we understand poetics to mean here a confirmation of academic criticism. There is a complete divergence between us on the meaning of the word "poetics," which I continue not to reserve for the school of professors or professors of schools.

Furthermore, I have nothing more severe for Bernstein than the words of Kim. Bernstein would relate nonsensical writing to the interests of professors . . . ! This is to accuse him as a Denise Levertov would, and as I more hesitantly would, despite all my admiration of him.

Let us also note that before Bernstein, Cage and perhaps Roussel, not to mention many others (I have already mentioned Duchamp), saw language as a system of differential relations organized by a set of rules that could be used for playing games. They saw this with great clarity and expressed it with great mastery, all the while circumventing the language of critical theory.

To be sure, there is in Bernstein, as Kim indicates, the profundity of what I would call an intuition of the inexhaustibility of meaning;

but it is obscured by his fondness for explanatory paradigms borrowed from philosophy. Kim tries to show that the stability of language as system and instability of each individual sign-signified relation can go together (here, again, I note a paradox). She could not succeed because the system is anchored in each user's provisional acceptance of the fixity of that relation. Let us add that if what Bernstein says about artifice is true, if poetry can be characterized as either absorptive or impermeable (but let us not forget that Bernstein himself rejects characterization), then we have not an inexhaustibility, but rather a *saturation* of meaning.

As to the status of nonsense, I am in accord with Kim (and Bernstein) and the critics of Bernstein, in saying that a form of production implies consumption (moreover, this is a tautology). Even nonsense can be consumed. But far from signifying the inexhaustibility of meaning, nonsense itself is the exhaustion, that is to say, the consumption of consumption. Thus, it is not true that to produce arbitrary meanings is to sever production from consumption. Moreover, if nonsense is, as Kim says in commenting on Bernstein, the poetry of communication, it cannot be the refusal of communication. Watten is more rigorous in this matter. But, in any case, whether we study the structures of communication, as in Watten, or communication's failure, as in Bernstein, the results are alike deserving of the epithet "language poetry." The very notion that there is one true language poet runs counter to the movement's overall doctrine.

Notes

The annotations are meant to supplement the text with a minimum of bibliographic and contextual information. Where possible, citations and explanations are grouped together. Full bibliographic information is only given with the first reference, and allusions are only identified when they first appear. Although tempted to do otherwise, I have not extended these notes to provide updates on the individual poets and institutions. *Simulcast*'s detailed portrait of the poetry world c. 1996 is itself an historical artifact. Updates, I fear, would only blur this fact by suggesting that the book's general perspective and particular judgments were objective, which was hardly the case—and hardly the point—of my method.

THE ANTI-HEGEMONY PROJECT

"The AHP": The source text is Poe's 1841 review of Lambert A. Wilmer's *The Quacks of Helicon: A Satire.*

72 *Ken Sherwood and Loss Glazier*

Coeditors of *RIF/T* (1993–1996), one of the earliest electronic poetry journals (archived at http://wings.buffalo.edu/epc/rift). Sherwood was a student in the Buffalo Poetics Program; Glazier, Director of the Electronic Poetry Center (EPC) (http://epc.buffalo.edu).

72 *chivalrous outcry*

"SHOULD WE OUT, BEN f? OR IS HE SELF OUTED? Some are too cruel, like the Watten one, for him to continue to hide, sniveling in the mire of his own petulance. But fabulous anyway. If I am wrong, I'll eat cake." James Sherry, message to the Poetics List, 14 February 1995.

72 *public statement . . . cooperative project*

Responding to the above, Chris Funkhouser wrote the Poetics List, 14 February 1995: "You (pl.) can OUT whomever you like, but to attempt to ascribe the work of the Anti-Hegemony Project to any one individual would constitute a whale-sized inaccuracy. So, bon appetite."

73 *The aggrieved poet himself weighed in with a bemused admission*

Ron Silliman's "bemused admission" was far more generous than Poe allows. His response, posted to the Poetics List on 2 March 1995, is well worth quoting at length:

> I've received a lot of backchannel queries about how I feel about the Anti-Hegemony Project's "alt.fan.silliman" sequence (which by my count stopped at around 25 messages).
>
> I don't feel badly. I don't feel "flamed." And I don't particularly think it was directed at me except in that "homage by ambivalence" sort of way. I (or at least a fictive Ron Silliman) was usually the object of some commentary that was being ascribed to somebody else on the list (tho I think one or two "authors" might not be up on email yet). Since they were the ones having phony words put in their mouths, I suspect that they might feel much more violated in that they were alleged to believe/say things they might not have any sympathy towards whatsoever. How does Lew Daly feel about being characterized in such a two-dimensional Elmer Gantry stereotype? It seemed to me throughout that whatever "meanness" existed in the sequence largely was involved in mangling those alleged voices.
>
> All the quotes of my work were generally accurate and so were a few of the critiques. (Yeah, I do use the anecdotal as a lever in my critical pieces and it's worth thinking about the consequences of that. I've been trashed for close reading before (by Don Byrd among others), as if the practice itself were politically incorrect (rather than the uses to which it once was put a full generation ago). But no, *Ketjak* is not a character. The comment on barfing in K was supposed to call up questions of gender, sexual practice and power. Those lines are grounded in autobiography, but that's not the point. I can't imagine having an R. Crumb cover. I loved the dream and have in fact stolen from it for a piece in progress, thank you very much. Most serious critique of all: not one comment about any of my last 6 books. . . .

The day before it all started, a lurker (you know who you are) wrote to me that one reason she posts so little to the group is the sense she has of active hostility on the part of particularly the younger participants toward us old-fart G1 types. People seem ready to jump all over a press like Sun & Moon while nobody trashes New Directions. I responded to her at the time that this was because New Directions was irrelevant, and that this kind of response seems to me precisely an index of anxiety that people may feel about a given person &/or institution. It's ultimately a definitional process. How do we differentiate ourselves from our "elders" especially when we admire their work and can't quite say why or how we ourselves are so unalterably *different?*

I told her that I thought we'd been just as bad in our 20s, although she personally denies it. (I don't: I got to really know Robert Duncan first when I wrote to the SF *Chronicle* in '66 saying that the bust of Lenore Kandel's *Love Book* gave writers and the ACLU the chance to extend the first amendment by arguing for the right to produce erotica that was not great literature or socially redeeming. Duncan went onto KQED television to read his open letter denouncing me. I was 19 at the time, an undergraduate at SF State, and a fun time was had by all. That was also the year I wrote to Pound telling him how he ought to conclude the *Cantos*—with a photo of the Hong Kong harbor, ancient boats bobbing in front of highrises in the smog-filled sky, carrying the poem's move to the graphic to a logical conclusion. I also wrote to Zukofsky, trying to get permission to publish *The Objectivist Anthology* & the Objectivist issue of *Poetry* as single volume. I no doubt explained to him in some very condescending fashion the importance of his own work. He sent back a very gracious note that's in the archives at UCSD: "No // but // sincerely, // LZ." I think that the evidence is clear that I was a total brat as a kid, but I only picked on poets who meant a lot to me.)

E-space merely changes the dynamics a little. It gives everybody on the list equal access in a way that sitting around the feet of a pontificating Duncan at a party never did. So it doesn't surprise me at all to see a dynamic I can still remember/recognize showing up here at all. It's no different from what the Apexers are trying to do in their editorials, but that's really the only other kind of venue young writers have for such a social move.

Ideally, though, e-space might actually change the dynamics over time. Maybe if all we simply acknowledge and presume the state of easy access (and, with it, the recognition that everybody's

> watching), we won't feel so intimidated by older writers who love to hear themselves talk. It would be interesting to see what might happen if younger poets could develop in a supportive setting and older ones wouldn't feel so threatened by difference among the next generation. How do we get there?
>
> . . . I do have one suggestion that I think would make for an improvement all around. When people send out parodies (even mean ones), have the courage to sign it or at least to send it from an email address that lets everyone know just who you are. Believe me, we don't bite. I think that a lot of the bad feelings I hear being expressed, both publicly and otherwise, have as much to do with the anonymity of the project as with anything that has ever been said. It's much harder to be an object of parody if you don't know where it's coming from.

The phrase "G1 types" refers to Steve Evans's distinction, offered on the Poetics List, between the generation of poets anthologized in Silliman's *In the American Tree* (Orono: National Poetry Foundation, 1986) ("G1") and those gathered in *Writing from the New Coast,* ed. Peter Gizzi and Connell McGrath (*O-blek,* no. 12, [Spring-Fall 1993]) ("G2"). For Evans's original post, see Joel Kuszai, ed., *Poetics@* (New York: Roof Books, 1999), 57–59.

74 *The palace . . . Rhode Island*

From an item, uncollected here, posted to the Poetics List, 4 February 1995.

76 Chain

A poetry journal co-edited by Jena Osman and Juliana Spahr, established in Buffalo in 1994.

76 *"American Book Awards"*

Douglas Messerli established the American Book Awards in 1994. A majority of the judges and winners were associated with his Sun & Moon Press. His poetry anthology, *The Other Side of the Century: A New American Poetry 1960–1990* (Los Angeles: Sun & Moon, 1994), is cited later in the essay.

80 *run amuck like a Zapatista*

The final entry in the AHP, not included here, was the long rewriting of a communiqué from "Subcommander Guantanamo Bey" (reprinted in *DIU,* no. 24a).

"An AHP Dossier": The source texts are news stories from the Clari.* News Net (documents nos. 1–8) and email postings from alt.fan.madonna (nos. 10–24). The individual pieces (and several others that remain uncollected) were sent to the Buffalo "Poetics List" in February and March 1995. The list archive at the EPC provides some of the context (http://listserv.acsu.buffalo.edu/archives/poetics.html), in particular the identities of people and topics of discussion satirized. Many of the satires also concern the Buffalo Poetics Program, information on which is also available at the EPC. The complete annals of the AHP are available in *The Little Magazine* 21b, *Visual Behaviors/Virtual Productions: The Paratarot Project* (http://www.albany.edu/~litmag/vo121b/poe/poe.html).

82 *Core Reserve*

Charles Bernstein's seminars at Buffalo went by the general name Core Poetics.

84 *chicken wings and bleu cheeze for visiting poets*

Free food served at the Central Park Grill in Buffalo, site of a poetry reading series hosted by Mark Hammond. "Chicken wings" were the subject of several silly poems posted on the Poetics List by Robert Creeley, Joe Amato, and others in April and May 1994.

85 *Nick . . . Alan*

Nick Lawrence and Alan Gilbert, then students in the Poetics Program. Gilbert was one of the editors of *apex of the M* (1994–1997), along with Kristin Prevallet (mentioned below), Pam Rehm, and Lew Daly.

85 *Sgt. Tedlock*

Dennis Tedlock.

86 *New Spirit*

One of the sections in *Writing from the New Coast.*

86 *"Wednesdays at Four Plus"*

The regular reading series at Buffalo.

87 *New York's Segue family*

Segue was an important early distributor of language writing books and journals. In 1987, The Segue Foundation sponsored renovation of an abandoned city-owned property in New York City. The building is now an artist's coop and performance space.

88 *Robert "Books" Bertholf*

Curator of the Poetry/Rare Book Room at SUNY Buffalo, site for many years of the Poetics Program reading series.

89 *Progress, Odes of Roba and Curve*

Books by Barrett Watten (New York: Roof Books, 1985), Clark Coolidge (Great Barrington: The Figures, 1991) and Andrew Levy (Oakland: O Books, 1994), respectively.

91 *radical transparency*

A phrase from "State of the Art," the polemical editorial to *apex of the M*, no. 1 (1994): "A radical transparency of language resists the notion that we are restricted solely to slippages within language to frustrate its conventional usages."

93 *Center for the Study of Accelerated Aesthetics*

Under the aegis of this "Center," Bill Howe's Tailspin Press produced a metafictional pamphlet about an imaginary Italian poet ("Francesca Cicchetto"), featuring an introduction by "Klaus Lorenz" (Nick Lawrence), Cicchetto's visual poems (realized by Bill Howe), and a commentary by "Nils Ya" (Benjamin Friedlander). See *Rognoni Sadiani* (Buffalo, 1996). The introduction ("Cut It Out") was first published in *C Theory* (http://www.ctheory.net) in October 1995.

95 *the Berkeley habitat Representations*

Jean Day succeeded Barrett Watten as managing editor of *Representations*.

96 *Poetry Flash and George Lakoff Inc.*

Poetry Flash, no. 147 (June 1985), included two long essays on language poetry, by George Lakoff and Robert Glück. Tom Clark's vitriolic response appeared in the subsequent issue, touching off an acrimonious exchange of letters that fractured the Bay Area writing scene. As in an earlier debate in *Poetry Flash,* much of the furor was focused on the work of Barrett Watten. For a contemporary journalistic account, see Gary Kamiya, "Can All the New Poets Put the Words Back Together Again?," *The Berkeley Monthly* 17:3 (December 1986): 23–29, 49–51.

99 *Jessica Lowenthal*

Then a student at Brown University, coeditor of *Black Bread* (1992–1994) with Sianne Ngai.

100 *lobbyist for poetic environmentalists*

Beginning in January 1995, Steve Evans and Jennifer Moxley coordinated a sustained campaign to defend the NEA from defunding. Their earliest events were a series of read-ins organized under the slogan "Freely Espouse today or Forcibly Emigrate tomorrow." For an overview of their efforts, see messages to the Poetics List between 14 January and 8 April 1995 with subject headings including the word "Espousing."

101 *Gary . . . Cass*

Gary Sullivan and Cass Clarke. Clarke adopted a variety of military and hunting metaphors in offering an explicitly Shelleyan defense of poetry (see, e.g., her messages to the Poetics List of 21, 22, and 24 February 1995 [subject headings "Romantic," "<No subject>," "flushing the quarry," and "Golden Whip"]). Sullivan was then offering spirited criticism of Marjorie Perloff (see, e.g., his messages of 22, 23, and 25 February 1995 [subject headings "Re: Perloff's Post," "To Cass, Marjorie, Ron, Charles," and "To Ira, & all"]).

102 *Yunte Huang*

Then a student in the Buffalo Poetics Program. His Chinese translations of Charles Bernstein, Hank Lazer, and James Sherry, produced with Ziqing Zhang, appeared in 1993.

103 *Donald Jaybird*

Don Byrd. Most of the other names are equally transparent. For the record, the cast of "alt.fan.silliman" is, in order of appearance: Kit Robinson, Lew Daly, Juliana Spahr, Eric Pape, Tom Mandel, Robert Kelly, Mike Boughn, Bill Luoma, Chris Stroffolino, Michael Amnasan, Loss Glazier, George Bowering, Bill Howe, Charles Bernstein (then holder of the David Gray Chair at SUNY Buffalo), Chris Funkhouser, Tony Green, Clint Burnham, Kali Tal, Joel Kuszai ("Mortified Botchup" an allusion to Joel's two cats), and Jennifer Moxley.

103 Toner *in* Sulfur

An excerpt from the long poem *Toner* in *Sulfur,* no. 24 (1989): 29–35, already brought out as a book by Potes & Poets Press (Elmwood, Connecticut, 1992). The other works by Silliman mentioned in this dossier include several sections of "The Alphabet": *ABC* (Berkeley: Tuumba Press, 1983), *Paradise* (Providence: Burning Deck, 1985), *What* (Great Barrington: The Figures, 1988), and the aforementioned *Toner;* the long poem *Ketjak* (San Francisco: This Press, 1978); the collection of early work *The Age of Huts* (New York: Roof Books, 1986); three essays from *The New Sentence* (New York: Roof Books, 1987) ("The New Sentence," "Migratory Meaning," and "Spicer's Language"); and the essay "Canons and Institutions: New Hope for the Disappeared" (in *The Politics of Poetic Form: Poetry and Public Policy,* ed. Charles Bernstein (New York: Roof Books, 1990).

104 *"To be a poet in this society . . . "*

Silliman, "Interview" (with Tom Beckett), *The Difficulties* 2:2 (1985): 46.

105 *Russia Trip*

Documented in Michael Davidson, Lyn Hejinian, Ron Silliman, and Barrett Watten, *Leningrad: American Writers in the Soviet Union* (San Francisco: Mercury House, 1991).

106 *"The goal of poetry . . . "*

Silliman, *The New Sentence,* 59.

107 *Samuel Delany . . . novel*

In the *The Mad Man* (New York: Rhinoceros, 1994), Delany

writes, "The Old Poet beamed at us. . . . The book in her lap was a trade paperback whose cover showed a power-cable pylon above a dark hill, a pastel bay in the distance backed with mountains and sunset clouds. Its title was *What,* and its author someone named Silliman" (307).

109 *neo-romantic Springsteen Rambo MLA sequence*

"To read this / as neo-romantic would be to equate / Springsteen's *Born in the U.S.A.* with the jingoism / of Rambo, charm songs for the MLA." Silliman, *What,* 28.

110 **JORIS**

Poet and translator Pierre Joris.

110 *Exploding Fibonacci?!*

Silliman based the structure of his long poem *Tjanting* (Berkeley: The Figures, 1981) on the Fibonacci number sequence.

113 *WE'RE THE POETICS PROGRAM AMERICA*

The core faculty pictured here are Charles Bernstein, Robert Creeley, Raymond Federman, Susan Howe, and Dennis Tedlock.

115 *his MLA thing*

Silliman delivered two papers at the 1987 MLA Convention in San Francisco, and they were eventually published as "Negative Solidarity: Revisionism and 'New American' Poetics," *Sulfur,* no. 22 (Spring 1988): 169–76, and "Poets and Intellectuals," *Temblor,* no. 9 (1989): 122–24.

POE'S POETICS AND SELECTED REVIEWS

"Letter to B——": The source text is Poe's preface to his 1831 *Poems,* with passages intercalated from the *Marginalia.*

123 *four Leninists in Buffalo*

The editors of *apex of the M.*

124 *"In passing with my mind . . .*

The Collected Poems of William Carlos Williams, Volume 1: 1909–1939, ed. A. Walton Litz and Christopher MacGowan (New York: New Directions, 1986), 205.

124 *a jointly written book about a week in Russia*

Davidson et al., *Leningrad.*

125 *"Because we are poets . . . had to be learned"*

Watten in Davidson et al., *Leningrad,* 36.

125 *"We can't identify . . . instances of panic"*

Hejinian in Davidson et al., *Leningrad,* 98. The colored ribbon and bilingual beasts mentioned below occur in Hejinian's poetry—

in *My Life* (Los Angeles: Sun & Moon, 1987) and "The Guard" (in *The Cold of Poetry* [Los Angeles: Sun & Moon, 1994]), respectively.

126 *"Who limits herself . . . conservatism"*

Carla Harryman, *The Middle* (San Francisco: GAZ, 1983).

126 *uphold it on the ground of realism*

Silliman titled his introduction to *In the American Tree* "Language, Realism, Poetry," and made the argument for realism more generally in the introduction of a previous anthology, published as a special issue of *Ironwood* (10:2 [Fall 1981]). "Inside Cheese" is an Alan Bernheimer poem in *In the American Tree.*

127 *as Spicer says*

In "Improvisations on a Sentence by Poe," *The Collected Books of Jack Spicer,* ed. Robin Blaser (Los Angeles: Black Sparrow, 1975) 69.

"The Poetic Principle": The source text is Poe's lecture of the same name. The poems quoted come from the following works: H.D., *Collected Poems,* ed. Louis L. Martz (New York: New Directions, 1983), 412–13 ("Sigil XI"); *The Collected Poems of Emily Dickinson,* ed. Thomas Johnson (Cambridge: Harvard UP), 3:936–37 ("The Mind lives on the Heart"); Gwendolyn Brooks, *Blacks,* (Chicago: Third World Press, 1987), 365 ("Jack"); Delmore Schwartz, *Selected Poems: Summer Knowledge* (New York: New Directions, 1959), 210 ("I Did Not Know the Spoils of Joy"); Walt Whitman, *Complete Poetry and Collected Prose* (New York: Library of America, 1982), 587 ("Riddle Song"); Marianne Moore, *Observations* (New York: Dial, 1924), 48 ("Radical"), and *Collected Poems* (New York: Macmillan, 1951), 37 ("The Fish"); Stephen Rodefer, *Left under a Cloud* (London: Alfred David Editions, 2000), 20–23 ("Brief to Butterick"); Joanne Kyger, *Just Space: Poems 1979–1989* (Santa Rosa: Black Sparrow, 1991), 115 ("DARRELL GRAY dies when I am in Mexico"); John Wieners, *Behind the State Capitol or Cincinnati Pike* (Santa Rosa: The Good Gay Poets, 1975), 155 ("Does His Voice Sound Some Echo in Your Heart"); *The Complete Poems of Charles Reznikoff, Volume 1: Poems 1918–1936,* ed. Seamus Cooney, (Santa Barbara: Black Sparrow Press, 1976), 127–29 ("Jerusalem the Golden").

129 *Nathaniel Mackey's* Song of the Andoumboulou

An ongoing sequence of poems published in Mackey's *Eroding Witness* (Urbana: U of Illinois P, 1985), *School of Udhra* (San Francisco: City Lights Books, 1993) and *Whatsaid Serif* (San Francisco: City Lights Books, 1998).

139 *Paul Muldoon's "The Soap-Pig"*

An elegy to Michael Hanifan from Muldoon's 1987 volume

Meeting the British, now in *Poems 1968–1998* (New York: Farrar, Straus and Giroux, 2001), 167–70.

139 The Wonderful Focus of You

A collection of poems brought out by Big Sky in 1980, subject of a short review by "Edgar Allen Poe" (based on the other Poe's review of Washington Irving's *The Crayon Miscellany*) published in *Passages*, no. 3 (28 May 1995): http://wings.buffalo.edu/epc/ezines/passages/passages3.

"Gertrude Stein: A Retrospective Criticism": The source text is Poe's "Rufus Dawes: A Retrospective Criticism."

145 *says Prof. Schmitz*

In "The Difference of Her Likeness: Gertrude Stein's *Stanzas in Meditation*," in *Gertrude Stein and the Making of Literature*, ed. Shirley Neuman and Ira B. Nadel (Boston: Northeastern UP, 1988), 148

145 *a solitary demurral, adventured by Prof. Davenport*

"Late Gertrude," in *The Hunter Gracchus and Other Papers on Literature and Art* (Washington, D.C.: Counterpoint, 1996), 187–91.

146 *several volumes of posthumous writings . . . Other attempts at selection*

The Yale Gertrude Stein consists of eight volumes published between 1951 and 1958. Richard Kostelanetz brought out his single-volume collection, *The Yale Gertrude Stein*, in 1980. The other Stein anthologies mentioned are *Selected Writings*, ed. Carl Van Vechten (New York: Vintage, 1972); *Look at Me Now and Here I Am: Writings and Lectures 1909–45*, ed. Patricia Meyerowitz (Baltimore: Penguin Books, 1971); *Really Reading Gertrude Stein*, ed. Judy Grahn (Freedom, CA: Crossing Press, 1989); and *A Stein Reader*, ed. Ulla Dydo (Evanston: Northwestern UP, 1993). Donald Sutherland's *Gertrude Stein: A Biography of Her Work* originally appeared from Yale in 1951.

148 *These lines are interpreted by Mr. Duncan*

In "Often I Am Permitted to Return to a Meadow," in Robert Duncan, *The Opening of the Field* (New York: New Directions, 1960) 7.

148 *Prof. Dydo avers*

In her *Stein Reader*, 569.

153 *"Patriarchal Poetry"*

Gertrude Stein, *Writings 1903–1932* (New York: Library of America, 1998) 567.

153 *Prof. Davenport hit the nail on the head*

Davenport, "Late Gertrude," 191.

154 *Miss Stein clung to her belief in inviolate national traits*

Gertrude Stein, *Wars I Have Seen* (New York: Random House, 1945), 8.

155 *"Before the Flowers of Friendship Faded Friendship Faded"*

Stein, *Look at Me Now and Here I Am,* 286–87.

157 *"Lifting Belly"*

Stein, *Writings,* 427–28.

"Mr. Rasula's History": The source text is Poe's review of Francis L. Hawks, *Contributions to the Ecclesiastical History of the United States—Virginia.*

159 *"poetry is well . . . pastime."*

Don Byrd, "Meter-Making Argument," *Epoch* 29:2 (1980): 178–83, quoted by Rasula in *The American Poetry Wax Museum: Reality Effects 1940–1990* (Urbana, Ill.: National Council of Teachers of English, 1996), 4.

159 *first conceived the idea*

See Jed Rasula, "The American Poetry Wax Museum," *Jimmy & Lucy's House of "K,"* no. 3 (January 1985): 69–72, and "Part of Nature, Part of—'US'? The Role of Critics and the Emperor's New Clothes in American Poetry," *Sulfur,* no. 9 (1984): 149–67. The latter concludes with "a year by year listing of books of poetry prominently reviewed in the trade press" from 1967 to 1981.

160 *"a theoretical scaffolding"*

Rasula, *The American Poetry Wax Museum,* 4.

160 *"Insofar as a canon* . . . membership."

Rasula, *The American Poetry Wax Museum,* 471.

160 *Mr. Nelson's* Repression and Recovery

Cary Nelson, *Repression and Recovery: Modern American Poetry and the Politics of Cultural Memory* (Madison: University of Wisconsin Press, 1989).

161 *"which enshrine . . . unorthodox."*

Rasula, *The American Poetry Wax Museum,* 460 and 463.

161 *"The Poundian lineage . . . booking agency."*

Rasula, *The American Poetry Wax Museum,* 113, 114.

162 *an early number of* Sulfur *magazine*

See Eliot Weinberger, "Pound after Torrey & Other Futures," *Sulfur,* no. 11 (1984): 158–68, and responses by Peter Michelson, Charles Bernstein, and Benjamin Friedlander, with Weinberger's reply, in *Sulfur,* no. 13 (1985): 161–69. The quotes from Weinberger and Bernstein that follow (along with their references to the Modernist poets) are taken from this exchange.

162 *Prof. Bernstein's "Pounding Fascism"*

"Pounding Fascism (Appropriating Ideologies—Mystification,

Aestheticization, and Authority in Pound's Poetic Practice)," originally published in *Sulfur,* now in Charles Bernstein, *A Poetics* (Cambridge: Harvard UP, 1992), 121–27.

164 *"Canto XCVI"*

The quoted lines that follow come from *The Cantos of Ezra Pound* (New York: New Directions, 1993), 684–86.

165 *as Prof. Perelman records*

Bob Perelman, *The Trouble with Genius: Reading Pound, Joyce, Stein, and Zukofsky* (Berkeley: U of California P, 1994), 179.

166 *"A Lustrum for You, E. P."*

The Collected Poems of Charles Olson, ed. George Butterick (Berkeley: U of California P, 1987), 38.

166 *as Prof. Davidson puts it*

Michael Davidson, *The San Francisco Renaissance: Poetics and Community at Mid-Century* (New York: Cambridge UP, 1989), 27, quoted by Rasula in *The American Poetry Wax Museum,* 221.

167 *"Lowell's seemingly . . . of the elite."*

Rasula, *The American Poetry Wax Museum,* 151, 90.

167 *"Lowell's evident dismay . . . regal attire."*

Rasula, *The American Poetry Wax Museum,* 254, 265.

168 *"the theoretically . . . language poetry."*

Rasula, *The American Poetry Wax Museum,* 222.

168 *"Tate, like Adorno . . . New Critical hegemony . . . "*

Rasula, *The American Poetry Wax Museum,* 92–95.

"Blockage, Breakdown, Baffle": The source text is Poe's review of the *Complete Poetical Works of William Cullen Bryant.* Except as noted below, the excerpts from Bernstein's work are taken from *Dark City* (Los Angeles: Sun & Moon, 1994).

172 *a reputable critic in a reputable biannual*

Keith Tuma, "Noticings," *Sulfur,* no. 35 (1994), 223.

174 *Prof. Perelman, in summing up his comments*

Bob Perelman, "A Note on 'Sentences My Father Used,' *The Difficulties* 2:1 (Fall 1982), 89.

174 *Prof. McGann, writing under the* nom de plume *Anne Mack*

Anne Mack, J. J. Rome and George Mannejc, "Private Enigmas and Critical Functions, with Particular Reference to the Writing of Charles Bernstein," *New Literary History* 22 (1991), 457.

174 *Mr. Silliman, who has said of an earlier work*

Silliman, *The New Sentence,* 181.

175 *The author of* Social Values and Poetic Acts

Jerome McGann in Mack et al., "Private Enigmas," 456, 458.

175 *I quote a few verses from "Gosh"*

In *The Nude Formalism* (a collaboration with Susan Bee), published as *20 Pages,* no. 3 (September 1989).

"Mr. Daly's Polemic": The source text is Poe's review of William Lord's *Poems*.

185 *her dissertation on Wittgenstein*

Rosmarie Waldrop, *Against Language? "Dissatisfaction with Language" as Theme and as Impulse Toward Experiments in Twentieth Century Poetry* (The Hague: Mouton, 1971).

THE LITERATI OF SAN FRANCISCO

The source text is Poe's *Literati of New York City,* supplemented with passages from his *Marginalia* and *Autography*. The specific matchups are noted below.

200 *Mr. Rodefer* . . . Four Lectures

Stephen Rodefer and his 1982 book of poetry (Berkeley: The Figures).

201 *Mr. and Mrs. Waldrop*

Keith and Rosmarie Waldrop. The former taught for many years at Brown University. The latter is editor and publisher of Burning Deck Press.

"Bob Perelman": Based on Poe's sketch of "George Bush," incorporating passages from "Epes Sargent," a comment on Coleridge's *Table Talk* from the *Marginalia,* and an entry on "Orestes Brownson" in the *Autography*. The quoted lines come from *Captive Audience* (Great Barrington: The Figures, 1988), 35–36. "China" first appeared in *Primer* (Oakland: This Press, 1981), "Seduced by Analogy" and "Picture" in *To the Reader* (Berkeley: Tuumba Press, 1984), "The Broken Mirror" and "Life Forms" in *The First World* (Great Barrington: The Figures, 1986), "Sex" in *Face Value* (New York: Roof Books, 1988), and "A Literal Translation of Virgil's Fourth Eclogue" in *Virtual Reality* (New York: Roof Books, 1993). *Chaim Soutine,* first published as a chapbook (Buffalo: Editions Herrison, 1994), appears in *The Future of Memory* (New York: Roof Books, 1998). All of these poems save "Life Forms" also appear in *Ten to One: Selected Poems* (Hanover, Wesleyan UP, 1999).

202 *a singular commotion*

A symposium on Perelman's *The Marginalization of Poetry* (Princeton: Princeton UP, 1996) moderated by Sean Killian at the Segue Performance Space in March 1997. The papers (including

Perelman's response) were published soon after as *The Impercipient Lecture Series* 1:4 (May 1997), and subsequently appeared in *Jacket,* no. 2 (January 1998) (http://jacketmagazine.com/02/marg.html).

202 *the editor of* Hills

Perelman edited 9 issues (1973–1983). *Hills,* nos. 6/7 (1980), *Talks,* was followed by *Writing/Talks* (Carbondale: Southern Illinois UP, 1985).

203 *Mr. Amnasan . . .* Ottotole

Michael Amnasan edited three issues (1985–89), the first in collaboration with Gail Sher.

203 *by Zora Neale Hurston*

In *Dust Tracks on a Road* (New York: HarperPerennial, 1991), 45.

203 *an essay in* New Left Review

Now the opening chapter of Fredric Jameson, *Postmodernism, or the Cultural Logic of Late Capitalism* (Durham: Duke UP, 1991).

204 *Watten's* Plasma/Parallels/"X"

A chapbook originally brought out by Tuumba Press (Berkeley, 1979), now included in Barrett Watten, *Frame 1971–1990* (Los Angeles: Sun & Moon, 1997).

"Andrew Schelling": Based on Poe's sketch of "William M. Gillespie," but incorporating two paragraphs from the sketch of "Evert Duyckinck." The quoted lines come from *The India Book: Essays and Translations from Indian Asia* (Oakland: O Books, 1993), 62. Andrew and I edited 9 issues of *Jimmy & Lucy's House of "K"* between 1984 and 1989.

205 *a conference on meditation and poetry*

"The Poetics of Emptiness: A Collaborative Gathering of Poets Who Meditate," held at Green Gulch Zen Center, 10–12 April 1987. The proceedings were published as *Jimmy & Lucy's House of "K,"* no. 9 (1989), *"The Poetics of Emptiness."*

"Robert Grenier": Based on Poe's sketch of "John W. Francis" along with several sections of the *Autography* (including, most notably, the entries on "Thomas Holley Chivers" and "Charles Anthon").

207 *abandoned print for calligraphy*

The turn to calligraphy occurs in his *What I Believe. Transpiration/Transpiring. Minnesota* (Oakland: O Books, 1993), a box containing handwritten and typewritten poems in black and white reproduction. For full-color reproduction, see the limited edition folio publications *12 from rhymms* (Scotia, NY: Pavement Saw Press, 1996) and *Owl on Bough* (Sausalito: Post-Apollo Press, 1997), and the on-line gallery of work available through the Light & Dust Anthology of Poetry (http://www.thing.net/~grist/1&d/lighthom.htm).

208 *"scrawl"*

From Leslie Scalapino's preface to Grenier's *What I Believe. Transpiration/Transpiring. Minnesota,* printed on the inside of the box: "Robert Grenier's 'scrawl' is comparable to Stan Brakhage's films which Brakhage described as poems."

208 *on a ping-pong table*

Of *A Day at the Beach* (New York: Roof Books, 1984), Grenier has said, "That was a structured narrative, laid out six poems at a time on the pingpong table with these various 'six' pages set up and various possibilities tried." Alastair Johnston, "Typwriter v Typeface . . . An Interview with Poet Robert Grenier," *The Ampersand: A Publication of the Pacific Center for the Book Arts* 6:2 (April 1986): 10

209 *Amy*

Grenier's daughter, much quoted in *Series* (Kensington, CA: This Press, 1978) and *Sentences* (Cambridge: Whale Cloth Press, 1978).

"Eileen Corder": Based on Poe's sketch of "Anna Cora Mowatt." The quoted lines come from "WARSHEPFASCADEFLATTEN," *'Aql,* no. 2 (July 1989): 20. *Busy Wrong: Two Plays* (Oakland: Jimmy's House of Knowledge, 1986), contains "Remember the Alamo Brand" and "Busy Wrong." *Unazonasacra* was published as *'Aql,* no. 4 (1992). The pamphlet of remarkable poems was *Braids* (San Francisco: Cultural Resistance, 1995).

209 *Poet's Theater*

Hills, no. 9 (1983), *Plays and Other Writing,* included a section of "Plays from San Francisco Poets Theater" (pages 5–93): Bob Perelman's "The Alps," Kit Robinson's "Collateral," Alan Bernheimer's "Particle Arms," Eileen Corder's "Under the Midwest," and Stephen Rodefer's "A&C." See also Kit Robinson, Eileen Corder, and Nick Robinson, "Poet's Theater: Three Versions of 'Collateral,'" *Poetics Journal,* no. 5 (May 1985): 122–38.

210 *Leslie Scalapino's* Leg

In *O One/An Anthology,* ed. Leslie Scalapino (Oakland: O Books, 1988) 137–49.

"Michael Palmer": Based on Poe's sketch of "Charles Anthon." The books mentioned are *Sun* (San Francisco: North Point Press, 1988) and *First Figure* (San Francisco: North Point Press, 1984), collected now with *Notes from Echo Lake* in *Codes Appearing: Poems 1979–1988* (New York: New Directions, 2001). Three issues of *Joglars* appeared between 1964 and

1966. Palmer co-edited the first two; Clark Coolidge produced the third on his own.

213 "Analytic Lyric"

See *Acts* 7 (1987), *Analytic Lyric?* In an editor's note, David Levi Strauss writes:

> This issue of ACTS is being sent out under the sign of "Analytic Lyric," a term which at this point in time must be followed by a question mark. That is how the term appears in one section of a talk given by Michael Palmer in Iowa City last year. . . . Michael begins with a discussion of Jack Spicer's work . . . , goes on to Hölderlin . . . as an early enactment of "the anxiety of signification" and "the problematics of self- expression," and then focuses on "two poets who are important to this notion of an analytic lyric"—Edmond Jabès and Paul Celan. . . . Michael proposes the relevance of this work to contemporary practice as a radical renewal of certain aspects of lyrical tradition. . . . I believe the poets in this issue of ACTS (and previous issues) participate, in various ways, in this struggle.

213 *photograph . . . made a stir*

See Tom Clark's cartoon in *Rolling Stock,* no. 6 (1983): 8: "Great Moments in the History of the Language School #43: MICHAEL PALMER IRONS HIS LEVIS."

"Nathaniel Mackey": Based on an entry on Tennyson in Poe's *Marginalia.* The quoted lines come from *Bedouin Hornbook* (Lexington, KY: Callalloo Fiction Series, 1986) 176. "Ohnedaruth's Day Begun" is a poem in *Eroding Witness,* 70–74; fourteen issues of *Hambone* appeared between 1974 and 1998. For examples of Mackey's criticism, see *Discrepant Engagement: Dissonance, Cross-Culturality, and Experimental Writing* (Tuscaloosa: U of Alabama P, 2000).

215 the various parts of "Mu"

Poems in *Eroding Witness* and *School of Udhra* subtitled "*'mu' first part*" and so on.

"Beverly Dahlen": Based on Poe's sketch of "Ralph Hoyt." The quoted lines come, in order, from *Out of the Third* (San Francisco: Momo's Press, 1974) ("Tree 5," "The Last Light You Came To"); "Forbidden Knowledge," *Poetics Journal,* no. 4 (May 1984): 5, 6; *A Reading 1–7* (San Francisco: Momo's Press, 1985), 120–21; *A Reading 8–10* (Tucson: Chax Press, 1992),

101, 51, 49–50; *A Reading 1–7,* 78; and *A Reading (11–17)* (Elmwood: Potes & Poets, 1989), 58. See also *The Egyptian Poems* (Berkeley: Hipparchia Press, 1983), reprinted in *Ironwood* 14:1 (Spring 1986): 133–45.

217 *"interminable"*

Dahlen's own description, echoing Freud: "I have been defensive about *A Reading,* wanting to postpone, or defer, conclusions or closure perhaps forever. It is the problem of the interminable." "Forbidden Knowledge," 10.

220 *"incisions of memory . . . rear up"*

Rachel Blau DuPlessis, *The Pink Guitar: Writing as Feminist Practice* (New York: Routledge, 1990), 111.

220 *the author of* A Blue Fire

James Hillman.

"Ted Pearson": Based on a passage on Shelley and Tennyson from Poe's *Marginalia,* lifted from his own earlier essay on Elizabeth Barrett Browning. The quoted lines come from Pearson's *Acoustic Masks* (Gran Canaria: Zasterle Press, 1994), 33. The other works cited are *Evidence 1975–1989* (San Francisco: GAZ, 1989) and *Planetary Gear* (New York: Roof Books, 1991).

224 *through the labors of Cid Corman*

Cid Corman, who featured Pearson in *Origin* (fourth series), no. 19 (April 1982).

"David Melnick": Based on Poe's sketch of "Piero Maroncelli." The works cited are, in poetry, *Eclogs* (Ithaca: Ithaca House, 1972), *Pcoet* (San Francisco: G.A.W.K., 1975), and *Men In Aida* (Berkeley: Tuumba Press, 1983), and, in prose, "On 'Quantity in Verse, and Shakespeare's Late Plays'" and "The 'Ought' of Seeing: Zukofsky's Bottom" (in *Maps,* no. 4 [1971]: 79–82, and no. 5 [1973]: 55–65, respectively).

"Stephen Rodefer": Based on Poe's sketch of "Laughton Osborn." The quoted lines come, in order, from "What I See in the Silliman Project," *Jimmy & Lucy's House of "K,"* no. 6 (May 1986): 140–44; "Dupe Check" [subsequently retitled "The Monkey's Donut"], unpublished ms.; "Automatic Toll of Criticism," *Ottotole,* no. 2 (Winter 1986–87): 128; "The Library of Label," *Dark Ages Clasp the Daisy Root,* no. 2 (February 1990): 22. The other works cited are "Prologue to Language Doubling," *Jimmy & Lucy's House of "K,"* no. 4 (June 1985): 74–76; "Chateau D'If," unpublished ms.; "Ted Greenwald, Writer-in-Residence March 2–5, 1982," *80 Langton Street Residence Program 1982,* 101–17.

226 *Mr. Messerli's "zoo"*

In the introduction to his anthology, Douglas Messerli writes, "For anthologies, too often, are like zoos which capture and cage 'types' of what they represent." *The Other Side of the Century* 34.

227 *recalls a well-known work by Edward Dorn*

"What I See in *The Maximus Poems,*" in Dorn's *Views* (San Francisco: Four Seasons Foundation, 1980), 27–44.

228 *breached decorum*

In a letter to the editor of *Poetry Flash* (no.136 [July 1984]: 7). The first paragraph reads:

> I REMEMBER THE ZUKOFSKY EVENING, reviewed by Mr. Levi Strauss in your June issue, fairly clearly, and just to be brief—for I can imagine that Barry Watten is probably at work this very moment in his own lengthy correction—I would like to say that Robert Duncan's literally taking over the podium from Barry Watten that night was both arrogant and annoying to those in the crowd (many) listening to the connections being proposed by BW, but it was necessary to keep the evening from getting boring.

228 *a symposium in the journal* Tyuonyi

Patterns/Contexts/Time: A Symposium on Contemporary Poetry, ed. Phillip Foss and Charles Bernstein, published as *Tyuonyi,* no. 6–7 (1990).

"Robert Duncan": Based on Poe's sketch of "Fitz-Greene Halleck." The quoted lines of Duncan's poetry come, in order, from *Bending the Bow* (New York: New Directions, 1968), 46–47; *Ground Work II: In the Dark* (New York: New Directions, 1987), 69; *The Opening of the Field,* 70, 71; *Ground Work: Before the War* (New York: New Directions, 1984), 73, 74; and *Roots and Branches* (New York: Scribner's, 1964), 122.

232 *"The Homosexual in Society"*

Now available in an expanded version in Duncan's *A Selected Prose,* ed. Robert J. Bertholf (New York: New Directions, 1995) 38–50. Ekbert Faas reports John Crowe Ransom's response in *Robert Duncan: Portrait of the Artist as a Young Homosexual in Society* (Santa Barbara: Black Sparrow, 1983), 151. "An African Elegy" appears in *The Years as Catches: First Poems (1939–1946)* (Berkeley: Oyez, 1966), 33–35.

233 *says Mr. Duncan's biographer*

Faas, *Robert Duncan,* 264. "The Venice Poem," first published in *Poems 1948–49* (Berkeley: Berkeley Miscellaneous Editions, 1949), is more readily available in *The First Decade: Selected Poems 1940–1950* (London: Fulcrum Press, 1968).

233 Passages

A sequence of poems that began in *Bending the Bow* and continues through the two volumes of *Ground Work*. *Of the War: Passages 22–27* (Berkeley: Oyez, 1966), which includes "Up Rising, *Passages 25*," became part of *Bending the Bow*.

234 The Structure of Rhyme

A sequence of poems begun in *The Opening of the Field*, continuing through *Roots and Branches* (New York: Charles Scribner's Sons, 1964), *Bending the Bow*, and the two volumes of *Ground Work*.

235 *a special issue of John Taggart's journal* Maps

Maps, no. 6 (1974): *Robert Duncan*.

235 *the still more clever conceit*

See Spicer, *The Collected Books*, 333.

"Carla Harryman": Based on Poe's sketch of "Ann S. Stephens," incorporating sections of "Emma Embury" and a line from "Richard Adams Locke." The books named or alluded to are, in chronological order: *Percentage* and *Property* (Berkeley: Tuumba Press, 1979 and 1982), *Animal Instincts: Prose, Plays, Essays* (Oakland: This Press, 1989), *Memory Play* (Oakland: O Books, 1994), and *There Never Was a Rose without a Thorn* (San Francisco: City Lights Books, 1995).

238 *the immortal author of* The Telling

Laura (Riding) Jackson.

"Ron Silliman": Based on Poe's sketch of "Evert Duyckinck," incorporating one paragraph of "Catherine Maria Sedgwick" and a line from "Nathaniel Willis." The books not already mentioned in these notes are, alphabetically: *Demo to Ink* (Tucson: Chax Press, 1992), *Jones* (Mentor, OH: Generator Press, 1993), *Lit* (Elmwood: Potes & Poets Press, 1987), *Manifest* (La Laguna: Zasterle Press, 1990), *N/O* (New York: Roof Books, 1994), ® (New York: Drogue Press, 1995), and *Xing* (Buffalo: Meow Press, 1996).

239 Socialist Review

Silliman served as Executive Editor and Collective member from issue 17:1 (January–February 1987) through 18:3 (July–September 1989). He remained a member of the Collective through 21:1 (January–March 1991), served as one of the journal's Associates through 24:4 (1994), and has been an Affiliate since 27:1–2 (1999).

"Benjamin Friedlander": Based on Poe's sketch of "Thomas Dunn English." "Insomnia" is quoted from *'Aql*, no. 2 (1989). I edited 8 issues of *Dark Ages Clasp the Daisy Root* with Andrew Schelling between 1989 and 1993.

"Tom Mandel": Based on Poe's sketch of "Henry Cary." The quoted stanzas come from *Letters of the Law* (Los Angeles: Sun & Moon, 1994), 26. The other works cited are *EncY* (Berkeley: Tuumba Press, 1978) (reviewed by Bruce Andrews in *L=A=N=G=U=A=G=E,* no. 8 [June 1979]; see "Encyclopedia (On Tom Mandel)" in *Paradise & Method: Poetics & Praxis* [Evanston: Northwestern UP, 1996], 178–81), *Central Europe* (Oakland: Coincidence Press, 1985) and *Four Strange Books* (San Francisco: GAZ, 1990).

"Steve Benson": Based on Poe's sketch of "Christopher Pease Cranch." The quoted lines come, in order, from *Reverse Order* (Elmwood: Potes & Poets Press, 1989), 59; and *Blue Books* (Great Barrington/NY: The Figures/ Roof Books, 1988), 126 ("The Busses") and 138 ("Dialogues"). The other works cited are *Dominance* (Oakland: Coincidence Press, 1984), *Briarcombe Paragraphs* (Paris: Moving Letters Press, 1984), and *The Busses* (Berkeley: Tuumba Press, 1981).

"Lyn Hejinian": Based on Poe's sketch of "Margaret Fuller." The quoted lines come from *Oxota: A Short Russian Novel* (Great Barrington: The Figures, 1991), 198; "Variations: A Return of Words," in Silliman, ed. *In the American Tree* 507 (the passage is somewhat different in Hejinian's *The Language of Inquiry* [Berkeley: U of California P, 2000]); *My Life* (Providence: Burning Deck, 1980), 11; *The Language of Inquiry,* 157 ("Ultimately") and 26 ("I think of you"); "The Inanimate Are Rocks, Desks, Bubbles," in *In the American Tree,* ed. Silliman, 49; *The Cold of Poetry,* 92. Other works cited, not already mentioned, are *The Cell* (Los Angeles: Sun & Moon Press, 1992) and "An American Opener [review of Paul Mariani, *William Carlos Williams: A New World Naked*]," *Poetics Journal,* no. 1 (January 1982): 61–65. "The Rejection of Closure" and "The Quest for Knowledge in the Western Poem" are now available in *The Language of Inquiry*.

247 *editor, or one of the editors of Tuumba Press*

Hejinian was in fact sole editor; her contributions to the press as author were *A Thought Is the Bride of What Thinking* (Willits, CA: Tuumba Press, 1976), *Gesualdo* (Berkeley: Tuumba Press, 1978), and *The Guard* (Berkeley: Tuumba Press, 1984).

247 *a poetic collaboration with General Watten's wife*

"The Wide Road," written with Carla Harryman, as yet uncollected.

252 *Susan Howe . . . her* Emily Dickinson

See, e.g., *My Emily Dickinson* (Berkeley: North Atlantic Books, 1985).

"Barrett Watten": Based on Poe's sketch of "Prosper M. Wetmore," incorporating a few lines from "Richard Adams Locke," and from the *Autogra-*

phy and *Marginalia*. The works cited are *Total Syntax* (Carbondale: Southern Illinois UP, 1985) and *Progress* (New York: Roof Books, 1985).

"Norma Cole": Based on Poe's sketch of "Frances S. Osgood." The quoted lines come from *Metamorphopsia* (Elmwood: Potes & Poets Press, 1988), 84; *My Bird Book* (Los Angeles: Littoral Books, 1991), 41 ("Gannet") and 23 ("Raven"); and *Mars* (Berkeley: Listening Chamber, 1994), 59 ("on the anniversary") and 68 ("Book, think"). *Mace Hill Remap* was published by Moving Letters Press (Paris) in 1988; "Desitution: A Tale" appears in *My Bird Book;* "Rosetta" appears in *Moira* (Oakland: O Books, 1995).

255 *"binding energy" (as DuPlessis put it)*
Rachel Blau DuPlessis, "Powetry," *Sulfur,* no. 36 (1995): 212.

259 *Scalapino's Gulf War anthology*
O/3, War (1993), edited by Leslie Scalapino.

"Kathleen Fraser": Based on Poe's sketch of "Lydia Maria Child." The titles mentioned are *What I Want* (New York: Harper & Row, 1974), *Each Next: Narratives* (Berkeley: The Figures, 1980), *Something (even human voices) in the foreground, a lake* (Berkeley: Kelsey St. Press, 1984), *Notes preceding trust* (Santa Monica: Lapis Press, 1987), and *when new time folds* (Minneapolis: Chax Press, 1993). For a sample of work from the cited books, see *il cuore: the heart: Selected Poems 1970–1995* (Hanover: Wesleyan UP, 1997). The essay "Partial Local Coherence," originally an afterward to an anthology of language writing edited by Ron Silliman for the journal *Ironwood,* is now available in *Translating the Unspeakable: Poetry and the Innovative Necessity* (Tuscaloosa: University of Alabama Press, 2000). *(How)ever* (1983–1992) was not a mimeo but photocopy magazine; the archive is now available on-line along with the journal's electronic continuation, *How2*, at http://www.scc.rutgers.edu/however. The quoted translation ("Excerpt from 'Sleep'" by "Amelia [sic] Rosselli") comes from *13th Moon* 11:2 (1993): 215. "Medusa's hair was snakes. Was thought, split inward" appears in *il cuore* at 67–68.

"Pat Reed": Cobbled together from Poe's sketches of "Anne Lynch," "Catherine Maria Sedgwick," "Frances Osgood," "Emma Embury," and "Richard Adams Locke," and from a short passage from the *Marginalia* (on "William Wallace"). The quoted lines of poetry come from *Kismet* (Oakland: O Books, 1990), 42, 56, and 93. The other books mentioned are *Sea Asleep* (Oakland: Coincidence Press, 1983) and *More Awesome* (Oakland: One Dog Garage, 1985). For examples of her prose, see *Surf Monkeys,* a "Choose Your Own Adventure" novel published under the name Jay Leibold (New York: Bantam Books, 1993), and *We Want to See Your Tears Falling Down* (San Francisco: Literatura de Cordel, 1996). The poets cited are Steven Farmer, Laura Moriarty, Larry Price, Diane Ward, and Benjamin Hollander.

"Kit Robinson": Based on Poe's sketch of "Mary E. Hewitt." The quoted lines come from *Balance Sheet* (New York: Roof Books, 1993), 31 ("The limitations") and 51 ("Pieced lines"), and *Oblek,* no. 7 (Spring 1990): 103 ("Nursury Rhyme"). The other works mentioned are *Chinatown of Chayenne* (Cambridge: Whale Cloth Press, 1974), *Ice Cubes* (New York: Roof Books, 1987), *Counter-Meditation* (La Laguna: Zasterle Press, 1991), and "In the American Tree" (first published in Robinson's *Down and Back* [Berkeley: The Figures, 1978]).

A SHORT HISTORY OF LANGUAGE POETRY

The source text is Jean Wahl's *A Short History of Existentialism.* My transpositions of Wahl's philosophers worked out as follows: Robert Creeley as Hegel; Clark Coolidge as Kierkegaard; Ron Silliman as Jaspers; Barrett Watten and Lyn Hejinian as Heidegger; and Charles Bernstein as Sartre. The characters comprising the discussion are based on the following philosophers: Nicholas Berdiaeff (Guantanamo Bey), Georges Gurvitch (Winnie Nelson), Alexandre Koyré (Wyman Jennings), Maurice de Gandillac (Nils Ya), Gabriel Marcel (Dirk Jefferson), and Emmanuel Levinas (Kimberly Filbee). I had toyed with the possibility of enacting an imaginary discussion by students in Buffalo's Poetics Program but feared putting words in my classmates' mouths would stir up too much bad feeling.

The text alludes in several places to titles of books by the poets in question, treating the titles as descriptive catchphrases for the work itself, and even as explanatory concepts. Note, in particular, excluding titles already mentioned, Clark Coolidge, *Sound as Thought: Poems 1982–1984* (Los Angeles: Sun & Moon, 1990), and Lyn Hejinian, *A Mask of Motion* (Providence: Burning Deck, 1977) and *Writing Is an Aid to Memory* (Berkeley: The Figures, 1978).

271 *roundtable discussion involving language writing*
Charles Bernstein, Ann Lauterbach, Jonathan Monroe, and Bob Perelman, "Poetry, Community, Movement: A Conversation," *Diacritics* 26:3–4 (Fall-Winter 1996): 196–210.

271 *charge made by . . . Blasing*
Mutlu Konuk Blasing, *Politics and Form in Postmodern Poetry* (Cambridge: Cambridge UP, 1995), 26, 27.

271 *"made thought" . . . "over-all equivalence of activity . . . "*
Barrett Watten, "The Bride of the Assembly Line: From Mate-

rial Text to Cultural Poetics," *The Impercipient Lecture Series* 1:8 (October 1997): 20, and *Total Syntax,* 56.

272 *Silliman . . . has asserted that the designation*

Silliman, "Negative Solidarity." For a response, see David Levi Strauss, "A Note on Us & Them," *Temblor,* no. 9 (1989): 121.

272 *what Bernstein calls*

In Charles Bernstein, *Content's Dream: Essays 1975–1984* (Los Angeles: Sun & Moon Press, 1986), 458.

273 *"obduration . . . mother of discourse"*

Clark Coolidge, "From Notebooks (1976–1982)," *Io,* no. 30, *Code of Signals: Recent Writings in Poetics,* ed. Michael Palmer (Berkeley: North Atlantic Books, 1983), 174, 177.

273 *"It's a constant . . . sufferance of thought"*

Stations, no. 5, *A Symposium on Clark Coolidge,* ed. Ron Silliman (Winter 1978): 14; Clark Coolidge, *Research,* (Berkeley: Tuumba Press, 1982).

274 *"I would like for writing . . . to be there"*

Coolidge, *Quartz Hearts* (San Francisco: This Press, 1978), 28.

274 *in a letter to Paul Metcalf*

Stations, no. 5 (Winter 1978): 29.

275 *"A tune . . . chords"*

Coolidge, *Solution Passage: Poems 1978–1981* (Los Angeles: Sun & Moon Press, 1986), 367.

275 *Coolidge's insistence*

In a transcribed conversation with Susan Coolidge and Barrett Watten, Coolidge likens his concept of "arrangement" to the "old alchemical notion that if you take objects, like the objects on this table, any objects, and arrange them in the correct order, that some incredible shift, or something, would happen. Something would be affected. Like the power is in the arrangement not the objects" (*This,* no. 4 [1972]). Regarding grammar, Coolidge comments in an author's note in *Quartz Hearts,* "It is in every sense a hinge work, reflecting a fresh interest in sentence structure as axial armature" (56).

276 *"gesture which is neither . . . affirm anything"*

John Ashbery, "Self-Portrait in as Convex Mirror," *Selected Poems* (New York: Viking, 1985), 190.

276 *"The Advantage . . . makes sense"*

Charles Olson, *Collected Prose,* ed. Donald Allen and Benjamin Friedlander (Berkeley: U of California P, 1997), 353, 184.

277 *"Parsimony . . .* mind of the reader"

Silliman, *The New Sentence,* 119.

278 *"to carve . . . words"*
Silliman, *The New Sentence,* 88

278 *"subjective . . . in the work"*
Watten, *Total Syntax,* 1, 9, 13, 65, 140.

279 *"active possibilities"*
Coolidge, *The Crystal Text* (Great Barrington: The Figures, 1986), 7.

279 *invented a formula*
Watten, *Frame,* 151.

279 *"a sequence . . . language only"*
Barrett Watten, "The Conduit of Communication in Everyday Life," *Aerial,* no. 8, *Barrett Watten: Contemporary Poetics as Critical Theory,* ed. Rod Smith (Washington D.C.: Edge Books, 1995), 37, and *Frame,* 171.

280 *"evidence"*
Watten, *Frame,* 269.

280 *"a baffle . . . everywhere"*
Coolidge, *The Crystal Text,* 89.

280 *"General . . . inheritance"*
Barrett Watten, *Bad History* (Berkeley: Atelos, 1998), 44, 45.

281 *as Watten notes . . . trip to Russia*
Manuel Brito, "An Interview with Barrett Watten," *Aerial* 8 (1995): 16; Watten in Davidson et al., *Leningrad,* 117.

281 *"the perception . . . issues forth"*
Watten, *Total Syntax,* 63–64, and in Davidson et al., *Leningrad,* 86.

281 *In a manifesto written by Watten with five other*
Ron Silliman, Carla Harryman, Lyn Hejinian, Steve Benson, Bob Perelman, and Barrett Watten, "Aesthetic Tendency and the Politics of Poetry: A Manifesto," *Social Text,* nos. 18–20 (Fall 1988): 271, 273.

282 *"a process set . . . one person"*
Watten, *Frame,* 67.

282 *"a manifest . . . manipulation"*
The Collected Essays of Robert Creeley (Berkeley: U of California P, 1989), 369.

282 *"sculptural . . .* time"
Watten, *Total Syntax,* 68.

283 *"La Faustienne" . . . "cogitation"*
Hejinian, *The Language of Inquiry,* 232, 345.

284 *"construction worker"*
Hejinian, *The Cold of Poetry,* 37.

285 *when Hejinian speaks of "The Person"*

According to Hejinian, "When I began the poem, or poems, called 'The Person,' one of my impulses was to write a work which would be to language what a person is to society" (Lyn Hejinian/ Andrew Schelling, "An Exchange," *Jimmy & Lucy's House of "K,"* no. 6, *Tuumba Press: A Survey* [May 1986]: 17). "The Person" now appears in *The Cold of Poetry*.

285 *"a whole . . . options"*

Hejinian, *The Cell*, 57, and in Davidson et al., *Leningrad*, 120.

286 *process of description . . . Retallack*

Hejinian, *The Language of Inquiry*, 158–59. See also Joan Retallack, "The Poethical Wager," in *Onward: Contemporary Poetry and Poetics: 20 Contemporary American Poets*, ed. Peter Baker (New York: Peter Lang, 1996).

286 *"Writing . . . findings."*

Hejinian, *The Cold of Poetry*, 124.

286 *"The wanton . . . outside it"*

Hejinian, *The Cell*, 96, and *The Language of Inquiry*, 105.

287 *"to provoke . . . experience"*

Lyn Hejinian, "The Quest for Knowledge in the Western Poem," in *Disembodied Poetics: Annals of the Jack Kerouac School*, ed. Anne Waldman and Andrew Schelling (Albuquerque: U of New Mexico P, 1994), 179–80. The passage does not appear in the version of the essay in *The Language of Inquiry*.

287 *"because . . . language itself"*

Hejinian, *The Language of Inquiry*, 49, 56.

287 *"as a spectator . . . being seen"*

Hejinian, *The Language of Inquiry*, 246.

288 *"the autonomy . . . strangeness"*

Hejinian, *The Language of Inquiry*, 94.

289 *Certain passages . . . challenge the Bay Area*

Bernstein, *A Poetics*, 16, 150, 178.

290 *having two forms*

Bernstein, *Poetics*, 53, 29. See also Bernstein's "Hearing 'Here': Robert Creeley's Poetics of Duration" in *Content's Dream*, 292–304.

290 *when he argues . . . skeptic*

Bernstein, *A Poetics*, 32, 34, 60, 71.

290 *"At the basis . . . ceding"*

Bernstein, *Content's Dream*, 174.

291 *"antiabsorptive / techniques . . .* impermeability*"*

Bernstein, *A Poetics*, 30, 68, 66.

291 *"the continuation . . . communication"*

Bernstein, *A Poetics,* 160, 178.

291 *akin in this respect*

Walter Benjamin, "N [Re the Theory of Knowledge, Theory of Progress]," trans. Leigh Hafrey and Richard Sieburth, in *Benjamin: Philosophy, Aesthetics, History* (Chicago: U of Chicago P, 1989), 64.

292 *This is not to say*

The poems cited in this paragraph appear in Charles Bernstein, *Controlling Interests* (New York: Roof Books, 1980), 39–47 ("Standing Target"), *Disfrutes* (Needham, MA: Potes & Poets, 1981), *Islets/Irritations* (New York: Jordan Davies, 1983), 36–45 ("Asylum"), *The Sophist* (Los Angeles: Sun & Moon, 1987), 44–50, 89–94 ("Dysraphism," "The Rudder of Inexorability"), *Rough Trades* (Los Angeles: Sun & Moon, 1991), 42–43, 89–106 ("Of Time and the Line," "Blow-Me-Down-Etude"), *Dark City,* 9–28, 85–101 ("Lives of the Toll Takers," "Emotions of Normal People"), and *My Way: Speeches and Poems* (Chicago: U of Chicago P, 1999), 58–62 ("Dear Mr. Fanelli"); and in Bernstein and Susan Bee, *The Nude Formalism.*

292 *a few rules-of-thumb*

Adrienne Rich, *What Is Found There: Notebooks on Poetry and Politics* (New York: W. W. Norton, 1993), 12–13; Alice Notley, "Epic & Women Poets," in *Disembodied Poetics,* 106; Frank Bidart, *In the Western Night: Collected Poems 1965–1990* (New York: Farrar Straus Giroux, 1990), 241.

293 *"Unconfusion . . . proof"*

Marianne Moore, "The Mind Is an Enchanting Thing," in *Collected Poems,* 135.

293 *"made poetry . . . same thing."*

Karl Shapiro quoted in Rasula, *The American Poetry Wax Museum,* 89.

293 *In the words of Jean Baudrillard*

Jean Baudrillard, *Simulacra and Simulation,* trans. Sheila Faria Glaser (Ann Arbor: U of Michigan P, 1994), 82.

294 *called for a return*

See Susan Schultz, "An Alphabet of Language Criticism," *Witz* 5:1 (Spring 1997) (http://wings.buffalo.edu/epc/ezines/witz/5-1.html): "At the [1996] Assembling Alternatives conference held at the University of New Hampshire . . . Bob Perelman opened his plenary talk with an unexpected defense of narrative and intelligibility. . . . The poems that he read during one of the long evening sessions contained the very qualities he was arguing for; they were neither nonnarrative nor unintelligible."

294 *Andrews, for his part*

Andrews, *Paradise & Method,* 28, 42, 52, 80, 81 and 106.

294 *Boone, among others*

See Bruce Boone, "Language Writing: The Pluses & Minuses of the New Formalism," *Soup,* no. 2 (1981): 2–9.

296 *"a heat-seeking . . ."*

Bernstein, *My Way,* 13.

298 *Grenier says somewhere*

Robert Grenier, *Attention: Seven Narratives* (Canton: Institute of Further Studies, 1985).

298 *"Words are as real . . . force field"*

Robert Grenier, "Notes on Coolidge, Objectives, Zukofsky, Romanticism, and &," in *In the American Tree,* 540.

298 *"clairvoyant" . . . "symbiosis"*

See Hannah Wiener, *Clairvoyant Journal* (Lenox: Angel Hair Books, 1978), and Grenier, *Attention,* 21.

298 *echo Emerson's acceptance*

Ralph Waldo Emerson, "Nature," *Essays and Lectures* (New York: Library of America, 1983), 32.

298 *"write nature"*

Perelman writes in an essay on Grenier, "[T]he desire to equate writing and nature and to write a natural lyric will come to dominate." *The Marginalization of Poetry,* 49.

299 *"last ditch . . . universe"*

Grenier, "Notes on Coolidge," 540

299 "I HATE SPEECH"

See Robert Grenier, "On Speech," in *In the American Tree,* 496–97.

302 *what Baraka refers to*

Adapted from a passage in LeRoi Jones, *Black Music* (1968; reprinted New York: Da Capo Press, 1998): "For certain, a great many who came and will come to see Monk come out of a health or unhealthy curiosity to see somebody 'weird,' as the mystique of this musician and his music, even as it has seeped down, distorted to a great extent by the cultural lag, into the more animated fringe of mainstream culture, has led them to believe" (29).

Permissions

Grateful acknowledgement is made to the following individuals and publishers for permission to use extended quotations from copyrighted works:

Alfred David Editions: for Stephen Rodefer, "Brief to Butterick," from *Left under a Cloud* (London: Alfred David Editions, 2000). Quoted by permission of Alfred David Editions, London UK. Copyright © Stephen Rodefer.

Robin Blaser, Literary Executor, Jack Spicer Estate: for Jack Spicer, "Improvisations on a Sentence by Poe," from *The Collected Books of Jack Spicer,* ed. Robin Blaser (Los Angeles: Black Sparrow Press, 1975).

The Estate of Gwendolyn Brooks: for "Jack," from Gwendolyn Brooks, *Blacks* (Chicago: Third World Press, 1987). Reprinted by consent of Brooks Permissions.

Chax Press: for excerpts from Beverly Dahlen, *A Reading 8–10* (Tucson: Chax Press, 1992).

Norma Cole: for "Raven," from *My Bird Book* (Los Angeles: Littoral Books, 1991).

Eileen Corder: for "WARSHEPFASCADEFLATTEN," from '*Aql,* no. 2 (July 1989).

Beverly Dahlen: for "Tree 5" and "The Last Light You Came To," from *Out of the Third* (San Francisco: Momo's Press, 1974).

Lew Daly: for excerpts from *Swallowing the Scroll: Late in a Prophetic Tradition with the Poetry of Susan Howe and John Taggart* (Buffalo, N.Y.: apex of the M supplement #1).

The Figures: for excerpts from Steve Benson, "Dialogues" and "The

Busses," from *Blue Books* (Great Barrington/NY: The Figures/Roof Books, 1988); Lyn Hejinian, *Oxota: A Short Russian Novel* (Great Barrington: The Figures, 1991); Bob Perelman, *Captive Audience* (Great Barrington: The Figures, 1988).

Kathleen Fraser: for her translation of Amalia Rosselli, from *13th Moon* 11:2 (1993).

Harvard University Press: for "The Mind lives on the Heart" by Emily Dickinson. Reprinted by permission of the publishers and the Trustees of Amherst College from *The Poems of Emily Dickinson,* Thomas H. Johnson, ed., Cambridge Mass.: The Belknap Press if Harvard University Press, Copyright © 1951, 1955, 1979 President and Fellows of Harvard College.

Lyn Hejinian: for "The Inanimate Are Rocks, Desks, Bubbles," from *In the American Tree,* ed. Ron Silliman (Orono: National Poetry Foundation, 1986).

Joanne Kyger: for "DARRELL GRAY dies when I am in Mexico," from *Just Space: Poems 1979–1989* (Santa Rosa: Black Sparrow Press, 1991).

Listening Chamber: Excerpts from Norma Cole's *Mars* courtesy of the author and Listening Chamber.

NCTE: for excerpts from Jed Rasula, *The American Poetry Wax Museum: Reality Effects 1940–1990* (Urbana, Ill.: National Council of Teachers of English, 1996). Copyright © 1996 National Council of Teachers of English.

New Directions: "Sigil XI" by HD (Hilda Doolittle, from *Collected Poems, 1912–1944,* Copyright © 1982 Estate of Hilda Doolittle. "CANTO XCVI" (17 line excerpt) by Ezra Pound, from *The Cantos of Ezra Pound,* Copyright © 1934, 1937, 1940, 1948, 1956, 1959, 1962, 1963, 1966, and 1968 Ezra Pound. Used by permission of New Directions Publishing Corporation.

O Books: for excerpts from Pat Reed, *Kismet* (Oakland: O Books, 1990).

Bob Perelman: for excerpts from unpublished correspondence.

Peter Owen, Ltd.: for excerpts from Gertrude Stein, "Before the Flowers of Friendship Faded Friendship Faded." Reprinted from *Look at Me Now and Here I Am: Writings and Lectures 1909–45,* Gertrude Stein, Peter Owen, Ltd., London.

The Estate of Charles Reznikoff: For "Jerusalem the Golden" by Charles Reznikoff. Copyright © 1977 Marie Syrkin Reznikoff.

Reprinted, with permission, from *Poems 1918–1975: The Complete Poems of Charles Reznikoff*.

Kit Robinson: for "Nursury Rhyme," from *Oblek,* no. 7 (Spring 1990).

Roof Books: "Dialogues" and "The Busses" were originally published in Steve Benson, *Blue Books* (Great Barrington/NY: The Figures/ Roof Books, 1988); "Counter-Meditation" was originally published in Kit Robinson, *Balance Sheet* (New York: Roof Books, 1993).

Ron Silliman: for his post to the Poetics List of 2 March 1995. Copyright © 1995 and 2003 Ron Silliman.

The Estate of Gertrude Stein: for excerpts from "Lifting Belly," from *Writings 1903–1932* (New York: Library of America, 1998).

Sun & Moon Press: for excerpts from Gertrude Stein, *Stanzas in Meditation* (Los Angeles: Sun & Moon Press, 1994). Copyright © 1956 Alice B. Toklas, renewed © 1980 Calman A. Levin, Executor of the Estate of Gertrude Stein. For excerpts from Charles Bernstein, *Dark City* (Los Angeles: Sun & Moon Press, 1994). Copyright © 1994 Charles Bernstein. For excerpts from Tom Mandel, *Letters of the Law* (Los Angeles: Sun & Moon, 1994). Copyright © 1994 Tom Mandel.

Index